AN AMERICAN LIFE

One Man's Road to Watergate

Jeb Stuart Magruder

AN
AMERICAN
LIFE

One Man's Road to Watergate

New York   Atheneum   *1974*

Copyright © 1974 by Jeb Stuart Magruder
All rights reserved
Library of Congress catalog card number 74–78466
ISBN 0–689–10603–3
Published simultaneously in Canada by McClelland and Stewart Ltd.
Manufactured in the United States of America by H. Wolff, New York
Designed by Harry Ford
First Edition

FOR GAIL

He's easy to get along with" has been your way of just sliding around. Now it can be a good way of communication, because more people can relate to your experience than they can, say, to Dan Berrigan's. It may be easier for them to learn through you.

To be Jeb is terribly valuable at this moment. His experience has been an All-American one."

The Reverend William Sloane Coffin, Jr.,
in conversation with Studs Terkel
and Jeb Magruder, Harper's Magazine, *1973.*

ACKNOWLEDGMENTS

I want to thank my attorney, James E. Sharp, for his tireless efforts on my behalf in the past year. I would also like to thank Patrick Anderson for his invaluable advice and assistance on this book. I am, of course, solely responsible for the book's contents.

J. S. M.
March 1974

CONTENTS

ILLUSTRATIONS

(FOLLOW PAGE 52)

Young Magruder, age 15
Pfc. Magruder, Korea, 1955
Jeb and Gail, March 1968, with Whitney, Tracy, Stuart, and Justin
Jeb and the kids, Christmas Eve 1970
The Magruders, with Jeb's mother, father, and brother
Gail and the children at the Inaugural Parade, January 20, 1973
John and Maureen Dean at the Senate Watergate committee *
Hugh Sloan, former Nixon campaign treasurer *
Maurice Stans, chief fund raiser for Nixon reelection campaign *
Charles W. Colson *
John D. Ehrlichman *
John Mitchell *
Herbert Kalmbach *
H. R. Haldeman, President Nixon's chief of staff, with the Chief Executive *
Frederick LaRue *
Egil "Bud" Krogh *
James W. McCord, Jr.*
E. Howard Hunt *
Herbert Klein with his successor, Ron Ziegler *
G. Gordon Liddy, former member of the White House "plumbers" squad *
Herbert L. "Bart" Porter *
Rob Odle, White House assistant and Presidential campaign adviser *
Gordon Strachan, Haldeman's chief political aide *
Robert G. Mardian, one-time Assistant Attorney General *
Richard Kleindienst before the Senate committee *
The Magruders with President Nixon
The Magruders with Clark and Barbara MacGregor

* All photographs with asterisk are from United Press International Photo

AN AMERICAN LIFE

One Man's Road to Watergate

PROLOGUE

RICHARD NIXON'S San Clemente estate is not impressive from the outside. It was once two separate properties, a private home and an adjoining Coast Guard installation. Today, as you approach it from the freeway, it might still be a naval installation, for all you can see is its gatehouse and uniformed guards; the President's home is hidden by a wall of trees and shrubs. But once the guards have waved you on, once the gates swing open and you are inside, you sense that you have left one world and entered another, very different one. The difference is more than simply that of leaving the gilt and clutter of Southern California to enter the grounds of a millionaire's ocean-front estate. The real difference is less tangible, an aura of power and promise and sophistication, a hint of decisions about to be made, an ever-present realization that when the President is here, this quiet retreat is the nerve center of the Western world.

I first entered the President's world on a bright afternoon in mid-August 1969. I was thirty-four years old and the head of two small cosmetics companies. I had been the Southern California coordinator for the 1968 Nixon campaign, and the President's chief of staff, Bob Haldeman, had invited me to San Clemente to talk about a job in the White House.

I had met Haldeman during the campaign, but did not know him well. A mutual friend of ours, Cliff Miller, a public relations executive in Los Angeles, had that spring been urging Haldeman to hire me to help organize a more effective White House public relations program. In June, I attended a luncheon speech that Haldeman made to a group of young executives in Los Angeles, and Haldeman sought me out at the end of his talk.

"Jeb," he said, "we don't know each other well, but I think perhaps you could help us in the White House. I'd like to talk to you about it."

I said I'd be happy to talk to him, and he suggested that the best time

3

might be later in the summer, when he and the President came for a stay at the San Clemente estate that the President had recently purchased.

In the next few weeks, Haldeman's young assistant Larry Higby called me several times to set up an appointment. One was canceled at the last moment before my mid-August appointment was finally set. When the day came, I drove the seventy miles down the Pacific coast to San Clemente in a state of high excitement. I had already discussed with my wife and my business partners the possibility that I might be offered a job in the White House. I tried, at that point, to appear casual about the possibility, but I knew that if Haldeman offered me a decent job I would take it.

I arrived at San Clemente in the early afternoon, was quickly cleared through the gates, and parked my car in the lot beside the compound where the President and his aides have their offices. The compound is on the site of the old Coast Guard installation; two hundred yards off to my right I could see the President's home, ringed by palm trees and clearly set apart from the working area. As I entered the compound I passed several of the golf carts that the President and his closest aides sometimes used to travel between the compound and the mansion. Those golf carts were prized status symbols in the Presidential circle.

Bob Haldeman greeted me warmly. I had worn a business suit, but he was wearing a sport coat, as the President and his aides usually did at San Clemente. Bob had developed a reputation during the campaign as a tough, demanding, difficult man, and the reputation was not entirely undeserved. Bob did not suffer fools gladly. But if he thought you could be useful to him—or to the President—he could be extremely charming and considerate. During my visit, he cut off all his phone calls and concentrated his attention entirely on me and the job I might do for him. It was immensely flattering that this powerful and self-confident man might want my help in solving a major problem in the White House.

I knew what the problem was, from my talks with Cliff Miller.

It was Nixon's terrible public relations, and it had been Richard Nixon's problem for all his political life. The problem encompassed many elements: the fact that Nixon was disliked and distrusted by many newspaper reporters; the fact that he was often stiff and ill-at-ease on television; the fact that he was somewhat awkward physically and had no talent for small talk. The difficulty had been minimized during the 1968 campaign when Nixon was presented to the public through a brilliant series of television advertisements, but now that he was President it was returning again. To some extent, as both Haldeman and the President realized, the problem was simply Nixon himself. He was not a lovable man and no public relations program was going to make him so. But, Haldeman felt, the problem was also an organizational one. There had been, he said, chaos in White House public relations during the first months of the new administration. Haldeman wanted someone to develop a plan to coordinate all the people and offices in the White House that dealt with the media and the public—Ron Ziegler's Press Office, Herb Klein's Office of Communications, the various speechwriters and consultants, the Congressional Relations Office, and so on. Haldeman was candid. He said the President understood he lacked the charisma or personal appeal of a Kennedy or an Eisenhower. He assumed, too, that he would never win over the liberal opinion makers in the media and elsewhere who had always loathed him. So the challenge was to develop a public relations program that could circumvent the liberal opinion makers and take the President's message directly to the people. He wasn't looking for someone to manage the White House public relations program, only for someone to devise a structure through which *he* could manage it. The idea was that, if I was chosen to put together the structure, we could figure out later where I would fit into it.

As we talked, I had one specific goal in mind, as a result of my talks with Cliff Miller. If I went to work in the White House, I did not want to be seen as someone who was coming in to solve Nixon's dilemma. I knew from Cliff that over the years several men had been seen in Nixon's eyes as the miracle workers who were going to banish the problem, and as it had persisted they had inevitably fallen from Nixon's grace. Bob Finch and Herb Klein were two major examples. In recent years, the men who had gained influence with Nixon had been tough, efficient managers like Bob Haldeman and John Mitchell, men who loathed the media as much as Nixon did and had as little to do with it as possible. I knew, therefore, that if I went to the White House it was important that I be perceived as a manager, not as a public relations man, for to be perceived as the latter was almost certainly a one-way ticket to nowhere.

Bob and I talked for almost three hours, about the situation and about my ideas and background. Finally I asked impatiently, "Bob, are you offering me this job?"

"No," he replied calmly. "Not yet."

He asked if I would write him a report on how I would approach the job we had discussed. I thought that somewhat impractical, since I didn't know the people involved, but I agreed to do as he asked.

Near the end of our talk, Bob leaned back in his chair and spoke of what it had meant to him to work in the White House. "Here you're working for something more than just to make money for your company," he said. "You're working to solve the problems of the country and the world. Jeb, I sat with the President on the night the first astronauts stepped onto the moon. I listened as he spoke to the first men on the moon. I'm part of history being made. When I come back to California and see my old friends, and they talk about their business problems, those problems seem mundane to me now."

I was moved by his words, for I too had been a businessman who was instinctively drawn toward politics. Part of the appeal of politics, certainly, had to do with my ambition. I had decided early in life that simply to make money was not enough. I saw that the really important people in America aren't those who are merely rich, but those who have political influence as well.

But I was drawn to politics by conviction as well as by pure ambition. I had worked for Richard Nixon in two Presidential campaigns because I believed that his essentially conservative political philosophy was what America needed. As a college student, majoring in political science, I had learned I was more comfortable with the conservative point of view than with the liberal. I wanted to see less big government and more individual self-reliance. By 1969 I was no longer the fiercely ideological conservative I had been in 1960—I liked winning elections, not winning arguments—but I believed in Richard Nixon and I looked upon the possibility of a job in the White House as a chance to serve my country's interests as well as my own.

Bob did not offer me a job that day. I assumed he wanted to discuss me with the President first. At the end of our meeting he suggested that I talk with several of his aides. My first talk was with Larry Higby. Larry was an extremely slight, serious, prematurely balding young man in his mid-twenties. While a student at UCLA he had worked part-time for Haldeman at J. Walter Thompson and had followed Haldeman into the 1968 campaign, then to the White House. It was obvious that Haldeman thought highly of him. One reason, I learned, was that Larry had overseen the renovation of the San Clemente compound and had done an excellent job. Larry and I walked out to the lovely cabana that sat on the bluff overlooking the ocean. As we talked, we drank a beer and watched young surfers ride the waves on the ocean below us.

Larry made one comment that I suspected was highly significant: "Jeb, one thing that bothers me, and perhaps bothers Bob too, is that you've moved around a good deal. We know you've been moving up the ladder, but you *have* changed jobs a lot."

I assumed he was reflecting Haldeman's concern that I might use the White House as a steppingstone to a higher-paying job in business, so I answered carefully. I said that one reason I'd held five jobs in the eleven years since I'd graduated from college was financial. But I added that in at least one instance I had changed jobs because of politics. I was young and independent, and when my boss had given me the choice between my job and my political activity, I'd quit my job. So, I told Higby, given my love of politics, it wasn't likely that I'd hurry away from a job in the White House.

Larry seemed satisfied with my answer, and soon we left the cabana and returned to the compound, where I talked with three other Haldeman aides, Dwight Chapin, Ken Cole, and Alex Butterfield. Like Higby, Chapin and Cole had both worked at J. Walter Thompson, as, indeed, had Press Secretary Ron Ziegler, whom I met later that day.

Chapin was then in his late twenties and was serving as the President's appointments secretary. I liked him immediately. He was a positive, creative, self-confident young man. Some people, confronted with a problem, tend to throw up their hands and say, "This is hopeless." Dwight was one of those people who greet each new problem with, "Sure, we can solve this," and proceed to do so. There was never any question of Dwight's resenting me or thinking that I might be any threat to his power; he was sure of himself and he looked on other capable people as potential allies, not as threats.

We discussed the President's public relations difficulty. In essence, Dwight said, "We've got the pieces, we've got good people, but it's a disaster organizationally. Herb Klein isn't managing it. Bob can't manage it, I can't manage it, but *somebody's* got to manage it." I was tremendously impressed with Dwight—he seemed to me to be the sort of bright, dedicated young man that every President should have serving him.

Ken Cole, the next Haldeman aide I spoke with, was a husky, handsome man in his early thirties. Ken wasn't as positive as Dwight. He seemed to look upon me as another PR man, and he didn't think the White House needed another one. His attitude was: Damn it, why don't we just quit worrying about public relations and worry more about matters of substance? Unlike Dwight, who still believed the problem could be solved, Ken doubted that it could be and thought the best thing was just to stop worrying about it. That might not have been bad advice, except for one thing: The President was still anxious about it, and determined to have it beaten.

Alex Butterfield was the only one of the four Haldeman aides who was older than I. Alex was a former air force colonel who had been handling some public relations projects for Haldeman but not, I gathered, entirely to Haldeman's satisfaction. Alex was an extremely pleasant man and a hard worker, but he didn't always perform fast enough to satisfy Haldeman's demands. Nor did he have the background for public relations work. Later, Alex was put in charge of the paperwork coming and going from the President's office and he did an excellent job. His real celebrity came, of course, in the summer of 1973 when he revealed the fact that President Nixon had taped his White House conversations.

By the time my talks were over, it was almost six o'clock, and I returned to Haldeman's office. Bob had invited me to attend a reception the President was giving for a group of newspaper and television people, the first time the media people had been invited socially to the President's new home.

When Higby, Haldeman, and I left the compound, Haldeman's golf cart was not waiting outside. He became furious. He turned on Higby and gave him a brutal chewing out. I couldn't believe what I was hearing. It was a gorgeous evening and it wasn't going to hurt us to walk, rather than ride, the two hundred yards to the President's house. But Bob told Larry in cold, clipped, scornful terms that keeping track of the golf carts was part of his job, and if he couldn't do the job Bob would find someone else who could.

The tirade ended in a minute or two and we proceeded on to the reception. It occurred to me that Bob's treatment of Larry might have been calculated for its impact on me, that Bob might have been warning me not to come to work for him unless I was willing to take plenty of heat. If so, the warning was wasted. I wanted the job, no matter what the conditions. I suppose I still had the illusion that *I* would never be the recipient of a dressing down like that. I would in time be disabused of that notion.

However, as I thought about it, I decided that Bob might have been genuinely angry about the missing golf cart. That might not make much sense in the ordinary world, where we take for granted a certain amount of inconvenience in our lives—that some days the car won't start or the furnace won't work. But the White House or San Clemente is not the ordinary world. In just a few hours at San Clemente I had been struck by the sheer *perfection* of life there. The flower gardens were perfectly trimmed, the communications system was perfectly tuned, limousines and helicopters and airplanes awaited Haldeman's pleasure. After you have been spoiled like that for a while, something as minor as a missing golf cart can seem a major affront.

The reception was being held beside the President's swimming pool, which stretches between the house and the nine-hole pitch and putt golf course. Haldeman left us after a moment; he was not much for small talk. I took a gin and tonic from one of the white-coated Filipinos who moved among the guests. There were fifty or sixty reporters and news executives present, including some whose faces I knew from the evening news shows. Higby and Chapin and I stood to the side and chatted for a while. Press secretary Ron Ziegler joined us for a minute or two. Chapin had already told me that Ziegler might be an obstacle in any effort to coordinate the White House public relations operation, and when Chapin explained to him why I was there, Ziegler seemed cool toward me. He struck me as an insecure person, and one who would definitely be a problem if I got the job.

For me, the evening's highlight came when the President walked out onto the terrace and spoke briefly to his guests. I had never had strong feelings about Richard Nixon personally. I was a party man, not a Nixon man. But it would have been difficult not to be impressed by him as he stood there by the pool, relaxed and tanned and gracious, and welcomed his guests to his new home. Even his severest critic would have been disarmed, I think, and moreover would have felt a pang of sympathy for this one man who was called upon to face such vast national and international problems. Nixon didn't even know that I was there, but if there had ever been any doubt that I was ready to work for him, it would have been gone by the time he ended his remarks by the pool.

I didn't want to outstay my welcome, so after half an hour or so I said my good-byes and started the drive home. In minutes I was out the gates and back to reality, just another commuter on a crowded freeway. But I had had a glimpse of something better, and as I drove up the Coast with the summer sun falling into the ocean off to my left, my hands were trembling. I was an ambitious man, a man with a craving for power, and I wanted more than I had ever wanted anything to return to work in that world of power and challenge and opportunity I had just left.

I had a long talk that night with Gail. She did not share my excitement. We had four children and in ten years of marriage we'd lived in six houses in three cities. Now we were settled in a house in the Santa Monica Canyon, a house we both loved and that Gail had worked hard to restore just as we wanted it. She had no desire to move to Washington and have to adjust to new schools and new friends and new stores. We both knew that in years past my political activity had put a strain on our marriage. But Gail understood too what an opportunity this might be for me. She asked, "Do we have any choice?" and I said no, if the job was offered I'd have to take it. She asked me at least to talk to her again before accepting an offer, if Haldeman made one, and I said I would.

With Gail's help, I quickly wrote the report that Haldeman had asked for and sent it to him. Then I settled back to wait for his decision, my anxiety increasing as each day passed.

One day while I was waiting I had lunch with Bob Abernathy, a TV reporter with KNBC in Los Angeles, who had previously been a reporter in Washington. Bob and I had gotten to know each other because we attended the same church. It had occurred to me that, for all my enthusiasm, I knew almost nothing about Washington or about working in the White House. So I asked Bob what he thought I should do.

"Take the job," he told me. "Don't worry about the money or the title. If they want you to be a mailboy, take it. It's the chance of a lifetime."

Two weeks passed before I heard from Haldeman. His office called on a Friday in late August and asked if I could come to San Clemente the next Monday.

That Monday morning, as I was leaving the house, my back went out. Gail says she saw it happen from the head of the stairs, saw me step off the bottom stair onto the parquet floor and suddenly jerk with pain. It was as sudden and as painful as if someone had hit me with a baseball bat. My back problem had begun when I strained it playing too much tennis as a teen-ager. In later years, the pain would return occasionally when I was under stress, as I had been those two weeks waiting for Haldeman to call.

I should have called a doctor and gone to bed. Instead, despite the worsening pain, I drove on down to San Clemente. I'd have kept that appointment if I'd broken my leg. Nor did I mention my discomfort during our talk, lest Haldeman think I had a health problem.

Bob offered me a job on his staff, pending a permanent assignment, with the title of Special Assistant to the President. The position was by Presidential appointment, a status symbol that Cliff Miller had urged me to fight for. I realized that despite the title I would be more an assistant to Haldeman than to the President, but that was all right with me.

The only problem was salary. I had been paying myself about $35,-000. Bob offered me $27,500 and a promise of quick raises if all went well. He liked to start people low and use raises as an incentive to get more work out of them. I didn't argue. I accepted the job on the spot, thus breaking my promise to Gail to talk with her about it. Bob wanted me to start as soon as possible, and I said I would need a month, until October 1, to settle my business affairs. Actually, when I got home that afternoon, I went to bed and stayed there for two weeks, because of my back problem.

I was on my way to the White House. It meant a financial sacrifice, it meant leaving a home I loved and a business I had just started, but those things didn't seem to matter. As I drove home to break the news to Gail, I was filled with excitement and anticipation. This was the chance I had been waiting for all my life. The Magruder family had, over the years, known its ups and downs, but now I was one of the Magruders who was on the way up, all the way to the top.

CHAPTER I

Starting Out

ACCORDING TO family legend, our ancestor Alexander Magruder came to America from Scotland in 1659 as an impounded prisoner. He had been on the losing side in one of the wars between Scotland and England and was sent to America in exile. Once he arrived in Baltimore, Alexander Magruder did well for himself. He married William Penn's secretary's daughter, and Penn granted him some land in southern Maryland, where for two centuries the Magruders were tobacco farmers. My great-grandfather, Thomas Jefferson Magruder, was the first of the family to go into trade. During the Civil War he opened a shoe store in the District of Columbia. Actually, he was a Confederate agent, and he would load up hearses with shoes and boots and take them across the Potomac to Confederate troops in Virginia. While Thomas Jefferson Magruder was working behind the lines, another of my ancestors, John Bankhead Magruder, served as one of Robert E. Lee's generals, and in 1862 he and his men stopped McClellan from taking Richmond.

Thomas Jefferson Magruder's shoe-smuggling operation was uncovered and he was jailed, but later released through the intercession of Governor Peabody of Massachusetts, who was also a shoe dealer. He then proceeded to Baltimore, where he opened the Magruder Shoe Company and in time became the biggest shoe jobber in the South. My father says that Thomas Jefferson Magruder was so pro-southern that when

13

Lincoln was assassinated he refused to let his church lower its flag to half-mast.

His son, Robert Magruder, who was my grandfather, grew up in Baltimore and served as county supervisor from 1895 to 1898, when he ran for Congress. It must have been an unusually expensive campaign, because, as my father tells the story, Robert Magruder lost all his money as well as the election. As a result, in 1899, when my father was three, Robert Magruder and his family moved to Staten Island, New York. He operated a number of credit firms there, then became a minor official of the Johnson Shipyard Corporation at Mariner's Harbor, Staten Island. But in 1916 he became an important figure in the corporation when he personally obtained contracts from the U. S. Shipping Board for the construction of three cargo ships for $900,000. In August of 1917, when the president of the shipyard entered the army, Robert Magruder was elected to succeed him.

He had become a man of wealth and prominence, but it all came tumbling down in June of 1921 when he was indicted on charges of misapplication of some $300,000 from the Mariner's Harbor National Bank. It was charged that my grandfather had conspired with one Sylvanus Bedell, who was the cashier of the bank and whom my grandfather had made the treasurer of the shipyard corporation. The charge was that when Robert Magruder presented checks to the bank for which the shipyard had no funds, Bedell would take money from other accounts to cover the checks. Magruder's defense was that the Shipping Board had been late in paying his company some $450,000 and that he had been forced to do what he did in order to get the cargo ships built on time.

As my father tells it, it was Attorney General Harry Daugherty who caused the Shipping Board payments to be late, and it was the same Daugherty who forced the indictment and prosecution of my grandfather. Daugherty himself later was indicted, of course, for his role in the Teapot Dome scandals, the first U. S. Attorney General to be so disgraced.

In any event, my grandfather was tried, convicted, and sent to jail for six months. In 1925, not long after his release, his wife, Elizabeth Thomas Magruder, died—of a broken heart, my father says. My grandfather died the following year.

All this had a profound effect on my father, Donald Dilworth Magruder. He had grown up on Staten Island in comfortable circumstances. In 1914 he was accepted at Princeton, but he saw that war was coming, so rather than start college then he went to work as a salesman for a printing company. He liked the business enough to start his own printing company, with his older brother Hamlin, the next year. He was, in those days, an outstanding horseman, and in 1916 he joined the New York National Guard's famous Squadron A, the last cavalry division in the U. S. Army. The next year he joined the 27th Infantry Division and was sent to France as a sergeant in charge of a machine-gun battalion. He received two citations for bravery in battle.

After the war, he and his brother operated the printing company on Staten Island, and my father also took a job with his father's shipyard corporation. It was about that time, as a handsome, highly eligible young bachelor, that he met my mother, Edith Woolverton. My mother was born in New Jersey in 1901, but a few years later, after her father died of malaria in the Canal Zone, her mother moved herself and her five children to Staten Island, where she operated a rooming house.

My grandfather's downfall came during my parents' courtship. The family was wiped out financially by the scandal and the trial, and my father, at age twenty-five or so, found himself in greatly reduced circumstances. It would seem that he lost more than money. Two of his older brothers went on to successful business careers, but my grandfather's disgrace seemed to take some spark or drive from my father. Perhaps he had seen too much of the fruits of ambition. I think he accepted at that early age that he would never be wealthy again. He married my mother in October of 1923 and lived a quiet, respectable, family-centered life thereafter, operating his printing company until his retirement in 1967.

My brother Don, who was named for our father, was born in June of 1930, and I arrived in November of 1934. Since my father was both a Civil War buff and a horseman, he named me for his favorite Confederate general, Jeb Stuart, his ideal of a hard-riding cavalry officer. I can remember seeing my father ride a few times when I was quite young. He was into middle age by then but he rode beautifully, always wearing a treasured pair of riding boots from his days in Squadron A.

In 1937 he paid $5,000 for a small frame house at 442 Home Avenue, in the Fort Wadsworth section of Staten Island, where I grew up and where my parents lived for thirty years. I remember my father as a hard-working man, a man of habit, a man who usually seemed preoccupied with his own thoughts. He fixed the family's breakfast each morning, then set off to deliver the previous day's printing and to seek new orders. His printing shop, although the largest on Staten Island, was not very large. It had a printing plant downstairs and a stationery and office-supply store upstairs. He employed an assistant, two salesladies, and four or five printers. He was not, as best I can judge, an aggressive businessman. He told me after his retirement that during his almost fifty years in business he usually earned about $5,000 annually and that it was not until his final few years that his profits rose as high as $10,000 a year. These were not starvation wages, to be sure, but neither were they the earnings he had aspired to as a young World War I hero with a rich father and a seemingly limitless future.

He was a quiet man. He was known for his courtly southern manners, but he was usually content to let my mother do the talking. He came home each evening after work, had one drink, read the paper, and then napped on the sofa while my mother prepared dinner. After dinner, my parents and my brother and I might sit and talk, out on the porch if it was summer, or my father might read some new Civil War history. He was usually in bed by 10:30. He and I had an affectionate relationship without really being close. We rarely disagreed. By contrast, my mother and I often disagreed, sometimes heatedly, but we were close. She was the greatest influence on my youth.

My mother's high hopes for me triggered my youthful ambitions. My father never spoke of his lost wealth, but, out of his presence, my mother often did. She would say to my brother and me—not bitterly, just wistfully—how nice it would have been if we'd been wealthy, and she would recall her courtship, when my father had called for her in his Cadillac convertible. She felt that life had been harder for her than it should have been, and she wanted her sons to achieve the success that her husband had not. Both Don and I felt the pressure, and as it turned out I was the one who came closer to achieving her high hopes for us.

We were not poor, but my brother and I grew up knowing that we had less than many of our friends, and certainly less than our mother wanted us to have. We had all the necessities of life, but there was not a lot left over and we always tried to economize. One of my father's economies was to keep, well into the 1950's, an old coal-burning furnace. He would shovel the coal in himself, then several times a week he would sift through the ashes to find the little pieces of coal that had slipped through the grate and could be used again. I took over this job when I was old enough, but after I went off to college in 1952 my mother finally persuaded him to buy an oil furnace because he was just too old to go on shoveling coal all winter.

I was eight or ten years old before I learned about my grandfather and his trial. I happened to come across a sheaf of clippings about the trial up in our attic. I went to my father for more information, but about all he told me was that his father had been the innocent victim of dishonest bookkeepers—I suppose he meant Sylvanus Bedell, my grandfather's codefendant. I grew up thinking that my grandfather had died before coming to trial. It was not until many years later—during a talk with my father in 1973—that I learned the truth, that my grandfather had actually gone to prison.

My parents never had the money to go out often, but my mother loved to cook and to entertain, and she always looked forward to entertaining members of our family at Christmas. She could be demanding and argumentative, but she was also attractive and gregarious, and she had many friends.

It was her habit, whether she was at home alone or had guests, to prepare tea and cakes each afternoon. This and other mannerisms made her stand out in our neighborhood of working-class and middle-class families. I remember once when I had a fight with another neighborhood boy, he yelled at me, "You think you're better than the rest of us!"

I didn't think I was better, but in my early years I was living a kind of dual existence. My parents consciously gave my brother and me a taste of upper-class living—we did the things the rich did that weren't expensive. For example, we'd go over to Forest Hills for the tennis matches, or drive to Princeton or West Point for football games. (During the war years, when Glenn Davis and Doc Blanchard were Army's legendary Mr. Inside and Mr. Outside, my dream was to be a West Point cadet.) Sometimes in the summers we'd drive to one of the New Jersey resorts and spend a day or two at a good hotel. And in the summer of 1942, when I was seven, we were given the use of relative's house in a very nice town on Cape Cod. I was awed by the elegance of the other houses there and I made up my mind to see the inside of all of them, which I did by meeting people on the beach and wangling invitations.

A case of pneumonia caused me to miss more than half of the second grade. The principal said I'd have to take the grade over, but my mother wouldn't hear of it. She declared that she'd work with me after school until I'd made up the work, and she did. She was protective of me, but she didn't want me to be a mama's boy. Once when an older neighborhood boy named Red Mahoney had been pushing me around and I complained to her, my mother said, "Go punch him in the nose and he won't bother you anymore." I gave Red a bloody nose and afterward we became friends. My mother liked that. She was aggressive in her way, as aggressive as the circumstances of her life would permit, and she wanted me to be more aggressive than my father was.

I went to a neighborhood elementary school through the sixth grade, then for the seventh and eighth grades I attended P.S. 13, which was located in a tough Italian neighborhood. I remember being shocked when one of my seventh-grade classmates, a well-developed Italian girl, told me about her sexual experiences, which she said included hanging out at the train station and having sex for money. Hard drugs were not unknown at P.S. 13, nor was serious fighting. Once an Italian boy drew a knife on me, which was not the way I'd learned to fight. I managed to get by, and was even elected president of my class one year, but we WASPs never felt entirely comfortable there. You always felt it was touch and go as to whether you'd get home unscathed.

The public schools didn't have organized sports until high school, but I had begun playing tennis when I was thirteen and it became my main sport. My parents encouraged my tennis. They belonged to an old, inexpensive club, and I began spending most of my free time there. By the time I was fifteen I was entering junior tournaments around the New York area. In one tournament, when I was sixteen, I played Ken Rosewall, who murdered me. But I was good by local standards.

I attended Curtis High School, which was the oldest high school on Staten Island and probably the best academically. Both my parents had gone there. We lived in another school district, but we got permission for me to go to Curtis, which had about two thousand students, with a good mixture of WASPs, Italians, and blacks. I was elected a class officer once or twice, and I was the treasurer of Arista, our school honor society. I had, even then, a greater-than-average interest in political affairs. I took an active part in political discussions in my classes, and politics was often discussed in our home. I can still remember my father's outrage when Truman upset Dewey in 1948. My father had admired FDR enough to vote for him in his first two campaigns, but he loathed Truman. My father's political views were very much those of a conservative Southerner, including his views on race.

My grades in high school were usually in the nineties, and I was on the honor roll. In addition to my classroom studies, I had begun reading a lot on my own. F. Scott Fitzgerald and John O'Hara were two of my favorite writers. Fitzgerald's stories about ambitious young men who yearned for the world of the rich struck very close to the reality of my own life.

Besides my tennis, I was on the school swimming team. I became one of the top-rated swimmers in the New York area. My specialty was the butterfly breast-stroke, and in my senior year I wasn't far off the world record for schoolboys.

I dated a lot in high school, and in my senior year I began to go steady for the first time. Her name was Charity—she had a sister named Faith— and she was a tremendous girl: beautiful, a cheerleader, a class officer, probably the most popular girl in the school. Our romance lasted through my senior year and my freshman year in college, and there were several times when we were close to eloping.

My social life increasingly caused conflicts with my mother, who thought I was dating too much and staying out too late. You couldn't get a driver's license in New York until you were eighteen, but I managed to get one in Pennsylvania when I was sixteen, and my mother and I then began to have the standard arguments that teen-agers and their parents have about the use of the family car. My mother was also unhappy about the number of traffic tickets I was getting and the amount of beer I was drinking. But those were the usual problems; all in all my senior year was the best year that I was to have until after I graduated from college.

That fall I enrolled in Williams College. My family and I had previously visited several of the New England Liberal Arts colleges and Williams had been the one I admired most. I liked its small size and its first-rate athletic facilities and its beautiful setting, in the Berkshire Mountains in northwestern Massachusetts. My parents were pleased with my choice. My college costs would be a financial strain on them, but Williams had the kind of social status they wanted me to have.

As it turned out, my freshman year was quite a jolt to my ego. About half the boys in my class had gone to prep schools and they were more sophisticated socially and better prepared academically than I or most of the public high school graduates were. The prep-school boys knew how to dress in the perfect Ivy League style and they seemed to know all the best girls at the nearby girls' schools and what to say to them and where to take them. We high school graduates, by comparison, were country bumpkins—High School Harrys, still wearing our jeans and letter jackets. Naturally, we soon set out to equal the poise and sophistication of our "preppie" classmates.

In my classwork, I found that the good grades no longer came so easily. In my first semester, I made four C's and a B, and in my second semester, with some special tutoring, I improved that to two C's and three B's. There were great gaps in my education; I had read a lot of novels but I barely knew what a poem was. In general, I did best in the more subjective courses like history and political science, and worst in subjects like math and science.

In my social life, after having been a leader in high school, I found that I was just another student at Williams. The fraternity system was very important at Williams then. You pledged one of the fifteen fraternities in your freshman year and thereafter you were to a great extent ranked by the prestige of the fraternity you belonged to. The one I joined, Phi Delta Theta, was a good one, but not one of the two or three best. As it happened, by pledging Phi Delta Theta, I became involved in what was then a raging controversy. My pledge class included a Jew, and the fraternity's national office refused to admit him to membership, so we cut our ties to the national and became a local fraternity, called Phi Delta.

I thought the whole thing was ridiculous. I'd gone to high school with Jews and Negroes and people from every conceivable minority group, and I couldn't see how it was going to dishonor Phi Delta Theta to have one Jew in its Williams chapter. It certainly didn't bother me. I was more bothered, as time went on, by the obvious inequities of the fraternity system. About five percent of the student body wasn't invited to join a fraternity. These people were called "non-affiliates," and they included some of the smartest boys in the school. The non-affiliates would have won the academic trophy each year, except that the college never recognized them as a formal organization, so the trophy went to one of the fraternities.

Two of my three freshman roommates were non-affiliates. They were nice people and good students, but not socially skilled. The rejection hurt them and I felt bad about it. But of course I continued in my own fraternity and essentially I accepted the system. In those days of the so-called silent generation, most students did accept the system, whether it was the fraternity system, the political system, or the corporate system. Later, in the very different decade of the 1960's, Williams and many other colleges dropped the fraternities entirely.

Charity was a student at Cornell and I went to see her every weekend

I could. I was also on the swimming team. But essentially my freshman year wasn't much fun. Increasingly, I tuned out my studies and concentrated on girls and beer.

In the summer between my freshman and sophomore years in college, I broke up with Charity, after two years of what had seemed a serious romance. I just woke up one morning and realized that I no longer felt the same about her, that we both had changed since high school, and she was no longer someone I'd want to marry and spend the rest of my life with.

The other thing I remember from that summer was a job I had. I'd been working since my early teens. I started out making deliveries for my father's printing shop. One summer in high school I was a counselor at a camp in Massachusetts, and in the summer after my graduation I was a clerk for the First National City Bank, one of the biggest Wall Street banks. Then, that summer after my freshman year, a friend and I got jobs working on the assembly line of a New Jersey auto plant. It was the best pay I'd ever earned, about $150 a week, and also the hardest work I'd ever done. Fenders came at me along the assembly line and my job was to screw in the four bolts that secured a headlight. The fenders came relentlessly, like an advancing army, and I soon saw that I couldn't possibly keep up. Then my foreman explained to me that the trick was to screw in only the three outer bolts. The fourth bolt screwed in from the inside and if I didn't screw it in the inspector would never notice.

I did as the foreman suggested, and even then it was hard to keep up. I was working the night shift, getting off work at 4 A.M., then driving home and sleeping until noon. Some mornings I'd wake up in a cold sweat, after having a nightmare in which the assembly line was revolving around my bed. It was the worst experience I'd ever had. More than all my political science courses, that assembly line showed me the monotony and frustration of life as millions of working people know it. I didn't see how anyone could live like that for thirty or forty years.

I couldn't live like that for even one summer, and my friend and I quit after six weeks. We worked in an upstate New York resort for a few weeks, then spent the final weeks before school started living on the beach at Cape Cod.

At the start of my sophomore year I began dating a petite freshman at Smith. Our romance lasted through Thanksgiving, when she threw me over for a Princeton basketball player. I was crushed. To take my mind off my troubles, I joined a group of upperclassmen who played poker every night, sometimes until dawn. It wasn't unknown for someone to win or lose two or three hundred dollars in a night. I probably won more than I lost, but as my poker playing improved, my grades steadily declined. In the first semester I had all C's, and in the second semester four C's and a D.

I could afford the poker playing, because I was managing the student laundry. I probably earned three or four thousand dollars that year, and the job also enabled me to have a car, which underclassmen normally could not. Thus I had a way to drive to Smith and Bennington and Vassar for dates. Using the car for non-laundry purposes was against the rules, of course, but I was never caught.

I took one course in my sophomore year that would have an impact on my future. It was Fred Schuman's course in international relations. Schuman was a liberal, one of the first academics whom Joe McCarthy went after in his witch-hunting days, and he was still known to some of his critics as "Red Fred." But the thing that most impressed me about Schuman was that, despite his liberalism, he was an advocate of a tough power-politics approach to international diplomacy. We saw in his course that throughout history great nations had survived only if they combined military strength with diplomatic moderation—if, in Theodore Roosevelt's phrase, they walked softly but carried a big stick. If a nation was too weak, other nations would devour it. If, at the other extreme, a nation grew too powerful and too aggressive—Hitler's Germany being a classic example—then the balance of power would come into play, and the other nations would put aside their differences to defeat it militarily. It seemed to me, in my college days, that President Eisenhower understood this balance-of-power approach and followed it wisely. It seemed to me, too, that some liberals took a "soft" approach to international relations that was unrealistic about the world we live in.

I was soon to get a firsthand look at the world of power politics, as a soldier guarding the demilitarized zone in Korea. My sophomore year, all in all, had been a disaster. Soon after I got my grades, I realized I was wasting my time and my parents' money, and I made a quick decision. I would not return to Williams in the fall. I volunteered because I thought that two years in the army might make me more ready to settle down and get something out of college.

I worked for a month at a resort in Maine; then the army sent me to Fort Dix for my basic training. I rather enjoyed basic. It struck me as a program that was well organized and that had a clear purpose. I had no problem adjusting to the military; I'd had enough jobs over the years to learn to get along with all kinds of people. Still, as basic training ended, I decided that three years as an officer would be preferable to two years as an enlisted man, so I applied for Officer Candidate School. I was sent to Fort Sill, Oklahoma, for training as an artillery officer.

The twenty-two week OCS program was sheer hell for the first sixteen weeks or so, but it became bearable in the final weeks when you advanced to being a kind of upperclassman called a "redbird," in reference to the red patches you wore on your shirt. The week I became a redbird I bought a new Chevrolet on credit, which seemed a reasonable step for a man about to become an officer in the U. S. Army. It turned out to be my downfall. Fort Sill is a pretty dismal place, but I had found one bright spot in the person of a colonel's pretty blond daughter. One night when I was planning to take her out in my new car, my class was told to attend a study hall. We redbirds had often been cutting the study halls, and several of us decided to do so that night. I went on my date, and naturally that was the night they checked roll in the study hall. The next morning we were all called to see the commanding officer. We knew there would be some punishment; we hoped it would only be our being set back in training a few weeks. But the CO indicated we might all be booted out of OCS, as an example to the other men.

"Sir," I told the CO, "that would upset my father a great deal."

That was true. My father had been delighted at my becoming an officer. I think he had visions of another Jeb Stuart charging off to military glory. Later, when I told my father the news, he called my CO to try to win me a reprieve.

The CO was unmoved by the Magruder family's military tradition, however, and soon the word came that I and the other erring redbirds were now ex-redbirds, about to return to the ranks as privates. My orders were cut a day or two later, and I found I was on my way to Korea.

I had three weeks' leave before I was to report to Fort Lewis, Washington. I returned my Chevrolet to the dealer. The time did not seem ripe for a trip home. Instead, another ex-redbird and I decided to see Mexico. We hitchhiked to the border, then caught Mexican buses on to Mexico City and Acapulco, stopping off in various towns along the way. We had several close calls when we visited Mexican bars, in particular one time when we were so rash as to take out a couple of Mexican girls we'd met. Some of the local lads made it clear that we two gringos should disappear, pronto, which we did.

Eventually, we ran out of money and hitchhiked back to Dallas, my friend's hometown, where I checked in with one of those drive-a-car-to-California agencies. They gave me a car and a copilot, an old actor who'd seen better days but was headed back to Hollywood for one more try. I don't know how good an actor he was, but he certainly looked the part. He had long white hair and an aristocratic face and clothes that had once cost a lot of money, but which too had seen better days. He talked a good deal, quite eloquently, and his stories often began, "Young man, when I was playing opposite Garbo in 1930 . . ." He was rather shaky, and although he hadn't been drinking that day, I thought it would be best if I did most of the driving. However, in the late afternoon of our first day on the road, somewhere in west Texas, I let him drive while I took a nap in the back seat. He proceeded to side-swipe a truck and our car landed on its side in a ditch. I climbed out of the wreckage without a scratch, but the old actor was in pretty bad shape. The truck driver and I got him out of the car and eventually an ambulance came and carried him away. There wasn't anything I could do for him, so, after I had called the drive-a-car agency and told them the bad news, I hitchhiked on west. Three young hoods in a Cadillac picked me up. They had guns and kept talking about the stickups they'd pulled. If they were trying to scare me, they succeeded, but they got me to Los Angeles nonetheless, and from there I made my way to Fort Lewis. Soon I was on a troopship bound for Korea.

There isn't much I can add to the extensive literature on life in the U. S. Army. Essentially, as an enlisted man in peacetime, you play the army game, which means that you do as little as possible for the army and as much as possible for your own comfort. I started out on guard duty near the DMZ. The cease-fire had been signed, but there were still occasional outbursts of sniper fire across the DMZ. The weather was terrible and life was pretty grim. Life in our six-man tent became even grimmer than usual when one of the tentmates developed a particularly malodorous case of VD. I had nowhere to go but up, so I applied for radio operator's school. I'm not very mechanical, and I never really learned to operate a radio, but after eight weeks I became a radio operator nevertheless. I was still near the DMZ but at least I was working indoors. Later I was chosen for the Eighth Army honor guard, and sent to Seoul. I thought I would be performing at military ceremonies, but instead I found that the honor guard's main honor was to guard the homes of generals. I was out in the cold again. But at least, by cultivating the company clerks, I was able to wangle three or four R&R trips to Tokyo instead of the one I was entitled to.

Korea was also a dramatic course in applied political science for me. I was living in a country that had been ravaged by war, and where millions of people were living in poverty that was unimaginable by American standards. I tried in my spare time to get to know the Korean people as best I could. I didn't speak the language, of course, but many of the Korean officers, and even some of our Korean houseboys, spoke English, and they made it clear to me that the Syngman Rhee government was a ruthless dictatorship. My Korean experience raised more questions than it answered, and it made me more anxious to continue the study of political science when I got back to college.

Because I was returning to college, I was discharged early, in June of 1956, after twenty-one months of service. I got myself on a plane back home, rather than a troopship. When the plane stopped for fuel in Hawaii, several of us realized that the army didn't much care about our whereabouts at that point, so we stopped off for a few days on the beach before continuing our flight back to the States.

When I returned to Williams in the fall, most of my old friends had graduated. I dropped out of my fraternity and became something of a loner during my final two years. I developed an interest in classical music and began to build an extensive record collection. I was far more concerned than I had been with my studies and my future. Partly because of my Korean experience, I decided to major in political science. I was not a campus politician—activism would come later—but I had always had an instinctive personal interest in politics. I'd realized early in life that people usually liked me, that if I was pleasant to people I could usually get what I wanted. I always tried to make people comfortable when I dealt with them. In that sense, I'd been a political animal since boyhood. Now I wanted to study the practice of politics on the national and international levels.

Williams' political science department contained a number of outstanding professors. Besides Fred Schuman, whose international relations course had made such a lasting impression on me in my sophomore year, there was James MacGregor Burns, whose course on modern American politics I took in my senior year. It was an exciting and timely course, with often heated discussions of such matters as the New Deal reforms, the Yalta Conference, the Marshall Plan, Truman's seizure of the steel mills, and the two Eisenhower–Stevenson campaigns.

Burns was a liberal, a very ideological man, but he didn't push his views in our classroom discussions. In those discussions I usually found myself coming down on the conservative side of the issues. I didn't think an ever-expanding federal government, such as we had seen under Roosevelt and Truman, was the answer to the nation's social problems. I admired Roosevelt as a great national leader, but it seemed clear to me that his social programs had not ended the Depression—the war had done that. It seemed to me that certain of Roosevelt's programs, such as the Rural Electrification Administration, that had been valuable in the 1930's had by the 1950's become self-perpetuating bureaucracies that only wasted the taxpayers' money. The "liberal" programs of the New Deal and Fair Deal seemed to me often to be more distinguished by good intentions than by effective results. Increasingly I found myself drawn to the conservative approach to government, with its emphasis on individual effort and self-reliance.

My political views had been forming all my life, of course, as most people's do. My father's southern-style conservatism was an influence on my early years, and many of my friends' parents were well-off and Republican. By the time I entered college, in the fall of 1952, I was pro-Eisenhower, so much so that on the morning after the Presidential election I razzed a Stevenson supporter in my fraternity until he almost hit me. I was unhappy that morning with the news that Senator Henry Cabot Lodge had been defeated by young John F. Kennedy. Throughout my college years, Eisenhower was President and I shared the widespread belief that the country was doing quite well under his leadership. So, despite the teachings of some outstanding liberal professors, I remained a conservative, which meant that in terms of party politics I was a Republican.

In my junior year I made all B's, quite an improvement over my pre-army grades. Thanks to the GI Bill, a partial scholarship, a college loan, a bank loan, and part-time jobs, I no longer needed money from my parents to meet my college expenses. That winter I sold Prince Matchabelli perfume at Williams, mainly to other students for Christmas gifts, and that led to the job I held in the summer between my junior and senior years. I was one of about thirty college students in the Vick Chemical Company's summer sales program. The company's best-known product was Vicks VapoRub, but it sold a complete line of patent medicines. Our summer began with a training program during which we were taught a carefully designed sales pitch. Then we were given a car, an area to work, and a tough sales quota to meet. I worked first in the New York/New Jersey area, then in western Kentucky.

In either place, the approach was the same. You would call on a druggist, and begin your sales pitch with some innocuous comments like "Nice day" or "Well, fall's coming, isn't it?" Once you had the druggist nodding in the affirmative, you slipped into your routine . . . special discounts . . . buy now, pay later . . . and so on. You'd set up your counter display, managing to knock your competitor's displays off the counter in the process. Finally as a parting touch, after you'd made the sale, you'd slap a decal on the druggist's window. That was a remarkable decal. It was made of plastic that couldn't be scraped off. To get rid of that decal you had to change windows.

Once in a while there'd be an unpleasant scene when I'd call on a druggist who'd dealt with one of my predecessors in years past, who had loaded up the druggist with a lot of merchandise he couldn't sell and might have a hard time returning. By the end of the summer I was bothered by the ethics of what I was doing, but the fact remained that I did it well, and I received a reward as the program's top salesman that summer.

During that summer, too, I began a romance that led to my friendship with Williams' new chaplain, the Reverend William Sloane Coffin, Jr.

Her name was Judy, she was from New York, she had attended Vassar, then the University of Michigan, and she was one of the most beautiful girls I had ever seen. As my senior year began, we were very much in love. We felt a great physical attraction for one another, one that caused us both to be uncertain as to how far we should carry our relationship. Finally I went to Bill Coffin for advice. He was not much older than I and we hit it off immediately. In the spring I took his course in ethics, which was often conducted at his house over a beer, and sometimes I'd babysit for him when he and his wife went out.

Our talks soon moved from my original problem into many other areas. I was a veteran, older than most of the students, beginning to be concerned about right and wrong, beginning to see a lot of hypocrisy in the world around me, and Bill was one of the few people on campus who wanted to talk about the things that disturbed me.

We talked a lot about the fraternity system. Bill loathed its inequities and cruelties. I didn't disagree with him, but most fraternity men resented his outspoken opinions, and Bill was becoming the most controversial man on campus. That year a fraternity man was killed in a private plane crash and Bill delivered a eulogy for him. But the eulogy, most listeners thought, became an attack on the fraternity system. In effect, Bill said it was the fraternity system, with its emphasis on drinking and hell-raising, that caused the young man's death. Not long after that eulogy someone fired a shotgun blast through Bill's living room window.

That set off an even greater controversy, with most people deploring the violence and a few fraternity men saying it was too bad he hadn't been standing in front of the window when the shot was fired. My impression was that Bill gloried in the controversy. He seemed to believe in confrontation. He would go up to someone at a party and tell him he was a racist or an exploiter or whatever. When Bill went to a hotel he would ask the clerk if it admitted Negroes, and if it didn't he would go elsewhere. I admired his courage, but I questioned his confrontation tactics. I didn't think many people could live their lives that way. My observation, in the army, in college, and elsewhere, was that most institutions are political in nature and that you made your way in them only by adroit maneuvering. It seemed to me that, Bill Coffin aside, most people got along in the world by being flexible in their attitudes, not by moral confrontation. My impression was that it didn't pay to challenge the system, because the system was stronger than any individual. I still believe in the need for compromise; the difficulty, I would learn in later years, is to decide when to compromise and when to take a stand on principle.

My greatest concern that spring was what I would do after graduation. I saw myself heading for a career in business, yet I had doubts that a career in business was what I wanted. Men like Burns, Schuman, and Coffin had made me realize there were more important things in life than making money. I had a feeling that I wanted to do something more meaningful. I wanted to go to graduate school, but I already was more than three thousand dollars in debt to a bank and to the college, and I didn't want to sink deeper into debt. I gave brief thought to divinity school and to the foreign service, but neither was a serious possibility. Colleges like Williams seemingly existed to prepare young men for careers in business or law or medicine.

The corporate recruiters came to Williams all spring, and I was one of the most sought-after seniors. I had my military service out of the way, I had good grades, and I had experience as a salesman in my summer and part-time jobs. I didn't doubt that I could do well in business, but I questioned whether that was what I wanted. I was groping for answers, for alternatives, in my talks with Bill Coffin, for he too was concerned that Williams students were programmed to be interchangeable parts in the corporate machine. Yet I wasn't sure that Bill's views, or my doubts, had much relationship to the real world we lived in—the world of the assembly line where you left off the fourth bolt, the army where you hustled your way to a good deal, the cough-syrup business where you sold druggists merchandise they didn't need. I was confused and troubled. I increasingly realized that I had grown up without any firm set of beliefs, except for the business ethic, the success ethic. I was groping for something better in my talks with Bill Coffin, but perhaps it was too late.

Five or six corporations invited me to join their sales programs. The one that most interested me was Armstrong Cork. I visited its headquarters, liked its people, and was made a good offer, one I should have accepted. Instead, I accepted an offer from IBM. I still don't know why. IBM was famous in those days for its corporate regimentation—its trainees sang the company songs and couldn't wear colored shirts and that sort of thing. Moreover, to do well at IBM I would have to master the technology of its various computers, and I had always been weak in math and science. I sensed I was making a mistake to go with IBM but I did it anyway. I suppose it was because of IBM's aura of power and prestige. My college generation tended to make too many judgments on the basis of externals—we wanted to wear the "right" clothes and to belong to the best fraternities and to date the girls from the richest families. IBM had all the externals, all the status, so when it offered me a job some part of me, the ambitious part, couldn't refuse it.

I went to Hartford to begin IBM's training program almost immediately after my graduation in early June. I wanted to start earning money, paying off my debts, and perhaps thinking about marriage to Judy, whom I'd been seeing on weekends throughout my senior year. I got a room in a Hartford boardinghouse that was perhaps the most dismal place I'd stayed since the troopship that took me to Korea. It happened that my first days with IBM coincided with a crisis in my romance with Judy. She had another boyfriend, one who'd been away at a military academy but now was back, and she felt that she must choose between us. Thus, for a hectic week, I was spending my days trying to comprehend IBM's computers and my evenings driving a hundred miles to plead my case with Judy. My mind wasn't on my studies and I failed my first five daily tests. Then Judy informed me that she'd decided in favor of the other fellow.

At that point, I said to hell with it. I went to my supervisor's office the next morning and told him I was quitting the training program. He was flabbergasted.

"I don't understand," he said. "Nobody quits IBM. Don't you realize that in five years you can be making $18,000?"

I was unmoved. I left IBM's offices, put my things in the 1953 Plymouth I'd bought from my uncle, and set out for California.

CHAPTER II

The Corporate Ladder

I WAS BOUND for San Francisco. I'd passed through the city twice when I was in the army and, like countless others, had thought it the most beautiful of American cities. I didn't know anyone there, and I was almost broke, but I was confident that I could find a good job.

On my first morning in San Francisco I wandered around its business district. I happened to pass a spectacular new building that was under construction. A sign said it was to be the new headquarters of the Crown Zellerbach Corporation, and also gave the corporation's existing address, which was a few blocks away. I didn't know anything about Crown Zellerbach, but I admired its taste in architecture, so I walked down to its offices and said I was looking for a job. It happened that they had one opening in a new sales training program, and I was hired as a $390-a-month trainee.

Soon after I was hired, I exchanged letters with the director of placement at Williams. I wanted to tell him about my new job and to explain why I had left IBM. I discovered that he was furious with me. I had been his prize catch for 1958 and I had let him down. I tried to justify my departure from IBM, but it was no use. My sin was unforgivable.

Crown Zellerbach, as I soon learned, is the world's second largest paper company. Its year-long training program was divided into two parts. For the first six months, we trainees spent our mornings in classroom study and our afternoons in on-the-job training in the order department. In the second six months we were to be sales trainees in San Francisco, but I was told I had done well enough to skip that phase and go directly to Los Angeles to begin as a full-fledged salesman.

During my training period, in the last half of 1958, I was dating some airline stewardesses and also, thanks to a friend with social connections, some San Francisco debutantes. Still, I thought to call a girl I'd met the year before when I was at Williams, Gail Nicholas. We had double-dated once when she was at Vassar, and I knew she had transferred to the University of California's Berkeley campus. When I called, Gail deflated my ego by saying she didn't remember me, but I nonetheless went to see her at the Kappa Kappa Gamma house at Berkeley and soon we were dating steadily.

That Christmas I visited Gail's home in Los Angeles and met her parents. Gail's father, William Howard Nicholas, a successful lawyer, had been the only son of Mormon parents who around the turn of the century had left their farm in Indiana and headed west. They had first stopped in Salt Lake City, where one day the Mormon elders told Gail's grandfather they thought he should take a second wife. Her grandmother didn't care for the idea and insisted they leave Salt Lake City that very day, which they did. They moved first to Oregon, then to Los Angeles, where Howard Nicholas grew up. He attended Berkeley, then the Harvard Law School, and returned to Los Angeles to practice law. His specialty was the law regarding water rights and he used to joke that the Colorado River had put his children through college—he had argued a case regarding rights to that river all the way up to the Supreme Court. One lawyer and rising political figure in Los Angeles in the postwar years was Richard Nixon, and Gail remembers Nixon occasionally coming to their house during her childhood.

Gail went east, as her mother and older sister had, to the Dana Hall preparatory school in Boston, and she then decided to stay in the East and attend Vassar. But she found she didn't like Vassar. She was accustomed to the friendly informality of California, and she found life at Vassar too formal and the students too cold and distant. So she transferred back to Berkeley where, when I met her, she was an extremely popular coed.

Gail had all the external qualities that I—like most young men of my generation—had always sought in the girls I dated. She was pretty and popular and from a well-to-do family. But Gail had more than those external qualities. Gail had a maturity and an honesty and a depth of character that exceeded any I had known in other young women I had dated. She was an exceptional person, and as 1959 began we found ourselves falling in love.

After my transfer to Los Angeles in January, I often went to San Francisco to see Gail on weekends, and after her graduation in June she returned to her home in Los Angeles where we continued to date. In my work, I had been assigned to what we called "missionary" selling, which meant I was not dealing with Crown Zellerbach's established customers, but was going in cold to companies to sell them our products. It's the hardest kind of selling, but I did well enough to be given a promotion at the end of the summer. I was to be transferred to Kansas City. In Los Angeles I'd been part of a large sales force, but in Kansas City there would be only two older salesmen and I covering a four-state area.

The transfer threatened to end my romance with Gail. She was visiting with friends in the Sierras when I got the news in mid-August, and she was to leave soon for several months in Europe. Impulsively, I drove up into the mountains and told her we must be married right away or we would inevitably drift apart. She was uncertain. She wanted to take her European tour and, beyond that, I think she was not entirely sure she was ready for marriage. But at length she agreed, and we were married on October 17, 1959 in Los Angeles.

Neither of us had been anxious to move to Kansas City, and our life there got off to a bad start because I had done a terrible job of selecting our first apartment. It was a tiny, dark, gloomy furnished apartment with ugly furniture and a lumpy, three-quarter-size bed. Moreover, we soon realized that the apartment building was primarily a home for old people. Some of the old ladies were fascinated to find some newlyweds in their midst and sometimes we would catch them listening outside our door. Some nights we were awakened by the arrival of ambulances, and one night by fire engines when one woman accidentally set her bed afire.

Gail became pregnant not long after our marriage, and after a few months we moved to a better, larger apartment, one that would have a room for the baby. We began to make friends with other young couples that we met at church or through my work. I played some golf and we went to University of Kansas football games and soon we were enjoying ourselves socially.

In my work, I traveled a good deal through Iowa, Kansas, Missouri, and Nebraska. I visited a lot of small town food lockers, to sell our locker paper, and I also sold paper bags, toilet paper, gum-label tape, and other products to wholesalers. Gail often accompanied me on my travels and we discovered some of the oldest and dustiest hotels in the Middle West. Several of the states were dry, and we were fascinated to be told in restaurants that they didn't serve drinks but it was all right if we wanted to bring in a bottle in a paper sack.

I had a good job but not an exciting one. The most memorable experience of my year with Crown Zellerbach was a conflict I had with our home office. I noticed a snarl in our ordering system and proposed a solution to it. I soon found out how hard it is to get anything done in a large corporation. No one said I was wrong, but the attitude at higher levels was: "But that's how we've *always* done it!" Eventually my idea was accepted, but it was a discouraging process. It taught me a lot about how a corporation works. It wasn't enough to be right, you had to sell yourself. You had to negotiate within the corporate hierarchy, to give a little here to get a little there.

My job left me dissatisfied. I had energies I wasn't using. Gail and I had our friends, and I read a lot and listened to my record collection, but still I was restless, and in the fall of 1960 I found an outlet for my energies in Richard Nixon's campaign for President.

I had no strong feelings about Nixon at that point, but he seemed well qualified to be President and he offered a continuation of the Eisenhower policies I had admired. Certainly I preferred him to Kennedy; like most of my Republican friends, I thought Kennedy was rash and immature and that his election would be a disaster.

Through friends who were active in the party, I became the ward chairman for an urban ward in Kansas City a few miles from our apartment. I worked one precinct myself and directed the volunteers who worked the other precincts. We did all the things you do in precinct work —went door to door, passed out pamphlets, drove people to the polls, and so on. I enjoyed the work immensely. I like dealing with people face to face, and I got much more pleasure out of selling a political candidate I believed in than in selling Crown Zellerbach's paper products to Midwestern wholesalers.

I got to know my counterpart, the Democratic ward chairman. He was an older man, very pleasant, a veteran of the Pendergast machine. We had a drink together on election night, soon after the polls closed. That was entertaining, but the rest of election night was all downhill. Nixon was losing, and the mood at our headquarters was one of despair. It was hard to accept defeat after all that work and emotional involvement.

Still, I had been bitten by the political bug, and I looked forward to future campaigns. But, as it developed, they were not to be in Kansas City.

Our son Whitney, named for one of Gail's brothers, had been born on September 20, and I began to give increasing thought to my future. I felt that I needed a master's degree in business administration to advance in the corporate world. I applied to, and was accepted by, both the Harvard and University of Chicago business schools. During the Christmas holidays, Gail and I took our infant son to Staten Island to meet my parents, and we made a side trip to the Harvard Business School. We stopped off in New Haven to spend an evening with Bill Coffin and his wife. Bill had become the chaplain at Yale. He and I had corresponded occasionally during the two years I'd been out of Williams. Our letters were not profound, just exchanges between two friends about new jobs and new children and the like. Our evening with the Coffins was extremely pleasant, but I could sense that Bill and I were living in different worlds; he was still concerned with ethical and philosophical questions, and I was trying to cope with the more tangible problems of the business world.

The Harvard Business School was impressive but financially out of my reach. To go there for two years I would have had to borrow more than $10,000 and it didn't seem worth it. The University of Chicago offered an MBA program at night, so that a student could hold a full-time job and attend classes in the evenings. That was what I decided to do.

I also visited Chicago during the Christmas holidays, and I was interviewed by Booz, Allen and Hamilton, the management consulting firm. I was offered a job as the manager of its Chicago office. My superiors at Crown Zellerbach, when I told them of my plans, offered to transfer me to their Chicago office, but I declined the offer. I felt that Crown Zellerbach was a good, solid company, and that if I stayed with them I would move steadily up the executive ladder. But I wanted to rise faster than that. Booz, Allen had more glamour; it seemed to be where the action was. So I joined Booz, Allen early in 1961 as a "consultant," the title they gave their junior employees. What that title really meant was that you had no tenure. My salary was $8,000, a thousand dollars more than I'd been making at Crown Zellerbach.

We lived in the Chicago area for five years and we loved it. We thought it an exciting, dynamic city, a good place to work, a good place to make friends, a good place for politics. However, our first apartment there, as in Kansas City, left a lot to be desired. It was a third-floor walk-up in Evanston, just a short ride on the "L" from downtown Chicago. The apartment was on the top floor, exposed on all four sides, and the winter winds whistled into it from Lake Michigan, only a block away. To make matters worse, the apartment manager turned off the furnace at night, and when he turned it back on in the mornings it took several hours for the heat to get back to the top floor. Some nights Gail and I were afraid that Whitney was going to freeze in his crib and we'd bring him in bed with us to keep him warm. This was not an easy time for Gail, with one small child and, before very long, a second on the way. The washing machine was in the basement and when she wanted to wash Whitney's diapers, and couldn't get both him and the dirty diapers down the stairs, she would drop a bag full of diapers off our back porch and they would land with a mighty splat in the alley.

My salary didn't leave us much extra money. Fortunately, we had received as wedding gifts a lot of linens, china, silver, appliances, and so on, which kept down our spending in our early years of marriage. And Gail used her imagination a lot. When we moved to Chicago, the moving company had packed some of our things in very solid boxes. Gail saved two of the boxes and covered them with tablecloths and we used them for end tables for several years.

I was quite busy, of course, with my job and my classes two nights a week and my studies most other nights. And we soon made friends and had a fairly active social life. Yet, as the months passed, I again had the feeling of restlessness I'd known in Kansas City, and once again I turned to politics to cure it.

One day in January of 1962 I had lunch with Ned Jannotta, a former Princeton football star who was then a rising young Chicago businessman. When I mentioned my interest in politics, Ned said he had a friend who was going to run for Congress in the Thirteenth District, which was the district I lived in. Ned asked if I'd like to work in the campaign. He added that his candidate, Don Rumsfeld, didn't have much chance of winning, but that the campaign might be fun nonetheless. I quickly accepted.

Don Rumsfeld was then twenty-nine years old. He had grown up in Winnetka and had been a star athlete at New Trier High School; his old high school friends would form the base of his political organization. He had gone to Princeton, been a pilot in the navy, worked in Washington as a congressman's administrative assistant, then had returned to Chicago to be a stockbroker. He had no overwhelming qualifications for Congress, but he was young and attractive and energetic, with good social connections and plenty of loyal friends to help him.

Ours was a predominantly Republican district, so the crucial election was the Republican primary in early April. An opening existed because the incumbent, Representative Marguerite Stitt Church, was not seeking reelection. The front runner seemed to be state representative Marion E. Burks, a likable, middle-aged political pro who had the support of most party regulars. Rumsfeld's candidacy was something of a Young Turk movement against the regular party organization.

I became Don's chairman for the third ward, which stretched along Lake Michigan in the southeast section of Evanston and included many apartment houses. Wherever there are apartment houses there are unregistered voters, and our job was to get those people registered and to persuade them to vote for Rumsfeld.

Don worked hard and stressed his personal appeal. We held dozens of coffees in supporters' homes, where Don would speak informally to twenty or thirty voters. He wasn't a particularly good speaker at first, but he improved as the weeks went by. More important, with his crew cut and his boyish good looks he projected honesty and sincerity, and thus was able to arouse an enthusiasm that his opponent could not.

My job was to harness that enthusiasm in an effective volunteer campaign. Eventually we had more than a hundred volunteers working door to door in the third ward alone. Our opponent, Burks, was from Evanston and I think he took it for granted. My impression was that his party regulars were lazy and complacent. Meanwhile, our volunteers were working hard, and eventually we carried the third ward by a three-to-one margin.

The Rumsfeld-Burks race might have been close but for a scandal that destroyed the older man's chance to win. I think Don would have won without the scandal, but it certainly accounted for his landslide margin.

Burks was the chairman of the board of the Central Casualty Insurance Company. In January, the Chicago *Sun-Times*, which had endorsed Rumsfeld, revealed some serious financial troubles at Central Casualty. Then the state insurance commissioner halted Central Casualty from doing business because some $1.5 million of its funds was missing. Burks was never accused of any personal wrongdoing, but Central Casualty's collapse certainly embarrassed his candidacy. We did everything we could to keep the issue alive. Don never mentioned it in public, but whenever Burks spoke we would send our people to pepper him with questions about the scandal. He wasn't adroit enough to cut off discussion of the issue; instead, our people's questions would make him angry and flustered.

Rumsfeld won the election with 42,000 votes to Burks' 17,000. He singled me out for praise at his victory party, and a little later my work in the third ward was featured in a *Sun-Times* "anatomy of a victory" article. Again I had been an effective political organizer, and I was beginning to think that I might want to organize a campaign of my own someday. I'd learned that winning was a lot more fun than losing. And I had learned, too, from our stacking of our opponent's audiences, that practices that might not seem ethical were nonetheless common in the heat of a political campaign.

I didn't participate in Don's successful campaign against a Democratic opponent that fall. Gail was expecting our second child, and that summer we bought our first home, a $30,000, three-bedroom house in Northbrook, Illinois, a suburb about twenty miles from Chicago. Our son Justin was born on October 19, and Gail was busier than ever, caring for two small sons and getting settled in a new house. Both boys had health problems when they were young. Justin was allergic to milk products and for a time suffered from earaches. Then, that winter, when Justin was an infant and Whitney was two, Whitney woke up one morning with his eyes crossing. We took him to a doctor who horrified us by saying Whitney might go blind unless he had an immediate operation. The operation was performed a few days later in the Michael Reese Hospital, which is located in the middle of a slum in Chicago's South Side. Gail stayed at Whitney's side throughout his three days in the hospital. It was a profoundly depressing time for her. After the operation, Whitney's arms were strapped to his sides so he wouldn't scratch at his eye patches.

Whitney's operation was a success. He was left with tiny scars in the whites of his eyes, but his vision is perfect. And Gail, once the crisis was past and Whitney was back at home, could begin to enjoy our new home. She also began to do hospital volunteer work. One day, while working in a hospital, she met the real estate agent who had sold us our Northbrook home, and he commented on how much happier she looked than when he had first met her a year earlier. It was true. The combination of having her own home and my reducing my political activity had lifted Gail's spirits considerably.

Despite our move, I remained friendly with Don Rumsfeld. As the new Republican congressman, he made his peace with the party organization and was permitted to name a number of precinct captains. He chose me to be one of the precinct captains in Northbrook. Later, I was the cochairman of one of the "leadership conferences" he sponsored, at which several hundred party workers met for a day with party leaders to discuss means of more effective political action.

That September, just before Justin's birth, I had changed jobs again. It was Booz, Allen's policy to automatically let go some of its junior employees whenever its projected workload fell below a certain point. I had been moved from managing the office to hiring new employees. When the workload dipped that summer, and no one was being hired, I was dispensable. They offered me a job in their research division but research didn't interest me. Fortunately, I had become friendly with Jim Allen, one of the founders of Booz, Allen. Once, when he wanted his Bentley with him during a Florida vacation but didn't want to drive it down himself, Gail and I had driven it down for him. It was a memorable trip. We cruised through the South like royalty, leaving in our path hundreds of awed motorists and service-station attendants.

When I told Mr. Allen of my situation, he called the Jewel Tea Company, which was one of Booz, Allen's major clients, and recommended that they hire me. I started at Jewel in September of 1962 as a management trainee at $10,000 a year.

Jewel was then the nation's fifteenth largest retailer, selling some $800 million worth of merchandise in its food stores and its drugstores. Like most food chains it is essentially regional—distribution problems make national food chains almost impossible in the United States—with more than two hundred stores in the Chicago area. The point I would stress about Jewel, however, is not that it is big, but that it was the best-run corporation I ever worked for.

Most large organizations—corporate, governmental, military, or whatever—become rigid. They resist change, they discourage creativity, they expect people to wait for slow, automatic promotions. Jewel was the opposite of that. Since its founding around the turn of the century it has had a tradition of young, innovative leadership, and of excellent relations with both its employees and its customers. In its corporate headquarters, only the top officials have private offices. Everyone else, including high-level executives, sits at a desk in one big room, rather like a newspaper's newsroom. The idea is to encourage communication and innovation by breaking down bureaucratic barriers, and it works.

Jewel developed excellent loyalty among its customers because it dealt fairly and honestly with them. There are plenty of opportunities for a large retailer to cut corners. One common way is to advertise low-priced "specials" that will draw customers into the store, then to conveniently run out of the specials soon after the doors open. Jewel didn't do that. Nor did its buyers, to my knowledge, ever take bribes from manufacturers, another fairly common practice. Jewel was a hard-driving, competitive company, but it had a tradition of ethical dealing that started at the top and permeated the entire corporation.

All this made Jewel an enjoyable place to work. If you were young and ambitious, you felt that someone was listening to your ideas and that you had a good chance to move up in the company. Perhaps to the outsider all food stores seem much the same, but at Jewel you felt you were giving the public superior value and the public knew and appreciated that fact.

The dominant figure at Jewel during my three-and-a-half years there, the man who symbolized its traditions of youth and innovation, was Donald Perkins. At the time I was hired Don was a thirty-six-year-old vice-president, and the next year he became Jewel's president. Don was a self-made man who had worked his way through Yale, gone to the Harvard Business School, started with Jewel as a route salesman in 1953, and become a vice-president at thirty-three. When I was hired, Don was in charge of a new training program for people with MBA degrees, and I was its first trainee. One aspect of the program was that each trainee had a sponsor from the top levels of the company. Don was my sponsor, and he became a good friend.

In that training program, you learned the business, as Don had, from the bottom up. You worked in Jewel's stores as a checker and a bagger and also you worked for a while as a route salesman. Jewel's routes were throwbacks to a simpler era when salesmen went door to door rather than customers' driving miles to supermarkets and shopping complexes. Jewel's men still make their rounds each week in many cities, wearing their brown coats and carrying baskets containing tea, soap, candy, jellies, and other wares. These routes add up to a $100 million a year business. I worked on routes in Chicago, Baltimore, and Philadelphia that fall; I was on my route during the Cuban missile crisis. The routes were fun, but when my training ended Don Perkins had a much more difficult assignment for me.

Don had been responsible for Jewel's purchase of a chain of Boston-area discount houses called the Turnstyle stores. I was assigned to the

Turnstyle Division, and was soon caught up in its problems, which were both organizational and philosophical. The organization problems arose from the fact that our Chicago-based executives were trying to run the Turnstyle discount stores in Boston and also to open five similar stores in the Chicago area. We were spread too thin. I would fly to Boston several times each month, but the job just couldn't be done on a commuting basis.

The philosophical conflict was even worse. Jewel's tradition was to sell quality merchandise in a fair, ethical way. Turnstyle's was the discount-house tradition of selling low-quality merchandise by means of hard-sell advertising. The executives who had worked at Turnstyle for years wanted to cling to their old tricks, while those of us from Jewel wanted a new approach that would be based on selling good merchandise in volume and gradually building a good reputation.

It was a difficult situation. People who couldn't conform to the new approach had to be fired. Jewel had traditionally been a paternalistic company, one that dislikes firing anyone, but in this situation there was no choice. When a corporation is losing money, the game can get very tough.

I advanced quickly in the Turnstyle Division. I started as an assistant to the advertising manager. After a few months the advertising manager was moved out and I replaced him. His mistake had been in spending too much of his time on creative questions. I had an assistant to concentrate on creating the ads; what I was supposed to do was to find ways to cut the costs of our advertising program. For example, I took Turnstyle's printing and engraving away from one printer and I placed it with a new printer who would do comparable work for less money. To make this change, I had to fight Jewel's advertising executives, who wanted to leave the printing where it was for reasons of convenience, but I pleased top management because I saved money.

As advertising manager, I reported to the merchandise manager. He and the operations manager were equals—neither was the boss. Perkins had created this difficult situation to see which man would emerge on top. Eventually the merchandise manager won the battle and was promoted to vice-president in charge of the Turnstyle Division. I was moved up to replace him as merchandise manager. At the age of thirty-one I was earning $22,000 and my future with Jewel looked excellent.

In the fall of 1963, just as I was starting with Jewel, I became active in the Goldwater movement. Charles Barr and Patricia Hutar, who headed Goldwater for President in Illinois, asked me to be in charge of the Thirteenth Congressional District, where I had worked the previous year for Don Rumsfeld. Don encouraged me to accept. Goldwater had not yet acquired an extremist image. He was seen as a conservative, but as a reasonable, honest, attractive man, a candidate who was acceptable to all but the most liberal elements of the party. Rumsfeld and I were typical of the young Republicans who saw him at first as a strong candidate, only to be disillusioned by his inept performance once he got the nomination. As the party's candidate, he should have broadened his base, made his peace with the liberal elements he'd bested for the nomination. Instead, he made his "extremism is no vice" acceptance speech, chose an obscure and ultraconservative running mate, and adopted a no-compromise stance that could only lead to disaster. As Goldwater's campaign chairman for our district, I was plagued by the zealots who flocked to his cause. They were uncontrollable. They cared nothing about the Republican Party, only about their hero, whose statements encouraged their excesses. I was soon in sharp disagreement with an avid Goldwater loyalist about a book, a hatchet job on Lyndon Johnson, that she and the Goldwater loyalists wanted to distribute as part of our campaign. I said no, and when she went over my head, the state leadership backed me up. But it didn't matter; her people distributed the book anyway. They weren't interested in the nuts and bolts of precinct work, only in smearing Johnson. (Johnson was doing some smearing himself, of course, notably with the "Daisy Girl" television commercial which implied that Goldwater favored the nuclear incineration of little girls.)

The campaign was not far along before I was completely disillusioned. Many moderates were dropping out of the campaign, but I chose not to, because I assumed that if I left I'd be replaced by one of the zealots. I stayed because I wanted to do what I could to keep the extremists under control and to hold the party together for future, happier campaigns.

I viewed myself as a moderate Republican. I liked winning elections and the way you won was not by being ideological, but by working with all possible elements of the party. At the same time I was working for Goldwater I was also doing all I could for Charles Percy, the liberal Republican candidate for the Senate. But as the Goldwater campaign went on I found that, simply because I was involved in it, many people assumed I was an extremist. I had to explain to reporters that no, I wasn't in the John Birch Society. I sensed that my involvement was hurting me with some people at Jewel, because the Goldwater campaign had become a joke and I was part of it.

Still, I made the best of things. I had learned one lesson from the 1960 campaign that I applied to the 1964 campaign. In 1960 my friends and I had thought the world would end if Kennedy was elected; Kennedy was elected and the world didn't end. After that, I was never quite so doctrinaire in my politics again. During the campaign, our local paper, the Northbrook *Star*, had an article on me that was headlined:

GOLDWATER BACKER MAGRUDER HAS EVEN TEMPER,
HIGH BOILING POINT

That headline resulted from an incident at a luncheon when the reporter saw a critic of Goldwater berate me rather heatedly about my candidate, and I used a soft answer to turn away her wrath. I tried to get along with everyone; that was my instinct, in politics and elsewhere. You accomplish more that way. When the Goldwater campaign was over, most of the people who worked in it were, politically speaking, dead in the water. I was one of the few exceptions. I had made the best of a bad situation and I sensed that my political stock had probably risen a little.

The worst thing about the Goldwater campaign was its impact on my marriage. Our third child, our daughter Tracy, was born on May 9. Gail at that point had three children under the age of four, no household help, and a husband who was preoccupied with a new job and a Presidential campaign.

Gail was not uninterested in politics. She had been a political science major in college. She had given a coffee for Don Rumsfeld in our third-floor walk-up in Evanston, and she had attended Young Republican meetings with me and had been active in the League of Women Voters. In 1964, her own political views led her to be pro-Goldwater. Still, that was not enough to compensate for the strain of raising three children virtually single-handedly. Naturally I rationalized my political activity— I was working for the greater good—but it was not so easy for Gail.

Part of the problem was that, while Gail cared about politics, she didn't care for precinct-level political activity. She liked many of the young people we met in campaigns, but she felt that a lot of the political veterans were losers who flocked to political campaigns because no one was ever turned away there. She felt that some who weren't losers were generally the sort of people who couldn't be trusted.

Certainly, after a few campaigns, I knew exactly what she meant. But I had led a less sheltered life than Gail and I was more willing to take people as I found them. That was part of the challenge and the fun of a campaign: to bring order out of chaos. Which was fine for me, but no consolation for Gail in the difficult year of 1964. It was the first time that my political work had caused serious problems for our marriage, and I resolved not to let it happen again.

I wasn't politically active for a year following the Goldwater campaign. I was chairman of Northbrook's March of Dimes Campaign, and involved in other civic activities, but not until late in 1965 when Dick Ogilvie, the sheriff of Cook County, asked me to work on his race for president of the Cook County Board of Supervisors, did I return to politics.

Dick Ogilvie was a short, compact, rather tough-looking man—he had scars on his face from his World War II service—who had a lot of ambition and a lot of talent. He once told a friend of mine, "If I had Magruder's looks and personality, I could be President." He had done quite well with his own looks. During the Eisenhower years he was a U.S. Attorney who won public attention by getting a conviction of Tough Tony Acardo, the reputed Mafia leader. I first met him in 1962, during the Rumsfeld campaign, when Ogilvie ran successfully for sheriff. He had been an excellent sheriff and by 1965 he had his eye on the next step up the ladder that would eventually lead him to the governor's mansion.

I was one of several people who met with Ogilvie for breakfast once or twice a week that winter to begin putting together a campaign organization. Then, early in 1966, with the primary coming in June, he asked me to be his campaign manager. I agreed and began working part-time in his campaign office near the sheriff's office.

I was excited about it but worried about problems with Gail if I combined my job and another political campaign. But I thought I saw a solution. I proposed to Don Perkins that Jewel give me a six-month leave of absence. It happened that Perkins was a friend of Ogilvie's, so I thought my request would be granted. Perkins spoke to the board of directors and they turned me down. They didn't want to set a precedent of employees' taking leave for political activity. I thought it was a short-sighted decision, that it would be good for Jewel to have an executive who was rising in Republican circles, and that more generally it was good policy for corporations to encourage their people to be active in public affairs.

I was frustrated and angered by the decision. Moreover, Jewel had recently sent a man about my age to Boston to run the Turnstyle stores there, and I thought I should have been given the job. I was discouraged, and I proceeded to make the worst possible decision: in May of 1966 I quit my job. It was the worst mistake of my business career.

I think, looking back on it, that I was simply too immature to cope with the multiple pressures I was under, and so I made an irrational decision. I should have dropped out of the campaign, or worked on a limited basis. Certainly, I shouldn't have walked out on a company that had been so good to me. If I had dropped out of the campaign, Ogilvie would have understood, and he would still have wanted me to help when (as it turned out) he ran successfully for governor in 1968. Then I might have taken my leave of absence to join in his administration. But that was not the course I followed, and in 1966 I was starting over, both in business and in politics, in California.

I had come to know a corporate recruiter in New York whose biggest client was the Broadway-Hale department store chain in California. He mentioned that spring that if I was available he had an interesting opportunity for me with Broadway-Hale. After Jewel turned down my request for a leave of absence, I was on a vacation trip to California, and I talked to Broadway-Hale's president, Ed Carter. He said he had a job for me in corporate development at a salary of $30,000. The job was vague and I should have been suspicious, but I was impatient so I took the job on faith.

I returned to Chicago and broke the news to Ogilvie. He wasn't upset to lose a campaign manager; he was a highly confident man and he knew he'd find someone else to do the job. Then I told Don Perkins, who was quite disturbed. He invited me and Gail to his home one Saturday afternoon to talk things over. Don had bought a beautiful old home in an exclusive suburb. It was set far back from the road and surrounded by trees. Gail and I often went driving on Sunday afternoons and looked at old homes, the kind we hoped to own someday, and Perkins' house was the sort we dreamed of. Gail had been horrified when I told her I'd decided to leave Jewel, in part because she was fond of Don Perkins and felt he was the sort of man she liked to see me associated with. That afternoon, at Don's house, he spoke of my unlimited future with Jewel. Certainly I had reason to think that within a few years I would be a vicepresident in charge of one of Jewel's divisions, and that if all went well I might someday succeed Perkins as president. But I told Perkins my mind was made up: I was going to take the job in California.

First, I took Gail on a trip to Europe for the month of June. It was our first long vacation alone together in six years of marriage. We flew to

Rome and then rented a Fiat and drove north through Italy into Germany and Switzerland and eventually flew to England. We stopped in the Alps and did some hiking. We tried to find little out-of-the-way restaurants, and often we'd buy some wine and cheese and picnic by the side of the road. Once I bought some cheap Italian wine and we were having a picnic beside the river when we found that the wine was just too bad to drink. A couple of Italian hobos were sleeping nearby on the river bank. I gave them the wine, which they thought was fine—they drank it on the spot.

In Rome, we stayed in a little hotel in a room that looked out on the Borghese Gardens. There was a statue in the museum there that I thought looked like Gail, and after that I'd sometimes call her Gail Borghese. She says it's the only nickname I've ever had for her.

We drove through the English countryside and one night stayed in an inn in Windsor, on the Thames, that had once been Christopher Wren's home. It was there that Stuart, our fourth child, was conceived.

We returned to Los Angeles on the Fourth of July, excited about my new job and the new life we were starting. I called Ed Carter the next day and said I was ready to go to work. It was then that the trouble began.

Carter told me he'd decided not to start me in the corporate headquarters, but in the company's Broadway Division, which operated twenty-seven Broadway department stores in Southern California. There, after a few days of awkward interviews, I realized that no one had any idea of what to do with me. Apparently Ed Carter had thought I was a promising young fellow whom he ought to hire, but had neglected the detail of having a job for me. And I had neglected to look before I leaped.

My new superiors were bothered that I had no department store experience, and some I think were resentful of my salary. I felt that, given my experience at Jewel, I could quickly adjust to a department store operation, but the Broadway people thought I should undergo basic training, department by department. I was sent for six months to run one floor of a department store in Century City, in West Los Angeles. I was a glorified floorwalker, at $30,000 a year. I couldn't believe it.

I soon realized that I had made a terrible mistake, and I called Don Perkins and admitted it. He invited me to come back to Chicago and talk to him. I did, and although he was unhappy with me he said he'd talk to his executives about taking me back. A few days later he called and said I could return to Jewel.

But by then I was having second thoughts. I feared that I'd look like a fool if I went limping back to Jewel only a few weeks after resigning. And Gail, who hadn't particularly wanted to return to California in the first place, certainly didn't want to pack up and move cross-country again. So I told Perkins I was sorry, but I guessed I'd stay with Broadway after all. He was furious, and justly so.

Those first months at Broadway, performing trivial work in a Century City department store, were easily the low point of my business career. I might have sought another job, but having made one stupid move, my instinct was not to risk another. I resolved to stick it out, to make the best of a bad thing, at least for a while.

I survived that frustrating period primarily by concentrating my thoughts on my family. Gail was tremendously helpful and understanding, and the children were an endless source of pleasure to me. Our fourth child, Stuart, was born on March 24, 1967. Gail had always been a wonderful mother and I, despite my work and my politics, had tried to give the children all the time and attention I could. During our last two summers in Chicago we rented a house at White Lake, Michigan, and spent as much of our time there as possible. When Whitney became six, he and I entered the YMCA's Indian Guides program for fathers and sons, and I later participated in the same program with Justin and Stuart in Los Angeles and Washington.

That summer in California, we first rented a house in Malibu, then bought a lovely, modernistic home in the Santa Monica Valley about a mile from the ocean. The house had been designed by either Frank Lloyd Wright or one of his students. It was in an L shape, with the inside of the L composed mostly of glass walls that looked onto a garden where a beautiful olive tree grew. The house was designed so that its windows caught the sunlight to best advantage. We almost never needed artificial heat. There was a big outdoor balcony, high up in the trees, where we liked to sit in the evenings. Gail loved the house, and took charge of having it painted and the installation of new floors and a new kitchen. We finally could afford household help for Gail, and when she wasn't working on the house she was busy renewing her friendship with girls she'd known in school, as well as with her sister, Ruth, who lived close by.

We enjoyed California's outdoor life. I liked body surfing, and many evenings we'd all go down to the ocean to swim together. We rode bicycles a lot, and sometimes we'd visit Gail's grandfather's ranch near San Diego where we could ride horseback.

Cooking is one of my hobbies, and most Sundays would begin with my fixing pancakes for the family. Then we'd go to church, then perhaps out to some inn for Sunday dinner. Or we might go for a visit with Gail's sister and her husband and their eight children. We spent two Easter Sundays with Ruth's family, and it was quite a sight to see all our children dashing around their two acres of land in search of Easter eggs, accompanied by her children's two dogs, numerous rabbits, and guinea pigs.

It was a good time for us. We were enjoying our lives, and my job, although it was never good, was getting better. After my six months of basic training, I was made an assistant buyer of cosmetics. Most young assistant buyers were paid about $7500; I was making four times that. After a couple of months I went to my boss and said my situation was ridiculous. He agreed, and I was promoted to being the chief cosmetics buyer for the twenty-seven Broadway stores, with responsibility for purchasing some $7 million of cosmetics annually. I liked the job. If you did well, you were largely left on your own. You sought out new and attractive products, and you tried to negotiate the best possible deals with the cosmetics companies on promotion, advertising, and so on.

I spent a year as the cosmetics buyer, then I was promoted to be one of Broadway's ten merchandise managers, at a salary of $35,000. That meant that after a year and a half with Broadway I'd worked my way back up to the level I'd been at when I left Jewel. In each case, I was responsible for a division with about $30 million in annual sales. My view was that I had needed a few months of training at Broadway but that a year and a half of training had been absurd.

The worst part was that, having worked my way back to a responsible level, I saw that I really wasn't interested in my new job. There was nothing creative about it. I had ten buyers reporting to me, and I functioned mainly as an accountant, keeping tabs on their profits and losses, gross margins, markdowns, and other data. I had the additional problem of not getting along well with my immediate boss, the vice-president of the division. He had wanted someone else in my job, but the president of the division had insisted on me.

Once I had been promoted to merchandise manager, and found that I still was bored with my job, it was only a matter of time until I left Broadway-Hale. When Gail and I left Chicago a neighbor of ours, an older woman who was a good friend of Gail's, said to her in parting: "Gail, whatever you do, keep Jeb out of politics." But it wasn't that easy.

I was restless, and politics was in my blood. Once again I turned to it as an outlet for my frustrations.

In the summer of 1967, at a party, I met Ed Blessing, a man about my age who was helping organize a Nixon for President campaign in California. Blessing reported to Bob Nesen, a Cadillac dealer (and later Assistant Secretary of the Navy), who in turn reported to Bob Finch, the Nixon adviser and then lieutenant governor of California, who was directing the Nixon effort in the state. I began working with their group. I assured Gail it was only a minor, part-time effort for me, but when Blessing separated from his wife and left the state, I replaced him as an organizer.

The Nixon campaign was in the hands of young, relatively unknown men like Blessing and myself because Nixon wanted to avoid antagonizing Governor Reagan, who also aspired to the Republican nomination. He therefore wanted his campaign to have a "low profile," and that meant using little-known figures rather than his prominent political supporters whose ties went back to the 1960 campaign and before. Also, many of those older men didn't want to have to choose between Nixon and Reagan at that point. Eventually, Nixon agreed not to challenge Reagan in the California primary, so our organizing efforts were not directed at the primary but at building a campaign organization.

I became the Southern California coordinator, with responsibility for Los Angeles County and ten surrounding counties. We worked out of an office on Wilshire Boulevard and in the preconvention months we made good progress toward building a precinct organization for Nixon. But in its final months, the Nixon campaign in California became a fiasco, a disaster. In memory I see it as hundreds of men and women fighting for personal glory and for the candidate's ear, and spending most of their time discussing which government job they'd get after Dick was in the White House. Nixon won California despite his organization there, not because of it.

There were two reasons for the fiasco. The first was Bob Finch. Bob was virtually incapable of making decisions. He was such a total political animal that he seemed to agree with everyone; you'd think you had a decision, then he'd talk to someone else and he'd change his mind. He was nervous and erratic and he just couldn't say no to anyone.

That led to the next problem. Once Nixon was nominated, all Nixon's old guard from his past campaigns came scrambling aboard the bandwagon. Most of them should have been given honorary titles and kept out of the day-to-day campaign operations. But Finch couldn't say no to any of them, so they were given operational jobs that they were unable or unwilling to perform.

The only significant function of a state organization in a Presidential campaign is basic precinct work—to identify your supporters and get them to the polls. The state organization has no significant media or advisory role, because the candidate is dealing directly with the national media and is getting his advice from his personal staff. But the old-line Nixonites who were taking over our campaign weren't interested in precinct work. They wanted to devise grand campaign strategies and to give advice directly to the candidate. Countless times, when a problem would arise, one of them would declare, "By God, I'm going to talk to Dick about that!" It was ridiculous. Most of them hadn't talked to Nixon since 1962, and weren't destined to be talking to him again any time soon.

We had a lot of large meetings at which various people made impassioned speeches and nothing was accomplished. Finch would announce decisions that would later be reversed and in general no one knew what was going on. At one memorable meeting at the California Club, one gentleman in his eighties introduced another gentleman in his eighties who was the new head of some aspect of the campaign. The second gentleman, it was explained, would surely do an outstanding job, because he'd performed the same function for Wendell Willkie in 1940. I almost broke up. *That* was the 1968 Nixon campaign in California.

Our precinct organization never reached its full potential because neither Finch nor his old guard advisers cared about it or put sufficient resources into it. Nor did Nixon's national staff choose to put any money into our precinct work.

We had some limited funds which the old guard wanted to put into newspaper ads. The fact is that newspaper ads have almost no impact in a Presidential campaign; they can be used for certain specific functions, such as soliciting money or volunteers and discussing certain complex issues, but it is television ads that influence how most people are going to vote. But the old guard had their media strategies that they were determined to test out in newspaper ads, although the money would have been far more effectively spent on telephone banks and other precinct operations.

The final indignity came when Nixon's campaign manager, John Mitchell, and his deputy, Peter Flanigan, bypassed our state organization entirely and set up their own precinct operation in California. They did this in a number of states. It was a slap in the face to the state organizations, but it was not a bad idea. Rather than fight with our top-heavy, fouled-up organization, they simply ignored it. They would rent offices in a city, have phones installed, and hire women to make calls. They would get a list of registered Republicans and then call voters at random and ask if they'd like to be Nixon block captains. If the voter agreed, he was sent campaign literature, sign-up sheets, registration information, and the like. There was an obvious duplication of efforts with our state organization as well as with the regular Republican Party organization, but duplication is not necessarily harmful in a political campaign.

When the national staff set up its boiler room operation in California, they called me for help and I did what I could. I didn't resent their bypassing our organization; in their position I'd have done the same thing.

Eventually I phased out of the campaign. You couldn't get decisions from Finch, you were always out on a limb, and nothing was being accomplished. There were bright moments. Nixon came to Los Angeles and we turned out a big crowd for him. I met Haldeman once or twice, quite casually, when Nixon was in the state. But eventually I eased myself out of the campaign and I don't think I was greatly missed.

Early in 1968, not long after I'd been promoted to merchandise manager with Broadway, I began to talk to two men about the three of us starting our own business. They were Bill Sawyer, a buyer with Broadway, and Jerry Mendelson, who had been the sales manager for a cosmetics company. They would run the new company, and I would stay with Broadway, but would contribute my part-time advice and assistance.

That spring we began Cosmetics Industries, Inc., which served as the sales representative for a number of cosmetics companies in California and other western states. This business started off well and soon we began a second company, Consumer Development Corporation, to manufacture and market a hosiery product and a cosmetics product. This too did well, but we needed capital to expand our manufacturing programs.

During the Nixon campaign I had become friendly with a lawyer named Waller Taylor II, who was a friend of Bob Finch's. I told Waller about my businesses, and he agreed to invest a substantial amount of money in them, enough so that he and I became the two major stockholders. As 1968 progressed, Waller was urging me to leave Broadway and devote myself full-time to our companies. I was uncertain, but in December I had a difference with my boss at Broadway, the vice-president with whom I'd never gotten along. We agreed that the best solution to the problem was for me to resign.

I went to work early in 1969 as the president and chief executive officer of our two small businesses. I did so with no great excitement. It was a practical matter. The companies needed me and I was available. I couldn't in conscience refuse to go, and there was always the possibility that the businesses might be very profitable. But, as I started my new job, I did give my partners one candid warning: Nixon was President, and if I got a chance to go to Washington, I would take it.

Not long after the election, in late November, Finch called me to New York to talk to him. He was then scheduled to be Secretary of Health, Education, and Welfare. It was a typical Finch meeting—everything was vague and uncertain. "Jeb, I need you down there," he told me, but it was never clear what he needed me for. At one point he was saying I might be an Assistant Secretary. That was absurd, given my age and qualifications, but I didn't think so then. I was excited. I had the book that lists all top-level government jobs and I was studying it to see what position might be worthy of my talents. One of my boosters with Finch and later with Haldeman was Ed Carter, with whom I'd remained friendly despite my leaving Broadway-Hale.

Finch had me come to Washington in January to talk to H.E.W. officials. It soon became clear that he had no specific job in mind and that my background had not prepared me for most of H.E.W.'s social service programs. Eventually, Pat Gray, Finch's executive assistant, found me a good job that I was qualified to perform. Gray was the balding ex-naval officer who had known Nixon as Vice President, whose administrative ability did much to hold H.E.W. together during Finch's tenure, and who eventually served briefly as acting Director of the FBI. But by the time he found me a job, I had thought things over carefully, and I had declined the job, despite my desire to go into the administration. I saw that H.E.W. was an administrative monstrosity; I felt that Finch was a terrible administrator; and my instinct was that the whole thing was going to be a fiasco, one that I had best avoid.

So I stayed in California and then, a few months later, Bob Haldeman invited me to come to San Clemente to talk about a job in the White House.

Young Magruder, age 15

Pfc. Magruder, Korea, 1955

Jeb and Gail, March 1968, with Whitney, Tracy, Stuart, and Justin

Gail and the children at the Inaugural Parade, January 20, 1973

FACING, ABOVE: The Magruders with Jeb's mother, father, and brother

FACING, BELOW: Jeb and the kids, Christmas Eve, 1970

Maurice Stans, chief fund raiser for Nixon reelection campaign, before the Senate committee, June 13, 1973. Jeb and Gail Magruder in the background

FACING, ABOVE: John and Maureen Dean near the end of the fourth day of Dean's testimony before the Senate Watergate committee, June 28, 1973

FACING, BELOW: Hugh Sloan, former Nixon campaign treasurer, testifying before the Senate committee

H.R. Haldeman, President Nixon's chief of staff, with the Chief Executive

FACING: Charles W. Colson (ABOVE LEFT); John D. Ehrlichman (ABOVE RIGHT); John Mitchell (BELOW LEFT); Herbert Kalmbach (BELOW RIGHT)

Herbert Klein with his successor, Ron Ziegler

G. Gordon Liddy, former member of the White House "plumbers" squad, wearing handcuffs, brushes past newsmen in basement of the Criminal Courts Building, Los Angeles, December 1973.

ABOVE LEFT: Herbert L. "Bart" Porter pleaded guilty to one count of lying to the FBI, January 28, 1974.

ABOVE RIGHT: Rob Odle, White House assistant and Presidential campaign adviser

LEFT: Gordon Strachan, Haldeman's chief political aide

Robert G. Mardian, one-time Assistant Attorney General

Richard Kleindienst testifying before the Senate committee,
April 10, 1973

The Magruders posing with President Nixon back in happier times, December 21, 1969

The Magruders with Clark and Barbara MacGregor at the Republican Convention in August 1972

Chuck Colson chairing a meeting that included Magruder, Fred Malek (fifth from right), and Rob Odle (sixth from right), May 8, 1972

Nixon meets with J. Willard Marriott, Magruder, Dwight Chapin, and Stephen Bull, December 12, 1972.

Magruder during his testimony before the Senate committee, June 14, 1973

The Magruders arrive in London, June 30, 1973, for a brief vacation, perhaps the last together for some time.

CHAPTER III

Inside the Oval Office

ON THE MORNING of November 5, 1969, after I had been working in the White House for a month, I was sitting in the President's office listening spellbound as an exultant Richard Nixon savored his most recent political victory.

We've got those liberal bastards on the run now, he was telling us in a proud monologue; we've got them on the run and we're going to keep them on the run.

Two nights before, he had gone on television to announce his plan for U. S. troop withdrawals from Vietnam and a larger military role for the South Vietnamese armed forces. The speech had been intended to deflate the resurgent antiwar movement, and the press and public reaction had been excellent. Now, as a way of saying thanks to the people who had helped him meet the crisis, Nixon had invited several members of his staff in for coffee.

Bob Haldeman was there, and Henry Kissinger, Ron Ziegler, Herb Klein, Dwight Chapin, speechwriters Pat Buchanan and Ray Price, and myself, the only newcomer in the group.

Nixon slumped contentedly in his chair, his feet up on his desk, a pleased smile on his face, as his monologue continued. In politics, he said, the best defense was a good offense; we'd floored those liberal sons of bitches with the TV speech and we'd never let them get back on their feet. His language was rough, but his tone was one of satisfaction, not anger. We'd won a big battle, he stressed, and we had the team now to keep on winning.

We all shared his satisfaction and his relief. The tension had been building in the White House for weeks. The antiwar movement had staged its nationwide moratorium rallies on October 15 and was holding a massive demonstration in Washington on November 15. But the President, with his announcement of troop withdrawals, had cut them off at the ankles, or so it seemed.

Nixon went around the room with a word or two for everyone. When he praised Kissinger, his foreign affairs adviser cautioned that, while we had indeed turned a corner, a satisfactory settlement to the war might still be a long way off. Nixon praised the speechwriters for their work on his speech. Then he turned to me and Chapin and recalled the stacks of telegrams we'd had waiting on his desk the previous morning, and the excellent wire-service picture they'd made.

"Those telegrams were great," he said to Chapin. "You and Jeb got those, didn't you? I heard you had a little trouble."

"At first, the Western Union people said it wouldn't be possible to get them delivered the next morning," Chapin explained. "Then I called the president of Western Union and he said it *would* be possible."

Nixon grinned and turned to Pat Buchanan, the very conservative, very combative ex-newspaperman who prepared his daily news summary as well as writing speeches.

"Pat, how were the televison reports last night?" he asked.

"They were all good except one," Buchanan said, and named a network correspondent who we felt often showed an anti-Administration bias.

Henry Kissinger broke in.

"Well, Mr. President, that man is an agent of the Rumanian government."

He explained that the correspondent was on a retainer to provide Washington reports to the Rumanian government, which is, of course, a Communist government.

"That's right," the President said angrily. "That guy is a Communist."

He looked at me.

"Jeb, you're our new ramrod around here. Get the word out on that guy."

I saw Herb Klein turning white.

"Yes sir, Mr. President," I said.

The talk passed to other matters, the butler moved among us with hot coffee, and a little later, the President stood up, the signal that the meeting was over. I returned to my office in the White House basement, across from the Mess and around the corner from Kissinger's suite of offices. Everyone else may have forgotten the matter, but I had received a direct order from the President to get the word out on the television correspondent's alleged ties to the Rumanian government. I didn't waste any time in soul-searching—I'd already seen, in one month in the White House, that those assistants who tried to second-guess the President's judgments didn't last long in his favor. So I passed the word about the correspondent to some friendly reporters.

The next thing we knew, the correspondent was in Herb Klein's office demanding to know the whereabouts of this son of a bitch Magruder who was calling him a Communist. Klein, who often found himself in jams like that, apologized profusely; Magruder, he explained, was a new man who'd made a mistake, and it would never happen again.

Other things would happen, however, for if there was any one lesson I took away from that meeting it was that the tough antimedia line I'd been hearing from Haldeman for a month didn't originate with Haldeman, it came straight from the President himself.

I had no bias against the media at that point. I'd had very little dealing with the national media. I thought a disproportionate number of reporters and commentators were liberals, but I realized that we Republicans had our friends in the media too. But the important point was my realization that if I wanted to do well, I'd better take the line that Nixon and Haldeman took. There just wasn't any room for debate on the issue. The media were out to get us, so we'd get them first. In my early days, I'd sometimes tell people like Dwight Chapin or Larry Higby, "You guys are paranoid. Look what the media did to Teddy after Chappaquiddick. They do it to everybody, not just us." But that kind of argument fell on deaf ears.

When I arrived at the White House, a shakedown was in progress. Some of the staff's influence was increasing, and that of others' was lessening. I saw that those who were losing influence were those who were seen as "soft" on the media or on liberals in general, including Herb Klein, whose future as Director of Communications was in doubt, and Bob Finch, who was on his way out as Secretary of Health, Education, and Welfare. Those whose influence was intensifying were the hard-liners—Bob Haldeman, Attorney General John Mitchell, and soon,

Presidential counsel Charles Colson—men whose contempt for the media and for our liberal critics equaled Nixon's own.

For my own part, the choice was clear. I had bounced around for several years, not having a job I really liked since I'd left Jewel, and now I had a job I loved, one that might be a springboard toward unlimited success.

"Jeb," I told myself, "you're not going to screw this one up. You like this job and you're going to do what they tell you."

The first time I went to the White House I got lost. That was in late September, when Gail and I flew to Washington to begin house-hunting. I called Haldeman, who invited us to lunch. We were both excited, and I was nervous about being on time, so we left early for the short drive from our temporary apartment to the White House. I had reckoned without the White House security system, however. I didn't know which gate to enter, and when I would ask one guard he would motion me on toward the next gate. I must have missed a gate, because we drove all the way around the White House before we finally found the correct gate, the one on Pennsylvania Avenue outside the West Wing.

Larry Higby greeted us warmly, then escorted us into Haldeman's office, where our lunch was served. At that time, Haldeman had an office next to the President's, with French doors opening out onto a small garden he'd had constructed. We had a leisurely lunch, one in which we saw Bob Haldeman at his best, as he dealt with a new staff man and, perhaps more important, a new staff man's wife. He and his wife had known Gail and her family in Los Angeles, and he was solicitous about our move and the house-hunting and the schools our children would enter in Washington. He stressed that there were still problems in the White House organization, that it was not yet the efficient, effective machine he wanted, but he was counting on me to help him toward that end. He admitted that the hours would be long and the work hard, and that my family would be called upon to make a sacrifice, but he stressed too the tremendous opportunity my new job presented for me—and my family—to share in national and international events. Haldeman was reflective, considerate, and tremendously impressive, and Gail and I left his office on a cloud. Haldeman had even arranged, after we left him, for a guide to take us on a special tour of the White House, to cap off the afternoon.

A few days later I started to work. On my first day, Haldeman had me into his office for a long talk about how he hoped to see the White House public relations apparatus improved. He gave me eight remarkable memos that the President had written to him about his concept of Presidential public relations. I was assigned an office in the White House basement, down the hall from Henry Kissinger's suite of offices and near the White House Mess, where I would often eat lunch and, until Gail arrived in Washington, dinner.

During the afternoon, I was in my office reading the documents Haldeman had given me when he called and asked me to hurry back to his office because there was something he wanted me to see. The something, it developed, was a reception in the Green Room of the White House for eight or ten new ambassadors to the United States who had come to present their diplomatic credentials to the President. In the past, each newly arrived ambassador had come for a private audience with the President. But President Nixon, Haldeman explained to me, didn't care for that formality; he regarded it as wasted time. Thus, he and Haldeman had worked out this new procedure, with the new ambassadors coming to the White House in a group, with each given only a minute or two alone with the President in the Green Room. This reception was the first test of the new procedure, and Haldeman wanted me to join him in seeing how it worked. It worked fine, from his and the President's point of view, although some diplomatic feathers were ruffled in the process.

My own first meeting with the President came, as I recall, in my second week on the job, when Haldeman took me into the Oval Office for a brief handshake and great-to-have-you-aboard chat. I was struck by how ill at ease the President seemed in greeting me. This was in contrast to how good he was with groups and in receiving lines; he seemed to have geared himself for dealing with masses of people, not individuals. One of the things you noticed in an informal meeting with him was how his hands shook; when he drank coffee, there was an embarrassing rattle of cup against saucer. I took that to be the result both of nervous tension and of his lack of physical dexterity. One of the younger White House aides told me a classic story about Nixon's physical awkwardness. At a bill-signing ceremony, a pen had been placed in front of the President on his desk with its top off. Nixon picked it up, put its top on, and tried to sign the bill with the top on the pen. Realizing his mistake, Nixon took the top off the pen, started to sign his name, but only managed to jab himself in his left hand. At that, he dropped the top of the pen to the floor, and total chaos ensued, as half the Cabinet dropped to its knees trying to find the top of the pen.

I would like to try to convey the mood that existed in the White House during my first months there, the crucial months of the fall of 1969 when the President faced his first challenge from the antiwar movement, a challenge that did much to shape the Administration's thinking about its critics and how to deal with them. But before I get to the specific events of those months let me introduce some of the people I was meeting and starting to work with. And the man to begin with, the one figure who was absolutely central to the Nixon White House, is of course Bob Haldeman.

I was working directly for Haldeman in my first months in the Administration, and I would be working for him indirectly throughout my stay in the government. Almost everyone in the Administration was working, directly or indirectly, for Haldeman, because that was how *his* boss, the President, wanted it.

"Every President needs a son of a bitch," Haldeman used to say, "and I'm Nixon's. I'm his buffer and I'm his bastard. I get done what he wants done and I take the heat instead of him."

Bob was tall, crew-cut, self-confident, efficient, disciplined, impatient, tough, fair, and ultraconservative. He could be charming when time permitted—but time did not often permit. He dealt with most people by memo because memos were quick and impersonal; he could say no on a memo in one second, by checking the "Disapproved" box, while if he dealt with someone in person, it might take three or four minutes to say no and hear their complaints and get them out of the office. Chuck Colson used to say that he could sometimes get ten or fifteen minutes to shoot the breeze with the President, but he could never get that with Haldeman.

Haldeman had a fetish about memos. One of the first ones I sent him was returned with orders that it be retyped because of some minor defect in style—his name wasn't capitalized or something like that. He usually scribbled comments in the margin when he returned a memo to you, and we all awaited his comments like kids awaiting their report card. A "Good thinking" or "Excellent" could make your week, while a "NO!" or "See me!" could cast you into despair. Rob Odle, who became one of my assistants in 1970, used to collect Haldeman's memos, good and bad, and pass them around for all to see. We rationalized that even if he cut you to pieces, at least that proved he was thinking about you.

Haldeman could not tolerate vague or incomplete work. Once late in

1969, when Vice President Agnew was at a peak of controversy, Lyn Nofziger of our Congressional Relations staff sent Haldeman a memo that said in its entirety:

"Senator Allott was on ABC and CBS networks strongly defending the Vice President. It is possible that other senators also were interviewed."

Haldeman replied: "Obviously, it's possible. That is a totally useless piece of information. The point is—*were* the other senators interviewed?"

One of Haldeman's main jobs was to keep away from the President people whom he didn't want to see, a number that was ever increasing. People like Herb Klein, who had once had easy access to Nixon, found it existed no longer, and people like Vice President Agnew and the Cabinet, who expected access, found they could not get past Haldeman. Haldeman often took the blame for hurt feelings, but I never doubted he was doing exactly what Nixon wanted done.

Another person who was losing access to the President in those days was his long-time secretary, Rose Mary Woods. Administrative functions that she once had handled were being assumed by Haldeman and his staff, and both Chapin and Higby made it clear to me that I was to deal with her carefully, to do nothing that might worsen a delicate situation. Actually, in my occasional dealings with her, I always found her a pleasant and competent person. She had plenty of work to do. She knew *everyone,* going back twenty years in the President's career, and she was a useful contact with hundreds of political figures. You couldn't fool her; she knew who had done what and who had given what and where the bodies were buried. But, in the White House, she had to accept the fact that she, like almost everyone else, had to accept Haldeman's supremacy.

In time, Haldeman became so incredibly busy that most people had to deal with him through Larry Higby, his young assistant. Senator Robert Dole, when he was Republican National Chairman, used to complain that he would call to talk to the President, be switched to Haldeman's office, and wind up talking to some kid named Higby. For my part, on an average day, I might get one call from Haldeman—a "hot-line" phone connected our desks, but only he ever used it—and ten from Higby. It became a joke in the White House that there really wasn't any Haldeman, just Higby up there sending all those memos.

But Haldeman existed, and if he gave me an order, I assumed that either the President had specifically asked that it be done, or that Bob was operating within such well-defined guide lines that he knew what the President wanted without specific instructions. The result was the same: an order from Haldeman was an order from the President.

It was not wise to question directives from Haldeman, although it was sometimes possible to change his mind if you had your facts straight and could show him a better way to do something. One memorable occasion when Haldeman and the President changed their minds was the affair of the new White House guards' costumes.

Ken Cole and I walked out into the Rose Garden one morning to watch some ceremony and were astonished to see the guards wearing costumes that looked like something out of eighteenth-century Bavaria: peaked hats, long white coats with gold braid, striped pants—all in all, what one writer called a "comic opera motif."

"What have those fools done now?" moaned Ken, who had a cynicism that was rare in the White House. We didn't know who had done what, but we laughed our heads off, as did the reporters who were present.

Later that morning I saw Haldeman.

"Those uniforms are unbelievable," I remarked.

"The President and I wanted something more formal," Haldeman snapped. "And I don't want to hear any more about it."

He didn't hear any more from me, but the ridicule we received from the press and the public in the next few days caused the costumes to be stored in mothballs, to everyone's relief.

Haldeman was without question the best instrument Nixon ever found for accomplishing exactly what he wanted done. I never saw the slightest indication that Haldeman disagreed with anything that Nixon said or did. Haldeman never discussed his feelings about the President with me—it was not the sort of thing he would discuss—but he obviously believed that serving Richard Nixon was the greatest honor that could befall him. He was well known in the White House for his hobby of taking home movies of the President on every possible occasion. If Haldeman attended a Rose Garden ceremony, or went on a Presidential trip, there were two things he always did—first, he would make sure the event was handled correctly and second, he would pull out his camera and film the President.

Not everyone served the President in such a totally unquestioning manner. When I got to know John Mitchell, I saw that Mitchell sometimes disagreed with Nixon's hard-line approach to politics, but went along with it as a way of humoring his "client." But Haldeman was just as hard-line as Nixon. He hated Nixon's political enemies as much as

Nixon hated them. That, I think, was Haldeman's major flaw as a Presidential assistant—he lacked any independent vision that might have helped Nixon avoid mistakes.

The press secretary, Ron Ziegler, had first known Haldeman at J. Walter Thompson, and he continued to be Haldeman's man in the White House. Ziegler was a heavy-set, dark-haired young man whose great asset as press secretary was that he never uttered a syllable that had not first been approved by Nixon or Haldeman. That got him the job over Herb Klein and others who had been known now and then to express a personal opinion or an independent thought.

In those days the press was writing a lot about Ziegler's boyish charm and his winning smile and how it was impossible to get mad at him. I found Ziegler to be stubborn, unpleasant, barely competent, and power hungry, a man who resisted my reorganization efforts as a threat to his own plans for empire-building.

In my first weeks in the White House, Ziegler would now and then summon me to his office for an early-evening drink and chat. But once the pleasantries were out of the way, he'd attack.

Klein's Office of Communications, he would say, was a disaster and the only answer was for the entire media program to be put under his, Ziegler's, direction. It was true enough that Klein's operation was a disaster, but it was also clear to me, after seeing Ziegler's own operation, that he wasn't capable of taking it over. Our interests were in conflict: I wanted to see Klein's operation strengthened and Ziegler wanted to see it disintegrate, so he could pick up the pieces.

Ziegler not only would oppose my plans, but often he would become abusive in the process. Typically, after he downed a couple of stiff Scotches, he would inform me that I was a new man who didn't know the ropes and I'd do well to keep out of his way. I had a hard time controlling my temper. Ziegler, as far as I was concerned, was a former Disneyland guide who in his present capacity was scarcely more than a ventriloquist's dummy. But Ziegler had a big office, and he had access to the President, and he liked to throw his weight around. Once he had told me: "I see the President all the time, Jeb; it's important for you to get good grades with people like me."

My problems with Ziegler came to a head one afternoon in December when Cliff Miller and I went to see him about my reorganization plans. Miller was the Los Angeles public relations executive who had urged

Haldeman to hire me earlier that year, and who continued to serve as a consultant to the White House on public relations matters. A good-looking, well-dressed, persuasive man in his forties, Miller was the president of the T. R. Braun & Co. public relations firm, one that traditionally didn't do routine chores like writing press releases but concentrated on giving strategic advice to its clients. He had worked on several Nixon campaigns and campaigns for other Republican candidates. Miller himself struck me as a political moderate, but one who always expressed his views in terms of practicality rather than ideology. Haldeman used to sum up Miller's role as a White House consultant by saying that Cliff had the best job of all, because he only gave advice and never implemented it; if things went right he could take the credit, and if things went wrong he could say you had fouled up the implementation.

That day, with Miller accompanying me, I went through the reorganization debate with Ziegler once again, around and around, listening to all his criticisms and protests, until I'd had enough.

"Ziegler, all you've done is waste my time," I told him. "I'm sick of this."

"Well, you come in here with these organization plans and you don't even know what the hell's going on around here," he told me.

"I know that you're an obnoxious son of a bitch," I declared, "and that I'm not going to waste any more time on you."

I almost hit him. Fortunately, Cliff Miller persuaded me that it'd be best if we went on to our next appointment. Once I calmed down, I was not displeased about the exchange. Anger can be used to advantage; that was something I'd learned in the business world. Ziegler had been trying to push me around and it was just as well to get our differences out in the open. He'd dislike me, but now he'd probably leave me alone. That was more or less how it worked out. In the eventual reorganization, his Press Office remained independent, reporting directly to Haldeman, and there was minimal communication between his office and our Office of Communications. Which was fine with me.

I had far more respect for Herb Klein, the director of communications, a sleepy-eyed ex-newspaper editor whom Ziegler had beaten out for the job of press secretary. Herb did not fully share the prevailing paranoia about the media. He had the idea that if we treated reporters decently, if we were as candid and open with them as we could be, most of them would give us a fair shake. In short, he didn't view the media as enemies, simply as critics who, if properly handled, would probably give us our due.

His attitude had two results. First, it made Klein by far the most effective person we had in dealing with the press.

Second, it made Haldeman, Nixon, and others increasingly suspicious that Klein was not "loyal." Klein had been a Nixon man since the late 1940's, but now was suspected of being too "soft" or too "liberal" and was therefore being frozen out by Nixon and his new, hard-line advisers. Haldeman told me that Nixon had once considered not even offering Klein a job in the Administration. Haldeman already had picked Ziegler as his candidate for press secretary, both because he fit in with the youthful image the Administration wanted to project, and because Ziegler obviously would be no threat.

Eventually, Bob Finch came up with the idea of making Ziegler responsible for day-to-day press briefings, and of creating the Office of Communications, where Klein could direct a long-range public relations program.

The trouble with this plan was that Klein, while excellent with reporters, was a terrible administrator. He woudn't delegate authority and when he was traveling, as he often was, nothing got done. The President or Haldeman would ask for something but no one in Klein's office was authorized to provide it.

The problem was perhaps summed up by Herb's briefcase, which became White House legend. The joke was that everything went into Herb's briefcase but nothing ever came out—if anything was lost, that was the place to begin the search. Among other things it usually contained several pairs of the slippers that airlines give first-class passengers on coast-to-coast flights and that Herb would toss in atop the President's unanswered memos.

One Saturday morning, several of us were meeting in Herb's office, and the time came for him to leave to catch a plane. He kept on talking as he grabbed some of the mountain of papers on his desk and started piling them into his briefcase. The pile of papers in the briefcase went up and up and up, until Herb casually tried to close it. Naturally, it wouldn't close so Herb kept on talking to us as he pushed on it, then pounded it, but that briefcase wasn't going to shut. Colson and Chapin and I got up and tried to help, but it was no use. Finally, in desperation, Herb put the briefcase on top of his safe, sat on it, and bounced up and down until it shut. We were all roaring by then, but if you had to live with Herb's briefcase as the center of your administrative life, it wasn't funny.

Yet, whatever his state of disorganization, Herb had sound political judgment. Once, when Vice President Agnew was about to deliver the toughest speech of his career, Herb saw an advance text and was able to persuade Agnew that the speech went too far. Often he would give Nixon sound advice on how the press or public would respond to some hard-line tactic. But however good Herb's advice, it was generally not what Nixon wanted to hear, and he was steadily losing his credibility and his access to the President.

Yet Herb's problem was not entirely political. He seemed unable to sense the moods of this moody President. Once I was watching as Nixon walked into the White House library for a nationally televised interview. He had a way, before a speech or an interview, of blocking everything else from his mind. Yet you could see his concentration, his total inward-ness, etched in his face. He was like that as he walked across the down-stairs foyer toward the library. It was certainly no time to bother him. But Klein walked up to him and started a conversation. You could see the annoyance on Nixon's face—and you only had to annoy Nixon once or twice before you found that the door was locked, and Haldeman had the key.

Chuck Colson joined the staff shortly after I did. His arrival was part of the general staff shake-up that had also brought me in. Bryce Harlow pointed out at one meeting that we had no specific person to work with special-interest groups. He added that he knew a Washington lawyer he'd recommend, Chuck Colson. Colson was interviewed and hired, and I recall Harlow saying, just before Colson came to work, "Well, I warn you, we've got a tiger on our hands now; this Colson will chew some people up."

He was right.

I came to regard Colson as an evil genius. His brilliance was un-deniable, but it was too often applied to encouraging Nixon's darker side, his desire to lash out at his enemies, his instinct for the jugular. I would have to say that—granting always Nixon's central responsibility for what happened in his administration—Colson was one of the men among his advisers most responsible for creating the climate that made Watergate possible, perhaps inevitable.

When Colson came to work, Haldeman asked me to show him around, just as Chapin had shown me around. Chuck was then in his late thirties, an articulate, ambitious lawyer from Massachusetts who had once worked for Senator Leverett Saltonstall. He had come to Bryce Harlow's attention during the 1968 campaign when he had written some position papers, including one controversial paper on Securities and Exchange Commission policy. It was soon obvious that Colson wasn't going to be content with a second-level role in the White House.

He showed up in my office one Monday morning, not long after he'd arrived in the White House, in a state of great agitation. I asked him what was the matter.

"I went to church services yesterday," he said. "I went through the receiving line and shook hands with the President. Damn it, Magruder, *he doesn't know who I am!"*

The President would soon know who he was. Colson became the only newcomer to gain the direct access to Nixon that Haldeman, Ehrlichman, Kissinger, Mitchell, Shultz, and Connally among others enjoyed. Colson was the first person in the White House to see that we had a chance to cut deeply into traditionally Democratic groups, including Catholics and blue-collar workers, in the 1970 and 1972 elections. He persuaded Haldeman and Nixon that the special-interest groups he was working with were the key to those elections, and that the President should, therefore, hold meetings with their leaders. Colson of course would sit in on the meetings.

Nixon normally ignored staff people who sat in on meetings, but it is not easy to ignore Colson. He's one of the most persuasive men I've ever met. He could always see which way the President was leaning, and he would state brilliantly whatever the President wanted to hear. He could devastate those who disagreed with him. His tactic was always the same: he only wished to help the President, so if you disagreed with him, you must be disloyal to the President. From the first, he would challenge any of the senior advisers if he thought they were wrong—that is, he would challenge anyone except Haldeman and Nixon, who were never wrong.

Colson and I soon came into conflict. He wanted to get rid of Klein and take over the Office of Communications, and when I resisted him, we became antagonists. I wanted to win elections and strike back at our critics as much as he did, but I thought Colson's tactics were often too hard-line, too heavy-handed, and would prove to be counterproductive. For example, in 1972 he tried to get me to send a fake McGovern supporter to a homosexual rally, which I refused to do—not out of any charity toward McGovern, but because it was too likely that the trick would be found out.

Colson's ploys too often accomplished nothing. He organized the phony write-in campaign for Ted Kennedy in New Hampshire in 1972, which did us no good. He persuaded the President we had to infiltrate a group of Quakers who were carrying out an antiwar vigil outside the White House—which we did and which bore no results.

For all his scorn for Klein, Colson was as bad an administrator as Klein. Once, when the President was to make a speech to the Junior Chamber of Commerce in St. Louis, and the advance men were arranging a motorcade, Colson said he'd use his labor contacts to help turn out a crowd. He was assigned a specific block along the motorcade; he was to pack it with cheering hardhats. In fact, when the President's motorcade passed by, Colson's block was deserted—that was Colson: lots of talk and an empty block.

He had his successes, of course. He could always boast that he "got" Senator Joseph Tydings in 1970 by planting a story with *Life* magazine that accused Tydings of financial misdeeds. Another time, Colson brought me a picture of Ted Kennedy and a beautiful woman, who wasn't Mrs. Kennedy, together in Rome. He asked me if I could get it printed. I was able to peddle it to the *National Enquirer,* a scandal sheet, and it was later picked up by one of the news magazines. That was a small success for Colson, and it also illustrates another of his talents— he usually was able to stay in the background, to get other people to do the dirty work for him.

But the important thing about Chuck Colson is that from 1970 on, he was the man whose advice the President most often followed on politics and on the media. He arrived in the White House with one secretary and by the time he left he had dozens of people reporting to him. The rest of us would joke about Colson's ever-expanding empire—the Department of Dirty Tricks, we called it—and about the fact that none of us knew exactly what Colson was up to.

The joke would in time be on us.

During my first month in the White House, Haldeman arranged for us to spend a Saturday at Camp David talking with Henry Kissinger and John Ehrlichman, who was then emerging as the chief domestic-affairs adviser. The purpose of the meeting was to discuss ways that our public relations program could work more closely with their two offices. It was necessary for Kissinger and Ehrlichman to understand, as they did not at that time, that it wasn't enough for the Administration to do good substantive work, we also had to present our work to the public in such a way that it could be understood and appreciated.

In government, the line between style and substance, between image and reality, is often a narrow one. Who knows if a government program is a "success"? The Peace Corps, in spite of glowing notices in its first years, actually had very serious problems. But its excellent publicity, generated by the tireless Sargent Shriver, created a climate in which the agency could grow and improve, and reflected well on the entire Kennedy Administration.

In our case, we felt we faced special problems in selling the Nixon program. Our man lacked the warmth of an Eisenhower, the charisma of a Kennedy, or the flamboyance of a Johnson. He wasn't supporting the sort of domestic programs that had immediate popular appeal. So, as Haldeman and I stressed to Ehrlichman and Kissinger, we would have to work for everything we got. If they had some new program or new accomplishment, they should let us know in advance, so we could see that the President received full credit for it.

Both men were receptive to what we said. Ehrlichman, in particular, owed his increasing importance in the Administration to Haldeman's patronage, and was eager to cooperate. Ehrlichman had performed a secondary job in the campaign—he had been tour director, working out of New York—and had come to the White House as Counsel to the President, a good job but not a first-rank one. Both Arthur Burns, the economist, and Pat Moynihan, the Kennedy Administration social planner, had been active in domestic affairs in the early months of the Nixon administration, but neither had quite worked out. Burns was too verbose to please either Nixon or Haldeman, and he was eventually kicked upstairs to be chairman of the Federal Reserve Board. Moynihan, while personally liked, and admired for his brillance, was too liberal and independent to please Haldeman, and his sponsorship of the controversial Family Assistance Plan caused him to come under increasing criticism from the more conservative elements of the Administration. Eventually, Moynihan was relieved of his domestic affairs staff, made a Counselor to the President, and later ambassador to India, and the trusted, toughminded Ehrlichman moved in as director of the Domestic Council. Ehrlichman was more open and personable than Haldeman, and less disciplined—he tended to float in and out of meetings, and to stick his nose into everything that came along. However, I found Ehrlichman able and cooperative, although I usually dealt with one of his deputies, Egil (Bud) Krogh or Ken Cole.

Ken Cole, one of the young men I met on my first visit to San Clemente, had worked for J. Walter Thompson in his native New York, but he was by no means a typical gung-ho advertising man. I used to call Cole our White House cold-water man—whenever anybody was excited about a new idea, Cole would pour cold water on it. His attitude was that the burden was on you to prove an idea was workable.

In early 1974, Cole succeeded Ehrlichman as Assistant to the President for Domestic Affairs, but it was largely by accident that he became involved in the substance of domestic affairs instead of working with me on public relations. He began as one of Haldeman's assistants, but he moved over to become Ehrlichman's deputy for administrative affairs. Eventually, because he was extremely able and self-confident, he became Ehrlichman's chief deputy and had a role in overseeing virtually all the domestic agencies. Cole lived only a couple of blocks from me and we and our wives were friends. I enjoyed Ken's company and found his skeptical approach to government refreshing and often effective.

Bud Krogh, the other Ehrlichman aide I most often dealt with, was lean, intense, and probably the hardest-working person in the White House. Some mornings you would see Bud, his eyes bloodshot, his suit rumpled, and you would know he'd worked in his office all night to finish an assignment. He kept in shape for these marathon sessions by frequent jogging on the Mall and weight lifting and saunas in the White House exercise room.

Krogh had been a lawyer with Ehrlichman's firm in Seattle before coming to the White House. He supervised several areas of the government for Ehrlichman, including law enforcement and drug-related programs, and we often found ourselves working together—for example, in arranging a White House Conference on Drug Abuse, with him handling the substance and me handling the public relations. He always had a keen understanding of the need for publicity to enhance the substantive achievements of federal programs, and he and I had an excellent relationship.

Krogh, given his drive and intensity, was often maddened by the slow-moving pace of the bureaucracy. He used to say it would take six years to get the bureaucracy straightened out—to promote the people who would do what the President wanted done and to get rid of those who wouldn't—and he would have given his all for every day of those six years had not unforeseen events disrupted his timetable.

When Ehrlichman replaced Moynihan as the chief domestic adviser, that further expanded Haldeman's grip on White House operations. Through me he had effective control over public relations, and when Bryce Harlow left he soon had the Congressional Relations staff reporting to him. The only White House office he did not control was Henry Kissinger's.

Kissinger's attitude, at our Camp David meeting, was "I don't know anything about public relations, so you fellows handle it." In time, as we got to specific events, that shifted to "I don't know anything about public relations, but let me tell you what we ought to do."

Nixon and Haldeman had made a judgment, early in the administration, that Kissinger should not appear on television because of his thick German accent—his Dr. Strangelove accent, we called it. It may have been a poor decision. Certainly Kissinger was extremely effective in his private sessions with reporters. We began using him more in press briefings until finally Nixon and/or Haldeman began to fear that Kissinger was getting a better press than the President. Haldeman sent Klein a memo asking whether Kissinger's briefings were serving the President's interests as well as Kissinger's own. Klein responded that Kissinger was doing an excellent job and reflecting credit on the President. It was an accurate reply, but it may not have been what Haldeman wanted to hear.

Kissinger is a most sophisticated man, but sometimes naïve about public relations. Once, soon after I met him, I was having lunch at Sans Souci, the elegant French restaurant located just across Seventeenth Street from the White House, when Kissinger came in with Cristina Ford, Henry Ford II's glamorous second wife. After lunch, when I got back to my office, Kissinger called me.

"Jeb," he said, "you saw that I was having lunch with Mrs. Ford. I'd appreciate it if you'd keep that quiet."

I almost broke up. "Henry, *I* won't say anything," I promised. "But you're out of your mind if you think you can take Cristina Ford to Sans Souci and not have it make the gossip columns." Their luncheon was in the papers the next day naturally.

Another time, during the 1972 campaign, I was having lunch at Sans Souci with Henry Ford II's daughter, Charlotte Ford, who was helping on the campaign, and whom I understood Kissinger had been seeing. He came in with another woman, and during lunch came over and said to me: "Jeb, could you bring Charlotte by my office after lunch?" It was amazing how he seemed to juggle dozens of beautiful women, but we in the White House were most impressed by the dedication Kissinger brought to his work. He ran through aides at a remarkable pace, and he was almost always the last of the senior assistants to leave the office at night. The joke around the White House was that any man who worked that hard couldn't have much energy left over for serious romance.

Pat Buchanan had a beefy, beer-drinker's face and a cool, highly conservative outlook—he called Colson a "Massachusetts liberal." He had quit his job as an editorial writer for the St. Louis *Globe-Democrat* in 1967 to become Richard Nixon's first full-time assistant in his drive for the Presidency. Buchanan, having been with Nixon so early, felt some resentment toward the Haldemans and other managers who came in later and seemed to dominate Nixon's time. He was something of a loner who avoided staff meetings, and kept busy with his speechwriting and his supervision of the production of the President's daily news summary. In my first few weeks in the White House, when I had a project that required some writing, I went to Buchanan's office to see if he would handle it for me. Instead, he exploded.

"Damn it," he shouted, "I'm sick of Haldeman thinking I'll write junk for him and I'm sick of you new guys coming in here and thinking you're in charge of everything."

I told him that I was just doing what Haldeman had asked me to do, and when I got back to my office I sent him a note saying I was sorry if we'd gotten off to a bad start. We never had any problem after that, and during the 1972 campaign, when he was a chief political strategist, he and I worked together closely.

I mentioned my exchange with Buchanan to Dwight Chapin, who shrugged and said: "Pat has got to understand that things have changed since it was just him and Nixon. If he can't understand that he should leave."

Chapin was handsome and self-confident, and his influence went far beyond his official role as appointments secretary. He, like Ziegler, had worked with Haldeman at J. Walter Thompson, and as a very young man he had been an advance man on Nixon's 1962 campaign for governor. In the White House, he gave a lot of time and thought to all matters relating to the Presidential image. He played no operational role in the public relations program, but he was someone I consulted with closely.

Chapin, the person I felt closest to in the White House, might have been called Haldeman's Haldeman. He was just as rigid politically as Haldeman, but far more personable, and he often served as a buffer for Bob. When people were becoming furious at Haldeman's abrasive behavior, Chapin would go down to the White House Mess and talk about what a good job Bob was doing for the President. Chapin was also something of a practical joker; he and I once faked a memo from the President to the senior staff, saying that henceforth they should deal directly with the President, not with Ziegler, on press matters. Chapin sent a copy to Ziegler, who after a few hours of panic finally realized it was a joke.

In the mid-1960's, J. Walter Thompson had transferred Chapin to its New York office, and when Nixon, then a Wall Street lawyer, began gearing up to run for President, he hired Chapin on Haldeman's recommendation. Buchanan had been Nixon's first campaign aide, and Chapin became the second. Chapin sometimes told a story from that period that I think suggests why Nixon's public relations advisers eventually gave up on presenting him as a lovable man. Sometime in late 1967 or early 1968, when Nixon was an unannounced candidate for President, he and Dwight left Nixon's Wall Street law office, were driven to La Guardia Airport, and boarded the shuttle flight for Washington.

Once the plane was out on the runway, the pilot announced a delay in takeoff and Nixon began to chafe.

"I'm not going to sit here all day," he said finally. He got up and went to the stewardess and demanded to see the pilot. When the pilot came out, he announced that he was Richard Nixon and he wanted off the plane immediately. The pilot protested, Nixon insisted, and finally the pilot radioed the tower and a ramp was rolled out onto the runway so Nixon could disembark. Chapin said he never forgot the sick feeling he had as he and his boss climbed out of that plane while, in the background, the other passengers booed and hissed their future President.

CHAPTER IV

Learning the Ropes

THE WHITE HOUSE existed in a state of permanent crisis. There were the major crises—the antiwar rallies and the Haynsworth nomination when I arrived; the Cambodian invasion and the Carswell nomination the following spring—and when there was no major calamity there were always a dozen or so smaller crises brewing. Haldeman contributed to the constant state of emergency by his administrative style. He never said, "Get me this by next week"; it was always, "Get me this by 3 P.M." Everything was important, every detail, and the result was a highly charged atmosphere, one that encouraged a siege mentality.

This is not said in complaint. We savored the crises, the challenges, the combat. Richard Nixon once wrote a book in which he confessed to a certain love of crisis situations, and in time we all came to share that fatal fascination.

I had been hired to try to lessen the crisis atmosphere by developing a plan whereby we could better anticipate and deal with emergencies. My first weeks in the White House were largely spent in interviewing various people involved in the public relations program and in preparing my recommendations for Haldeman. At the same time Haldeman was increasingly giving me special projects. My memos from those first weeks reflect both our internal reorganization and the external pressures that preoccupied us, and by reviewing them I can perhaps suggest the mood of the White House when I arrived there in the late fall of 1969.

72

R N ON P R

During my first day in the White House, Haldeman had given me eight memos on public relations that the President had dictated for him on September 22. Haldeman commented that these memos might help me better understand just what the President expected from us, as indeed they did. Once I had read the memos I realized that the most sophisticated student of public relations in the White House was neither Haldeman nor Klein, but the President himself. He knew what he wanted, in general terms and in specific detail; all he lacked were the people who could implement his wishes.

The President's memos had been inspired by the fact that two great antiwar demonstrations were approaching, the national moratorium on October 15 and the rally at the Washington Monument on November 15. We all felt threatened, put on the defensive, by the imminence of these two well-organized, well-publicized demonstrations, and the President was taking the initiative in suggesting how we might counter our critics. But, more generally, the memos reflected the President's continuing discontent with the quality of his public relations in his first year as President. He recognized the absolute centrality of his own role: in one memo he said the "basic need is *not* PR—it's PO"—Presidential Offensive. He would do his share, if the rest of us would do ours.

Two of the President's memos, one short and one long, suggest the tone of all eight. In the short one the President stated his priorities:

> When we have our Public-Relations discussion on Saturday, I think we ought to put down five or six public-relations goals that we want to impress on the public consciousness. For example: hard work, dignity, staff treatment (compared with Johnson), boldness in offering new programs, world leader restoring respect for United States and the world, RN family, and others that may come to mind. Get Garment and Safire as well as Buchanan to give their thoughts on this.

The President's longer memo to Haldeman got into specifics, rather fascinating specifics, I thought. It reflected his preoccupation with Senator Edward Kennedy, whom he considered a formidable critic despite the Chappaquiddick incident that summer, and it suggests how he sized up Kennedy's political strategy. Because the memo was to Haldeman,

it sometimes contains abbreviations that Haldeman would understand—
K is Kissinger, E is Ehrlichman, and H is Haldeman himself. The memo
said, in its entirety:

September 22, 1969

MEMORANDUM FOR: MR. HALDEMAN
FROM: THE PRESIDENT

In memoranda in the future, I shall use the letters PR whenever
I am referring generally to a project I want carried out in the PR
front. Until we get a full-time man I think we need in this field, you
will have responsibilty for seeing that these decisions are implemented.

What is particularly important is that I be informed as to what
action has been taken and, if action is not taken, why the decision
has been made not to take it.

PR. The subject in this paragraph should be discussed only
orally. It involves the attack Teddy made on our Draft Statement
and on our Troop Withdrawal Statement which most critics, I think,
would agree was totally irresponsible. Any sophisticate, however,
would also agree that it was very clever for him to launch this
attack. He is trying to divert attention from other subjects which
could be quite embarrassing to him. The way for him to do it is to
enlist the McCarthy-ites and all the far-left on Vietnam, leading
up to the October 15 mobilization date for the college campuses.

We, however, ought to have the good sense to take this on in a
very effective way. I would suggest that one Senator with plenty of
guts should hammer him along the lines that Griffin did a few days
ago, and should quote directly from Hanoi's reaction to our troop
statement in which they used the Teddy quote against us with devastating effect. In fact, Buchanan's prudent primary group might get
a major mailing-out to editors and columnists in Massachusetts and
perhaps even nationally, just setting forth the Hanoi quote or, better
still, an editorial which takes that line. The devastating cartoon in
the New York *Daily News* could be used with good effect in this
respect. The best place from which this could be mailed would be,
of course, from Boston. Buchanan also should be able to get a
columnist or two (and Nofziger could help in this respect) to pick
up this line. I think Teddy's is the first round of Federal syllables
we are going to get on Vietnam leading up to October 15th. It is

absolutely essential that we react insurmountably and powerfully to blunt this attack. We cannot continue simply to leave this to Kissinger; he is over-worked and the few people that he can meet in a backgrounder don't cover enough ground. And, in addition, I don't want him to get into the Teddy Kennedy fight. I want this followed up by one of our best people and a report given to me on its progress.

PR. Every Monday, I want a week's projection as to what we anticipate will be the major opposition attacks so that we can plan our own statements with those in mind. I realize that we sometimes may not have such information, but on the other hand, a careful checking with the offices of Kennedy and McGovern et al will yield us some pretty good information as to what their plans are. Any newsman—maybe Mazo or somebody like that to build up his force and keep us informed. In this connection, I wonder if you might game plan the possibility of having some pro-administration rallies, etc. on Vietnam on October 15, the date set by the other side. Inevitably, whenever we plan something, they are there to meet us; perhaps we can turn the trick on them. Give me a report as to what you think is possible.

PR. I have completed a very thorough analysis of the reports made by HK, E and Harlow which were submitted to me at San Clemente. On the four PR fronts I asked for coverage. In general, I think I could sum up my reaction in this way—the only area where we really came through with a better-than-average grade (and here it was considerably better than average) was on Family Assistance and Welfare and the New Federalism. This was due to a plan executed and followed through. On the Foreign Policy front, on the Nixon Big Charge front, our record in the Congress and the others are performances considerably lower than average. The reasons are obvious. K is simply too busy to be charged with the responsibility for seeing that our actions are publicized. The same is true of Harlow on the Congressional front. I have reached the conclusion that we simply have to have that full-time PR Director, who will have no other assignments except to bulldog these three or four major issues we may select each week or each month and follow through on directives that I give but, more importantly, come up with ideas of his own. I think the Cliff Miller participation is better than what we presently have, but it will be inadequate on a part-time basis. I think that H is simply too busy on the Operational front to carry out this assignment. The same is true of E and K.

While I do not think it will be the best answer, perhaps we ought to enlist Safire in this respect. He seems to have a long-range view and although his PR ideas are not usually in tune with my own, he at least will have us do something and will be watching for all of the curves. I know this is a subject that troubles all of us, but I do not want to continue to slide along with what I fear is an inadequate response, and an amateurish response to what will be an enormous challenge in the next two or three months. This could be a subject for discussion and decision next weekend at Camp David, among other subjects.

I learned much from this memo. The President's comments on Bill Safire indicated that, to say the least, I was not working for a man who would be indifferent to my performance, but for one who would study and evaluate it. I learned, too, that the President's concept of public relations was a broad one that included intelligence-gathering, staging rallies, and prompting hostile letters to our critics. The President wanted to know what his Senate critics were up to—in advance. He suggested that friendly newsmen—like Earl Mazo, the one he mentioned—could serve, in effect, as political spies for us, and in time this desire for political intelligence was to be more broadly interpreted, until it was seen as including, among other things, wiretapping.

The President's candid evaluation of Bill Safire—that he respected Safire for having a "long-range view" but feared that Safire's "PR ideas are not usually in tune with my own"—rather accurately summed up the situation as I came to see it in the next few months.

Safire was a former New York public relations executive whose ties with Nixon went back to the 1950's. He had on his office wall the famous photograph of the Nixon–Khrushchev "kitchen debate" in Moscow in 1959. What most people didn't notice at first glance was that Safire was in the picture, too, cheering Nixon on. Safire sometimes managed to suggest that in some unspecified way he had helped stage that historic confrontation. He might have, for he was certainly one of the most creative men in the White House. He was a good speechwriter, but he was even more valued as an idea man, and as the man who could most often come up with the exact word or phrase the President was looking for to describe one of his programs. Safire was an energetic, personable man in his early forties, with a beautiful English wife and a taste for people and parties. That may have been his only drawback in the Nixon circle— he was known to go to Georgetown parties and associate with news-papermen and liberals. That was enough to make him suspect to a purist like Haldeman, and whenever there was a leak to the press Safire was one of the people who was automatically under suspicion. But, despite his consorting with the enemy, his creative talents were such that he was highly prized, as the Nixon memo suggests.

Most important to me, the Nixon memo once again underlined the tough, combative view of politics the President held. I eventually came to think of him as having a split personality where his public relations was concerned. On the one hand was the extremely astute student of media politics, one with a legitimate interest in presenting himself and his policies in ways that would strengthen his leadership. On the other hand was a politician who was absolutely paranoid about criticism, who took it all personally, and whose instinct was to lash back at his critics in ways that usually did more harm than good.

This duality about Nixon was reflected in his staff and its activities. As Nixon's memo suggests, he was still looking for the miracle worker who would solve his lifelong problem—"that full-time PR Director" who would "bulldog" all his projects through to completion. To an extent, I was hired to be that man, but I was never aggressive enough to make a major impression on Nixon, and it was increasingly to Chuck Colson that Nixon looked for the media tactics that could destroy his critics in the press, Congress, and elsewhere. The struggle between the two sides of Nixon was reflected in the power struggle between Colson and Klein, one that, as the months went by, was obviously being won by Colson.

GAME PLANNING

On October 9, barely a week after my arrival, I sent Haldeman a memorandum captioned: "Weekly News Calendar, Three Months Objectives, and Major Game Plan Program."

Essentially, I made three recommendations. The first, and most ambitious, was:

"To plan the general Administration objectives we will have to gather the four individuals most concerned with the long term goals of the

Administration. They are Messrs. Haldeman, Harlow, Ehrlichman and Kissinger. They would meet approximately once every three months to determine the objectives for the following three months."

The series of summit meetings I envisioned never came about. The White House was simply too geared to day-to-day events—a story in that morning's *Times;* a report on that evening's CBS News—for anyone of importance to think two or three months ahead. The important people were the ones who were on the firing line, not those who were pondering the future.

To carry out my second point, a Weekly News Calendar, I recommended a weekly meeting, at 10 A.M. on Wednesdays, of Haldeman (as chairman), Chapin, Ziegler, Klein, speechwriter Bill Safire, Harry Dent and Lyn Nofziger of the Congressional Relations staff, Ken Cole and Alex Butterfield of Haldeman's staff, and myself. The idea was that this group, which came to be called the Planning Objectives, or P.O. group, would discuss the major news stories coming out in the next week, and how they could be best presented and coordinated.

This P.O. group was also the focus of my third proposal, a system of Game Planning, whereby we would assign responsibility for major White House projects. As I said in my memo: "The Game Plan would be the tool used to take major objectives and plan them on a consistent long term basis. The Game Plan would only be used for major Administration goals, i.e., Vietnam, The Welfare Program, the Haynsworth Situation. The basic Game Plan would be assigned to an individual in our P.O. group who is most suited to handle the total preparation."

In short, one person should have responsibility for overseeing each major White House project. That may sound obvious, but the White House had not managed to reach that point of organization in the previous eight months.

Haldeman liked my ideas. Our P.O. group began meeting and the Game Plan concept became the way we managed White House affairs, under the direction of the P.O. group at first, then under my direction at the Office of Communications, where I had four assistants who worked as project managers.

TELEGRAMS

On October 11, as one of my special projects, Haldeman sent me a memo asking me to have some telegrams sent to one man who had supported the President's Vietnam policy and to three men who had opposed it. Interestingly enough, the supporter was Hubert Humphrey, and the critics were three Republican senators. Haldeman's memo read as follows:

> Would you please make sure that a hundred telegrams are sent to former Vice President Humphrey commending him for his courageous stand and thanking him for supporting the President in his statement yesterday.
>
> These telegrams should be sent from various points around the country and be worded individually.
>
> Also would you get with Nofziger and work out having people here at the White House assigned to Goodell, Mathias and Percy. Let me know who these people are today. Each of these people will be responsible to work out a program over the next week for sending letters and telegrams, and making telephone calls to Senators, blasting them on their consistent opposition to the President on everything he is trying to do for the country. This program needs to be subtle and worked out well so that they receive these items from their home districts as well as other points around the country.

This assignment was tied in with the growing criticism of the President's Vietnam policy and the moratorium rallies to be held a few days later, on October 15, and which many politicians were endorsing, much to our displeasure.

Two days later, I reported to Haldeman that the hundred telegrams to Humphrey had been sent. I had simply called Nixon loyalists in several states and asked them to send telegrams and to ask friends to do the same. Humphrey was not to know we had inspired the telegrams of congratulations, but was simply to get the idea that to support the President was good politics.

I said I would try to get copies of the telegrams, and Haldeman scribbled on my memo: "Be sure to get me at least a few to show the President as soon as possible. H." That suggested to me that this was a project the President had personally asked for, or at the very least it was one that Haldeman thought would give the President pleasure.

The next day I sent Haldeman a memo reporting that I had the telegrams on their way to Senator Percy and reporting where things stood regarding Senator Goodell of New York and Senator Mathias of Maryland. Of Senator Mathias, I reported:

> In discussing this situation with Stan Blair [a Republican leader in Maryland], he indicated that there was a meeting held in Baltimore between Mathias and some of his principal contributors. As a result of this meeting, Blair believes we are making some progress with the Senator and that a campaign along the lines we have mentioned would not only be unproductive but perhaps counter-effective.

Haldeman wrote in the margin: "*Absolutely* the wrong approach. See me!"

But that was only a warm-up for the next paragraph. I noted that I had spoken with Tom Huston, a White House aide with New York political contacts, and he felt that letters or telegrams would in no way alter Goodell's position on the war. Thus, I concluded, "I would agree with both the Mathias and Goodell situations and think we would do better to hold our fire in these cases."

Haldeman exploded. His reply began in the margin and spilled over onto the back of the page:

"This is pure BS—as *excuses*. I disagree 100%—and besides, this was an order—not a question—& I was told it was being carried out & so informed the P. Now let's get it carried out—and quickly."

Haldeman's scribbled chewing-out was followed by a face-to-face chewing-out.

Haldeman's chewings-out were much like his memos—terse and to the point. "You've done a lousy job on this," he would say. "You're not helping the President. Now get on the ball or we'll find somebody else to do the job." Once he had gotten his point across, he would proceed to other business. It was nothing personal; just a tactic to keep people on their toes. If you *really* displeased him you'd simply discover one day that you no longer worked in the White House.

After the memo and the chewing-out, I produced an avalanche of telegrams for Senators Mathias and Goodell. I think the episode suggests several things about Bob's style. In the first place, it could be argued that I was right and he was wrong about Goodell and Mathias. Goodell was a committed dove and we weren't going to change his mind with telegrams. Mathias was a closer case, but perhaps we should have deferred to the local Republican leader's opinion, instead of injecting our own.

But it was clear that the President wanted those telegrams sent. Haldeman always felt, and usually correctly, that he was fighting a battle against those of us farther down the line who were too lazy or timid or soft to do what the President wanted done.

THE PEACE MOVEMENT

On October 16, Dwight Chapin sent a long memo to Haldeman (with a copy to me) called "The 'Peace' Movement and November 15." The day before, on October 15, antiwar groups had staged the series of moratorium rallies all over the country, which had generally been peaceful and well publicized. The mass rally at the Washington Monument was set for November 15. Chapin's memo was intended as a game plan for the President for the remainder of the time leading up to November 15. I think this memo is worth quoting at length, because Chapin was one of the most intelligent people in the White House and his comments reflect both the mood as we contemplated our antiwar critics and the means at our disposal to counter them.

Here are some of the key points of Chapin's game plan:

> Following our discussion in the car tonight, the objective is to isolate the radical leaders of the "Moratorium" event and the leaders of the "Mobilization" committee. They are one and the same and their true purpose should be exposed. At the same time, those people who are loyal to the country and who have been disillusioned by the war should be pulled back into the fold of national consciousness.
>
> Key dates are now November 3 and November 15. The whole approach to the November 15 activity may be in seeing the right action is taken prior to November 15.
>
> For example, if the President should determine the war has to be escalated and it is announced November 3, unless the stage is properly set, the action will only fuel the November 15 movement. (If the President de-escalates the war on November 3, then the action can be built upon in order to head off November 15.)

PROPOSITION:

Only the President can work out the peace. He must be given the nation's support, trust, and understanding. Unity during the next few months is of primary importance.

ACTION TIMETABLE

October 17 to 20   Tone—very low key.

1. Congressmen and Senators who endorsed the October 15 activity are approached by moderates within their parties—told not to rush off on the November 15 thing—it is different.

2. The media is contacted—maybe by rumor—the same as above. Friendly columnists should be given the line—for Sunday stories and next week's articles.

3. The Cabinet, agency heads and other appropriate officials should be given some facts about the November 15 mobilization groups—they should start talking it down in private situations.

4. The Business Council in Hot Springs should adopt a resolution of Presidential support and put out a resolution to ask the business community to rally to the President at this time.

October 20–26

1. Congressional activity should be pressed hard—resolutions of support until November 3. Try to quiet all except the real fringe—talk responsibility. Congressional support is the main mode of public support for the moratorium group.

2. A full-fledged drive should be put against the media (the Gavin light at the end of tunnel theory). Letters, visits to editorial boards, ads, TV announcements, phone calls. (In New York, the networks should be visited by groups of our supporters—the highest level—and cold turkey should be talked.)

3. A representative of the Justice Department and a spokesman for the FBI should hold a press conference on Monday, October 20. They would brief the press with documented information on the leaders of the two movements.

4. The President should meet with Rogers, Laird, the Joint Chiefs of Staff, and others through the week. He should meet with friendly press and favorable publishers of papers—all of this for background only.

A Monday, October 20, press meeting should point up a dedicated President—not detoured by the Moratorium . . . a man who has been working for peace and has stepped up the activity. It

should not be an appeal—it is fact, he is strong, confident, unde-
terred.

He should not make a play for public acclaim—everyone is
serious and wants him to work for peace—unnecessary trips will
not fill the gap and have their risks. Public support will mean more
after November 3.

October 27 to November 3

Setting–speculation will be building.

All of the activity of the preceding week would be sustained at a
higher pitch. The President would spend most of the week meeting
advisors and talking about keeping the country together.

November 3 and after

The time to go for the display of support for the President is immediately after the November 3 speech. This—if done right—will
pre-empt much of the publicity which the November 15 group will
be trying to generate at that time. If properly handled, many of
those who might be considering becoming involved in the November 15 activity can be won over. It will also tend to make the
November 15 group more vocal—less rational and appear properly
as the fringe groups they are.

This would also be the right time for the appearance of pro-
Administration sentiment. It should be shown by all—each in their
own way—but what they do must be visible. It does not have to be
group-oriented—it can be as simple as everyone wearing a flag
lapel pin, writing letters to Congressmen and so on. It might be an
idea to ask the networks to tell it to Hanoi—what if the networks
were set as the sounding board for the vast segment of American
people who support the President and his peace efforts. Thousands
of wires, letters, and petitions to the networks. (Sign-up tables for
petitions to the networks in front of supermarkets.)

On Saturday—November 15—most Americans will do what
they normally do on a Saturday—go shopping, work on the lawn
or go to the ball games. Football games—half times—are the things
to shoot for—and the President should also attend a game that
weekend. It would work.

It did work. The President largely followed Chapin's game plan, down
to the final detail of the football game—for, as hundreds of thousands of
demonstrators gathered at the Washington Monument, the President let
it be known that he was watching the Ohio State game on television.

SHOTGUNS AND RIFLES

On October 17 I sent Haldeman a memo that was destined to be totally ignored. My memo was a failure because it suggested that Richard Nixon change his attitude toward the press, and that, as I came to realize, was not to be.

I made my suggestions as a result of having seen, in my first two weeks in the White House, an endless stream of memos pouring down on me, Herb Klein, and various others, each one demanding action to counter this or that bit of criticism in the media. There were too many demands, and too many of them were unreasonable. Herb Klein had told me, "I don't mind calling an editor when we have a case, but when you keep calling over nothing you lose your credibility." I had come to see that Klein was right—he was not "soft" on our critics, just realistic about how things worked.

I called my memo "The Shotgun versus the Rifle," because I wanted to suggest that we stop "shotgunning" our critics with our disorganized calls and complaints, and use a focused, "rifle" approach that might do more good.

To document my case, I attached a list of twenty-one Presidential requests for action on the media that various of us had received in the previous thirty days. They included the following:

—September 24: The President asks Peter Flanigan for a rebuttal to Ralph Nader's charge that the President pays little attention to consumer affairs.

—September 27: The President asks Klein and Ziegler to attack *Life* magazine's editorial accusing the administration of creating a Coherence Gap.

—September 29: The President asks Klein to counter Ralph Nader's charge that consumer adviser Virginia Knauer had little accessibility to the President.

—October 3: The President asks that we have the Chicago *Tribune* hit Senator Percy hard on his ties with the Moratorium peace group.

—October 8: The President asks Klein for a report on what action was taken concerning Senator Muskie's appearance on "The Merv Griffin Show."

—October 7: The President tells Klein to demand equal time

to counter John Chancellor's commentary on the Haynsworth nomination.

—October 8: The President asks Klein to tell Rogers Morton to take action to counter Howard K. Smith's remarks concerning the three House seats lost by the GOP this year.

—October 10: The President asks Klein for letters to the editor of *Newsweek* mentioning the President's tremendous reception in Mississippi and at last Saturday's Miami Dolphin football game.

The point of my memo to Haldeman was this:

> It is my opinion that this continual daily attempt to get to the media or to anti-Administration spokesmen because of specific things they have said is very unfruitful and wasteful of our time. This is not to say that they have not been unfair, without question many situations that have been indicated are correct, but I would question the approach we have taken. When an editor gets continual calls from Herb Klein or Pat Buchanan on a situation that is difficult to document as to unfairness, we are in a very weak area. Particularly when we are talking about interpretation of the news as against factual reporting.

Haldeman liked memos that suggested solutions to problems, so I gave him one. The way to turn the media around, I said, was not by phone calls from Klein, but by a "rifle" approach in which we would bring to bear our biggest guns on our critics. I suggested that we might begin an unofficial monitoring system of the media through the FCC to see if unfair coverage could be documented; we might have the Justice Department's antitrust division look into possible violations among various news empires; we might have the IRS investigate the networks and newspapers most hostile to us; we might play favorites with the media, as, I noted, the Kennedy Administration had; finally, we might have the Republican National Committee set up a major letter-writing program.

Four years later, when this memo was made public, it was cited as an example of my advocating strong-arm tactics against the media. That was not my intent. Whether or not the IRS or the antitrust division or the FCC would or could take action against our critics was far out of my control. The purpose of my memo was to tell Haldeman, not too subtly: "Get off our backs; if you want to blast the media, use your big guns, but don't expect us to do it for you with phone calls every morning."

My advice went unheeded. The President continued to be outraged by the news media, continued to fire off his requests, and we continued to struggle with them as best we could.

In time, my thinking about these requests began to change. I decided that my "Shotgun versus the Rifle" memo had been naïve, and probably irrelevant. No one was going to change Richard Nixon's way of thinking. It was basic to his personality to see himself surrounded by liberal enemies—in the media, in Congress, in the academic world—and to feel he must get them before they got him. If it made him feel better to think we were complaining to Cronkite or having letters written to *Newsweek*, then perhaps that would free his mind to concentrate on Russia and China and the other great issues that pressed upon him. That, essentially, is how we justified the endless trivia we performed—if it made him happy, it was worth it.

In November, a minor issue arose which suggests the atmosphere in the White House at that point. The President very much wanted to be *Time* magazine's Man of the Year, and Haldeman had ordered me to do whatever I could toward that end. I spoke to Jim Keogh, a Presidential speechwriter who had previously been an editor at *Time*. Keogh said that (1) the decision would be made by Henry Grunwald, *Time*'s managing editor, (2) Grunwald wouldn't be swayed by any letter-writing campaign we might stimulate on the President's behalf, and (3) he, Keogh, feared that Grunwald would choose Sam Brown, the New Left leader.

Sam Brown? He had achieved some minor celebrity in 1968 in Senator Eugene McCarthy's Presidential campaign, and in 1969 as an organizer of antiwar rallies, but he hardly seemed like the Man of the Year. It is a measure of the atmosphere in the White House that Keogh, a balanced man, a former editor of *Time*, could convince himself that our liberal enemies were going to glorify Sam Brown over Richard Nixon as *Time*'s Man of the Year.

A note from Dwight Chapin was more perceptive:

"Prediction—doesn't take much brains—the Time Magazine Man of the Year—will be the men of Apollo XI."

He was right, of course—*Time* chose the first men on the moon for its Men of the Year, not Sam Brown.

THE SILENT MAJORITY INSTITUTE

Lyn Nofziger was a stocky, bald, wisecracking ex-newspaperman of forty or so who had once been Governor Reagan's press secretary and who in the White House worked as a writer, often ghostwriting speeches for friendly members of Congress, and as a political odd-jobs man. There were two predictable things about Nofziger. He always wore the same outfit—dark blue suit, blue shirt, dark tie—and he always had the last word, usually a quip. And he got away with it because he was genuinely bright and funny—Haldeman would roll his eyes skyward at Nofziger's rejoinders, but it was impossible to get mad at him. I worked with him closely and liked him tremendously.

Nofziger was a hard-line conservative whose verbal barbs were often directed at Bob Finch for his misadventures at H.E.W.—Lyn's distaste for Finch had its origins back in the Finch-Reagan rivalry in California. Nofziger later came to loathe Chuck Colson—at bottom, I think he just couldn't believe that there was someone who was harder-line than he. Nofziger fought many battles with Colson, losing almost all of them, because for all his ability Lyn had a problem of not finishing jobs he had started, and perhaps because he basically didn't have Colson's instinct for the jugular.

One day in mid-December Nofziger sent around a detailed proposal for setting up what he called the Institute for an Informed America. This plan for a conservative "think tank," a "rightwing Brookings Institution," was one that the President gave top priority.

We felt that the existing foundations and nonprofit institutions, such as Brookings, were liberal oriented, consistently opposing our programs, and we wondered if we couldn't do something to achieve more balance. As Nofziger said in his memo, the purpose of the proposed IIA was: "To ensure that the American people have access to all sides of significant issues. Implicit here is the understanding that the media already gives emphasis to *one* side."

He proposed that the new Institute be located in Washington, that it have a budget of a million dollars a year, and that its staff include writers, researchers, public-relations experts, and film crews. This staff, working in close but unofficial contact with the White House, would issue statements and reports, sponsor seminars and debates, and otherwise promote conservative causes and Nixon Administration legislative proposals.

Chuck Colson, who had just come to the White House, fired me a memo saying he thought the proposal was excellent, and adding:

"My only comment is that I think Bob Haldeman very correctly feels that we should capitalize on the 'silent majority' name which has taken hold so well on its own as Bob pointed out at the Wednesday meeting. To do this I would think we would want to talk about this as the 'Silent Majority Institute' or just 'Silent Majority, Inc.' "

It was typical of Colson to applaud any suggestion of Haldeman's, even one as bad as this. Institute for Informed America had a certain dignity to it, but Silent Majority Institute sounded like a think tank full of hardhats. Neither Haldeman nor Colson was noted for his light touch.

Early in 1970, Colson sent me a friend of his who, he said, would make a good director for the proposed Institute.

I interviewed the man, who was retiring from the CIA and who struck me as bright, articulate, and highly conservative. As a follow-up to our talk, he sent me an outline of how he would operate the Institute. He added one significant element to Nofziger's plan: He saw the Institute as a base for covert political activity.

I told Colson I didn't think his friend was the right man for the job, because he had a cloak-and-dagger orientation and we needed a scholar, an elder statesman to promote conservative ideas. As it turned out, we never got our Institute into operation. But thanks to Chuck Colson we would see more of his friend, whose name was E. Howard Hunt.

The first months were hectic, but they were enjoyable too. I had never been happier in my work, and Gail, somewhat to her surprise, was finding that she enjoyed Washington almost as much as I did. By Thanksgiving, we were into our new home on Fort Sumner Drive, just across the Maryland line, and we used what free time I had in exploring the Washington area. Actually, despite my hours, I had more free time than in most of my jobs, because I didn't do anything else—if I wasn't at the White House, I was with my family. We took the children to the Capitol and to all Washington's monuments and museums. Some Saturdays the kids would come to the White House and we'd go for bike rides around the Ellipse. On most Sundays we'd eat at one of the many rural inns in the area, and we made trips to Mount Vernon and Monticello and other historic points. Between Christmas and New Year of 1969 we spent several days at Williamsburg. Gail, as a Californian, loved the distinct changes of season that Washington enjoys.

We were not very social. We saw some of my colleagues at the White House socially, and we went to an occasional embassy party, but our free time was family oriented. The children entered good schools, and Gail was pleased at the diversity of the student bodies—children from Spain, from Africa, from almost everywhere. I regretted the time my work kept me away from my family, but the children were old enough to know that I was working at a job I thought was important and that we could all take pride in. Washington was working out well for us.

CHAPTER V

The Office of
Communications

IT WAS OBVIOUS to almost everyone that something had to be done about Herb Klein's Office of Communications. Some people were urging Haldeman to get rid of Klein, but Haldeman understood Klein's value and therefore chose a compromise solution: early in 1970 I went over as Klein's deputy to administer and expand the Office of Communications, and Klein was thus freed to concentrate on his personal dealings with the press.

Klein at first resisted this plan as an affront to his authority. Haldeman sent Cliff Miller over to talk to Klein. I was told that Miller urged Klein to accept the new arrangement lest Haldeman take more drastic action. I followed up Miller's talk with a visit in which I pledged my loyal cooperation. Eventually Klein accepted the inevitable, perhaps in part because he saw that I could help him build up his office.

I came to have a great deal of respect for Klein, but there was a certain ambiguity in our relationship. Klein was my nominal boss, but Haldeman was my real boss, and from time to time that awkward fact came to light. Once, for instance, a memo on the Administration's civil rights policies leaked to the *New York Times,* one that presented the Administration in a bad light. A furious Haldeman called me and Klein with a plan to catch the person who'd leaked the memo. Haldeman suspected Len Garment, the Special Consultant to the President, who was one of the White House "liberals" and one who did work in the civil rights area. Garment, like Bill Safire, was automatically suspect whenever a leak occurred, because of his supposed liberal leanings and because he was known to associate with newsmen.

Garment was extremely smooth, well informed, and articulate—a perfect example of a sophisticated New Yorker. He had met Nixon in the 1960's when they had been law partners in New York. John Mitchell, who had been another partner in the firm, never trusted Garment or felt comfortable with him. 'Watch that Garment," he would tell me, "he's tricky." As it happened, I enjoyed dealing with Garment—I found him fascinating personally and I thought his political judgment was sound, although he sometimes tended more toward theoretical discussion than toward practical advice. He had worked on the effective advertising campaign in the 1968 election, and in the White House he dealt with minority groups and with Administration programs for the arts.

But he was never part of the White House inner circle, and when Haldeman suspected him of being the source of the civil rights leak, he came up with a harsh plan to try to prove it. He told Klein to call Garment and tell him point-blank he knew he, Garment, was the source of the leak because the reporter had told him. It was a bluff, but Haldeman hoped that Garment would blurt out a confession.

Klein refused to make such a call.

Haldeman was furious, and a few minutes later he called me and told me to call Garment. I did, Garment indignantly denied the allegation, and we never did find out who leaked the memo. I hadn't wanted to make the call any more than Klein did, but I was willing to put away my personal preferences to please Haldeman. Thus, I rose in Haldeman's favor, while he scorned Klein for being too "soft."

When I joined the Office of Communications early in 1970 I moved from the White House basement across Executive Avenue to an office in the Executive Office Building, that huge old Victorian fortress that some call a monstrosity and others call a masterpiece. I was assigned a big, high-ceilinged corner office on the first floor, one with a view of both the White House and Lafayette Park. The Executive Office Building once housed the Department of State, and I was told that my office had once been Cordell Hull's. Klein was next door to me in a huge office that once had been the Secretary of State's conference room; one of the adornments of Klein's office was the set of three side-by-side television sets that had once enabled Lyndon Johnson to watch three news shows at once; Richard Nixon had banished it from the Oval Office. Nixon's own "hideaway" office was in the middle of our corridor, with Colson's office past it and Len Garment's at the far end of the corridor.

When I joined the Office of Communications, Herb had four assistants, who were oriented toward providing Klein with a great deal of research information that he wanted, and not oriented to satisfying Haldeman's demands for action on various projects. There was no sense of urgency among Klein's staff and there was a good deal of resentment toward Haldeman for trying to push them too hard.

I felt that some personnel changes were needed, but I had no mandate to fire people. Klein, of course, never fired anyone; the only time I ever became angry with him was when I was insisting that a staff member who was ineffective had to go, and he kept insisting how valuable and loyal she was. In time, I was able to get rid of two people who I felt were hurting our operation, and I hired numerous others.

One person who caught my attention was a junior assistant on Klein's staff named Rob Odle, who was twenty-five years old and just out of law school. Haldeman had mentioned Odle to me as someone who was not being used to full advantage. Odle was an enthusiastic, fresh-faced young man who believed deeply in President Nixon and the conservative approach to government. He had worked for Klein during the 1968 campaign, and then had been put on Klein's staff at the White House but not given assignments equal to his abilities. I got Odle a raise in salary and made him the first of my new project managers. He worked with me throughout my stay in government and was to remain a friend after I left.

Eventually, I also hired Herbert (Bart) Porter and Gordon Strachan to serve as project managers.

Strachan was twenty-eight years old when I hired him, an aggressive, sometimes brash, extremely ambitious lawyer with the President's old law firm in New York. He was, however, a Californian by birth, and had been a campus leader at U.S.C., where he had known Chapin and Ziegler. Chapin had wanted to recruit him for the Administration, and first used him as an advance man in the New York area when we were planning the Honor America Day ceremony in the summer of 1970. That was just a part-time assignment, but Strachan came to Washington once or twice and met the younger men on the White House staff and we were all impressed with him. Chapin and I were always interested in recruiting bright young men for the White House, and we agreed we should offer Strachan a job. He came aboard in time to do some work for me on the advertising program in the 1970 campaign.

I found Strachan to be blatantly ambitious; I could imagine him developing into a Colson-style political operative. He was one of those people, like John Dean, who was capable and could be engaging, but who was obviously always studying all the angles and trying to manipulate events to his own advantage. Strachan sensed that the action in the White House was on Haldeman's staff, not Klein's. When I left early in 1971 to start up the reelection committee, Strachan moved over to Haldeman's staff, partly because he had become friendly with Larry Higby.

Bart Porter was another native Californian, one who sometimes spoke of how his parents had worked in the early Nixon campaigns and how he'd worn his first Nixon button when he was eight years old. Porter had been a marine officer, then a computer salesman in Phoenix, where he, like Strachan, had done some part-time advance work for us. When his computer firm had some difficulties, he came to us about a job. I hired him as a project manager, and he later worked for me at the reelection committee and on the 1972 Inaugural. Porter was capable, but he sometimes rubbed people the wrong way. Eventually, Porter's ambitions, and his unquestioning devotion to the President, were to lead him into serious difficulties.

Our Office of Communications also included Margita White as my administrative assistant, later Dick Howard as head of the speakers' bureau, and Al Snyder, who dealt with the television networks, particularly in placing Administration spokesmen on the Sunday interview shows. Eventually, I built up Klein's office from four assistants to about twelve.

Inevitably, our office spent a great deal of time reacting to the endless crises, major and minor, that afflicted the White House. But we also tried to develop positive programs that could get the Administration's case to the people. We were involved in media politics, and we were seeking not only to speak *through* the media in the usual fashion—press releases, news conferences—but to speak *around* the media, much of which we considered hostile, to take our message directly to the people.

Most often, we had to sell the President without his personal involvement in our efforts, for he and Haldeman believed that a President's popularity is subject to ups and downs, and that his personal efforts must be timed with extreme care. Throughout the spring and summer of 1970, as we struggled with the Carswell nomination and the Cambodian invasion, we would urge Haldeman to ask the President to speak out more, as a way of rallying support. "No," Haldeman would say, "he doesn't want to be overexposed. You have to figure ways to get the publicity without him. We can be down now, that won't hurt us. The important thing is to be back up by November."

We tried to devise an imaginative, aggressive publicity program. We did the trivia and the dirty tricks when we had to, but we also tried to explore every possible means to reach the public with a program that we all believed to be excellent. Some of these techniques at positive image building were our expanded White House mailing list, our series of regional press briefings, an effort to publicize the younger members of the Administration, an effort to exercise better control over departmental public relations, and an attempt to use the White House to focus national attention on the drug-abuse problem.

MAILINGS, BRIEFINGS

Rob Odle had discovered early in 1969 that the White House had no mailing list of any consequence. If someone wrote in and asked for a document—a State of the Union Message, say—it was sent to him, but there was no aggressive program to mail Presidential statements to a wide audience. The reason for this, I think, was that the press traditionally came to the White House, so there seemed no reason for the White House to take any initiative. We did not share that assumption. We felt that some of the reporters were inimical to us and that none of them, antagonistic or not, was going to print more than a fraction of the material we gave them. Why not, then, use direct mailings as a way of going around the White House press corps?

At the time of the nomination of Warren Burger to the Supreme Court, Klein suggested sending out a biography of Burger to every possible newspaper in the country. Odle hired a direct-mail firm to handle the mailing, which went to about 30,000 publications. Hundreds of editors wrote in to express their thanks for this attention, and thousands of small newspapers carried more information on Burger than they otherwise would have. From a political point of view, we had to assume that this kind of publicity helped generate a favorable climate for Senate confirmation, although in Burger's case confirmation was never in doubt.

We therefore proceeded to build up our mailing list until it was an extensive, sophisticated, entirely computerized operation. It was broken down into scores of groupings—daily newspapers, weekly newspapers, ethnic groups, geographical divisions, professional groups—so that by a computerized process any given statement or document could be sent to the precise group we wished. Major Presidential statements might be sent to all the 150,000 or so people on our full list, but we could also, by punching the right buttons, mail to middle-aged black dentists or the presidents of small Midwestern colleges or whatever.

Somewhat related to our mailings, but more controversial, was our program to stimulate letters to the editor and to members of Congress in support of the President. When I first arrived in the White House, our letter-writing efforts were on a hit-or-miss basis—someone would call a few friends and ask them to write letters. But by 1972 we had developed, at the Republican National Committee and at the Committee to Re-elect the President, an extensive and well-organized letters program. We had a woman in Washington working full-time, writing fifty or sixty individualized letters per week, which were sent to Republican loyalists to be signed and mailed to a designated publication. We found that fifteen to twenty percent of these letters would be published. We were also working with our state reelection committees to set up a grass-roots letters operation. We stressed positive, reasoned, factual letters—not attacks on our critics but support for the President.

Our objective, obviously, was to take full advantage of the space that most publications set aside for readers to present their views. *The New York Times'* columnists and editorialists might blast us, but we could at least get a rebuttal through their letters column. There would eventually be a good deal of criticism of our "faking" these letters. I saw nothing wrong with our letters program. The letters were prompted, but not faked—the people who signed them believed in the President's program and wanted to support him, and often there was nothing more they could do in support than to sign a letter. What we did, with considerable urging from Haldeman, was to organize and maximize the letter writing that was carried out on the President's behalf.

There was one occasion when we had two letters written that were questionable—the letters were devious, intended to trick two of our press critics, but the ploy was not without its humor. It came in December of 1970, at a time when we were concerned about the hard-line image the

President had projected during the fall's political campaign. Haldeman gave me specific instructions on letters he wanted sent to Hugh Sidey of *Life* and John Osborne of the *New Republic,* two columnists who wrote exclusively on the President. These were not to be angry or critical letters. On the contrary, they were to be supposed anti-Nixon liberals, thanking the two columnists for revealing Nixon as the shallow and dangerous man he so obviously was.

Thus, the letter to Osborne began:

"Let me begin by saying that I think you are the best political writer of our time. Your scathing attacks on President Nixon have delighted me beyond belief."

To our delight, not long after this letter was sent, Osborne wrote a troubled, soul-searching column in which he conceded "a quality of sour and persistent disbelief that I did not like to recognize but had to recognize in my own work and in my own attitude toward the President."

A similar letter to Sidey (". . . you have not been one of those who knocks Nixon all of the time; on occasion you have indicated that you think he has some redeeming quality") produced not a column, but a rather defensive letter of response in which Sidey promised "to review my writings of 1970" and asserted his "fervent desire that he [Nixon] succeed in the months ahead."

We doubted that, but at least we had him thinking.

Our regional press briefings were seen, like the direct-mail program, as a means of bypassing the Washington press. The first was held at San Clemente in June 1970 for national news executives. It featured a Mexican lunch at poolside, brief remarks by the President, and a full-scale foreign policy briefing by Henry Kissinger. The affair won us extensive publicity and good will, and we proceeded to have other regional briefings in New Orleans, Chicago, Hartford, and Des Moines. The President enjoyed the opportunity to get out of Washington to the heartland cities where he was greeted with enthusiasm, and the publicity continued to be excellent.

We viewed the briefings not only as news events, but as part of our effort in the Congressional campaigns. The location of the various briefings, and the editors invited, were tied to the key Senate races. There were other political considerations as well. We snubbed *The New York Times* and the Washington *Post* by not inviting their editor or publisher to the San Clemente briefing. That was not too bad, however, because the San Clemente briefing was on the West Coast, but we soon scheduled a briefing for East Coast publishers in Hartford, Connecticut, and a serious dispute then arose about whether or not to invite representatives of the *Post* and the *Times,* our two most influential newspaper critics. Klein and I sent Haldeman an invitation list including them, but Haldeman scribbled on our memo "No. Leave them off." Memos flew between us and Haldeman for several days, with Klein and me arguing that to omit the *Post* and *Times* was petty, and was the sort of thing that only made a bad situation worse. Finally Haldeman agreed to the invitations —and then the *Post* one-upped us by not sending a representative.

The *Times'* publisher, Punch Sulzberger, did attend the Hartford briefing, and he said to me at the end of it, "I don't agree with a lot the President does, but it's hard to stay mad at him after something like this." That was, of course, exactly what we hoped he would say.

AN IMAGE OF YOUTH

On April 15, John Ehrlichman, the domestic affairs chief, wrote Haldeman a memo in which he stated:

In terms of social programs, e.g., manpower training, antipoverty, environment, health and education, we are doing as much or more than Johnson or Kennedy.

In terms of sound legislation on the domestic side, experts agree that we have made more good proposals for significant reform (draft, post office, manpower, occupational health and safety, etc.) than any for ten years.

We have loaded aboard a lot of bright, young, able people who can present the President and his programs in an excellent light.

Nevertheless, among young business executives, among municipal officials and on the campuses we are epitomized by the by the Vice President, the Attorney General, and Judge Carswell.

We are presenting a picture of illiberality, repression, closed-mindedness and lack of concern for the less fortunate . . . I do not sense any existing activity on the part of Herb Klein or, for that matter, Ron Ziegler, to respond to this dilemma.

Haldeman passed this memo on to me, noting that he found it "disturbing" and asking me for comments and solutions.

I was in substantial agreement with Ehrlichman. I too was frustrated by the distance between the reality I saw daily of a young and energetic Administration and our image of an Administration of middle-aged businessmen in dark suits. After talks with Bill Safire, Dwight Chapin, Rob Odle, and others, I replied to Haldeman in a long memo of my own. I began:

> In analyzing the memorandum, one has to step back a bit and see why we are "epitomized by the Vice President, the Attorney General, and Judge Carswell." Some time ago, we quietly set out to recruit Middle America, the Silent Majority, or whatever we choose to call it, into our camp. We have done a good job—and the images which the Vice President and the AG project have been largely responsible. We have sent as our ambassadors to Middle America those men who best appeal to Middle America, and we have won the hearts and minds of Middle America.
>
> But in doing this we have alienated those people who are alienated by Middle America: the young, the poor, and the black. And perhaps we have also alienated those Eric Goldman terms the "Metroamericans," the counterpart to the Silent Majority; the under-40-college-educated urban-dwelling business and professional people who enjoy art, attend the symphony, and read *The New York Times Book Review*. The kind of people who have been turned off by the identification of the VP and the AG with a middle American they characterize as a fat, racist suburbanite sitting at home in front of the television watching a football game and drinking a half-case of beer.
>
> Thus, I am saying that to the extent we have succeeded in cultivating the vote-rich Silent Majority by identifying with it, we have alienated those who view the Silent Majority as bourgeois.
>
> Now to appeal to those outside Middle America (the young, the poor, the black, *most* of the Northeast, *all* of New York City, the "student community," much of the media, many of the "opinion molders," etc.) we have to send other emissaries. And that really is much of the problem: I do not think we have exploited the people in this Administration who project an image quite different than that of the Vice President, the Attorney General, and Judge Carswell.
>
> I would propose that we develop a major strategy to publicize the

fact the President has surrounded himself with bright, young, well-educated men who *care*. Men like Goldman's "Metroamerican," who, while moderate, have hearts and consciences. Men like Moynihan, Ehrlichman, Rumsfeld, Flanigan, Garment, Whitaker, and Haldeman.

In the margin, Haldeman added the names of Finch, Shultz, and Harlow to my list. I went on to note the objections to publicizing members of the White House staff—that they hadn't time for public appearances, that we didn't want to create the image of an all-powerful "palace guard," that a White House assistant who "goes public" may lose his effectiveness on the job, particularly if he becomes controversial. But, I said, all those objections could be met if we limited the aides' appearances and if we stressed "not that they're all that powerful, but that they're bright, young, and they're *here,* working on bold new programs which they can publicize best."

I outlined the sort of publicity I thought we could generate:

They can be on the cover of *Time,* on "The Johnny Carson Show," interviewed on a Sunday talk program, featured in the columns. If the decision is made to do it, they can project an image very different from that which the memorandum criticizes. And in projecting these people, the programs which they and the President care so very much about will be publicized, too. But of course none of this can be if they remain only "inside" people.

We can also begin to publicize, a little more, the second-level people in the Cabinet departments and White House. What sophisticated young professional man (or his wife) would not be interested in, say, an *Esquire* picture-story on the life-style of a Dwight Chapin or a Ron Ziegler, men who daily meet with the President and are not yet middle-aged?

This is the way to sell our programs, not just our men. Who, better than Marty Anderson, can "turn on" young people about draft reform? Marty, on television and in magazines, can do much for us in reaching the kind of people the memorandum to you discusses. And in doing this, he can sell our programs where others can't. Young Metroamerica won't listen to Mel Laird, but they will to Marty Anderson—not because Marty's any more liberal (he's probably *less* liberal than Laird) but because he's got more *hair,* a Ph.D., a sexy wife, drives a Thunderbird, and lives in a high-rise apartment. The story on Marty in the *Post,* attached, is really a good example. Why not balance the society pages with the Administration's young swingers as well as the Mitchells and the Agnews?

I noted also:

There are also bright young fellows in the Departments who probably have never had a column inch of publicity. John Dean, Dick Kleindienst's aide, is an example of a sophisticated, young guy we could use.

Haldeman wrote in the margin: "*Absolutely.* Really work on this."

Then, finally, I got back to the touchy question of whether the President would help us with my proposals:

Then, of course, we get back to the use of the President's time. An hour of his time gets more results than a month of game planning on our part, and here, too, it depends on the audience one wishes to please. If we want to cultivate Middle America, we invite Johnny Cash to the White House, or go to South Carolina for a stock car race. This is well and good. And successful. But if we want to make points with the kinds of people the memorandum in question seeks to impress, then the President attends the Philadelphia Symphony, hosts a party for Duke Ellington, etc. Perhaps we ought to make some additional suggestions along these lines— perhaps it would be well for the President to attend and be more identified with many more cultural events. And this office could let the President's private interest in cultural activities be more widely known (e.g.: how much of Metroamerica is aware that the President is so interested in classical music that in his office residence, and retreats, he's taken out Lyndon Johnson's telephones, and put in stereo tape decks)?

Haldeman, in his response to my memo, twice called it "excellent"— some kind of an all-time high in praise. I wish I could therefore report that my memo led to a sparkling new "youth" image for the Nixon Administration, but that was not to be. Although Haldeman liked my idea of calling attention to our younger people, he and Nixon could never break away from their basic belief that there was only one man in the White House who needed publicity, and his name was not Chapin, or Magruder, or Buchanan.

From my point of view, and that of the other White House aides, it was simply not worthwhile to seek publicity, unless Haldeman clearly changed his policy. If one of us made a speech, or gave an interview, Haldeman expected us to say exactly what he or Nixon would have said, and it isn't possible for anyone to parrot the party line all the time. Thus, when I occasionally made a speech, I always put it off the record, as did most of the other White House aides. It was simpler and safer that way.

My advice was not totally wasted, however. A few weeks later, during the crisis that followed the invasion of Cambodia and the shootings at Kent State, when tens of thousands of college students were in revolt against the government, we were forced to open up the White House and it was the younger aides who were used to meet with the angry delegations of students and who were sent to the campuses to speak. But, at least until Watergate brought some of us more publicity than we needed, the Administration's image continued to be that of bland middle-aged businessmen.

In retrospect, I think we made a terrible mistake in not having a more open administration. I wish that Haldeman, for example, had gotten out and talked to student groups. When Haldeman went on the "Today" show and called our antiwar critics traitors, he was reflecting our frustrations, but also his own insularity. We had a tendency, from inside the besieged White House, to lump all our critics together—all journalists were enemies, all Vietnam critics were radicals. If Haldeman had talked more to our critics, and seen that they weren't all radicals or revolutionaries, it might have made a difference. As it was, there was too little fresh air blowing through the White House, and we all tended to become caught up in the "enemies" mentality.

THE CABINET

As the government has continued to expand, a kind of centrifugal force has increasingly pulled the Cabinet-level departments outside the Presidential orbit. Most recent Presidents, Nixon included, have used a powerful White House staff to try to keep their Cabinet officials under control. There is a certain built-in friction in such an arrangement, particularly when some of the Cabinet members were men of political importance, such as former governors George Romney, Walter Hickel, and John Volpe, and former House leader Melvin Laird, four of the Nixon Cabinet.

From our perspective in the White House, the Cabinet officials were useful spokesmen when we wanted to push a particular line—on Cambodia, on Carswell, or whatever. From their perspective, however, it was often a rude awakening to have Jeb Magruder or Chuck Colson calling up and announcing, "Mr. Secretary, we're sending over this speech that we'd like you to deliver." But that was how it was. Virtually all the Cabinet members had to accept that they lacked access to the President and that their dealings would be with Haldeman and his various minions. There were some serious conflicts, and we in the White House sometimes tried to find some humor in the situation by inventing nicknames we privately used for several of the Cabinet officials—Laird was the Bullet, Volpe was the Bus Driver, Blount was the Postman, and so on. I don't recall that we had a nickname for Wally Hickel, who became something of a hero when he quit the Cabinet, but he was regarded, by most of us who dealt with him, as one of the most long-winded and egocentric men in Washington.

The Cabinet officials were, of course, often caught in the middle, between what the President wanted and what their bureaucracies wanted, and we in the White House sometimes became involved in battles to enforce the President's wishes. I was involved in two such battles that suggested to me the vast difficulty of any President's gaining control over the government.

One battle was with the Bureau of Labor Statistics (BLS), which puts out monthly figures on employment. These figures had traditionally been put in terms of the unemployment rate, which in 1970 was holding steady at about six percent. At the same time, while the unemployment rate was constant, the number of people holding jobs was at an all-time high, and getting higher each month. In other words, there seemed to be a hard core of six percent unemployables, but as the work force increased the new people coming into it were finding jobs. We saw no reason why the BLS couldn't stress the positive fact—a record number of jobs—at its monthly briefings, but the BLS did not agree. I spoke with its director, Geoffrey Moore, several times. I tried persuasion, and when that didn't work I finally told him, "Look, Mr. Haldeman says this is what the President wants. If you want to argue with Mr. Haldeman, fine. But if not, change your style."

The BLS changed its style, and eventually some of the networks began citing the number of jobs as well as the number unemployed. It was a small victory, one achieved only after a great deal of pushing, but it seemed to us outrageous that a bureau of the Labor Department should defy a reasonable request by the President.

My other conflict was with the FBI and it also had to do with the emphasis to be given some statistics.

We learned in mid-June that the FBI was about to issue its quarterly crime report, with the figures for the first three months of 1970.

The FBI's crime reports traditionally accentuate the negative—the increase of crime—as a means of, among other things, getting more money from Congress for the FBI. Rob Odle went over to the Justice Department and read the press release the FBI had drafted to go with the crime figures. Its lead, or first paragraph, was on the continued national increase in crime. However, Rob found two positive items in the statistics —the rate of increase for crimes of violence had gone down, as had crime in the larger cities. We asked the FBI to rewrite its release to lead with the good news, and, not entirely trusting the FBI to do our bidding, asked John Mitchell to speak to J. Edgar Hoover about the need for a new press release.

In the end, the press release was rewritten with the good news in the first paragraph and the bad news in the third paragraph. Any reporter who wanted to play up the bad news was free to, but we knew that many reporters would follow the style of the press release. It was not an inconsequential matter. If the wire services followed our lead, newspaper stories across the country would be headlined "Violent Crime Drops" or "Crime Down in Big Cities." And those headlines would suggest to millions of Americans that the Nixon Administration was keeping its promise to do something about crime. We felt that we were doing everything an Administration could do to reduce crime, and if there were legitimate statistics that gave us some credit for our efforts, we felt we deserved that credit.

DRUGS

The President and members of his Cabinet discussed the drug problem in America at a Cabinet meeting late in 1969, and one of the points made was how important television can be in reaching young people and making them understand the menace of drugs. This led the President to instruct Ehrlichman to see what could be done to further utilize television as a tool in the fight against drug abuse, and he asked me and Bud Krogh to work together on the project.

Bud and I soon discovered that the various federal agencies working on the drug problem take quite different approaches—some stress prevention, some stress law enforcement and control. The first meeting we called was hilarious—I couldn't believe those people were working on the same problem. Bud and I hoped that by getting all these people together we could work out some sort of system of priorities and central White House coordination. We encountered the usual hostility that White House people meet in the bureaucratic world; I recall one official of the National Institute of Mental Health who couldn't believe that Krogh and I weren't hard-liners who wanted to put kids in prison for smoking marijuana.

Everyone agreed that television was the single most effective means to reach young people and alert them to the hazards of drugs. The government already promoted public-service messages about drugs, but we wanted to encourage more *programing* on the drug danger. On April 8, we held an unprecedented Conference on Drug Abuse at the White House for about fifty of the nation's leading television producers. Haldeman at first hadn't liked the idea of a working conference in the White House, and one for people who mostly weren't our supporters, but we urged him to ask the President, and the President agreed to it.

Our program for the producers included remarks by Attorney General Mitchell and by John Ingersoll, the head of the Bureau of Narcotics, a visit with the President in the Oval Office, lunch at the Department of State, and a program in the White House theater. The program dramatized the drug problem and what the government was doing about it. It included a one-act play by some inmates of a federal drug-treatment center, a police informer's account of his experiences, and a demonstration of the police dogs that can sniff out marijuana.

The producers loved it, and in the weeks following they flooded us with letters about new drug-related programs. Shows like "The Name of the Game" and "Hawaii Five-O" added segments on the problem, new series were planned, and dozens of documentaries were produced. The success of the conference for the television producers led to a good deal of follow-up, including a Drug Abuse Prevention Week in May, a National Drug Alert in September, to coincide with the opening of school, and another White House conference in October, this time for radio station owners and managers. One of our hopes was to discourage disc jockeys from playing music and using jargon that glorified drugs.

I look back on these efforts in the drug field as a model of the way a President can use his prestige to publicize worthwhile causes. Our costs were minimal and the results, measured in terms of television and radio programing, were remarkable—millions of dollars couldn't have bought the antidrug television time that we got from one meeting at the White House. Our efforts also aided the passage of the Administration's new drug laws, which, among other things, reduced the penalty for the possession of marijuana from a felony to a misdemeanor.

This was the best kind of "Presidential Offensive," and the Administration would have been far better off if we'd spent more time on this kind of positive activity and less time plotting ways to blast our critics.

HUNTLEY AND BRINKLEY

But our critics were always with us, and there were many pressures to do something about them. I was involved in 1970 in efforts to counter criticisms by the NBC News team of Chet Huntley and David Brinkley. Brinkley was the one who we felt was most actively and obviously opposed to us—we felt that even when his words were "straight," he would indicate his scorn for the President by a raised eyebrow or a note of irony in his voice. We felt that his personal attitude reflected the liberal bias of the entire NBC News apparatus. Huntley was considered more middle of the road—it was not until he publicly denounced the President that we began to think about going after him.

Early in 1970, Pat Buchanan had completed a six-month study of both the quantity and quality of the NBC television news coverage of our Administration. He had his staff monitor the amount of pro-Administration and anti-Administration news, hoping to document our belief that NBC was sharply anti-Nixon. On February 5 Haldeman wrote to me:

> I'm sure you have studied that TV summary done by Buchanan, which is a devastating indictment of NBC especially of David Brinkley.
>
> Specifically, Brinkley was completely off base factually on his budget criticism, and we need to get that one straightened out.

The need, probably, is to concentrate on NBC and give some real thought as to how to handle the problem that they have created in their almost totally negative approach to everything the Administration does. I would like to see a plan from you . . .

I responded three days later with an eight-point plan. Among my recommendations were:

—That we have Buchanan's report released by the Republican National Committee to indicate NBC's unfairness.

—That we have a poll taken on Brinkley's credibility, as compared to Walter Cronkite's, and if it reflected a lack of credibility on Brinkley's part, get it out to the media.

—That we ask some Republican senators to criticize Brinkley's erroneous statement that more than half of the President's budget was for defense spending.

—That we have Budget Director Mayo meet with Brinkley in New York to discuss Brinkley's statement on the budget, then leak an account of their talk to friendly columnists.

—That we have major businessmen who were friendly with the Administration and advertisers on television complain to NBC's owners about Brinkley's coverage.

Haldeman wrote on my memo: "Jeb, Damn good! Hack away. H."

In July, Huntley, who was about to retire, was quoted in a *Life* magazine article as saying of Nixon: "The shallowness of the man overwhelms me; the fact that he is President frightens me." We thought the remarks —which Huntley later denied making—proved our point that these supposedly "objective" television newsmen were actually hostile to the President. A few days after Huntley's remarks appeared—and this was in the highly charged atmosphere following the Cambodia crisis—Larry Higby wrote:

We need to get some creative thinking going on an attack on Huntley for his statements in *Life*. One thought that comes to mind is getting all the people to sign a petition calling for the immediate removal of Huntley right now. The point behind the whole thing is that we don't care about Huntley—he is going to leave anyway. What we are trying to do here is to tear down the institution . . . Let's put a full plan on this and get the thing moving.

I responded with a four-page game plan that began:

Since the newscaster enjoys a very favorable public image and will apologize for his remarks, claiming to be misquoted, we should not attempt to discredit him personally. Also, since his remarks were expressed as an individual, we would have difficulty attacking his network directly. The focus of our effort should be to raise the larger question of objectivity and ethics in the media as an institution. To do this, we will have to turn objectivity into an issue and a subject of public debate.

I listed eighteen follow-up possibilities, including:

—Release the letter of apology to the press along with a gracious reply from the President. [Huntley had offered to write a letter of apology to the President for the remarks he denied making.]

—Plant a column with a syndicated columnist which raises the question of objectivity and ethics in the news media. Kevin Phillips would be a good choice.

—Arrange a seminar on press objectivity with broadcasting executives and working newsmen. Attempt to have this televised as a public service.

—Ask the Vice President to speak out on this issue. He could point out that the *Life* quote has proved his point.

—Have Dean Burch "express concern" about press objectivity in response to a letter from a Congressman.

—Arrange for an "exposé" to be written by an author such as Earl Mazo or Victor Lasky. Publish in hard cover and paperback.

—Produce a prime-time special, sponsored by private funds, that would examine the question of objectivity and show how TV newsmen can structure the news by innuendo. For instance, use film clips to show how a raised eyebrow or a tone of voice can convey criticism.

—Have a senator or congressman write a public letter to the FCC suggesting the "licensing" of individual newsmen, i.e., the airwaves belong to the public, therefore the public should be protected from the misuse of these airwaves by individual newsmen.

Very little came of these two game plans. We did leak to UPI Huntley's letter of apology to the President, although without the "gracious reply from the President" I had suggested—Haldeman vetoed that one. And we did arrange for Senator Robert Dole and some congressmen to denounce Huntley's comments. Perhaps a column or two was written. Not much else happened.

Not only did little come of my two game plans, little was expected to. To an extent, many of our lengthy game plans were bureaucratic exercises, ways of producing an illusion of activity when in fact little existed. Did anyone really think Victor Lasky or Earl Mazo was going to write a book about press objectivity? Can anyone imagine a "prime time special" on Brinkley's raised eyebrows? There was an element of fantasy about many of our memos and game plans. It was Haldeman's style to order you to do a hundred things by 5 P.M., in the hope that you might actually do twenty-five of them. For our part, we would rush him a list of twenty-five bold actions we were poised to undertake, when in truth five of them might ever occur. We did all we could, but there was no real way to bridge the gap between what we could actually do about our critics and what the President wanted done about them. The game plans could at least produce an illusion of action; Haldeman could at least show the President a piece of paper that might put his mind at ease.

CHAPTER VI

Carswell, Cambodia, and the 1970 Campaign

IN THE SPRING and early summer of 1970 Richard Nixon confronted two of the gravest crises of his crisis-ridden political career. He sought the Senate's confirmation of G. Harrold Carswell to the Supreme Court, and then he attempted to convince the American people that his ordering U.S. troops into Cambodia had been a necessary and effective action. In retrospect, I think these two battles were a turning point for his administration, for the passions and frustrations engendered by the Carswell and Cambodian conflicts shaped the political strategy the President followed that fall, which in turn led to the panic that gripped the White House early in 1971 and to the new tactics that were employed to ensure victory in 1972.

The Administration's determination to win the Carswell nomination was heightened by our defeat the previous November on the nomination of Judge Clement Haynsworth to the Supreme Court. We had all been embittered by that loss. We felt the conflict-of-interest charges brought against Judge Haynsworth were totally political—an excuse for Senate liberals to vote against a conservative nominee for the Supreme Court.

It was unthinkable that the President should suffer a second straight rebuff, and we made an all-out effort to ensure that he did not. Our effort

109

was coordinated by a task force that included Congressional Relations Director Bryce Harlow and Deputy Attorney General Richard Kleindienst as cochairmen, William Rehnquist and John Dean of the Justice Department, Senators Bob Dole and Howard Baker, and White House aides Colson, Klein, Nofziger, and myself. I was in charge of follow-up on the public relations decision made by the group.

We met at eight each morning to plan the day's pro-Carswell activities, and our meetings were increasingly punctuated by groans of frustration and hoots of disbelief as our nominee's ineptitude became more and more apparent. Carswell abundantly demonstrated his mediocrity whenever he appeared in public, and his Senate opponents would further document it with research into his scholastic and judicial record. At first, however, his mediocrity was an unspoken issue, one that might not have defeated him had not one of our Senate allies, Senator Roman Hruska, chosen to make it a public issue. In a televised interview, Hruska blandly declared that there were millions of mediocre people in America and they too deserved representation on the Supreme Court.

We couldn't believe it. That one remark made our nominee a national joke. And yet, to our group, Carswell's qualifications were not the point. Few if any of us thought he was well qualified for the Supreme Court, but the issue was that we could not endure a second straight defeat on a Supreme Court nomination. Haldeman had already called in Dick Kleindienst and told him that if Carswell wasn't confirmed, Kleindienst would be out of a job. As we understood the story, Kleindienst had come up with Carswell in the first place; he had acted, we were told, in great haste, having been ordered by the President to find a Southerner, almost any Southerner, to nominate after the defeat of Clement Haynsworth.

We had started out convinced that Senate confirmation for Carswell was assured, if only because so many senators didn't want to vote against the President twice in a row on this issue, but we began to see we were in trouble. Our task force discussed the wisdom of the President's withdrawing the nomination, and Bryce Harlow took the proposal to the President and Haldeman, who said it was out of the question. This was do or die.

We carried out on Carswell's behalf all our usual activities—a letter-writing campaign, speeches by friendly senators, calls to editors and broadcasters—but as the fight went on we were increasingly involved not only in pro-Carswell efforts but in a counteroffensive against his critics.

For example, in early April Haldeman sent me an editorial pointing out that Senator Birch Bayh, who was deploring Carswell's mediocrity, had himself flunked the Indiana bar exam the first time around, and urged us to push hard on this fact as a means of discrediting Bayh.

Haldeman also sent me a report that Clark Mollenhoff, the investigative reporter who was then on the White House staff, had sent to the President, indicating that both Senator McGovern and former Vice President Humphrey had lived in homes in the Washington area that were subject to restrictive racial covenants. Haldeman asked me to get this material to the press as a means of countering reports that Carswell owned property subject to such covenants.

I took this up with Herb Klein, who passed the information about McGovern and Humphrey along to a few reporters. Klein then sent a memo to Haldeman pointing out that, from a reporter's point of view, the information about the McGovern and Humphrey covenants was not worth a story unless they criticized Carswell for his covenant. Klein also reminded Haldeman that Nixon had once owned property subject to such covenants. Klein was perfectly correct in pointing out these facts but that was not what Haldeman wanted to hear.

At the height of the battle, Chuck Colson came up with a theory that the Senate could not reject a Supreme Court nominee because he was conservative and/or mediocre, but only on the grounds of impropriety. Colson proposed to have Senator Marlow Cook of Kentucky, one of the undecided senators, write the President for guidance, and for the President to respond with this theory of the Senate's proper role in the confirmation process. Everyone in our task force rejected Colson's proposal as both bad law and bad politics. Undaunted, Colson took his plan directly to Nixon, who liked it and sent the proposed letter to Cook. The reaction in the Senate was disastrous; it seemed to the senators that they were being told their role in the confirmation process was simply to rubber-stamp Presidential nominations. It could be argued that the Colson letter was the final straw, the one that caused Carswell's nomination to be defeated by a slender margin. But the President apparently did not think so, for Colson's star continued to rise.

The real loser, in the aftermath of the Carswell defeat, may have been Bryce Harlow, who was then a Counselor to the President. Harlow was a soft-spoken, gracious, politically astute man who had served in the Eisenhower White House, had been Procter and Gamble's Washington lobbyist, and was probably the one man in our Administration who was most liked and respected on Capitol Hill. He and I had lunch together frequently, and I often sought his advice. I remember him telling me once:

"We're here to bear the brunt of the President's problems. We take the heat, and if it costs us our jobs later, that doesn't matter, we've served our President well."

Despite Harlow's dedication and his political talents, I could see him, like Klein, losing influence with Haldeman and the President because he was too reasonable (i.e., "soft") in his attitudes toward Congress, because he was not a good manager, and ultimately because he "lost" the Haynsworth and Carswell nominations. He didn't lose them, of course, but someone had to be blamed.

The Senate's rejection of Carswell on April 9 caused all hell to break loose in the White House. The President was furious, and determined to turn the defeat into a political plus, by picturing it not as a setback to himself but as a rebuff to the South. He went on television that evening to warn that the Senate "as presently constituted" would never permit a Southerner to serve on the Supreme Court—a not too subtle bid for the South to elect Republican senators that November. Meanwhile, Haldeman was pressing me for action, and I quickly sent him a plan listing twenty-four actions that our task force would take. We would send copies of the President's statement to every southern newspaper; we would ask every southern governor to speak out; we would mobilize the Cabinet to deplore the Senate action; we were pondering a "Thank you, Mr. President" petition drive in the South, and so on. It was the typical crisis memo; twenty-four actions listed, and perhaps half of them ever carried out.

CAMBODIA

On the afternoon of April 30, Henry Kissinger briefed senior members of the White House staff on the speech the President was delivering that night. The President, Kissinger told us, would announce that U.S. and South Vietnamese troops were attacking Communist sanctuaries in Cambodia—a bold military move that he hoped would hasten the war's end.

As we watched the President deliver his speech that night, we saw we had trouble ahead. Not only was the President's military action controversial, but his tone in announcing it was too hard-line, too divisive.

"We live in an age of anarchy both abroad and at home," he declared. "We see mindless attacks on all the great institutions which have been created by free civilizations in the last five hundred years. Here in the United States, great universities are being systematically destroyed. . . . If when the chips are down the U.S. acts like a pitiful helpless giant, the forces of totalitarianism and anarchy will threaten free nations and free institutions throughout the world."

He went on to compare his decision on Cambodia with the great military decisions made by Presidents Roosevelt, Eisenhower, and Kennedy, and then to note that: "In those decisions, the American people were not assailed by counsels of doubt and defeat from some of the most widely known opinion leaders of the nation."

His speech was like a red flag waved in the faces of his critics in the Congress, in the media, and on the campuses. It would have been better if he'd simply announced the invasion without a speech, rather than make the one he made.

Our office undertook its usual back-up effort. Herb Klein sent the text of the speech and some background material on Cambodia to our mailing list of newspaper editors. We arranged for the College Republican National Committee to issue a statement supporting the President, as a means of balancing the student opposition. We got our spokesmen on television—for example, Vice President Agnew went on "Face the Nation" and Bob Hope on the "Tonight Show." The "Tell It to Hanoi" Committee placed pro-Nixon ads in more than forty newspapers.

Despite our effort, the situation across the nation was getting worse. Student demonstrations were shutting down scores of campuses. The President exacerbated the situation by speaking of "those bums" who were demonstrating on campus. Then came the tragedy at Kent State, and more and more demonstrations and finally the early college closings.

Even after Kent State, Nixon clung to the hard-line approach—his initial statement implied that it was the students' own fault they'd been shot, since they'd been somewhere they didn't belong. But it was clear that something had to give. We feared more demonstrations, more Kent States, a nation immobilized. The columnists were asking if Nixon could still govern, and some were questioning whether the Cambodian invasion was not a military failure. Finally, heightening the pressure, antiwar leaders scheduled a huge rally outside the White House on Saturday, May 9. How would we respond? With bayonets? With a wall of buses encircling the White House? In the final days before the rally, the President was under intense pressure from his Cabinet, party leaders, and advisers like Bob Finch and Herb Klein to soften his position, to shift to a more conciliatory approach. He had used the "I'm-watching-a-football-game" approach when the antiwar legions had gathered at the Washington Monument the previous November, but that was simply not going to work this time around, or so his more moderate advisers argued.

The President finally accepted the moderates' advice. He approved, a day or two before the Saturday demonstration, a plan whereby the younger White House staff people would go out and meet with demonstrators, and a telephone center would be set up to take calls from student groups arranging for them to meet with Administration spokesmen.

Then, in the early, predawn hours of Saturday, the President added a touch of his own. He had Dwight Chapin summoned to the White House, where he told Dwight that he had been unable to sleep, that he was troubled, and that he wanted to go out and talk with the demonstrators who were encamped on the Mall. His plan met vigorous resistance from the Secret Service—to them it was like Daniel entering the lion's den—but the President went ahead, and met at dawn with young people at the Lincoln Memorial.

From all reports, the exchanges were no more profound than one might expect at that hour, yet the President's action was highly significant. Most immediately, it meant that the Saturday afternoon headlines said "President Sees Demonstrators" instead of "Demonstrators Encircle White House." The President had taken the initiative, and to some extent blunted the impact of the massive demonstration. Beyond that, the President's action added momentum to our effort to "open up" the White House. We invited delegations of young people inside that day; I talked to several groups and even Haldeman met with some students. His meeting, I was told, went very well, for Bob could be extremely charming and persuasive when he chose to be. Perhaps no one's mind was changed, but at least we began a dialogue. The students saw that we were not bloodthirsty militarists, but people who sincerely believed the Cambodian action would shorten the war. For our part, we got a valuable reminder that many of our critics were reasonable and intelligent people, not Yippies and anarchists.

As a follow-up to the May 9 dialogues, our office arranged for eight of the younger White House aides to visit several dozen college campuses to discuss Administration policies. We felt these exchanges were valuable, and on July 24 I sent Haldeman a memo in which I proposed that we create a White House Youth Office which would work with young people, particularly students, in much the same manner that Len Garment worked with minority groups. I urged that we find a young person to head this office who was intelligent, articulate, and one hundred percent loyal to the President. Nothing came of my proposal, so I tried again in October, with a proposal that we begin a program in which twenty-six of the younger White House people would each visit two campuses a year, as a means of communication with the student population.

I knew why my proposal hadn't gotten anywhere, and I stressed in my October memo:

"This does not fly in the face of the Scammon thesis. Scammon's voter dislikes campus violence and the permissive educators. But even the Dayton housewife won't be upset if her President sends out his staff to talk things over with students."

The thesis I referred to, advanced by William Scammon and Ben Wattenberg in their book *The New Majority*, was that the crucial voter in America, the "average" voter, was a forty-five-year-old Dayton housewife whose husband worked in a factory and who was most concerned about the "social issue," i.e., crime, race, drugs, and permissiveness. This "Dayton housewife" simply personified what we usually called Middle America. And the reason my idea for a Youth Office never was approved was that Nixon and Haldeman believed that Middle America was so down on students that we might lessen our hold on Middle America if we made any overtures toward the campuses, or at least any well-publicized overtures. There was probably an additional fear that we'd never find a young person to be our youth spokesman who could be trusted to follow our line one hundred percent of the time—the risk of eventual embarrassment was high.

So our conciliatory gestures toward the May 9 demonstrators did not touch off any new "open door" policy toward the young. Once the pressure was off, the President reverted to his basic belief that there was more political advantage in isolating his campus critics than in trying to win them over.

The demonstration passed, and the crisis simmered on through May and into June. The President went on television early in June to tell the nation that the Cambodian venture had been a major military success, and our Office of Communications made an all-out effort to back up his claim. Not all our efforts were successful, however. I was involved in two that backfired, one rather badly.

The lesser incident began when Senator Edward Gurney of Florida suggested to our Congressional Relations staff the idea that we buy television time so that several of our Senate allies could state their support for the President's Vietnam policy. Senator Gurney was clearly excited at the prospect of the national television exposure, and he suggested Senators Dominick, Dole, McClellan, and Stennis as others who might join him for a panel discussion.

We kicked the idea around, but we saw several problems. Money was one, and also the timing—we were into June, probably too late to do us much good. Moreover, some of our supporters' views were more hawkish than ours, and we might be embarrassed by what they'd say. Haldeman considered all this and then told us to drop the idea.

Lyn Nofziger then suggested that since he had to deal with Senator Gurney frequently, it would be best if I broke the news to him of our decision. I accepted, somewhat naïvely, not knowing that Senator Gurney was famous for his temper. I went to Gurney's office where he and his administrative assistant greeted me warmly, thinking I had come with the final plans for the show that would make the Senator a national figure. Instead, I announced that we'd decided to kill the show, and Gurney exploded.

It wasn't a crisp, constructive, Haldeman-style chewing-out. It was a red-faced and profane tirade; I thought the man was going to leap across his desk and attack me.

"Where did the President find you blankety-blank idiots?" Gurney demanded. "There's not a one of you blankety-blankers who I'd let empty my wastebaskets. You—you've never worked in a campaign, have you?"

"Well, yes, Senator, as a matter of fact . . ." I began.

"Hell, no, you haven't," he continued. "You don't know a blankety-blank thing and now you've screwed up this television show, you've humiliated me—there's not much hope for the Republican Party as long as the President has morons like you working for him!"

It went on like that for a while until finally I made my escape. When I arrived back at the White House I described my encounter to Nofziger and Timmons; they were highly amused—they'd known that would happen, that's why they'd sent me.

The Gurney incident was annoying, but a struggle I had with Chuck Colson about our Cambodian follow-up was more serious. In late May Joseph Alsop published a violent attack on the antiwar movement; in effect, he called the antiwar people traitors. We discussed the column at one of our planning sessions and we agreed that it was a plus from our point of view. Then Chuck Colson had an idea: "Let's mail it out, over Herb's signature."

Klein was out of town, so it fell to me to oppose Colson's idea. Klein had always insisted that we mail out only factual material, not political propaganda, lest his personal credibility be endangered, and also so there would be no charges that we were using the White House mailing apparatus for political purposes. In my view, the Alsop column, however pro-Nixon, had no business being sent out from the White House.

Colson was unconvinced by my arguments, however, and he came back to me the next day.

"The President wants the Alsop column mailed out," he said. "Over Klein's signature."

I stalled, and when he was gone I called Haldeman and stated my objections again.

"No, the President wants it mailed out," Haldeman said. "So mail it out."

I did, and, predictably, we were severely criticized for using our mailing program for such blatantly political purposes. It was, once again, an instance of the President's buying Colson's heavy-handed tactics and rejecting advice that he viewed as "soft." It was also an instance of what I came to call our slippage problem. We had built up a tremendous mailing program, one that could do us endless good in positive, legitimate public relations efforts. But that same machinery could also do a great deal of harm. Later, at the Committee to Re-elect the President, our slippage problem grew worse and worse.

The Alsop column was sent out, with a cover letter from Klein, without Klein's knowledge. When he got back to Washington and found out about the letter, he was furious. He called me in and demanded an explanation. I pleaded innocence and ignorance, and called in Rob Odle and demanded an explanation from *him*. Rob then "confessed" his "guilt"—he said he'd authorized the mailing without clearing it with me or Klein. Klein chewed Odle out and then, because Klein was a decent and forgiving man, the matter was dropped.

Odle's confession was a total fiction, of course. I had authorized the mailing, on orders from Haldeman. I had an understanding with Odle and my other project managers that from time to time they'd be called in and expected to take the heat for something I'd done. The theory was that it was better that way. If Odle or one of the others took the blame for something like this, Klein could write it off as a young staff man making a mistake. But if the blame fell on me, we'd have to face up to the fact that it wasn't a mistake, that in a showdown I was following Haldeman's orders, not Klein's.

The Cambodian crisis was an interesting study in Presidential opinion making, or media politics, or whatever one chooses to call it. You had the President taking a bold military action that he believed would shorten the war and save American lives. You had a significant number of people who disagreed with him, from the students demonstrating on the campuses to the senators who were speaking out on Capitol Hill. In between, you had the majority of Americans, who didn't know what to believe, and whom both sides were trying to persuade, always with an eye on the fall elections.

From the President's point of view, he has a certain number of tools he can use in presenting his case to the American public—he can make speeches, his Cabinet can support him, and so on. In the Cambodian crisis, we expanded that list of pro-Administration tools to a record high—we did everything we could possibly think of. For instance, to take two diverse actions, we had a program whereby high school students distributed our literature on Capitol Hill, and we also arranged for a delegation of friendly governors, senators, and representatives to make a "fact-finding" trip to Vietnam, one whose outcome was not greatly in doubt.

In the short run, our massive effort was successful, for all the polls indicated that the majority of Americans believed the Cambodian invasion was a success. And yet in winning we may have lost. We may have become too confident that we could manipulate public opinion in a hard-line, rally-round-the-flag way. All the passions and frustrations of the Cambodian crisis would soon be channeled into the hard-line strategy we followed in the Congressional elections that fall, when the results would not be so satisfactory.

HONOR AMERICA DAY

The Honor America Day rally on the Fourth of July, one of our more ambitious attempts to mold public opinion in our favor, grew directly out of the Cambodian crisis. The idea sprang from a conversation between the President and Billy Graham.

"Mr. President, everyone talks about what's wrong with America," Graham said, as he later told me. "Why doesn't someone talk about what's *right* with America?"

From that remark the idea evolved of a patriotic rally in Washington on the Fourth of July that would give ordinary citizens a chance to speak out *for* America at a time when so many people were speaking out against her. Billy Graham, Hobart Lewis of the *Reader's Digest*, J. Willard Marriott, the hotel owner, all close friends of Nixon's, agreed to organize the rally, and I was their liaison with the White House, which is a nice way of saying I was assigned to make sure the event was run the way Haldeman and the President wanted it run. Staff from Marriott's corporation and other companies began to put things together, but it was soon clear to me that they couldn't bring off the rally we envisioned, in the six weeks or so available, without close supervision. Their first newspaper ad, for example, never quite made it clear what Honor America Day was; we got them an ad agency and the later ads were fine.

Actually, it *was* hard to explain Honor America Day, for it was an event that worked on several levels. To most people who attended, it was a patriotic Fourth of July ceremony, featuring a religious service led by Billy Graham in the morning and free, all-star entertainment in the evening. To us, it was a political event, one in which honoring America was closely intertwined with supporting Richard Nixon, and in particular with supporting his policy in Vietnam at a time when a great many people were opposing it with rallies of their own.

Another problem with the initial planning was that some of the organizers from the private sector seemed to think that a crowd would appear on its own, with no prompting. We in the White House didn't make that assumption, and we assigned Ron Walker, the head of our advance team, to make sure we got a maximum turnout. Ron's staff of some thirty volunteers—part-time helpers around the country, like Gordon Strachan in New York—carried out a telephone campaign, and also distributed some five million handbills in the Philadelphia, Washington, and New York areas.

Bob Hope helped recruit such entertainers as Glen Campbell, Red Skelton, and Vikki Carr, and Marriott himself, a leader in the Mormon Church, arranged for the Mormon Tabernacle Choir to perform. One of the highlights of the evening's entertainment was Skelton reciting the Pledge of Allegiance, and elaborating on its various points in an emotional statement of patriotism.

I was on hand for the full day's activities, often placing calls to Haldeman and Chapin in San Clemente to let them know how large the crowd was and how it was responding. We had, as it turned out, only one serious problem that day. Hundreds of hippies, who had for several years gathered at the Washington Monument on the Fourth of July for a marijuana "smoke-in," made several attempts to disrupt the Honor America Day events. The problem began in the morning, when a number of them jumped into the reflecting pool and started wading noisily toward the Lincoln Memorial, where Billy Graham was conducting a religious service before some 50,000 people. The police easily turned them away, but later in the day several hundred of them gathered on the hill at the base of the Washington Monument. From there, they looked down on the crowd beginning to gather for the evening's entertainment. In the early evening, as the crowd of an estimated half million began to form, many of them married couples with children, the hippies began to chant obscenities and to throw rocks and bottles.

Bud Krogh, whose duties included being White House liaison with the D.C. government, was there to work with the D.C. police on such problems, and he and I joined Police Chief Jerry Wilson as he charged around trying to rally his men to stop the troublemakers. The families were terrified to be attacked by this foul-mouthed, rock-throwing guerrilla army, and many of them were near panic. There was tremendous confusion. A second group of hippies had started throwing rocks up at the front of the crowd, near the bandstand, and Gail and our children were endangered there. Police Chief Wilson was hit by a rock and blood covered his face. To me, the whole episode was tremendously frustrating; I wanted to grab one of the troublemakers and say, "Look, we're not bothering you; why don't you leave us alone?" But they wouldn't leave us alone, and finally Wilson had to use tear gas to drive them away. The hippies managed to throw some of the cannisters back into the crowd, causing more discomfort for the people who'd come to watch the evening's entertainment.

Somehow, the show went on, and the demonstrators aside, we considered Honor America Day a success. All three networks carried the morning's religious ceremonies, and CBS carried the entertainment live in evening prime time. The evening's coverage was only obtained, however, after I persuaded Mr. Marriott to send a very strong telegram to the president of CBS when his network seemed to be backing out of its promise to carry the event. Our feeling was that the networks had given plenty of coverage to various antiwar rallies, and it was only fair that they give coverage to this pro-America rally.

My work on Honor America Day brought me in close contact for the first time with my future boss, Attorney General John Mitchell. He wanted to be kept informed on plans for the event, because of the Justice Department's role in its security arrangements, and because of his own personal interest in an event so closely aligned with the Administration's interests. I briefed him two or three times, and was profoundly impressed with him; I could see why he had become the strong man of the Nixon Administration.

He was more than a strong man: he was a kind of father figure to dozens of people in the top level of the Administration. Young men like John Dean and myself thought of him in those terms, and even the President seemed to regard him as a tower of strength, an equal, someone to take his troubles to and to be counseled by. Mitchell was a man who inspired confidence. He was physically imposing, he was a successful and self-confident man, and he always seemed in control of any situation. He was good-natured, soft-spoken, and philosophical. He could be tough, even cruel, to anyone who opposed him or annoyed him—as both Finch and Colson did from time to time—but to younger men who deferred to him, he was unfailingly tolerant and considerate.

He became the great conciliator in the Administration. When there were conflicts, and neither the President nor Haldeman wished to become involved, Mitchell was often the person the President turned to. I was in Mitchell's office several times when he got calls from Secretary of State William Rogers, who would be protesting some indignity at the hands of Henry Kissinger—typically, Kissinger would have taken some action or made some statement in the foreign policy area without informing Rogers or the State Department. "Now, don't worry about it, Bill," Mitchell would say. "I'll talk to Henry and we'll get this straightened out." There was no way to straighten out the Rogers–Kissinger problem (except by the eventual solution of making Kissinger Secretary of State) but Mitchell's great aura of serenity would usually ease the wounded feelings for the time being.

I always found Mitchell more of a political moderate than his public image suggested. Mitchell was a hard-liner in a philosophical sense—he wanted strong anticrime laws and conservatives on the Supreme Court—but he was not a hard-liner like Colson or Nixon in wanting to go after our critics with a meat ax. My impression was that he tolerated the "dirty tricks" approach as a means of humoring the President. He might acquiesce in dirty tricks for that reason, but it would not have been his instinct to initiate them. He had better political judgment than Colson or Haldeman. In his talks with me that summer and fall, he often warned me about the White House political strategy in the Congressional elections:

"Jeb, you people are hitting law and order too hard."

He was right.

THE CAMPAIGN OF 1970

Mitchell hated Colson. He often said that Colson had only joined the Administration because he wanted to build up his future law practice, that he wanted to become the Republican Clark Clifford. Colson apparently heard what Mitchell was saying, because he once made a point of showing Dick Moore, who was then a special assistant to Mitchell, a copy of his 1968 income tax return, which indicated that he had earned around $100,000 and thus didn't need the White House to build up his law practice.

Although Mitchell was then widely regarded as the President's key political adviser, it was actually the advice of Colson and Haldeman that Nixon chose to follow in 1970.

Traditionally, the party in the White House loses Congressional seats in the off-year elections. Presidents often choose to minimize their campaigning in those elections, lest they be blamed for their party's losses. Our original plan had been for the President to be only marginally involved in the Congressional campaigns. But Nixon and Haldeman became convinced that the President could rally the Silent Majority and perhaps even lead the Republican Party to majorities in the House and Senate.

We were going to win this historic victory by hammering at the law and order issue. It was a totally negative approach, one that combined the national fear of increased crime with undertones of racism. We would not emphasize our constructive achievements—new crime laws, more judges, more aid to police—rather we would damn our opponents as "radical liberals" who were soft on crime, who in effect were procrime. To a lesser extent, we appealed to patriotism on the war issue—the same radical liberals who were soft on crime at home were soft on Communism abroad. It was an approach that assumed little intelligence on the part of the voter, and assumed that cries of "law and order" could divert his attention from, among other things, the economic problems and inflation.

Some of us favored a more positive campaign strategy. On September 11, I sent Haldeman a memo that said in part:

> Our domestic record is one of reform, and it is a good record, and those attacking our record do so only to downgrade our country. We won't take a back seat to anyone on progress—and we haven't. . . . Let's tangle with them on a *philosophy* of government. The Establishment Democrats and opposition want a government that *tells* people what to do. RN wants a government that is responsive to all people, not just special interests.

But Haldeman didn't want philosophical discussions. He replied:

> The attached still doesn't do it. Read the Scammon memo again and then listen to a few of the Vice President's speeches and see if you don't get a better fix on what our theme is. We can't hit as many issues as you attempt to do—we have to hit two or three strong chords and stay with them. And it's imperative to our success that *you* clearly understand this.

At that point I gave up—I sent Haldeman a memo that told him what he wanted to hear:

> The Democrats should be portrayed as being on the fringes: radical liberals who bus children, excuse disorders, tolerate crime, apologize for our wealth, and undercut the President's foreign policy. . . . The rank and file Democrats thought theirs was the party of Kennedy and Truman, but that small noisy group of anti-everything radical liberals have made it the party of McGovern, Hart and Muskie—ultra-liberals who have deserted the party and deserted the country.

My idea of a first-rate political campaign is to wage a positive campaign, based on a debate of the real issues, and to back it up with a first-rate precinct organization.

There may be a place for tough tactics in a campaign, including negative ads that hit hard at the opposition, but I don't think an entire campaign should be negative in its approach or that the tactics used should be the kind that are so extreme that they backfire. Colson's approach was that issues and precinct organization weren't important, the only important thing was to clobber your opponent. I had stated my approach, and Haldeman had rejected it, so I fell in line behind the law-and-order theme.

We had been pushing the crime issue in a positive way through the year. On September 22 Haldeman sent me and Bud Krogh a memo that said: "The President wants some action on his frequently repeated instruction that there should be something coming out every day for public consumption on the issue of law and order, control of crime, tough actions against bombings, etc."

To carry this out, we set up a task force that included top-level aides at the Justice Department, the Treasury (for its involvement in drug control), and the White House. As it happened, the Administration was doing a lot to combat crime, and by seeking out and coordinating our news releases, we were able to provide virtually the story a day the President wanted. A memo that Rob Odle sent to Haldeman after the election suggests the kind of news we generated in the final weeks before the election:

OCTOBER 14—The White House Conference on Drug Abuse for radio executives, which produced a wire-service picture of the President with the police dogs that sniff out marijuana.

OCTOBER 15—The President signed the Organized Crime Control Act at the Justice Department, then visited the D.C. Police Department.

OCTOBER 16—The Attorney General held a press conference and dedicated the Indiana University Law School.

OCTOBER 17—The Attorney General received an award from the Association of Federal Investigators.

OCTOBER 19—Assistant Attorney General Bill Ruckelshaus began a series of Justice Department "visitations" to discuss the drug problem on college campuses. His first visit was to Mount Holyoke College in South Hadley, Massachusetts. Our memo notes that "Ruckelshaus' speech is broken up by pot-smoking co-eds; nevertheless, Justice Department's hard line is evident in media throughout the country."

OCTOBER 20—The President visited injured policemen in Kansas City.

And so it went, right through the election, with special emphasis on supporting the police, and combating skyjackings and drugs. All of this was good public relations and good politics—we were fighting crime and we deserved credit. The problem was that, once they got out on the stump, the President and the Vice President tended to forget about our positive achievements and spend their time blasting Democrats as pro-crime.

In addition to the news we could generate, we wanted to develop a series of tough newspaper ads for use by our candidates, stressing both law and order and Cambodia, and painting our opponents as soft in both areas. On September 11, Haldeman wrote me:

> Please try to develop an ad that can be run hitting the radical liberal theme of the Vice President's speech with specific focus on Cambodia.
>
> Even the Lou Harris poll now shows that the public reaction is 2 to 1 favorable regarding Cambodia as we have a real asset if we figure out how to use it.
>
> The thing to do is to make an asset for us out of those who took a position against Cambodia. The ad should talk about the radical liberals and then probably list them by name—that is, those candidates that we're trying to defeat this fall—pick up some of the quotes as the Vice-President did in his speech of things that they said at the time about the Cambodia operation and then make the point of how wrong they were.
>
> You probably ought to get Buchanan to give you some guidance on how to put this thing together. It should be a very tough ad and could be very effective if done right.

I had some ads drafted, but Haldeman said they weren't tough enough, and at that point Colson injected himself into the situation. Colson was operating on a sort of free-lance basis. Certain people like Harry Dent and Murray Chotiner had responsibility for overseeing key Senate races, but Colson floated about and injected himself into whatever issues or campaigns interested him, presumably with the President's blessing.

Dent and Chotiner were then the two top political aides in the White House, the men who dealt with governors, state chairmen, and other party figures, and reported on their needs to Haldeman and the President. Chotiner was, of course, the better known of the two, having been regarded as Richard Nixon's political mentor and/or hatchet man from the time of the first Congressional campaigns. I never found that Chotiner lived up to his sinister reputation. He always struck me as a reasonable man with good political judgment. At the time I knew him, of course, he was somewhat out of favor, and he never had the responsibilities that he believed he should have. My chief memory of Murray, who died early in 1974 of injuries suffered in an auto accident, was of a man who was always extremely considerate toward my family. Once on a flight to California he went out of his way to amuse the children, and to talk to Gail. A great many political figures, in the same situation, never had a word for anyone's wife or children, unless they thought it would work to their advantage.

Dent, the other top political operative, had originally worked on Strom Thurmond's Senate staff and his knowledge of southern politics had made him the leading southern spokesman in the Nixon Administration. He was low-keyed, a storyteller, extremely easy to work with, and extremely effective.

On the issue of the newspaper ads, Colson called me, Nofziger, Dent, and Chotiner to his office and outlined for us a series of attack ads he had in mind. It was all innuendo—you questioned a man's patriotism, his intelligence, his morality, his manhood, anything you could get away with. We were all appalled. The ads just went too far—you didn't just question your opponent's judgment on Vietnam, you had to put blood on his hands. Dent, Chotiner, and I felt that Colson's approach would be counterproductive, that it would arouse sympathy for the men it hoped to defeat. I thought it noteworthy that Murray Chotiner, who for twenty years had been stereotyped as a hatchet man, was in 1970 protesting—in vain—that Colson's tactics went too far.

The result was that in 1970 we had two distinct ad programs, the "positive ads" and the "negative ads." The positive ads were simply traditional newspaper ads that dealt with the issues and urged the election of a Republican Congress to support the President. Both types were run in newspapers around the country, sponsored by various committees that Colson had set up. During the final weeks of the campaign, there was quite a struggle as Dent, Chotiner, and I tried to persuade Haldeman to spend less money on Colson's negative ads and more on our positive ones. We got some cutbacks, and in the end we spent $133,000 on the positive ads and $110,000 on the negative ads.

I had the responsibility of placing both sets of ads with our ad agency and because of this it was later charged that I had masterminded the "dirty" ad campaign, but in truth that honor belonged to Colson.

Colson took a special interest in Senator Joseph Tydings' race for reelection in Maryland. One of his ads that ran in the Washington *Post* asked in big black letters: WHAT KIND OF MAN IS JOE TYDINGS? and then proceeded to make clear that Tydings was the sort of man who was soft on crime, who didn't back up our boys in Vietnam, and who was most at home with Yippies and anarchists. Colson also planted the story in *Life* that charged Tydings with influence peddling. The charge was later shown to be false, but not until after November 3, when Tydings was defeated. After that, whenever you pointed out one of Colson's blunders to him, you could be sure he'd reply, "Yeah, but I'm the guy who got Joe Tydings."

The key mistake in 1970 probably was not in using the law-and-order approach, or even in overusing it. There is no question that the issue had strong appeal to the voters. The real blunder was in our timing. Richard Nixon had for many years said that campaigns must not "peak" too soon, but that is exactly what happened in 1970. We hit the law-and-order theme too soon, we peaked perhaps a month before the election, and we therefore left time for the Democratic candidates to present themselves as being just as opposed to crime and violence as our candidates. In Illinois, for example, Senator Ralph Smith had used some tough television spots linking Adlai Stevenson III to crime and permissiveness, so Stevenson began wearing an American flag pin in his lapel and emphasizing his law-enforcement record. We joked about the Democrats lining up to pin on their sheriff's badges, but the fact was that our poor timing allowed most of them to pin on their badges in time to save themselves.

Behind all the slogans and the sheriff's badges, there was a real issue struggling for attention. There *is* a basic difference between the way liberals and conservatives approach the crime problem. Liberals tend to put more emphasis on prevention, on human weakness, on society's responsibilities. Conservatives, in the 1970 campaign, put more emphasis on control and on strict laws. It is by no means an easy question; experts with no political axes to grind are split on whether, given limited funds, priority should go to prevention or control. But politically there can be no doubt that the average American is more interested in having a cop on the beat than having a social worker in the neighborhood. We had a good case, and we should have made it in a straightforward, positive manner, instead of overstating and distorting our case.

Part of our peaking too soon was caused by Vice President Agnew. By midsummer he was charging around the country grabbing headlines with tough speeches about "radiclibs" and "rotten apples" and "effete snobs." The speeches were necessary, for fund-raising purposes, but someone should have told him to hold down the rhetoric. Many of us had mixed feelings about Agnew's rhetorical rampage. We enjoyed what he was saying, but we sensed he might be going too far. Agnew, of course, was having the time of his life. He'd been frozen out by Nixon for almost two years, but now the eyes of the nation were upon him and he gloried in the attention. He was getting tremendous publicity as our cutting edge, the spokesman for the Silent Majority. That was fine, but he should have held his fire for a couple of months, or the President should have reined him in.

But, as it developed, the President was caught up in the passions of the campaign season, and he too would soon charge into the battle.

The original plan was for the President to do little or no campaigning. Our speakers' bureau set up its program on that assumption, and therefore stressed speeches by Cabinet members and other surrogates, including the President's two daughters. But the President changed his strategy. We never knew exactly why. No doubt he savored the challenge, scented victory in the autumn air, and perhaps he disliked playing a passive role while Agnew was out there reaping all those cheers and headlines. So he set out on the campaign trail, delivering the same law-and-order message as Agnew, although in a slightly more elevated tone. But once he had committed himself and his prestige, emotions inevitably began to escalate, until it all culminated in the fiasco that ended our campaign.

There were two fiascoes, really, a smaller, warm-up fiasco on the Friday before the election, and then, on election eve, a fiasco of truly Presidential proportions.

The curtain raiser on Friday night came when some antiwar demonstrators threw rocks at the President's car as he left a rally at San Jose, California. There were reports from the scene that the President had taunted the demonstrators by standing on the roof of his car and waving his arms at them. But no matter. The President persuaded himself that this was the last straw, that national outrage over an attack on the President would trigger a Republican landslide. The next morning Haldeman called my office with orders that we stress the San Jose incident in every possible way over the weekend. He sent along a statement Jim Keogh had written ("On Friday night in San Jose, California, a vicious mob of militant demonstrators attacked President Nixon. . . . It was the most severe attack on a President since the assassination of John Kennedy") that we were to give to the Vice President, to all the Republican candidates, and to other Administration spokesmen to play up over the weekend. Meanwhile, Ziegler was giving skeptical newsmen an inch-by-inch, scratch-by-scratch tour of the President's supposedly battered limousine. It all added up to overkill, another instance of Nixon trying to make mountains out of molehills. Left to itself, the San Jose incident might have added up to a slight plus for us, but our hard sell, plus the suspicion that Nixon provoked the demonstrators, took the edge off it.

Such was the overheated atmosphere during the final weekend of the campaign when a major blunder was made concerning the President's final television appearance.

On that Saturday morning, as far as I was concerned, the campaign was over. Our plan had called for two final television appearances by the President: first, a half-hour, nationally televised speech he delivered in California on Friday night, shortly before the San Jose incident; second, a number of four-and-a-half-minute spots to be run during the half-time break of several professional football games on Sunday afternoon. I was proud of these spots because they represented a purchase of local time on a national basis, which normally is not possible. The spots would be shown on a local basis, focusing on various key Senate campaigns, and would feature four minutes of the local candidate and a half minute of the President. I'd been in New York for several days, tying down all the details of this purchase, and when I was finished I thought we'd given our Republican candidates an excellent political package that fall: the President and Vice President had stumped for them all over the country, we'd had our newspaper ads, then the President's Friday night speech, and finally the Sunday afternoon spots.

Early on Saturday afternoon, I was sitting down for a leisurely lunch at the Toll House Restaurant in Silver Spring, Maryland, with my wife, children, and my visiting parents, when my Page Boy began to beep. I went to a pay phone and called the White House switchboard, where an operator told me Air Force One was calling me.

My heart sank. Calls from Air Force One were a joke among those who didn't often travel with the President. He and Haleman and Chapin and others in the traveling entourage would get up there, thirty thousand feet above the earth, and something would happen to them. It must have been the closed-in atmosphere, or perhaps the plane's well-stocked bar, or something about the altitude that made them feel God-like, but they would invariably begin to rain down calls upon us mere mortals back on earth, and there was no way to talk to them or reason with them.

"Mr. Magruder, this is Air Force One," the military operator said. "I want to advise you this is not a secure telephone. We have Mr. Klein for you."

Actually, he referred to Klein by his military code name, which I forget. The President was Searchlight, and Ron Walker, our chief advance man, was Roadrunner, but the others escape me now.

"Jeb, the President just made this tremendous speech in Phoenix," Klein shouted. He had that near hysteria in his voice that they always had when they called from the plane. "Is there time to get it on the networks?"

Oh, no, I thought.

"It's possible, Herb," I told him. "But it wouldn't be easy. What kind of speech was it?"

Klein indicated that the President had given the radiclibs hell, then said he'd be back in touch soon. I returned to my lunch, but soon my Page Boy beeped again. This time it was Chapin, who raved for a while about the President's great speech in Phoenix and the need to get it on the networks. I continued to discourage the idea, because I knew it would be almost impossible, in the time available, to get the film to Los Angeles, edit it, and send it over the network lines to New York. Eventually Chapin signed off and I returned to lunch, but soon Air Force One called again, and this time it was Higby, who said Haldeman wanted to talk to me.

"Get us a half hour on all three networks, Sunday or Monday night," Haldeman told me.

I didn't argue. I asked a few questions, like where was the tape of the speech—it was on its way to California, where Bill Safire was in charge of editing it—and then I got to work.

I called the networks, whose spokesmen at first said that what we asked was impossible, because the time was already sold. Eventually, however, they said they would sell us some time, but they would have to offer equal time to the Democrats. A group of Democrats raised the money to put Senator Muskie on as their party's spokesman. The networks said they could not free more than a total of thirty minutes, so we and the Democrats could each have fifteen minutes, back to back. All this involved extensive negotiations—my records show that I made or received forty-three calls at my home that Sunday.

The final issue was who would go first, the President or Muskie. Both sides wanted to go first, because of the high "tune-off" factor on political broadcasts. The networks suggested that we flip a coin, but I insisted that since we had first requested the time, we should have our choice, and that was the decision.

The Republican National Committee reluctantly put up the money, and on Monday morning I flew to New York with three checks for about $50,000 each in my pocket, one for each network.

At the first network I went to, one of the top executives said:

"Say, do you want to see this tape of yours? It's terrible."

I had talked to Bill Safire, who had edited the speech down to thirteen minutes, earlier that morning. "It's a little rough," he had said, "but it's *realistic.*"

I quickly watched the tape, and it *was* terrible. It was the wrong speech to show on television. The President had delivered it at a Republican rally. It was a fighting, arm-waving, give-'em-hell, law-and-order speech, fine for a rally, where the partisan audience gets caught up in the excitement, but completely wrong to send into the quiet of people's homes. Moreover, the sound was bad, often inaudible. The tape was in black and white, and some imperfection caused a jagged line to run down the middle of the picture. Finally, because the speech had been edited down to thirteen minutes, it was disjointed to the point of irrationality.

I was speechless when I finished watching the tape, and a network executive added to my panic by saying:

"Of course, I can't show you the Muskie tape, but I'll tell you this—it's first-rate!"

I called Chapin.

"Dwight, believe me, this speech will be a disaster."

"Safire says it's good," Chapin insisted.

Finally I called Haldeman in California. I told him my objections to the film, and I offered him a positive alternative: If the President would go to NBC's studio in Burbank that night, he could address the nation on live television.

"No, the President is going to Riverside to speak for George Murphy," Haldeman said.

"Hell, Bob," I said, "Murphy is already down the tube. You've got to do something to stop us from showing this disaster."

"You say it's bad, but Safire says it's good," Haldeman said. "He's the creative guy and you're the manager. The decision is made. We go with it."

So we went with it.

And it *was* a disaster. I was part of a group that watched in the White House that evening as the President and Muskie appeared on the screen—watched in mounting shock and dismay.

The President's inaudible, disjointed, black-and-white, law-and-order tirade was followed immediately by Ed Muskie, in living color, sitting in an armchair by a crackling fire, speaking in the voice of sweet reason. The contrast was devastating. It was like watching Grandma Moses debate the Boston Strangler. The networks were soon flooded with calls from angry Republicans who charged the networks with sabotaging the President. They were wrong; the President's own people had sabotaged him.

Herb Klein was in California on Election Day, but a group of us decided to have an election-night party in his office, complete with drinks and wives, as we awaited the results that we hoped would give us control of the next Congress. By the time the evening was over, that hope was gone. We had picked up a net gain of two Senate seats, not nearly enough for a Republican majority, and we had lost nine House seats. We had also lost a shocking eleven governorships. Actually, as off-year elections go, our Congressional results were not bad. The problem was that the President had put his personal prestige on the line and had suffered a sharp political setback. What was worse, the *style* of his campaigning had caused many commentators to say—and many people to believe— that he had degraded his office. All this was to have several consequences.

Most immediately, life became rather difficult for Bill Safire for a few days. The President ordered him to write a report on why he had urged using the edited version of the Phoenix speech on television, which was rather like writing a speech defending Pickett's charge. Bill hung on somehow, but I always thought I would have been fired if I had not been firmly on record against using that speech.

Sometime the next year, I was reading a book on the Nixon Presidency by Rowland Evans and Robert Novak, and I was surprised to find an account of the election-eve fiasco that erred in only one detail—it blamed me instead of Safire. I confronted Safire with it.

"Bill, that obviously came from you. I can't believe it."

"Jeb, I was just trying to get your name in the book," he told me.

In the longer run, the 1970 disaster persuaded the President that he must change his tactics for 1972, that he must take the "high road" when he ran for reelection. The election-eve television shows had positioned Senator Muskie as the likely Democratic candidate in 1972, and in early 1971 the polls were showing him ahead of the President, a fact that led to panic, to a thirst for political intelligence, to new tactics and new people. At least the dirty tricks had been out in the open in 1970; in 1971 they went underground.

CHAPTER VII

Moving On

TWO DAYS AFTER THE ELECTIONS, I entered the hospital to have my gall bladder removed. I was there for nine days, then at home for three weeks. I thus had plenty of time for reflection, and my main thought, as I looked back over my first year in Washington, was that it was time for me to leave the White House.

I wasn't enjoying my job as much as I had at first. Occasionally I'd be involved in something I thought was worthwhile, like the drug conferences, but most of the time I was overseeing an endless stream of trivia, and doing so under constant pressure. The other factor was Colson, who seemed about to force Klein out. I didn't want to work for Colson and I was tired of fighting him, so the obvious thing to do was to move on.

But where? I thought I could probably get a job at the Assistant Secretary level in one of the departments, but it would have been the same sort of job I had, a move over but not a step up. I thought my best strategy would be to work in the 1972 campaign and use it as a springboard to a senior job in the second Nixon Administration. I assumed that John Mitchell would direct the campaign, and I resolved to speak to him when I got back to work. If I did well during the campaign, and thus had the support of both Haldeman and Mitchell, I would not lack for opportunities in 1973. My hope was that I might be made the director of some independent agency, something like ACTION or the Environmental Protection Agency. I was tired of being a staff man and I looked forward to having my own program to manage.

134

While I was in the hospital I received flowers and a letter from the President, an example of Haldeman's thoughtfulness. I also received a handwritten, extremely nice letter from Haldeman himself. He spoke highly of my work and said he was looking forward to my return and to our next two years together. A letter like that made it all seem worthwhile, for Bob's compliments, being rare, were all the more appreciated.

Soon after I returned to work in December, Gail and I went to church services at the White House. We went through the receiving line after the services and shook hands with the President. He made a point of chatting with us and complimenting my work for a minute or two.

"Jeb's looking a little thin from that operation, Gail," he said. "You'd better fatten him up."

I was surprised and pleased both that he remembered about my operation and that he remembered Gail's name. It was a nice personal touch from a man with many other things on his mind. Mainly, I recall that as the first of the two times he ever personally thanked me for my work.

Colson had used the campaign as an excuse to move deeper into our public relations program. He was taking over the use of our mailing lists, he had pushed his negative ad program, and he was generally injecting himself into every corner of our operation. During the antiballistic missile struggle, he and I had an angry exchange over his sending memos to the President in which he took credit for the things our office was doing to support the ABM. I told him, "Look, Chuck, we don't want to be involved in your special-interest groups; can't you stay out of our operation?" His standard reply was that he was only trying to help the President—and that meant nothing was off-limits to him.

In October, after Colson called the three network presidents on a matter that was clearly Klein's to handle, Klein sent him an angry memo that said in part:

> I thought we had a clear agreement you would not be calling them without consulting me. . . . Your continued calls have caused network heads to ask me privately—are you leaving? What has happened to you? With actions like this you make my work harder. Are you promoting the idea of taking over my contacts and Ron Ziegler's? They think so and tell me.

It was a sad memo, really, and a sad situation. Klein had been a Nixon loyalist for twenty years, but now Colson's star was rising and Klein's was falling.

During the Christmas holidays I ran into Colson at a cocktail party, and we had a talk about the situation.

"Jeb, you don't seem willing to work with me and cooperate with me," he said.

"I have no problem working with you," I told him. "But that doesn't mean I agree with everything you want to do."

"You know Klein's got to go," he said.

"Herb can be useful if he's properly directed."

"He can't be properly directed. He's got to go. The President wants him out."

"I think it'd be a serious mistake to lose Herb."

"You know, Jeb, your refusal to cooperate with me could be construed as disloyalty to the President."

I just walked away. Colson had never blinked an eye. It was classic Colson: if you're not pro-me, you're anti-Nixon.

In January, after getting Haldeman's approval, I went to the Justice Department to talk to Attorney General Mitchell about working in the campaign. He knew me from my White House work, but he hadn't known that I'd had campaign experience—in California in 1968 and in various campaigns before that. He couldn't give me an immediate answer, but he encouraged me, and I went away thinking that something might be worked out.

It seemed to me that if Mitchell ran the campaign he'd need someone like me who knew the White House people and could be his liaison with them. Haldeman and Mitchell got along well, but Mitchell thought most of the White House staff people were too young and too pushy—eager beavers like Higby and Strachan who were forever pestering his people about trivial matters. Haldeman, for his part, didn't think much of Mitchell's top aides, Dick Kleindienst and Bob Mardian, both of whom were old Goldwater people from Arizona and were not well attuned to the Nixon–Haldeman style of operation.

It often seemed to me that there were two distinct operational styles to be seen in Washington, the political and the managerial, and that while it would have been useful to combine the best of both, success in the Nixon Administration depended largely on managerial skills. The skills that politicians cultivate—a talent for small talk, an ability to be all things to all men—can be good for winning elections but very bad for any sort of managerial assignment. In the Nixon Administration, Bob Finch was the archetypal politician, and Bob Haldeman the archetypal

manager. Typically, a politically oriented figure would come to Haldeman and say, "Let's do a favor for old Charlie; he helped us out in
1960," and Haldeman would reply: "So what?" Haldeman existed only
to serve Richard Nixon, and Richard Nixon, despite all his political success, was never a natural or comfortable politician. He was by nature a
manager, a man who wanted to run things. The 1968 Nixon–Humphrey
campaign was a classic encounter between a manager and a politician,
and once in office Nixon became more and more the secluded, above-the-
battle manager. I considered John Mitchell the one man in the Administration who best combined political and managerial talents. He
understood the need for handshaking and backslapping with the state
chairmen, and he also knew how to run a department or a campaign.
Haldeman could never bring himself to chitchat with politicians, most of
whom bored him, and he and Nixon became more and more isolated
from the political realities that existed beyond the White House gates.

My own role was that of a manager with political experience. Haldeman had confidence in me, but it was not true, as some writers have
suggested, that I was a Haldeman man who was forced on Mitchell as a
means for Haldeman to control the campaign. Mitchell viewed me as
someone he could work with, and someone who could also work effectively with the White House. Given all this, it seemed likely that there
was a role for me to play in the 1972 campaign structure.

Early in 1971, Haldeman assigned Fred Malek to evaluate the Office
of Communications. Haldeman had recently brought Malek to the White
House to replace Harry Flemming as the director of personnel, or chief
talent scout. Malek was a husky, tough, gruff, aggressive West Point
graduate and onetime Green Beret, who'd been a successful self-made
businessman before entering the Administration. I respected Malek's
managerial ability, but he wasn't someone I cared for personally.

Sally Quinn, who at that time was with the Washington *Post*, wrote an
article that described Fred Malek as a man who, every morning while
driving his old Mercedes to work, whizzed past a long line of cars
waiting to get onto the George Washington Parkway and cut in at the
head of the line. It was an apt story, and it called to my mind an experience I had with Malek after we had been working together a while. He
and I and our wives and children, and two of his aides, were going up
to spend a weekend at Camp Hoover, a rustic retreat in the Blue Ridge
Mountains that President Hoover had often used.

You reach Camp Hoover by a private road that runs off the Skyline

Drive. The camp is located about a mile from Big Meadows, a tourist stop on the Skyline Drive. About a half mile down the mountain from Big Meadows is a garbage dump where bears come almost nightly to eat and where tourists often go to watch them. The Park Service officer who admitted us onto the private road to Camp Hoover explained that if we wanted to see the bears we could drive part way to the dump, but we mustn't drive all the way lest we scare them off.

We were in two cars, mine and Malek's Mercedes, and I was in front. I drove to within about two hundred yards of the dump, then we got out and walked the rest of the way. We found about a hundred tourists standing around in the dusk like an audience in an amphitheater, waiting for the show to start. We joined the people, most of whom were speaking in whispers, and then we were horrified to see Malek arriving in his Mercedes, honking his horn for people to get out of his way. He had decided to drive up, so he could watch the bears without getting out of his car.

The people were appalled, then furious. They began shaking their fists and making angry remarks, and Malek kept honking his horn until we thought some of the tourists might drag him out of his Mercedes and tear him apart. Then Malek began yelling for me and Gail to come join him. We ignored him. We didn't want anyone to know we had anything to do with him. And, needless to say, the bears never came that evening. Malek had ruined everyone's evening. When we finally got back to Camp Hoover, one of his assistants said to him:

"Fred, why didn't you *order* the bears to come?"

Malek, of course, never understood why we were annoyed with him.

In any event, Malek was the efficiency expert whom Haldeman had chosen to evaluate Klein's Office of Communications. I took Malek's "evaluation" to be a put-up job, engineered by Colson, as part of Colson's effort to get rid of Klein.

I went to see Haldeman and tried to discuss the Colson–Klein situation with him. In effect, I told him that if he wanted Colson to take over the Office of Communications, that was his decision—I disagreed, but if it was going to be done, it should be done with a minimum of bloodshed. Haldeman would give me no hint of what was coming. Perhaps he didn't know. My guess was that Colson had convinced the President that Klein had to go, and Haldeman didn't want to make an issue of it. Certainly the major issue was what happened to Klein, the President's old friend, and not what happened to me. But it was a confusing and discouraging time for me. I didn't know if my campaign job would come through, and I didn't know if I might come to work one morning and discover that Colson was my new boss. So, while I waited for word from Mitchell, I concentrated on the business at hand, which was to present a positive picture of the President to offset the strident image of the campaign.

We redoubled our efforts to convey "the human side of the President." We suggested ideas for feature articles about the President and his family to writers and magazine editors. We tried to encourage friendly writers to undertake books about the Nixons. There was a long and unsuccessful effort to get one or both of the Nixon daughters to write a first-person account of White House life. Our efforts to stimulate books were hampered by an apparent feeling in the publishing world that Kennedy books sold but Nixon books didn't.

In particular, we kept looking for the slogan that would capture the essence of the Nixon Administration. We had been seeking our "New Frontier" for two years and never found it. Various slogans came and went—the New Federalism, the New American Revolution, the Generation of Peace—but none ever caught on, and the President kept prodding us to find the one that would. In November, a week or so after the election, Bill Safire told the President that the prefix "Mr." can be highly effective and impressive—Mr. Republican, Mr. Conservative, Mr. President—and he therefore suggested a campaign to identify Nixon as Mr. Peace. As Safire noted, 'Mr. Peace, of course, leaves all other Misters behind."

That was perhaps not one of Safire's best ideas, and the President did not order us to immortalize him as "Mr. Peace," but in January of 1971 he at last found his slogan. He found it when he went to dedicate the new Eisenhower Republican Center in Washington. As he was waiting to speak, he noticed an open door in the back of the hall. Inspired by this, he put aside his prepared text and spoke of the need for the Republican Party to be "the party of the open door."

The next day Haldeman sent out a memo saying:

> The President is very anxious to get the "Open Door" concept used as frequently and widely as we possibly can.
> From now on the "Open Office Hours" should be called the "Open Door Hour" and the 5 o'clock sessions with Congressmen, Senators and other people should be billed as "Open Door" sessions. This should be tied to the statistics on the number of people the

President has seen, and so forth, and build on the theme that he's the most "Open Door" President in history.

This request set off a flurry of activity. We sent the President's remarks to our mailing list and we sent engraved, framed copies to the nation's three thousand Republican county chairmen, with the suggestion that they put a plaque saying "The Party of the Open Door" outside the county headquarters. The Republican Party paid for this mailing. It was in the new Open Door spirit that we had the signs changed that were hung outside the White House on the days it was closed to visitors. The existing signs simply said CLOSED TO VISITORS, but after a great many memos passed between Haldeman, Ziegler, Chapin, Klein, myself, and others, we agreed that was too negative and we therefore ordered new, more positive signs saying CLOSED TO VISITORS TO-DAY—COME BACK TOMORROW.

One idea we sometimes kicked around in the White House was changing the name of the Republican Party. We felt that in the minds of too many average Americans "Republican Party" meant the party of the rich and privileged. One way to attract Middle Americans to our cause might be by offering what seemed to be a new party. The title that most attracted us was Conservative Party. Haldeman was interested in this idea, as was Harry Dent, but nothing ever came of it.

This was the sort of trivia I had grown very tired of, and yet, along with the slogans and the trivia there was important work to be done. One of our basic postelection decisions was that there was an urgent need to make the Administration's domestic program more visible and understandable. Our domestic record at that point had been a mixed one. We had won, or were about to win, Congressional passage of the crime and drug bills, and postal reorganization, and part of our revenue-sharing program, but we had been unable to pass the Family Assistance Plan, the bill for government reorganization, or the rest of the revenue-sharing program.

Government reorganization and revenue sharing were of particular importance to us. They were cornerstones of the New American Revolution that the President had proclaimed in his State of the Union Message in January of 1970. Granting the rhetorical overkill of the slogan, we felt these were extremely important measures. Our reorganization plan was intended to streamline an executive branch of government that in many ways was decades out of date. The President accomplished what changes he legally could by executive order, but many important changes could only be achieved by Congressional action, and we faced opposition both from our own bureaucracies and from Congressional leaders, both of whom had a vested interest in preserving the status quo. We felt that our reorganization plan was in no way a partisan issue; it was simply a matter of wanting an efficient and effective government apparatus. Our bipartisan approach to the issue was reflected in the makeup of a Citizen's Committee for Government Reorganization that we helped set up in April, which had as one of its cochairmen Terry Sanford, the former Democratic governor of North Carolina, and included among its members Joe Califano, Lyndon Johnson's former Special Assistant, and Wilbur Cohen, who was Johnson's Secretary of Health, Education, and Welfare.

Revenue sharing was more controversial. The President proposed to return money, and therefore power, to the state and local governments, to the maximum degree possible. The idea was that money should be spent at the lowest possible levels—in Washington when necessary, but in the state houses and city halls when possible. There would be stress on block grants instead of categorical grants; that is, on grants with no strings attached, so that local officials could set their own priorities. This concept was indeed revolutionary in that it challenged the liberal assumption of nearly four decades that all possible decisions should be made in Washington. It was a clear-cut issue—centralized government versus local decision-making. The liberals in Congress were able to bottle up our plan, but we kept fighting for it, and hoping that we could at least take the issue to the voters in 1972. Before the election, general revenue-sharing passed, but, to date, the many specific revenue-sharing plans are still bottled up in Congress.

To try to generate grass-roots support for our program, we began a series of Regional Domestic Program Briefings which was an outgrowth of our successful briefings on foreign policy. Actually, there were two types of briefings. The President personally participated in several regional press briefings. These were supplemented by more local visits by Administrative spokesmen such as Ehrlichman, Finch, and Rumsfeld. These local briefings were, of course, another way we could get around the Washington press and take our message directly to the people.

Mitchell called me to his office around the first of March and said he and Haldeman had agreed that I should leave the White House to begin the planning for the 1972 campaign. It was a typical informal talk with

Mitchell; there was no mention of what title or permanent role I might have. He simply said I'd work on the initial planning and that I should be thinking about other people I'd need to help me. He stressed that I shouldn't worry about what the candidate would do—what line he would take, what policies he would follow—but should concentrate simply on putting together the best grass-roots campaign in history. We were both fascinated by the technology available to us—the use of computers in mass mailings, for example—and we both agreed that we had the time and the money to make this the best campaign ever.

Mitchell called a meeting a week or so later to which he invited me and three other men who were going to work on the campaign: Herb Kalmbach, the tall California lawyer who handled the President's personal legal affairs, was to be one of the campaign's chief fund raisers; Hugh Sloan, one of Chapin's assistants in the White House, was to be the campaign's treasurer; and Harry Flemming, who had formerly been the White House personnel chief, was to set up Nixon organizations in each state.

I was pleased to see Kalmbach. I didn't know him well, but he was known as one of the most engaging men in the Nixon circle. I was less pleased to see Sloan and Flemming.

Sloan was a Princeton graduate and navy veteran who had gone to work for the Republican National Finance Committee in 1966, when he was in his mid-twenties, and had worked as assistant finance director of the Nixon–Agnew campaign in 1968. After the election he was assigned to Chapin's staff, handling detail work on the President's appointments schedule. He hadn't entirely pleased Chapin, however, because he wasn't aggressive enough, didn't take the initiative on solving problems, and I knew that Chapin was using the campaign job as a way of getting rid of him. Although I didn't expect to have many dealings with Sloan, I felt that to be a poor way to staff the reelection committee.

Harry Flemming was somewhat similar. His father had served in the Eisenhower Cabinet, and Flemming was an Alexandria, Virginia, businessman and city councilman a year or two younger than I. He had been in charge of personnel for the White House, but he had not satisfied Haldeman, who had eased him out to make way for Fred Malek. I didn't think Flemming was qualified for this major campaign assignment, and I didn't look forward to working with him for a year and a half on the campaign.

Mitchell outlined the roles that each of us would play: Kalmbach would raise money; Sloan would keep track of it; I would be in charge of planning; Flemming would work with state party leaders. There was never any thought that we would run the campaign through the Republican National Committee rather than set up our own Nixon organization. The essential problem is that your fifty state chairmen are elected within their states, and they may or may not be competent or loyal to your candidate. You make use of state organizations wherever you can, but few Presidential candidates, of either party, have seen any alternative to setting up their own organization.

Mitchell told us there were going to be three basic rules in this campaign:

First, no credit cards. This rule resulted from his discovering, after the 1968 campaign, that advance men and others with credit cards had run up some $3 million in unpaid bills.

Second, he, Mitchell, would control all spending; except for petty cash, no money was to be committed without his personal approval.

Third, there would not be a lot of hangers-on in this campaign, particularly women whose role might be other than political. Our Administration had acquired a sexless, straight-arrow image, which was fine but not entirely accurate. Mitchell wanted to minimize that aspect of this campaign.

After the Mitchell meeting I talked to Haldeman, and we agreed I should stay at the White House until about the first of May, so I could wind up some ongoing projects. Haldeman spoke with enthusiasm about my new job. "You've got a great opportunity to build a campaign from the ground up," he told me. "This is the most important thing we'll be doing in the next two years."

Throughout March and April, my thoughts were increasingly on the campaign, but I was also involved in the continuing struggle over the Office of Communications. Cliff Miller and I had been urging Fred Malek, as he conducted his evaluation of the Office of Communications, that Herb Klein should be kept on. Colson knew we were lobbying against him and was furious with us. Finally a meeting was held in Klein's office to discuss Malek's recommendations, which were that, in the interests of more effective management, Colson should take over the direction of the project managers and the speakers' bureau, while Klein should retain the liaison with the television networks and the job of answering certain Presidential mail, keeping one writer on his staff.

Both Colson and Klein angrily resisted Malek's proposal—Klein because he was losing two-thirds of his office, Colson because he wasn't getting it all. Cliff Miller and I spoke in favor of the plan, as one that would give Klein more time for the thing he did best—his personal dealings with newsmen—and would free him from administrative "details."

Another issue was who would replace me as Klein's deputy. Colson won a voice in the naming of my successor, who eventually turned out to be Ken Clawson, a former reporter for the Washington *Post,* who was more Colson's deputy than Klein's, and who in his attitudes toward the media proved to be a junior edition of Colson himself.

But my thoughts were less and less on the Klein–Colson struggle and more and more on the campaign. I told Mitchell and Haldeman I wanted to take two of my White House assistants with me, Rob Odle to handle administration and Bart Porter for general operations. I also needed someone to head up our research program, and I was fortunate to find Bob Marik, a man in his early thirties who had both a Ph.D. and business experience, and who had been serving as a consultant in the Office of Education. Marik performed brilliantly throughout the campaign. He'd never been in a campaign before, but he proved to have more political perception than most veteran politicians. He ran our direct-mail and telephone programs, and he became our best strategist on the shifting political trends and issues of the campaign. Later, he received a top management position at the Office of Management and Budget.

I went to the Committee to Re-elect the President (which was officially titled the Committee for the Re-election of the President, and will be remembered by history as CREEP) at a salary of $38,500, a raise of several thousand dollars over my White House salary. I resigned my Presidential commission, the President and I exchanged letters, and I moved a block up the street to CRP's new offices at 1701 Pennsylvania Avenue.

I was pleased and excited—to be out of the White House power struggles, to be working on a national campaign, to be working for Mitchell. I knew the pressures would be great, for there is a high mortality rate in any Presidential campaign, but I thought I could survive as well as anyone. I was moving up to a new plateau, the most challenging one of my political career. There was only one small, sour note as we entered our new political headquarters. CBS had gotten wind of our new offices and sent a camera crew to photograph them. Hugh Sloan happened to walk out the door into the cameras and, not being experienced in dealing with the media, instinctively put his arm across his face in the classic pose of the bank robber hiding his face from the photographers.

It was not exactly the image we wanted for the Committee to Re-elect the President.

CHAPTER VIII

The Committee to Re-elect

As we set up the Committee to Re-elect in the spring of 1971, the President's popularity was lower than it had ever been. In May, the Harris Poll showed him running behind Senator Muskie in a projected 1972 election by 47 to 39. We had no way of anticipating the boosts we would receive in the next eighteen months—the public acceptance of the wage-price controls, the China and Russia trips, the blunders of the McGovern campaign. Yet we knew we had one priceless asset: time. We were starting our campaign a year earlier than whomever the Democrats would nominate in the summer of 1972. The Democratic candidate might equal us in campaign spending, his people might be as able and dedicated as ours, but there was no way he could make up for our year's head start.

At the White House we had often talked about long-range planning, but we rarely did it—we were almost entirely crisis-oriented. The most exciting thing about our work at CRP was that we *did* plan ahead, and as the months went by we saw our plans transformed into what we believed would be one of the best-organized, most scientific Presidential campaigns in history. The significance of the 1972 Nixon campaign—which Theodore White called "a science-fiction preview of future politics"—has been obscured by Watergate, but its lessons will not be ignored by the politicians of both parties who plan future Presidential campaigns.

At the top of the CRP apparatus, its unofficial but very real boss was the Attorney General, John Mitchell. In April, early in our planning, there had been some confusion when Bob Finch got the idea that he might head the campaign. Finch had performed so poorly as Secretary of Health, Education, and Welfare that in mid-1970 he had been replaced by Elliot Richardson and brought back to the White House. Unfortunately, there was little for him to do, and he spent a great deal of his time in California, presumably with an eye on his own political future. That was fine with Haldeman, who wanted Finch out of the White House, but it wasn't fine with Governor Ronald Reagan, Finch's old rival in California politics. Their mutual distaste went back at least to 1966, when Finch, running for lieutenant governor, ran ahead of Reagan, who was elected governor. Finch had a habit, when in California, of calling news conferences, and his comments would usually outrage Reagan. For example, Finch would speak out in favor of our Family Assistance Plan, which the more conservative Reagan opposed. When Finch arrived in California, Mitchell would start getting furious calls from Reagan. And since Reagan, not Finch, was the political power in that key state, Mitchell would often get on the phone to suggest to Finch that he tone things down while in California.

The President gave Finch the idea that he might play an active role in the campaign, and Finch therefore began discussing plans and strategies with me. But he was uncertain of his role, and little was accomplished. Once Finch went out to California and told the state's Republican Central Committee that CRP would pay some $60,000 of the cost of a sophisticated program to computerize voter data. He had absolutely no authority to make such a commitment, but he came back to Washington and asked me for the money. I told Mitchell, who was furious—we wondered if the computer program might appeal to Finch mainly for its utility in some future Finch campaign—but eventually we paid the money rather than offend the California party leaders.

Not long after that, Finch went to Mitchell to discuss their respective roles in the coming campaign. Mitchell made it clear that he, Mitchell, would be in charge of the campaign, and that if Finch had any doubts he should talk to the President. We didn't see much of Finch after that.

As our planning developed, I reported all major issues and decisions directly to Mitchell, but it was also necessary to keep Haldeman involved. I reported to Haldeman through Gordon Strachan, who had become Haldeman's assistant for political matters. At first, when I had a memo to take to Mitchell for a decision, I would make a copy for Haldeman but hold it until I had taken Mitchell his copy. But Haldeman told me this was not satisfactory. He wanted to see the decision memos in advance. My concern was that he might embarrass me by calling Mitchell about a memo before Mitchell had read it. "Just don't sandbag me, Bob," I told him, and Haldeman agreed not to contact Mitchell about a memo until Mitchell had read it.

My first important job at CRP was to divide the campaign into planning task forces, which included advertising, youth, polling, candidate support, research, the convention, direct mail, media, minorities, administration, and so on. My three initial assistants, Rob Odle, Bob Marik, and Bart Porter, each served as project manager for several of these task forces, and I headed the initial planning for one, advertising.

We understood the dangers of a committee like ours seeming to work in isolation, so we asked some major Administration figures, like Rumsfeld and Buchanan, to serve as chairmen of the task forces. In some cases, these top-level chairmen made an important contribution to the planning, in other cases they did not, but in either case they could not complain that they had been ignored.

Four areas of planning that occupied a great deal of CRP's time in 1971, and that deserve individual mention, were our polling, our advertising, our youth program, and the struggle over the location of our National Convention.

THE CONVENTION

The Republican National Committee consists of party leaders from every state. It has a paid staff in Washington and a national chairman, who is in theory selected by the National Committee members but who, when a Republican occupies the White House, must be the President's man. The President's first national chairman, in 1969–70, was Rogers Morton, the big, white-haired, easy-going congressman from Maryland. But as passions flared in the 1970 campaign, Morton had struck many at the White House as not tough enough in his attacks on the Democrats, and early in 1971 he was made Secretary of the Interior and replaced as national chairman by Senator Bob Dole of Kansas. Dole was handsome, articulate, ambitious, and more partisan by nature than Morton. To an extent we needed Dole to be our cutting edge in 1971–72 because Vice President Agnew was assuming a more statesmanlike role in preparation for the 1972 elections.

Dole was a hard-hitting, outspoken conservative, quite able and willing to take on Democratic Chairman Larry O'Brien, the Senate doves, and other of our critics, but even Dole was not always harsh enough to satisfy some of the White House hard-liners, in particular Chuck Colson. From time to time Colson would send Dole a speech he wanted Dole to deliver. Typically, it would be the kind of speech that accused our anti-war critics of treason. Dole was in a difficult position; in effect he had four constituencies: the President, the National Committee, the voters back in Kansas, and to an extent, the Senate, since there are limits on the kinds of personal attacks senators traditionally make on one another. Sometimes, when Dole felt that Colson was trying to push him further than he should go, he would call me and ask that I show the proposed speech to Mitchell for his judgment. Usually Mitchell would agree that the speech should be toned down or scrapped.

Once, in early 1972, I attended a large luncheon meeting of the Republican National Committee at the Washington Hilton. I was up on the speaker's platform with other Administration figures. Mitchell and Dole were sitting at the front speaker's table, and I was in the second row, with Colson sitting two seats down from me. A day or two earlier, Colson had sent Dole one of his "treason" speeches and Dole had discussed it with Mitchell, who agreed it should not be delivered. Before lunch began, Dole walked back and started talking with me.

"Jeb, I've got one of those God-damned speeches from Colson," he said, rather loudly. "What am I supposed to do? I can't say that stuff."

All this was obviously for Colson's benefit, to use me to give Colson a public chewing-out. My instinct was to avoid a scene.

"Senator, maybe you should talk to the Attorney General," I said.

Dole wandered over to Mitchell, but in a minute he was back.

"I talked to Mitchell," Dole said. "He says this Colson speech is junk and I ought to forget it."

"Well, I guess that's what you should do then," I said. Dole wandered off, and after a while I sneaked a glance at Colson, who was staring at his plate, red-faced with anger.

Unfortunately, we didn't scrap all of Colson's speeches. This was another instance of what I called our "slippage" problem. Under constant pressure from Colson, Mitchell would sometimes tell Dole to tone down a hard-line Colson speech but to go ahead and deliver it. We would compromise, we would give Colson half a loaf, which was usually more than we should have given him.

The first major decision in our planning for the 1972 Republican National Convention was where it should be located, and a controversy soon developed that caught Bob Dole between his one-man Presidential constituency and his official constituency of the Republican National Committee.

The National Committee had appointed a site-selection committee whose six or seven members were examining the merits of several cities that were interested in playing host to our convention, including Houston, Miami Beach, Louisville, and Chicago. However, the President one day informed Haldeman that he wanted the convention in San Diego.

One reason for the President's choice was simply convenience: he could stay at his San Clemente estate and fly over to the convention by helicopter when he was needed. But the more important reason was political. California was a crucial state, the state with the biggest bloc of electoral votes, and a state we had carried by a relatively narrow margin in 1968. The publicity that would surround a Republican Convention in California might be enough to lock up California for the President before the campaign had even begun.

Bill Timmons of the White House Congressional Relations staff was in charge of convention planning. Timmons, a Tennessean who had served on Bill Brock's Congressional staff, had worked on the 1968 convention and was considered politically astute. When he got word from Haldeman that the President wanted the convention in San Diego, Timmons went out to check the facilities. He reported back that the hotel and arena facilities were adequate, but just barely, and that security might be a problem, but that, if the President insisted, a convention *could* be held in San Diego.

Our convention-site deliberations were taking place at the same time that the Justice Department was moving toward its controversial July 1971 settlement of antitrust suits against the International Telephone and Telegraph Company. Timmons told us that ITT had offered $400,-000 in cash, services, and discounts to the Republican Party if we used the new Sheraton Hotel in San Diego, owned by one of ITT's subsidiaries, as Nixon convention headquarters. I took that as a not unusual public relations gesture—presumably, the presence of the President and party leaders in the new hotel for a week would be worth $400,000 in publicity. It was only later that Timmons mentioned to me the government's antitrust suit against ITT and the possibility that the $400,000 offer might become controversial. I spoke to Mitchell about this law suit, and he assured me there was no problem.

The problem, it seemed then, was the site-selection committee. The National Committee was meeting in Denver in July to decide, among other things, on the convention city. I was sent out to the meeting to make sure that San Diego was the choice. Gail and Rob Odle went with me, and I expected a semivacation, but it turned out to be a hectic trip.

We had one loyalist on the site-selection committee who supported us on San Diego. The rest of the committee members wanted the convention to be in Miami Beach, and their attitude was, "To hell with the White House—this is our decision."

I stayed in the background, dealing with Dole, whose job it was to bring the site-selection committee around. He knew what was expected—Mitchell had made that clear to him. But he began to waffle when faced with the site-selection committee's objections. He could probably ram San Diego down their throats, but there might be protests and embarrassing charges that he was a White House puppet.

Dole and I had no personal conflict. He understood that I was there representing the President's wishes. Dole's problem was that it wasn't enough for him to tell the site-selection committee that Jeb Magruder wanted the convention in San Diego. To save face, he felt that he needed to say he'd gotten the final word from the President, or at least from Haldeman or Mitchell. Perhaps he hoped he actually could get the President to accept Miami Beach.

"I've got to talk to somebody, Jeb," he told me in desperation.

I could see the problem ahead. The President wouldn't talk to Dole, nor would Haldeman. They didn't want to talk to politicians unless it was absolutely necessary. They wanted other people, presumably Mitchell, to handle the face-to-face political affairs. Mitchell was good about holding Dole's hand, but Mitchell was in Europe. I tried to reach him there, but I could never get him and Dole on the phone at the same time. Finally, I called Haldeman.

"You've got to talk to Dole," I told him.

"No, I won't talk to him," Haldeman snapped. "You tell him the President wants San Diego."

"I have told him. But I'm not sure I can get it done."

"You'd better get it done," Haldeman said.

Finally, Dole capitulated. He told his site-selection committee that if the President wanted the convention in San Diego, it would just have to be San Diego. So we got our way, although as it turned out we were to reverse ourselves a few months later, and go through an even worse fight to get the convention *out* of San Diego.

POLLING

One of our most important activities in 1971 was setting in motion an extensive polling program, the results of which were absolutely basic to our campaign. The polls helped shape our advertising, our geographic target areas, our youth program, our telephone and direct-mail programs, and virtually every other area of the campaign.

We hired Robert Teeter, a thirty-three-year-old vice-president of Market Opinion Research in Detroit, to direct our polling program. Bob was both a sophisticated political analyst, an expert on ticket-splitting, and a trusted Republican—for pollsters, despite the objectivity of their work, tend to become identified with one party or the other, and once a firm is identified with one party, the other party usually won't employ it.

In September Bob Teeter sent Mitchell a long memo outlining the most extensive polling program ever undertaken for a Presidential candidate. He was not proposing—and we did not want—the kind of polling that tells you that your candidate is leading by 60–40, or trailing by 55–45 or whatever, on a national basis. You can get that from the Gallup Poll in the newspapers each week. Rather we wanted polls that showed in depth the attitude of voters in key states. We expected a close election, one that would be decided in a handful of the larger states, and those were the states on which we would focus our polling. Near the end of the campaign, we switched to a fifty-state strategy, but at the outset our focus was much narrower.

We wanted a scientific campaign. We wanted to base our decisions on facts, not someone's hunches. How did people in south Texas feel about busing? Should we stress revenue sharing in California? Should the President be smiling or somber in a poster directed at youth? Teeter's polls were the way we proposed to answer such questions.

Teeter outlined, at a cost of some $600,000, four separate "waves" of polling:

A first wave, in December of 1971, of about 13,300 interviews—about seven hundred interviews in each of fifteen of the target states, which included California, New York, Pennsylvania, Texas, Illinois, Ohio, and other of the larger states, as well as in five important primary states: Wisconsin, Maryland, Oregon, Nebraska, and New Hampshire.

This first wave of polls would give us basic information on which to plan our strategy in the primaries, and it would also give us base-line data against which to measure later changes in voter attitudes.

A second wave, in June and July, of seven hundred more interviews in each of the fifteen target states, to measure voter trends after the primaries and to help us reevaluate our list of priority states.

A third wave in late August, of seven hundred voters in each of ten target states, to test voter attitudes after both parties had nominated their tickets, to see how issues were then perceived, and to identify groups of undecided voters.

Finally, a *fourth wave* of continuous telephone polling in the target states in the last six weeks of the campaign.

Teeter attached to his proposal a copy of the eighty-odd questions he would have our interviewers ask voters in the first wave of polls. It was a detailed, often highly subjective interrogation. It asked for reactions to the President's Vietnam policy, his China policy, his economic policy. It asked what the voter thought about busing, and how long he would be willing to have his child ride on a bus—ten minutes? thirty minutes? forty-five? It asked if the voter would be willing to pay higher taxes if the money were used to clean up the environment. It asked, "What two or three words do you think best describe Richard Nixon as a person?" It asked the voter to rate Nixon and Senators Muskie, Humphrey, and Kennedy in terms of specific descriptive terms, such as "courageous," "fair," "warm," "untruthful," "arrogant," "wishy-washy," and "deceptive."

The poll was conducted and when the results began to come in early in 1972 we studied them carefully for the guidance they might give us on our campaign strategy. Teeter's initial conclusions included the following:

—Past party voting behavior is the single most important factor which affects the Presidential vote. The classification of voters into behavioral Republicans, Democrats, or ticket-splitters accounts for almost three times as much of the variance why people vote for or against the President than any other variable. [In other words, traditional Democrats tend to vote Democratic, traditional Republicans tend to vote Republican, and the election is decided by independents and ticket-splitters.]

—The next most important factors affecting the Presidential vote are the voters' perceptions of the President's trust and his issue-handling ability. . . . To a lesser degree, the Presidential vote is related to perceptions of competence—experienced, trained, and informed.

—The only individual issues which appear to have any significant independent effect on voting are Vietnam, inflation, and general unrest. Vietnam and inflation were also, fortunately, the issues that the President was seen as handling well, and his ability to handle the general unrest problem was rated about equally to that of his opponents.

—The issues on which the President is rated relatively poorly—crime, drugs, and unemployment—do not appear to affect Presidential voting to any major degree. [This finding, that the President got poor marks on crime and drugs, was a disappointment to me, because we'd worked hard to show how much the Administration was doing in those areas; but it pointed up again the difficulty of dramatizing the results of complex domestic programs.]

The polls showed that people saw Nixon as informed, experienced, competent, safe, trained, and honest. He was not seen, relatively speaking, as warm, open-minded, relaxed, or as having a sense of humor. The average voter, in short, saw Nixon as a competent, experienced leader, but not as someone for whom he felt any personal affection. One of the most significant poll results was Nixon's high rating for honesty. "Tricky Dick" was dead; we simply didn't have to fight that issue in 1972.

The poll results suggested a campaign that would say to the voter not "You like Nixon" but "You need Nixon." In fact, our entire advertising campaign was based on the President's performance, with almost no reliance on personal appeal. Eisenhower could stress personal appeal—"We Like Ike"—but ours was a you-need-him slogan: "Now More Than Ever." That slogan was chosen over "President Nixon for President," which echoed the "Governor Rockefeller for Governor" slogan in New York a few years back. We took polls that showed that "Now More Than Ever" had more voter appeal than "President Nixon for President," but the fact remained that we were stressing Nixon's incumbency in every way we could. When we called our campaign committee "the Committee to Reelect the President," Larry O'Brien had protested angrily: "Why don't they use Nixon's name? Are they ashamed of him?" But we knew what we were doing. Richard Nixon was not beloved, but President Nixon was respected.

Some of our other first-wave polling results were:

—The President was relatively weak with older voters, whom Teeter called "the single most important group in the election." He urged renewed attention to older voters, with emphasis on taxes and inflation, the two issues that most concern them. As a result, the President met with several "senior citizen" organizations and spoke to one of their conventions, and various Administration spokesmen did the same.

—The President was running poorly with voters aged eighteen to twenty-four, so poorly that Teeter recommended that we end all activity among young voters, on the theory that if they voted at all they'd vote against us by a high percentage.

—Perhaps most important, the polls showed that as election year began, relatively few people were undecided about the President—some were for him, some were against him, but few had no opinion.

This fact led eventually to a major campaign decision: we made no effort to persuade undecided voters to vote for Nixon. We would, rather, stress getting our decided pro-Nixon voters to the polls.

We would, in short, stress organization, not persuasion. If you have a high degree of undecided voters, you stress persuasion, via television, direct mail, and so on. But if the voters are decided, you are wasting your time on persuasion—your job is to get your people to vote. That is what we did. As the campaign progressed, we continually cut back our advertising and put more money into storefront headquarters, telephone campaigns, direct mail, and get-out-the-vote programs.

We at CRP faced a certain problem with our polling program because of the extreme secrecy the President demanded on all polls. I'd encountered this when I was in charge of polling at the White House. I was under strict orders from Haldeman that no one but he should see poll results. Once Ehrlichman was furious when I refused to show him some new polls, but all I could tell him was to get Haldeman's permission. There was, of course, a legitimate concern about leaks, but the fact remained that polls were pointless if no one knew their findings.

When Teeter's first-wave results were ready to be shown to Mitchell, I routinely informed Gordon Strachan that Teeter and I would be going to Mitchell's office for that purpose. Strachan called me back a little later.

"Bob doesn't want you to attend that meeting on the polling results," he told me.

"That's ridiculous," I protested.

"It's an order from Haldeman."

I repeated the conversation to Mitchell, who dismissed it with a wave of his hand. "Don't worry about it," he said. "Just come to the meeting. I'll handle it."

After my initial shock, I didn't let myself be offended by Haldeman's order. I decided that Nixon had probably said to him, "Don't let anybody but Mitchell see those polls," and as usual Haldeman had taken him literally. Nothing more was said about it.

ADVERTISING

One major breakthrough in the 1972 campaign came with our decision in the summer of 1971 to form our own advertising agency.

The decision grew out of top-level dissatisfaction—Nixon's, Haldeman's, and Mitchell's—with the way the advertising was handled in the 1968 campaign. That year, the Nixon campaign had followed tradition and hired an ad agency, Fuller, Smith and Ross, then sent some top Nixon people, including Len Garment and Frank Shakespeare, over to head up a Nixon group within the agency. The external result had been a brilliant series of television commercials, but internally there had been a great deal of confusion, expense, and conflict. In effect, the Nixon campaign not only paid the salaries of people like Garment and Shakespeare, but also paid the agency its 15 percent commission, which in 1968 amounted to some $1.5 million, on the total of ten million spent on advertising.

Haldeman had told me before I went over to CRP that I should look carefully at the possibility of our starting our own agency for the campaign. I talked to advertising people throughout May and early June, and on June 30, I sent Mitchell a memo outlining our three alternatives.

First, I said, we could hire a large agency and create our own group within it, but that was ruled out on the basis of the 1968 experience.

Second, we could hire a large agency and simply leave the advertising program up to it. The problem there was one of control. Not the least of the pitfalls was the fact that so many of the creative people in advertising are liberal Democrats. There was the risk of leaks, and Joe McGinniss' "exposé" of our 1968 advertising campaign, *The Selling of the President,* had increased that concern. Beyond that was the question of loyalty and dedication. We couldn't expect liberals to pour their hearts into the Nixon media campaign, but it didn't seem easy to find conservative copywriters. I talked to two staunch Nixon supporters who headed a large ad agency in Chicago. I'd thought the political climate there might be more favorable to us than in New York. They wanted our account, but after they'd checked into it they told me: "We'd love to do it, but we can't put the team together."

I urged upon Mitchell the third alternative, that we form our own agency. By so doing, we could control hiring, salaries, and loyalties. We could base people in Washington or New York, at our convenience, and we could minimize the usual agency excuses and delays. It would be difficult for us to pull together the people for a year's assignment, but no more difficult than it would be for an established agency to expand to handle our multimillion-dollar account. Moreover, to form our own agency might save us a million dollars. I proposed that we put together a skeleton team in November, then expand it in July for the actual campaign. I estimated that this could be done for $1.8 million. By contrast, if we hired an agency and spent $20 million on advertising, we would pay it $3 million in commissions. By that estimate, our own agency would save us $1.2 million—but even that saving, I stressed, was less important than the element of control.

My plan was approved, and our next job was to find the right person to be our director of advertising. Garment, Chapin, Safire, Miller, I, and others interviewed perhaps a dozen senior advertising executives, and we all agreed that the outstanding candidate was Peter H. Dailey, who headed his own advertising firm in Los Angeles.

Dailey was a Nixon loyalist, a one-time football star at UCLA, and a friend of Haldeman's. Mitchell interviewed him in October and shared our enthusiasm, and Dailey joined CRP soon thereafter. By the end of the year Dailey had a small staff working on the basics of our advertising campaign. Our immediate goal was the primaries, which would begin in the early spring, and in which the President faced opposition from the Republican left in Congressman Paul McCloskey and from the Republican right in Congressman John Ashbrook. We had initially planned to use the primaries to test out our advertising program, and particularly our television commercials, but that turned out not to be necessary.

YOUTH

Bob Teeter, on the basis of his first-wave polls, had recommended that we halt all activity among young people, lest it prove counterproductive. He was concerned (as were many others in the Republican Party) that if we registered young voters, we would just be registering people who would end up voting Democratic. Furthermore, there was the risk that activity by young Republicans would only inspire a greater amount of counteractivity among young Democrats.

From a purely statistical point of view, Teeter's recommendation was perhaps sound. But we rejected it because we believed there were other considerations. From a public relations point of view, for example, it would have been devastating if the word had gotten out that the President had written off youth. We felt the President's record would appeal to young voters, if we could get it across to them. We made our campaign plans on the assumption that the President would have ended the war in Vietnam by Election Day, and we counted on that to defuse a lot of anti-Nixon feeling among the young. In addition, the President was in the process of ending the draft, and he had signed the bill that granted the vote to people aged eighteen to twenty. There had been a sharp disagreement in the White House when the President signed the voting bill. Some advisers had urged a veto, lest he enfranchise the voters who would defeat him in 1972. I wrote a memo urging that he sign the bill. I knew that young voters traditionally don't vote in significant numbers, and I thought the positive impact of the President's signing the bill would offset the supposedly liberal leanings of the young.

To head up our youth program we chose Ken Rietz, a sophisticated, extremely talented man of about thirty who had been a partner in Harry Treleaven's political-management firm, and who had proved his political ability in the 1970 Senate race in Tennessee. Ken had managed Congressman Bill Brock's campaign against Senator Albert Gore. Because of his opposition to the war, Gore had hundreds of antiwar volunteers from all over the country working on his campaign. Brock, perhaps, had fewer young volunteers, but thanks to Ken Rietz they were better organized than Gore's and they did much to bring about Brock's victory. We wanted that repeated on a national scale in 1972.

Ken believed that most young people are not ideological, but are highly susceptible to peer-group pressure. Thus, if the Youth for Nixon groups are holding rallies and receptions and registration drives, these activities become the "in" thing to do and attract activity by more and more young people. You get the young people involved through peer-group pressure, then you direct their enthusiasm into useful campaign activities.

Ken joined CRP as youth director in the summer of 1971, the first of our new division heads. By September he had submitted to me a plan for a "demonstration project" of voter registration in Orange County, Florida, which includes the city of Orlando. Ken's plan was to carry out in November a complete canvass of the country to identify and register new voters who supported President Nixon. Ken called this a demonstration project because he was well aware that many Republican leaders took the view that Teeter had suggested, that youth was a sleeping giant we should not disturb. The staff of the Republican National Committee strongly believed that we shouldn't activate youth. Senator Bill Brock, as national chairman of our youth campaign, argued strongly on behalf of an all-out effort among young voters. Nixon and Haldeman were receptive to youth activity, not so much for its substance—voters registered, volunteers enlisted—as for its PR benefits.

The President was fascinated with mock elections on college campuses. Throughout 1971 I kept getting memos from Haldeman: "The President wants to know what you're doing about the mock elections." In truth, we weren't doing much then, since the proper time for the mock elections was the spring and fall of 1972.

But the President's PR instinct was sound. It is not hard to win mock elections, and each one the President won on a college campus would help knock down the idea that the kids were all against him.

We hired one young man whose main job was to visit college campuses and encourage student governments to sponsor mock elections. When elections were called, he would work through pro-Nixon students to make sure we won them. It wasn't very hard. Most students were apathetic, so if you organized your people and got them to the polls, you'd win. Whenever possible, our man would see that the voting booths were located in out-of-the-way places and the elections held at odd hours, all with the intention of keeping the vote low. The result was that in

1972 the President won more than a hundred mock elections and the publicity added to the momentum of our youth campaign.

As 1972 began, Ken Rietz had youth registration drives planned for New Hampshire, Pennsylvania, and several other states. He was setting up a national Young Voters for the President Committee that included famous athletes, show-business figures, and student-body presidents. What Ken Rietz did, in those early months when the President's status with young people was extremely uncertain, was to create a framework we could later build on. When, in the final months of the campaign, young people began to move toward the President, we had an organization that could make maximum use of them.

THE ACCOUNT

Back in March, when Mitchell told me he wanted me to set up the re-election committee, he said near the end of our meeting:

"By the way, Jeb, I have a problem I'd like you to help me out with."

I leaned forward eagerly, anticipating my first big assignment.

"My wife, Martha, has become rather well known," he continued.

"Yes, sir, I know she has," I said, my excitement waning. Managing Martha was not part of my game plan.

"She's getting flooded with requests for speeches and interviews," Mitchell said. "She needs professional guidance. She can help the Administration, if she's used properly. So I wish you'd give her a hand."

I said I'd be glad to assist his wife, and a few days later I invited Mrs. Mitchell to my White House office for a talk. I asked Bart Porter to join us, for I planned to give him the day-to-day responsibility for helping her. Martha couldn't have been more charming that day—she was all southern drawl and good intentions. "I just want to help Mister President," she said—she always referred to Nixon as Mister President—"and I have all these letters and all these people wantin' me to come talk and I just don't know *what* to do. But now that I've got you two fine young men to help me, I know everything will be just *fine*."

From our point of view, Martha had an important public relations potential. At that point, she was probably the third most sought-after Republican in America, trailing only the President and the Vice President. Her husband had told me she wasn't good at delivering speeches, but there was no reason she couldn't travel extensively and make the sort of informal remarks she excelled at.

Using advertising jargon, we called her "The Account"—Bart Porter was in charge of The Account. As it turned out, he was the first of several people to come to grief trying to handle that account, for we soon learned that Martha was a southern charmer one moment, and absolutely impossible the next.

We, like the rest of America, learned that Martha liked to use the telephone at odd hours. During the Memorial Day weekend I took my family to Ocean City, and one night the phone rang, waking me up.

"Jeb, do you know where _____ is?" she asked, naming one of her secretaries, an attractive, unmarried young woman.

I was too annoyed to be polite. "Martha, it's midnight and if she's not at home she's probably in bed with some guy."

"I hadn't thought about *that*," she admitted.

"What do you need her for?"

It developed that she didn't really need her for anything—she just felt like talking. I suggested she quit bothering people and go to bed, and hung up. But Martha was not easily discouraged. There was, I came to realize, a certain pattern to her late-night telephone calls. The Mitchells rarely left their Watergate apartment in the evenings. They didn't go to restaurants or theaters because Martha was obsessed with the idea that someone would try to assassinate them. Both of them had received more than their share of threatening letters, but they had FBI protection, and Martha's fears seemed to me to go beyond the rational—she imagined that people were following her, and that sort of thing. Nor did the Mitchells often go out socially, because Martha's reputation for erratic behavior had become such that many hostesses were unwilling to run the risk of inviting her to dinner. So they stayed at home, usually alone except for their daughter, Marty, and their cook, Julia. If any of Mitchell's political associates dropped by for a drink, Martha would soon make it clear, by dirty looks or indignant comments, that we were not welcome. So they spent most evenings at home alone. Both of them might be drinking, but he held his liquor better than she did. Eventually he would go to bed, and that was when she'd get on the phone, a lonely, frustrated woman who would pour out her soul to her secretary or a wire-service reporter or virtually anyone who would listen to her.

That fall Bart Porter and I accompanied Martha to Los Angeles where she was taping the "Merv Griffin Show" and a "Laugh-In" show.

She was on her best behavior on that trip. I think she was nervous about her performance on "Laugh-In," although she needn't have been, because she had natural gifts as an actress and comedienne. Martha did a "Laugh-In" skit that featured her trying to place one of her telephone calls with Lily Tomlin, who had made famous the character of the snoopy telephone operator. It was a funny skit, but as we watched the rehearsals we noticed that as soon as a scene was over Miss Tomlin and the others in the cast cut off the laughs and were quite abrupt with Martha. I assumed this was for political reasons. I don't think Martha ever noticed, however, because she was so concerned about her performance.

Our policy, as we attempted to direct her public appearances, was to present her as a personality but never as a spokesman on matters of substance—she was appropriate for "Laugh-In" but not for "Meet the Press." She yearned, of course, for a more substantive role; thus her midnight pronouncements to wire-service reporters. There was never any question of our stopping Martha's public appearances, for she loved the limelight, but we tried to direct her so she'd be helpful to us, or, failing that, so she'd do as little harm as possible. Mitchell never interfered with or questioned our handling of his wife, and for our part we never went to him with our problems—he *knew* the problems, and he didn't want to hear about them.

Bart Porter lasted on The Account until one evening that fall when he was attending a horse show at the D.C. Armory and was paged over the loudspeaker. When he got to the phone, it was Martha, who was calling about some extremely trivial matter. Porter told her rather tersely that she shouldn't bother him with trifles and hung up the phone.

"I don't wish to deal with that Mr. Porter any longer," she informed me the next morning. "He is *not* a gentleman."

Porter thus left The Account and was replaced by Glenn Sedam, a lawyer in his thirties who had come to CRP from the Republican National Committee. Glenn had been a kind of pinch hitter for us, performing various troubleshooter assignments, and managing Martha fitted into that category. He had spoken to me that fall about his desire to be CRP's general counsel, but I was afraid he was not experienced enough. Also, Glenn was rather lawyerly, and I wasn't sure he could move at the fast pace our general counsel would have to maintain. Certainly my putting him on The Account was a mistake. His rather nervous manner drove Martha up the wall, and Martha drove him up the wall. For Martha, if any little detail displeased her, would fly into a rage. We had done some scheduling for Tricia Nixon Cox, and she could be an extremely demanding young lady, but Tricia was an angel compared to Martha. Sedam was constantly in my office pleading to be taken off the assignment, but I had to tell him to hang on, until finally Martha told me she'd had enough of his assistance.

Martha always wanted to hitch a ride on Air Force One when the President was traveling. However, the President wanted absolutely nothing to do with her. Dwight Chapin, who approved the passenger list for Air Force One, once told me:

"We've dealt with that woman since 1968 and we're sick of her. The President doesn't want her anywhere near him. I'm not going to talk to her. She's your problem, you handle her."

A kind of routine developed regarding Martha and the President's trips. To begin with, she always found out about his trips almost immediately after they were scheduled—she had an amazing intelligence network. Then she would call me, talking in her most sugar-sweet southern tones. That was the tip-off. If Martha played a southern belle, she wanted something—the thicker the drawl, the bigger the favor. When she was on the rampage, the Scarlett O'Hara accents disappeared entirely.

"Jeb," she would drawl, "I understand that Mister President is goin' to Los Angeles, and it just so happens that I have a speakin' engagement out there the same day."

That was another of her tricks. When she learned that the President was going somewhere, she would quickly arrange an appearance of her own, so she'd have an excuse to fly out with him.

"Jeb," she would continue, "you know that Mister President has told me, 'Martha, you just call anytime you want to fly with me,' so why don't you call over and make the arrangements for me?"

I would promise to check into the matter, and my next move would be to call Chapin, who would say something like:

"No, damn it, no! I'm not going through this again!"

"Dwight, I have to work with this woman," I would tell him, "and you've got to help me out."

The point was that you just didn't tell Martha that the President didn't want her on the plane. If you told her that she'd ignore you and get on the phone herself and cause even more confusion. Our solution, therefore, was to devise some elaborate story to explain why she couldn't make this particular trip with the President. Once, for example, we persuaded her that some particularly unpleasant politicians would be on the flight, men who weren't gentlemen at all, and with whom it certainly wouldn't be appropriate for her to travel. Another time we went to great lengths to get her on a television show at a time that would make it impossible for her to make a trip with the President.

Martha was convinced that Haldeman and Chapin were conspiring both to keep her off Air Force One and to come between her husband and the President. She was half right. They weren't conspiring against Mitchell, but they were certainly conspiring to keep her out of the President's hair.

"Jeb," she would say indignantly, "if Mister President only knew what was happenin' to me I'd be on that plane faster'n you can shake a stick. It's that awful Haldeman and that awful Chapin who're tryin' to keep me away from Mister President. They know how much he likes to talk to me and how much he values my advice. I think I'll just *call* Mister President and tell him what those awful men are doin' to me."

You didn't want to push Martha too far, because you didn't know what she might do or say, so sometimes she would wear us down and get on Air Force One. Then it became a problem for Chapin and others on the flight to keep her away from the President's private cabin. Most of us wouldn't go within twenty feet of the President's sanctuary unless summoned. Chapin sometimes told with disbelief of the time he virtually had to restrain Martha physically when she decided she had to have a private chat with Mister President.

I should add that my wife's view of Martha Mitchell is more sympathetic than my own. Gail saw Martha as an insecure woman, one needing constant reassurance, who had married a cold, driven man who denied her the love and encouragement she needed. Gail did not see a great deal of Martha, but she was present the day Martha taped "Laugh-In" and she was stunned by the rude treatment Martha received from its cast. After the taping, Gail and I, Gail's sister Ruth, and Martha went to dinner, and Martha was nervous and upset. "Did I do all right?" she kept asking. "Was it funny or was it just dumb?"

"My heart went out to her," Gail said later. "She was so bouncy and funny, but she was like a child, always seeking your approval. She might have been entirely different if she'd married a warmer man, instead of one who froze her out of his life."

Gail's view of the Mitchells reflects her general belief that almost all the men at the top of the Nixon Administration, myself included, were driven by ambition to a point of all but inexcusable neglect of their wives and children. Looking back on it all, I agree with her.

SLIPPAGE

Throughout 1971 we at the Committee to Re-elect received a certain amount of sniping from people at the White House who felt we weren't producing enough "results." Haldeman and his aide Strachan, or Colson and his aide Dick Howard, would ask indignantly: "What the hell are you guys *doing* over there? What are we *getting* for all that money?"

I understood how they felt. If I'd still been at the White House, battling crisis after crisis, I'd probably have been complaining about those memo writers at CRP too. But I *was* somewhat annoyed by one standard complaint: that our offices at 1701 Pennsylvania Avenue were too lavish. The offices *were* nice—1701 Pennsylvania Avenue, a half block from the White House, is not Washington's low-rent district. We had our burnt-orange pile carpeting and our color-coordinated decor and good furniture and office equipment. I happened to get an office with its own bathroom, complete with a shower, which was great—it meant that on nights when I worked late, then went straight out to dinner, I could shower and change first. But I nonetheless disliked the criticism, coming as it did from people who were themselves enjoying the ultimate luxury of the White House, which made our CRP offices look like the YMCA. We at CRP hadn't sought the offices at 1701. (After a while, we just called it 1701.) One reason we'd chosen 1701 was its proximity to the White House. Another was that it also contained the Washington offices of Mitchell's law firm. It was Mitchell's plan to resign as Attorney General early in 1972 and return to his firm, and from that base direct the reelection campaign.

Along with the sniping about our lack of results and our lavish lifestyle, there was growing pressure for CRP to engage in intelligence-gathering activities. "Why can't you guys find out what Muskie is up to?" the White House people would ask. I was by no means surprised by the requests. The White House had always wanted political intelligence, and the May Day demonstrations, followed by the leak of the Pentagon Papers in June, had intensified the pressures to find out what our "enemies" were up to. The basic problem, which had always existed and was growing worse, was that the President and Haldeman believed that Communist groups were funding the antiwar activists, and when the FBI or the Justice Department's Internal Security Division couldn't find proof of that, Nixon and Haldeman would write off those agencies as inept and want their own investigators who could do the job.

I talked to Mitchell, and we both agreed that it would be appropriate for CRP to gather information on what the Democratic contenders were doing, and particularly Senator Muskie, who then seemed the front-runner for the nomination. Mitchell's attitude struck me as ambivalent; he agreed that we needed intelligence, but he wasn't excited about it.

I asked Ken Rietz if he had any ideas on how we might gather intelligence on Muskie. I thought he might have one of his young people go volunteer to work in Muskie's headquarters. Ken said he would look into it, and a week or two later he came back to me and said he could plant someone as Muskie's driver, but that we would have to pay the man $1,000 a month. I reported this to Mitchell, who approved the expenditure. Again, he wasn't enthusiastic; I think he saw $1,000 a month as a cheap way to get the White House off our backs.

Rietz did not explain the details to me, but it later came to light that he had contacted a government employee he knew, a man called Fat Jack Buckley, who had a background in investigative work, and Buckley made contact with a retired taxi driver who successfully volunteered to serve as Muskie's driver. The irony was that Rietz, the amateur in cloak-and-dagger affairs, had done the job professionally; our agent was two steps removed from CRP and had no idea he was reporting to us. Later, we would be confronted by "professionals" in espionage who did not bother to take that basic precaution.

Bart Porter, who was in charge of our spokesman resources—or surrogate—program, became the man who paid our agent in the Muskie camp and received the documents he sent back. This was another example of our slippage. Porter had been in charge of petty cash for the office, so it had seemed logical that he should handle the payments for our intelligence-gathering operation. Mitchell had given Porter authority to go to Hugh Sloan, Jr., CRP's treasurer, and draw the cash he needed.

Our agent obtained several Muskie documents, at least two of which we made use of. One was a memo in which several of Muskie's foreign policy advisers were urging left-wing policies on him. We passed this on to columnist Robert Novak—we may have simply mailed it to him anonymously; I don't recall—who used it in a column on December 12 to accuse Muskie of surrounding himself with left-wing advisers. The other memo detailed Muskie's position on a tax initiative in California, and I used it to plant another Evans-Novak column that was embarrassing to Senator Muskie.

After that fall, we set up our "Sedan Chair" program of harassment against the Democratic contenders. This grew out of talks I had with Dwight Chapin and Ron Walker, the chief White House advance men, both of whom were fascinated with "black advances"; that is, pranks that disrupt your opponent's campaign. We had in mind the kinds of stunts that Democratic prankster Dick Tuck had carried out against Republicans over the years—picking up the campaign staff's laundry and not returning it, summoning the press to nonexistent 6 A.M. news conferences, and so on.

I was not aware that Chapin had already recruited an old friend of his, Donald Segretti, to carry out black advances—or dirty tricks, as it became known—but I agreed that it would be good for CRP to have a man skilled in that technique. Walker said he knew a young Californian who could do the job for us. In October, Porter and I had lunch with the fellow, whose name was Roger Greaves, and he was hired as our black advance man. Porter gave him the code name Sedan Chair, in honor of a military exercise of the same name he'd participated in while a marine.

Sedan Chair was with us for about three months, was paid some $3,800, and accomplished very little. He spent most of the time in California where, on two occasions, he arranged for young people with pro-Nixon signs to be at the Los Angeles airport when Senator Muskie arrived. I understood he carried out some similar activities in New Hampshire and Florida, two key primary states for the Democrats, but I was not close to his activities. He reported to Porter, and I was only informed if he did something significant, which was not often. Early in 1972 Porter told me that Sedan Chair was folding.

"He doesn't like the work," Porter said. "He wants to quit."

"Fine," I said. "Just get us another guy."

I got a call in September from John Dean, who said he wanted me to have lunch with him and Jack Caulfield, an investigator on the White House staff who, Dean explained, wanted to start a private-investigation firm and hoped that CRP might be a client.

John Dean was someone I'd known since my arrival in Washington.

I'd first met him in early November of 1969, when he chaired a meeting I'd attended at the Justice Department. The meeting was to discuss the government's response to the November 15 antiwar demonstration, and I was impressed with how smoothly he handled himself. John was about thirty then, an acute young lawyer who considered all the angles and who obviously was on the rise. He was a legislative aide to Dick Kleindienst, the Deputy Attorney General, but he soon was working closely with Attorney General Mitchell and he regarded Mitchell, as I did, with great respect and affection.

Dean and I saw each other fairly often and we got along well. In mid-1970, when John Ehrlichman offered him the post of Counsel to the President, Dean came to my office in the White House to ask my advice.

"I'm just not sure I want the hassle," he said. "I like Mitchell, I like my job at Justice, and I'm not sure it'd be smart to come over here."

"Take it," I told him. "You can handle the White House, and that is where the action is. Besides, when you're ready to go back to private practice, it won't hurt to have the White House on your résumé."

Dean continued to impress me after he came over to the White House. We tended to view the White House in the same light, with a certain irony and a certain detachment. I remember when the Senate rejected Carswell, and others were furious, Dean and I took the defeat philosophically—we thought we'd probably gotten what we deserved on that nomination. I thought that Dean, Chapin, myself, and a few other of the younger White House people had an understanding of the President's dual personality. Unlike Finch and Klein and some of the others, we accepted the President as he was. If he was paranoid about criticism, if he didn't want to deal with us face to face . . . well, he just *was*, and if you wanted to work in the White House you had better accept those facts. Dean took it all with a grain of salt, as I tried to, so we always felt a certain instinctive kinship.

I knew Jack Caulfield less well. Jack was about forty, a chunky Irishman who'd started his career as a policeman in New York, but won a promotion to detective and specialized in "terrorist organizations." During the 1960 Presidential campaign he helped guard candidate Nixon when he was in New York, and he held a temporary security job with the 1968 campaign, one that led Ehrlichman to hire him, in April of 1969, to be a special investigator on the White House staff. Caulfield's office was next to Lyn Nofziger's office in the Executive Office Building and I'd see him there from time to time. He was always very hush-hush about his work, but he seemed to be particularly active during antiwar demonstrations, so I assumed he was investigating antiwar leaders and other of our political opponents.

Dean, Caulfield, and I had lunch at the White House Mess. Caulfield explained that he hoped to start a private-investigation firm—code-named Sand Wedge—that could do work for both CRP and the Republican National Committee, as well as for corporate clients. The firm would provide both security services and covert intelligence-gathering, Caulfield said. John Dean added that both Mitchell and Haldeman were interested in Sand Wedge. The plan had an extra boost in that one of Caulfield's partners was to be Joe Woods, the former sheriff of Cook County, who was Rose Mary Woods's brother.

I told Dean and Caulfield that they should get back in touch with me if they got Caulfield's firm started. CRP had adequate security, but I felt we needed a professional intelligence-gathering operation, and if Mitchell and the White House wanted Caulfield, he was fine with me. However, Dean called me in early November and told me to forget Sand Wedge.

"It fell through," he said. "Jack couldn't put it together."

"We need something," I told him. "If we're going to play this cloak-and-dagger game, it's silly to have Rietz and Porter in charge."

"Maybe we could combine the intelligence job with the general counsel," Dean said. CRP needed a full-time lawyer, and Dean had been trying to find us the right man. "I'll check into it."

Early in December, Dean called with good news.

"I've found you a general counsel," he said.

"Great! Who is he?"

"His name is Gordon Liddy," Dean said. "He's just what you've been looking for."

CHAPTER IX

The Liddy Plan

G. G O R D O N L I D D Y entered my life on Friday afternoon, December 3, 1971, when John Dean brought him to my office for what I thought was to be a job interview. But Dean soon disabused me of that notion.

"Jeb," Dean said, "the Attorney General thinks Gordon is the ideal man to be your general counsel."

Our meeting, thus, was a formality. I was annoyed, but I trusted Dean's judgment. He recommended Liddy highly, so I was willing to give Liddy a try.

Certainly, as Liddy outlined his background, he seemed well qualified: He had been an FBI agent in the early 1960's, then an assistant district attorney in Dutchess County, New York. In 1968 he had run against Congressman Hamilton Fish, Jr. in the Republican primary. He ran as a tough, law-and-order conservative—his campaign slogan was "Gordon Liddy doesn't bail them out—he puts them in"—and although he lost in the primary, he remained the Conservative Party nominee. However, a deal was apparently struck, for Liddy withdrew from the general election and Congressman Fish, once reelected, recommended Liddy for a job with the Nixon Administration. Liddy landed at the Treasury Department, where he worked on drug-law enforcement and vigorously opposed gun-control legislation. Eventually he worked with Bud Krogh on drug-

170

related projects, and Krogh was so impressed with him that he brought him over to the White House staff.

Liddy was vague about what he'd been doing at the White House. I assumed he'd been working with Krogh on drug legislation. Actually, it later became known that, in the aftermath of the Pentagon Papers leak, Krogh had been put in charge of the investigatory unit that became known as "the plumbers" (because its job was to stop leaks). Liddy had worked with him on the plumbers unit, with the break-in at the office of Daniel Ellsberg's psychiatrist as one of their major undertakings. That was carried out during the Labor Day weekend, about three months before I met Liddy. All this was unknown to me at the time I met Liddy. My only inkling of the plumbers unit had come in a talk I'd had in July with David Young, who was an aide to Henry Kissinger, and with whom I sometimes played tennis.

Young and I had lunch at the Federal City Club and he asked my advice about a job John Ehrlichman had offered him. The idea was that he would work with Krogh on a small, confidential unit that would investigate the Pentagon Papers affair and other national security leaks. Young was willing enough to leave Kissinger's staff. He was working himself to death, like all Kissinger's aides, and he was in his mid-thirties, a bit too old for that kind of staff job. My advice to him was to take the job if it seemed likely to be a springboard to a higher-level job, the kind that involved a Presidential appointment.

Young took the job, and later I'd sometimes see him outside his new office in the Executive Office Building with "The Plumbers" on the door. I'd ask him how it was going, and he'd shrug and say something noncommittal. Later, he commented once that he thought they'd caught the man who leaked some confidential papers on the India-Pakistan conflict to Jack Anderson in December of 1971. I suppose if I'd put two and two together I might have concluded that Liddy had been working with Young and Krogh on this special-investigations unit, but that never occurred to me, nor did Liddy volunteer the information. I knew only that he was a lawyer whom Bud Krogh recommended highly, and that Dean and Mitchell wanted to hire him.

On that first afternoon, Dean, Liddy, and I discussed the work I'd expect from our new general counsel. There were two basic areas of concern for me. One was primary-election laws. The President had agreed to enter all twenty-three of the Presidential primaries in 1972. (He had agreed to do so on the condition that he would not campaign in any of them, which we at CRP agreed was a good strategy.) I expected our general counsel to become expert on the filing laws in the primary states, so there could be no legal slipups that would keep the President off the ballot. Secondly, a new campaign-finance law was moving through Congress and we wanted our general counsel to advise us on it. The new law had two main parts, one regulating fund raising, which would primarily concern our finance committee, and another putting limits on media spending, which I was concerned with.

As we talked, Dean added that there was another area that Liddy could handle for us—our intelligence-gathering program.

"No sweat there," Liddy said. "I know that cold. I'm up on all the latest equipment and techniques. I can get you anything you want."

"That's good, Gordon," I said. "We definitely need some professional guidance in that area."

Liddy started to work for us about ten days later, on Monday, December 13. There was a slight hitch because he wanted a raise, to about $25,000 as I recall, and we had a policy that everyone came to CRP at the same salary he'd been making. Since Dean was Liddy's sponsor, I bucked the request to Dean, who eventually got Haldeman's approval for the raise.

On Liddy's second day with us, I called him to my office for a more detailed talk about his work. There were some aspects of his intelligence work I wanted to discuss, but I had barely mentioned the subject when he said:

"Turn on your radio."

"Do what, Gordon?"

"Your radio. Turn it on."

"I don't want to listen to the radio, Gordon. I'd like to finish our talk."

"Don't you understand?"

"I guess not," I admitted.

"You see that building over there?" he said.

"Yes, I see it." My office had a large window overlooking Pennsylvania Avenue, and directly across the street a new office building was being constructed.

"Well, there might be somebody over there listening to us."

"Listening to us from across the street?" I was too intrigued to be angry.

"That's right. There's a new honing device that can pick up vibrations across a street and through a window. That's why we need the radio on, so they pick up the wrong vibrations."

I shrugged and turned my radio on. He was, after all, a professional, and anyway a little music wouldn't hurt anything.

I called in Rietz and Porter and told them that Liddy would be taking over their intelligence activities—Rietz's driver in the Muskie camp and Porter's Sedan Chair. Later, we discussed Liddy's budget. He asked how much he could expect.

"Well, we're spending four or five thousand dollars a month," I told him. "You'll have to work within that framework."

"Four or five thousand?" Liddy said. "Dean told me I could have a million dollars for intelligence-gathering."

That was a rather stunning statement, but I didn't know what Dean or others in the White House had in mind, so I told him:

"Gordon, a million dollars is a lot of money. You'd better get a plan together for the Attorney General that will justify that kind of money."

"Oh, I'll justify it," Liddy said. "Don't worry about that."

A day or two later, when I introduced Liddy at a meeting of our senior staff, I ventured a little joke:

"Gordon's talents aren't just legal. He's going to be our supersleuth."

I glanced at Liddy and saw him flush, and he said little during the rest of the meeting. When it was over he pulled me aside and said angrily: "I can't do this job unless I have my anonymity. Are you trying to blow my cover?" I mumbled my apologies. The irony of the situation was that Liddy constantly boasted about his exploits. The classic instance, which came to light later, was after he and E. Howard Hunt had pulled the break-in at Ellsberg's psychiatrist's office. They flew back to Washington and, to impress two stewardesses, boasted that they'd just pulled a big national-security job. They were traveling under false names, and they fuzzed up the break-in story, but they said enough that when the Watergate scandals broke, the stewardesses recognized their pictures in the papers and called the FBI.

As the days passed, I came to realize that our new general counsel was, to put it mildly, a character.

The first thing you noticed about Liddy (who didn't have his moustache in those days) was his handshake—he greeted you with the proverbial "viselike grip," one that would leave you with a sore hand if you weren't careful. He was not a big man, but he was in good shape, a cocky little bantam rooster who liked to brag about his James Bond-ish exploits. He liked to tell, for example, of the time he supposedly jumped from a moving car and outdrew a "most wanted" fugitive, and about the time he supposedly led a drug raid on Timothy Leary's house.

Liddy particularly liked to impress women. Rob Odle used to tell the story of his wife's first meeting with Liddy:

"I came out of a meeting and Lydia was waiting for me and she said, 'Rob, I just met the most amazing man. He showed me how you could kill someone with a pencil.' " It was Liddy, of course.

Liddy's method of killing someone with a pencil, incidentally, involves bracing the eraser end of the pencil in your palm and ramming the sharp end into the victim's neck, just above the Adam's apple. He recommends that the pencil be freshly sharpened.

Liddy had some larger-than-life campaign posters, with a picture of himself shining a police spotlight at a crowd of angry blacks, that he would give to any woman who'd take one. And there was the time in February when he appeared at the office with his hand bandaged. I ignored the bandage at first, but after he'd worn it a week I finally asked what the problem was.

"I was meeting with some important contacts," Liddy whispered in his most conspiratorial manner. "I had to show them I could take it. So I held my hand to a blowtorch. That's what you call mind over matter—mental discipline."

"Are you serious?" I asked.

"Sure I am," Liddy said. "I burned my nerve endings. But I never flinched, and it was worth it."

The true story of the bandaged hand leaked out later. Liddy had held his hand over a burning candle to impress some friends.

True to the James Bond tradition, Liddy loved guns. One of the stories from his days as an assistant district attorney concerned the time he was summing up a robbery case before a jury, and pulled a pistol from his pocket and fired it into the ceiling to make a point.

Liddy once remarked to me:

"Jeb, did you know I have a gun that will shoot underwater?"

I thought about that one a minute.

"Gordon, when are you going to be shooting anybody underwater?"

"I might have to sometime," he said. "You never know what might happen."

I had a friend who lived near Liddy in Chevy Chase, Maryland, who told me that Liddy was often angered because the neighborhood kids made too much noise to suit him. One evening at dusk, my friend said,

Liddy crouched on the roof and when the kids ran through the alley he leaped down and waved a gun at them. As a result, the neighborhood parents asked Liddy to move, and he did.

One rainy day, Liddy came to my office to discuss a legal matter, and when we finished, I grumbled about some columns Jack Anderson had been writing that were embarrassing to the Administration.

"Boy, it'd be nice if we could get rid of that guy," I commented.

Liddy left, and a moment later Bob Reisner, my administrative assistant, burst in with a look of horror on his face.

"Did you tell Liddy to kill Jack Anderson?" he asked.

"What?"

"Liddy just rushed past my desk and said you'd told him to rub out Jack Anderson."

"My God," I said. "Get him back in here."

Reisner found Liddy before he left the building, fortunately.

"Gordon," I told him. "I was just using a figure of speech, about getting rid of Anderson."

"Well, you'd better watch that," Liddy said with annoyance. "When you give me an order like that, I carry it out."

Another time, Liddy told me that when he was with the FBI he'd been part of a secret "hit squad" and that he'd once killed a man. As Liddy told the story, he'd hidden in a garage until the victim arrived, overpowered him, put a rope around his neck, and hanged him from a rafter.

"Then you know what happened?" Liddy said, shaking his head. "I found out he was the wrong guy. I've always felt bad about that."

Liddy may have made the story up, but he told it convincingly and I believed him. I'd never known anyone like him, and I was beginning to wish I'd never met him. Yet there was a certain inevitability about Liddy. My personal distaste for him aside, he seemed like the right man for the dual job we envisioned. He wasn't really a good staff man, because of his lone-wolf style, but he performed his legal duties adequately. As far as his intelligence duties were concerned, he seemed extremely well qualified. He was no goon or second-story man. He'd been with the FBI, he'd been an assistant district attorney—he was, in short, a professional, and ours was a campaign that looked to professionals for guidance. Based on his background, we had to assume Liddy knew what he was doing. Once you accept the premise of no-holds-barred intelligence-gathering, G. Gordon Liddy is what you wind up with.

After Liddy had been with us a few weeks I gave him his first political intelligence assignment. We received reports from various sources about the Democratic Presidential hopefuls and some of them seemed worth checking out. We had a report that Senator Muskie, who supposedly was the champion of the environmentalists, had a big financial backer who was one of Maine's leading industrial polluters. I asked Liddy to check this out—not necessarily personally, but to get the facts. He chose to go up to Maine himself and he came back a few days later empty-handed. I didn't push the matter, but subsequent newspaper stories indicated there was indeed something to the charge. That was something else I eventually realized about Liddy: he liked the shoot-'em-up exploits, but he wasn't interested in the dull fact-gathering that was often what we needed.

Around the middle of January, Liddy told me he was ready to make his intelligence-gathering presentation to the Attorney General. I scheduled an appointment with Mitchell on January 27, and I also invited John Dean, since he had recruited Liddy and expressed interest in his intelligence plans.

Just before we left for the 4 P.M. meeting, Liddy was racing around CRP's offices looking for an easel. He had some charts for his presentation, he explained, but the charts would be no good without an easel. I had Bob Reisner look for an easel, and when none could be found Bob called Mitchell's office to see if they had one over there.

Bob Reisner was an extremely intelligent twenty-five-year-old whom I had hired a month earlier. He was a graduate of Yale, where he played on the lacrosse team, and of the Harvard Business School. After getting his business degree, he had taken a job at H.E.W., helping set up the new Environmental Protection Agency. He had caught the eye of our talent scout, Fred Malek, who suggested that he talk to me about a campaign job. Bob was short, serious, extremely bright, always conservatively dressed, and as far as I was concerned he was the perfect staff man.

I had interviewed several people about being my administrative assistant. I was looking for my Higby—for by then, in honor of Haldeman's right-hand man, we had begun calling any perfect staff man "a higby." Most ambitious young men with Reisner's ability wanted to jump right into a decision-making job. Reisner was obviously going to make plenty of decisions before his career was over, but he realized that for the time being he could learn as my assistant. He was tremendous about adjusting his methods to suit my preferences, about helping me get my work done on time, about seeing that papers reached me in the form I wanted them, and a million other things. The only problem with Reisner was that he was too good for me to keep long. In the summer, when Clark Mac-Gregor replaced Mitchell as campaign director, Reisner left me to be MacGregor's executive assistant, and after the election he went to a high-level job at the Office of Management and Budget.

After the last-minute runaround about an easel, Liddy and I took a limousine to Justice, and rode the elevator up to the fifth floor, where the Attorney General's office was located. I had a key to the Attorney General's private elevator, but the public elevator was just as quick, and I always enjoyed the walk through the halls of the Justice Department. It struck me as the most impressive of the government buildings, with its dark-paneled walls and its WPA murals and the dark-hued portraits of past Attorneys General that lined the corridors. There was a special aura about Justice—its lawyers seemed never to dash about in confusion like the bureaucrats at so many government departments, but to move through those quiet corridors with a sense of dignity and purpose.

Dean met us in the Attorney General's reception room and we went in promptly at four for our appointment. Mitchell did not work in the huge, ceremonial Attorney General's office that most of his predecessors had used. Instead, he used a small office just off the ceremonial office. I always thought it characteristic of Mitchell to use the smaller office: he was a self-effacing man, not overwhelmed with the glory of himself as Attorney General.

Something of a routine had developed for my meetings with Mitchell. I'd always take two copies of whatever memo or decision paper I wanted to discuss with him, one for him to read and another for me to follow along on. Mitchell's desk was always piled high with papers (unlike Nixon's desk, which was always perfectly clean) and whenever I gave him a paper I'd always make a point to remember which pile he put it on. Then, when I'd return a few days later, and he'd start searching for the paper, I could point to the right pile and say, "General, I believe it's right here."

The meeting with Liddy was unusual in that I hadn't reviewed Liddy's plan in advance, as I normally would before I took a division head to see Mitchell. I think that reflected the fact that already I felt uncomfortable with him and a certain tension was developing between us. He had been outraged when Rob Odle had found it necessary to move his office from the fourth floor, where most top CRP officials were located, to the eighth floor. "If I'm the general counsel of this committee I've got to be where the important people are," he'd roared at me. In general, Liddy made it clear that he considered it an indignity to have to report to me, instead of dealing directly with Mitchell.

We took our places around Mitchell's desk. I was immediately to his right, then Dean, then an empty chair that Liddy put his gear on, then Liddy, a bit to Mitchell's left. The meeting began with Liddy outlining how the new election law would affect our campaign spending. That took five or ten minutes, then he moved on to his intelligence-gathering presentation. An easel had somewhere been found, and Liddy unwrapped a package that contained six or seven professionally prepared charts, each with a code word at the top that indicated one aspect of his proposal—the code words included "Gemstone" and "Target."

Liddy moved briskly and confidently into his presentation. He was the complete professional—James Bond meeting with "M." He threw a lot of jargon at us, "buzz words," I called them, like "interdiction" and "safe house," and other, more technical words that I didn't understand.

"Now, Gordon, what does that word mean?" Mitchell asked several times.

None of us was prepared for the nature of the plan that Liddy was outlining with such self-assurance. It was, as John Dean said later, mind boggling. It included mugging squads, kidnapping, sabotage, the use of prostitutes for political blackmail, break-ins to obtain and photograph documents, and various forms of electronic surveillance and wiretapping.

The mugging squads, he explained, could rough up hostile demonstrators. The kidnapping squads could seize radical leaders—he mentioned Jerry Rubin and Abbie Hoffman—and hold them in a "safe house" in Mexico during the Republican Convention. He also had a plan for the Democratic Convention.

"We'll sabotage the air-conditioning at the arena," he explained. "Can't you see all those delegates sitting there dripping wet in 120-degree heat on national television?"

He wanted to employ call girls, both in Washington and in Miami Beach during the Democratic Convention, who would be used to compromise leading Democrats. He proposed renting a yacht in Miami Beach that would be set up with hidden cameras and recording devices. The women would lure unsuspecting Democrats there for what would be, unbeknownst to them, a candid camera session.

"These would be high-class girls," Liddy stressed. "Only the best."

Liddy's presentation went on for nearly a half hour. It would be, he promised, the most complete operation of its kind ever undertaken, and it would more than justify the million dollars needed to carry it out. John Dean said later that Mitchell winked at him during one of Liddy's more fanciful proposals. Certainly I was stunned. The whole thing was, as Mitchell said later, beyond the pale.

When Liddy finally finished, there was a long silence. Liddy stood there, perhaps waiting for cheers and applause. Mitchell puffed on his pipe for a minute, then said:

"Gordon, that's not quite what we had in mind, and the money you're asking for is way out of line. Why don't you tone it down a little, then we'll talk about it again?"

That was Mitchell's understated way of expressing his displeasure with the more extreme aspects of the plan—the call girls and the kidnapping squads. Yet Mitchell did not reject the entire plan, for we all felt there was a need for intelligence-gathering, and we were interested in the wiretapping aspects of the plan.

We discussed the plan for a few minutes, but our talk was awkward because Liddy was so obviously stunned at Mitchell's disapproval. My impression was that Liddy thought his plan already had White House approval and the meeting with Mitchell was only a formality. He explained in more detail some of the elements of his plan. For example, he explained that the proposed kidnap squads would seize radicals, inject them with some drug that would render them unconscious, and carry them unconscious to the "safe house" in Mexico. "They'd never even know who had them or where they were," he promised.

But no one shared his enthusiasm for this aspect of his plan, and Mitchell ended the meeting by telling Liddy he should come back with a less expensive plan that focused on intelligence-gathering and countering demonstrations.

Liddy was despondent as we left the Attorney General's office, and Dean and I both tried to encourage him.

"Cheer up, Gordon," I said. "You just tone the plan down a little and we'll try again."

"I thought that was what he wanted," Liddy said incredulously.

"It was just a little too much, Gordon," I told him, and Liddy agreed that he would present a new version that would eliminate the call girls and kidnapping squads and concentrate more on the wiretapping.

Back in my office, I routinely called Gordon Strachan and outlined

Liddy's proposal, for him to pass on to Haldeman.

Liddy quickly got back to me and said he was ready to present his toned-down proposal, and I arranged a second appointment with Mitchell at 11 A.M. on February 4. This time, I reviewed Liddy's proposal in advance, and I was pleased to see that his proposed budget had been cut to $500,000 and the substance of the plan now focused mainly on the wiretapping and electronic surveillance. Ths time, instead of using charts, he had his proposal typed on standard-sized paper.

Once again Dean joined us, and once again we had an inconclusive talk with Mitchell. Liddy had not specified the targets for wiretapping, but in discussion we agreed that priority should go to Larry O'Brien's office at the Democratic National Committee in the Watergate complex, to O'Brien's hotel suite in Miami Beach during the Democratic Convention, and to the campaign headquarters of whoever became the Democratic nominee for President. O'Brien had emerged in the past year as the Democrats' most effective spokesman and critic of our Administration.

Liddy still wanted to use call girls in Washington, but the others of us were skeptical and discouraged that plan. We agreed that we should have the capacity to break up hostile demonstrations, and that we needed agents who could get us information on possible disruptions at our convention. Mitchell was still concerned about the plan's price tag and told Liddy he should cut back on his costs, then we could discuss the plan again.

Mitchell, during the discussion, told Liddy that he had information that a Las Vegas newspaper publisher, Hank Greenspun, had some documents in his office that would be politically damaging to Senator Muskie. Mitchell said he would like very much to know whether these documents could be obtained. Liddy beamed and said he'd check out the situation.

So the second meeting ended with Liddy's plan still dangling. None of us was quite comfortable with it, yet all of us felt that some sort of intelligence-gathering program was needed. We knew the daily pressures from the White House for political intelligence, and I think we had a sense that this was how the game was played. During the discussion of wiretapping and break-ins, John Dean had said:

"I think it is inappropriate for this to be discussed with the Attorney General. I think that in the future Gordon should discuss his plans with Jeb, then Jeb can pass them on to the Attorney General."

There was a long delay, almost two months, before I was able to arrange a third meeting on Liddy's plan. The main reason for the delay was that Mitchell was increasingly preoccupied with the Senate inquiry into the ITT affair—the alleged relationship between the government's settlement of antitrust suits against ITT and ITT's offer to donate some $400,000 in cash and services to the Republican Convention. Mitchell was resigning as Attorney General to become full-time campaign director, and his deputy, Dick Kleindienst, had been nominated to replace him. Kleindienst's nomination had cleared the Senate Judiciary Committee, but when Jack Anderson published the Dita Beard memos that suggested a tie-in between the antitrust settlement and the campaign contribution, Kleindienst asked that the hearings be reopened so he could rebut the charges. As a result, both Kleindienst and Mitchell were required to testify in detail on the ITT settlement, and there were later charges that both had perjured themselves.

I had no knowledge of the facts of the ITT affair; I only knew that by early March, when Mitchell came over as campaign director, it was almost impossible to get time with him except on the most urgent campaign business, and neither Mitchell nor I considered the Liddy plan to be a high-priority matter.

Liddy apparently complained to Colson about the delay, because Colson called me about it one evening.

"Why don't you guys get off the stick and get Liddy's budget approved?" Colson demanded. "We need the information, particularly on O'Brien."

"It's under consideration," I told him. "We'll get to it as fast as we can. You know the problem with Mitchell."

I also had a call, sometime in February, from Colson's aide Dick Howard, who'd formerly worked for me, saying that E. Howard Hunt had finished his work as a White House consultant and might be very valuable to us in CRP's intelligence-gathering. I'd met Hunt only once, more than two years before, when I'd interviewed him about the proposed "Silent Majority Institute," and it wasn't clear to me how Hunt could be valuable to us. I told Howard to have Hunt call Liddy, who could hire him if he wanted to. Eventually, Liddy did hire Hunt, who, as it developed, was an old friend of his.

Liddy's operation was of minor concern to me at that point. The important facts, in those early months of the election year, were that the primaries were starting, and that our CRP operation was rapidly expanding, to the point that I found myself all but overwhelmed by the work that was pouring in on me. Mitchell was virtually unavailable, and I had all of our division heads except Harry Flemming reporting directly to me. Here, to suggest the size of our operation, is a list we compiled in early March of our operating divisions, the division heads, and the proposed budget for each division:

DIVISION	DIVISION HEAD	BUDGET
Convention	Timmons	$475,000
Candidate Support	Magruder/Odle	1,400,000
Polling	Teeter	750,000
Political and State Support	Flemming	4,000,000
Spokesman Resources	Porter	790,000
PR/Media	Miller/Shumway	750,000
Research, Direct Mail, Telephone, Planning	Marik	7,000,000
Citizens' Committees, Women, Special Groups	Hutar/Chotiner	2,500,000
Advertising	Dailey	12,750,000
Campaign Materials	Dailey	1,500,000
Administration	Magruder/Odle	282,000
Office Administration	Odle	500,000

A few of the division heads need identification. "Miller" was Cliff Miller, my friend from Los Angeles, who was acting as a consultant on our media planning. "Shumway" was DeVan Shumway, a former UPI reporter in California who had worked for Herb Klein and me at the Office of Communications and then had come over to be CRP's press officer. "Hutar" was Patricia Hutar, the Republican leader in Illinois, with whom I'd worked in the Goldwater campaign in 1964. "Chotiner" was, of course, Murray Chotiner, the President's old friend, who had a law office at 1701 and was advising us on citizens' groups and special interest groups.

Our budget chart had a footnote under "Administration" that explained that its $282,000 included salaries for "guards, drivers, secretaries, professionals, Liddy, E. Nixon, etc." E. Nixon was Ed Nixon, the President's younger brother, a pleasant, likable, undemanding man who obviously was not close to the President but wanted to help him in any way he could. Mitchell had sent him to see me that winter with an indication that I should hire him. I assumed that Mitchell was acting on instructions from the President. Ed Nixon had, I was told, run the mail room in the 1968 campaign. In the 1972 campaign, he eventually became one of our Presidential surrogates, one who ranked well below the Cabinet members, or Julie or Tricia, but who nonetheless could be dispatched to minor Republican functions. I found it extremely useful to have Ed on our staff. In any campaign there is a constant stream of local party leaders coming in who feel they must talk to someone, hopefully someone important who can solve whatever their problem is. We often directed such people to Ed Nixon, for who could complain if they'd talked to the President's brother?

As 1972 began, and CRP's operations rapidly expanded, we had several new people join the staff in top positions, among them Fred LaRue and Bob Mardian.

Fred LaRue, who was about six years my senior and became one of my closest friends in Washington, was an introverted, soft-spoken Mississippian whose life had been haunted by tragedy. Fred's father, Ike LaRue, was an oil man and a cousin of the Texas oil millionaire Sid Richardson. Ike LaRue was sent to prison in Texas for banking violations, and upon his release started over in the oil business in Mississippi. In 1954 he and his sons, Fred and Ike Jr., struck oil in the Bolton field, twenty miles from Jackson, and made a fortune. Then, three years later, in 1957, during a duck hunting trip in Canada, Fred LaRue accidentally shot and killed his father.

LaRue continued in the oil business, and also became a behind-the-scenes power in Mississippi politics. He had ties to both parties, for although a Republican he was close to Democratic Senator James Eastland. In 1964 he was a major contributor to the Goldwater campaign, and in 1967 he became an early and substantial contributor to the Nixon cause. In the process he became a close friend of John Mitchell's. When Nixon became President, LaRue moved into an office in the White House. He had no title and was paid no salary, but Mitchell and other top figures consulted him on political affairs, particularly with regard to southern politics.

LaRue had neither the desire nor the talent for an out-front role. He was homely, had extremely poor eyesight, and was not a good public speaker. His talents were for a backstage role. Because he was likable, sincere, and politically astute, he was excellent at dealing with people and in negotiating internal problems, such as the disputes we at CRP had with the Republican National Committee over its campaign role. Mitchell had the highest regard for LaRue, and around the first of the year he sent him over to CRP "to help out," with no clear-cut title or assignment.

At that point, the two top men at CRP were myself and Harry Flemming, who was in charge of our state campaign organization. Flemming was supposed to be selecting our Nixon chairmen in each state, building contacts with state Republican organizations, and generally setting up our grass-roots campaign organization. Unfortunately, Flemming was not doing the job. He was slow in picking our state chairmen and the ones he picked often weren't satisfactory; he didn't have a budget; he had personality clashes with the rest of us—his operation was simply a mess. My only serious criticism of Mitchell as an administrator was that he tended to be too tolerant of unproductive underlings, and Flemming was a prime example.

When LaRue came over to CRP, Flemming immediately viewed him as a threat, while I, for my part, viewed him as a godsend. Flemming resisted LaRue's attempt to move into an office near his own, so I arranged for LaRue to have an office next to mine. Soon, an informal arrangement evolved whereby LaRue would sit in on most of the meetings held in my office. Whenever I could turn over responsibility for a project to LaRue, I was glad to—I needed all the help I could get. LaRue was no threat to me. He had no desire to be a manager, only to advise. We became so close, both professionally and personally, that people in the office used to refer to us jointly as "Magrue."

Bob Mardian could hardly have been more different. If Fred LaRue came into a room, you'd hardly know he was there. If Bob Mardian came into a room, he'd be into an argument with someone in five minutes. Mardian was a balding, muscular, aggressive, and volatile Arizona conservative, the son of an Armenian refugee whose sons built a multi-million-dollar construction company in Arizona. They also became politically active. Mardian's brother Sam was once the mayor of Phoenix, and Mardian managed Senator Goldwater's campaign in several western states in 1964. He was brought into government first as general counsel of H.E.W., then as head of the Justice Department's Internal Security Division. He soon became known as an extreme hard-liner with regard to radical groups. Tom Charles Huston once said of Mardian, "He doesn't know the difference between a kid with a beard and a kid with a bomb."

When Mitchell came over to the campaign full-time in March, Mardian came with him, advising him on the ITT controversy and looking around for a niche in the campaign for himself. I think that he at first aspired to my job, but when he saw I was well entrenched he then began moving in on Flemming, who was a good friend of his. The trouble was that it didn't seem that Mardian would be any improvement over Flemming. You just couldn't deal on a rational basis with Mardian. If you asked his advice on something, he'd take that as a sign of weakness and try to take over whatever it was. If you had a disagreement, he'd fly into a rage, pace around the room, and start shouting that he knew what was right and you didn't know anything.

I enjoyed Mardian socially. He was extremely bright, and he was an outspoken, colorful character, fun to see at a party or to play poker or gin rummy with. And I realized that he had been tossed into a typically confused campaign situation, with no niche of his own, and no guidance from Mitchell. Given his nature, it was natural that he would fight for someone's job, but understanding that didn't make him any easier to deal with.

A fight began between Flemming and Mardian over control of the state campaign program. Mitchell tried to resolve the problem by dividing the state program into five regions, with five men, including Mardian and Flemming, each in charge of one region, all reporting to Mitchell, but that wasn't workable.

The situation was further complicated by the arrival of Fred Malek on the scene. Early in the year, when I found myself overwhelmed with work, I had talked one Saturday morning with Mitchell and LaRue and we agreed that Malek, who was then the White House personnel chief, might be someone who could help us. I suggested that he might oversee our various citizen's groups, such as youth, the aged, Spanish-speaking voters, and so on. I wrote a memo that Mitchell sent to Haldeman asking that Malek be assigned to CRP. Haldeman agreed to let Malek work with us part-time, while continuing his personnel duties.

However, once the extremely aggressive Malek got to CRP he wanted more than a part-time role. Like Mardian, I think that he first wanted my job, then, seeing it wasn't available, went after the state organization. Eventually, in the late spring, Malek got Haldeman to assign him to conduct a "study" of the state campaign operation. Malek's studies were, of course, the kiss of death—after he studied Herb Klein's Office of Communications, Klein lost two-thirds of his office and almost lost his job. I viewed Malek's study as a ploy by which Haldeman intended to put Malek in charge of the field operation. That was fine with me. As it turned out, the ploy proved unnecessary, because when Mitchell resigned in July, Flemming lost his main supporter, and it was an easy matter for Haldeman to move Malek in over him.

My main concern in February, as Liddy awaited a third meeting with Mitchell, was the March 7 primary election in New Hampshire. We had two goals in New Hampshire: to test our campaign techniques and to demolish the President's two Republican challengers, Congressmen Ashbrook and McCloskey. The early polls looked so encouraging that we decided not to spend any money on television advertisements. Instead, we chose to rely heavily on an extensive direct-mail program, one that, as I told Mitchell in a memo, reflected "the best that is known from both the commercial and political worlds."

Our plan featured three mass mailings.

First, on January 27, we sent a third-class, bulk mailing to every registered Republican in the state. The mailing included a personalized computer letter from our New Hampshire reelection committee chairman, a "Re-Elect the President" window sticker, a volunteer card, and a business reply envelope. This was a relatively hard-sell mailing, designed to establish personal contact with the party faithful and to encourage volunteer work and/or financial contributions.

Our second and third mailings went to registered independents as well as Republicans. We assumed that the majority of independents would choose to vote in the more hotly contested Democratic primary, but we hoped some could be persuaded to cast a vote of support for the President.

The second mailing went out on February 10, first-class, with a stamp rather than bulk-rate postage (to add the personal touch), and contained another personalized letter—that is, a typed form letter that began Dear Mr. Jones rather than Dear Fellow Republican. The mailing also included a brochure on the President's stand on major issues.

The third mailing, on February 25, also first-class with a stamp, included another personalized letter and a sample ballot.

This direct-mail program was tied in with our telephone program. Our telephone canvassers noted on IBM cards whether each Republican voter was favorable, unfavorable, or undecided about the President. If the voter was undecided, the volunteer would note on the card what issues most concerned the voter; this card was fed into a computer, which sent that voter a letter with material on the President's position on the issue in question. This letter would then be followed by a second phone call to see if it had caused the voter to decide in favor of the President; if so, the voter would be called in the get-out-the-vote drive at the end of the campaign.

This program in New Hampshire came at a time when we were still experimenting with techniques to persuade the undecided voter. Eventually, our experience in the early primaries, plus Bob Teeter's first-wave polls, led us to halt this kind of persuasive activity, and to concentrate instead on getting our sure pro-Nixon voters to the polls.

The direct-mail operation in New Hampshire seemed to work well, and it was subjected to follow-up analysis that led to modifications and improvements in subsequent primaries. Yet our mailing program, which was entirely legitimate, was subject to the kind of slippage that afflicted so many aspects of the campaign.

The problem, once again, was Chuck Colson. He was obsessed with the idea of instigating a write-in vote for Senator Kennedy in the Democratic primary in New Hampshire. His idea was that if enough Democrats could be persuaded to vote for Kennedy—who wasn't on the ballot and said he wasn't a candidate for anything—it would cut into Muskie's vote, sow ill will between Kennedy and Muskie, and generally create confusion among the Democrats. Naturally, Colson wanted to use our mailing lists and wanted us to pay the several thousand dollars that the postage and other costs would come to. I discussed Colson's scheme with Mitchell, and we were both dubious about it. We liked the idea of sowing disunity among the Democrats, but we weren't convinced that one mailing would do very much. It seemed like a large outlay for a dubious result, so we stalled, hoping Colson would drop the plan.

Then, one day in February, I was in the White House and encountered Colson just outside the President's office.

"We've got to get that mailing going," he told me. "I've just come from talking to the President and he thinks it's crucial."

I returned to my office and called Haldeman, who told me that what Colson said was true, the President did want the pro-Kennedy mailing in New Hampshire. I reported to Mitchell and we agreed to go along with the plan. Once again, it was what I called a throw-away decision, a matter of Mitchell's going along with some dubious White House plan because it would please the President or because it was just too much trouble to argue about it.

Colson's aide Dick Howard had a Democratic friend named Robin

Ficker—he'd once run for Congress in Maryland on the slogan "My Friend Ficker"—who was persuaded to implement the Kennedy write-in scheme. Ficker announced he was starting a draft-Kennedy movement—which Kennedy immediately repudiated—and proceeded to mail out the letters urging Democrats to write in Kennedy's name on the primary ballot. There was no follow-up beyond the one mailing and the whole thing was a waste of time and money—fewer than a thousand voters wrote in Kennedy's name, and most of them probably would have done so without the mailing. It was a typical Colson fiasco.

I was also involved in a fiasco of my own that winter, one that related to two of our major political preoccupations—winning California, and the electoral threat posed by George Wallace. The Alabama governor was a constant concern to us. If he ran in 1972, would the third-party split help us or hurt us? The equation was a complex one, but the consensus was that he would hurt us, and there were constant discussions and plans on how to keep him out of the race, ranging from preempting him with go-slow school integration policies to our putting several hundred thousand dollars into the campaign of the man who ran against Wallace for governor in 1970. The ongoing White House concern about Wallace was reflected in a constant stream of memos from Haldeman asking us for up-to-the-minute reports on how many state primaries Wallace would be able to enter.

It was against this background that in the fall of 1971 I considered a plan that had been proposed to us to get Wallace off the ballot in California. I don't recall how the plan got to us, but it made its way to me and I gave it serious attention and discussed it with Mitchell and others.

The plan came from one Bob Walters, a man who had been the leader of Wallace's American Independent Party in California but had been ousted in a power struggle. As Walters explained it, he was one of the party's moderates and he had been forced out by party extremists. In his disenchantment, Walters had come to believe that Wallace was surrounded by extremists and Richard Nixon now embodied the ideals of the Wallace movement.

His plan was based on the fact that, to be on the ballot in California, a party must have a certain number of registered voters. The American Independent Party had more than the required number, but Walters proposed to send other disillusioned Wallacites door to door to persuade their friends to reregister as Republicans—or as Democrats, for that matter. If enough members of the American Independent Party reregistered, the party could not qualify for the ballot in 1972. Such was Walters' proposal. We had lawyers in California check it out, and they said it was legally sound, although later we came to have doubts about that, because the law was somewhat ambiguous. But we took the plan to be legally sound, and all our political contacts in California stressed that Wallace was a serious threat to our hopes there, and that keeping him off the ballot was highly desirable.

While in California on other business, I arranged to meet Walters at the Polo Lounge of the Beverly Hills Hotel for a drink and a talk. He was a presentable-looking man and seemed quite reasonable and sincere.

"Wallace on the ballot will hurt you," he said. "All we've got to do is get our people who are disgruntled to go around and talk to their friends and get them to switch parties. Then Wallace is off the ballot and your problem is solved."

Walters wanted $10,000 to carry out his plan. This would go, he said, to pay the canvassers, to pay for literature they would distribute, and to pay for the registrars who, under California law, could accompany the canvassers door to door and reregister people on the spot.

With Mitchell's approval, we gave Walters the $10,000 to implement his plan. To ensure secrecy, I gave it to Lyn Nofziger (who was then the Republican National Committee's director of communications, but later became director of our reelection committee in California) in cash, and he gave it to a friend of his who passed it on to Walters.

Walters had estimated that for the $10,000 he could reregister some 10,000 Wallace voters, but of course it did not work out like that. I never saw Walters again, but we received two or three progress reports from him that indicated there wasn't much progress.

He was unable to find enough disgruntled Wallacites to do the canvassing, so (we didn't know this until much later) he hired members of the American Nazi Party as his canvassers. The mind boggles at the thought of the Nazis trying to convert the Wallacites to Republicanism. In any event, the whole thing came to nothing. It just fizzled out, for as the months passed and the President's popularity rose, we were less concerned about a Wallace candidacy. In retrospect the episode was one of the stupidest things I became involved in, but at the time to keep Wallace off the California ballot for $10,000 seemed like the bargain of the year.

Bart Porter burst into my office one day in February with some bothersome news:

"Allan Walker just called," he said, referring to the director of our reelection committee in New Hampshire. "He says there's some guy up there who claims he's been sent by the White House to harass the Democrats. Do you know what's going on?"

"No," I said, "but I'll bet I know where to find out."

I called Gordon Strachan, but he claimed to know nothing about the mysterious prankster. I was skeptical, but I let the matter drop. Then a little later, the director of our Wisconsin primary campaign called with a similar complaint; a prankster with crazy ideas had come into the state and his schemes threatened to backfire and screw up the campaign. Again I called Strachan and again he denied knowledge. This led me to play a little bureaucratic game. I sent Mitchell a memo entitled "Potentially Embarrassing Situation," which explained about the mysterious Wisconsin/New Hampshire prankster and expressed my suspicion that someone in the White House was responsible for him. I said it was important that we at CRP know about this person and exercise control over him, lest he harm the campaign.

I routinely sent a copy of the memo to Strachan for Haldeman. As I'd hoped, the memo caused Haldeman to level with us. He had Strachan call me and say that yes, they did indeed have a prankster in the field. I asked that their prankster make contact with Liddy, so we could supervise his activities. This was done, and I learned later that Liddy had assigned Howard Hunt to oversee the prankster, who turned out to be Donald Segretti. At the time, I didn't know Segretti's name, or have any interest in his activities. I just wanted to see that he was supervised so he would cause us no problems in the future.

Gordon Liddy, as March began, was anxiously awaiting a third chance to sell Mitchell on his spy plan, but I simply couldn't get time with Mitchell on anything as minor as that in the midst of the ITT controversy.

I had a couple of assignments for Liddy while he waited. We had received an interesting report about Jack Anderson. It alleged that a college in Maryland that one of Anderson's children attended owned some valuable land on the Chesapeake Bay, and that Anderson had told college officials he'd use his political influence to get them some substantial federal grants if they'd sell him some waterfront land at bargain prices. I asked Liddy to investigate the report, and again he came back empty-handed.

We also had a tip from Kevin Phillips, the conservative columnist, that the Democratic Party might be involved in a kickback scheme in connection with their convention. The report was that the Democrats would lease space at the convention to an exposition company, which would then rent space to individual exhibitors and kick back part of the fee to the Democrats. Liddy went down to Miami Beach to investigate. He had another man call a Democratic Party official and pose as a businessman who wanted to rent space at the convention. Liddy taped their conversation, in which the businessman said something like, "I'd sure like to see some of my money go to the Democratic Party," and the Democratic official said something like, "Well, that might be arranged."

Liddy played me the tape, which was ambiguous—the Democrat might just have been stringing the "businessman" along—but which seemed to me to merit further investigation. Larry O'Brien, the Democratic chairman, was continuing to give us a hard time, particularly on the ITT affair, and if we could implicate him in a kickback scheme it would do much to discredit him. So, after Liddy played me the tape, I said, "Fine, Gordon, find out some more," but he never produced anything more on the alleged kickback scheme.

One Friday in mid-March I encountered Liddy in CRP's third-floor reception area. At the time, I was highly annoyed with Liddy because he had been late in giving me some legal reports, and his delays were causing me to get static from Mitchell and Haldeman. There was no excuse for the delay. If he had too much work to do, he was free to hire other people. I hadn't asked him to go personally to Maine or Miami Beach to check out the political reports—only to have them checked out. The problem, as I saw it, was that Liddy preferred the cloak-and-dagger assignments, even if it meant neglecting his duties as general counsel. I simply wasn't comfortable with Liddy and he, for his part, made it clear that he considered me too young and inexperienced to be telling him what to do. So, at this particular encounter, I let my annoyance show.

"Gordon, where are those reports you promised me?"

"They're not ready," he said angrily.

"Well, the delay is causing me problems," I told him. "If you're going to be our general counsel, you've got to do your work."

As I spoke, I put my hand on his shoulder.

"Get your hand off me," he shouted. *"Get your hand off me or I'll kill you!"*

That was just Liddy's tough-guy talk, but I dropped my hand and walked away, back to my office. The more I thought about the scene, the angrier I became. The situation was intolerable, so after a few minutes I called Sally Harmony, Liddy's secretary, and asked her to have Liddy come up to my office.

Fred LaRue sat in on my meeting with Liddy, for I welcomed his advice on this sort of problem.

Liddy came in, still boiling with anger.

"This isn't working out, Gordon," I said. "I can't work with people who talk about killing me. We've got to have a change."

"That's fine with me," he said. "I'm sick of screwing around with a punk like you."

Liddy never minced his words.

My original thought had been to fire him outright, but then a compromise idea occurred to me. Maurice Stans had recently resigned as Secretary of Commerce to be the chairman of our Finance Committee. He needed a full-time lawyer, and Liddy had already done legal work for him.

"Maybe you should go work for Stans," I said.

"That'd be fine with me," Liddy said. "I respect Stans. He knows the score."

"I'll talk to him," I said. "What about your intelligence-gathering?"

"You can let Hunt run it," Liddy said. "Or you can drop it—you don't seem very interested in it."

"Maybe we shouldn't make any quick decisions," LaRue interjected. "Maybe Gordon should keep on with the intelligence program."

"We can decide later," I said, and the meeting broke up with the future of our intelligence-gathering operation up in the air.

Once Liddy left my office, however, he had second thoughts about turning over his cherished spy program to Hunt, because he called John Dean to enlist his support, and Dean called me a little later.

"Jeb, you don't want to let your personal feelings about Liddy get in the way of an important operation," he said.

I had to agree that was true.

That afternoon, I went to see Strachan at the White House and we discussed the Liddy problem. He too urged me to put aside my personal feelings, because we needed the intelligence-gathering program and Liddy was our number-one professional in that area. Strachan walked back to 1701 with me—it was raining, I recall, a cold blustery March afternoon—and I remember him commenting:

"Liddy's a Hitler, but at least he's our Hitler."

So, finally, it was agreed that Liddy would transfer over to the Finance Committee as its general counsel, but continue to report to me as our intelligence chief. I never consulted Mitchell. This was the sort of problem LaRue and I handled on our own. I might have fired Liddy, but the others convinced me that he was too valuable to lose. So he moved his office again, down to the second floor at 1701, where Maurice Stans was in charge of campaign fund raising and Hugh Sloan was in charge of keeping the financial records of the campaign. I chose Glenn Sedam to replace Liddy. I had passed over Sedam the first time around, but after the Liddy experience I was glad to have a conventional, quite lawyerly lawyer as our general counsel.

Mitchell had resigned as Attorney General around the first of March to be the full-time campaign director, but he had continued to be preoccupied with the Senate hearings on the ITT affair. Near the end of the month he flew down to Key Biscayne for a vacation. Before he left, he told me that after he'd had a few days rest I should come down and he would address all the campaign decisions that had been piling up for weeks. I flew down on Wednesday, March 29, checked into the Key Biscayne Hotel, and called Mitchell's house. Fred LaRue, who was staying with the Mitchells, answered the phone and said he would come over and pick me up. I changed into informal clothes and met LaRue for the short ride across the island.

Key Biscayne is a small island just offshore from Miami. In size it is much like Miami Beach, a few miles to the north, but the two are entirely different in the way they have developed. Miami Beach became a gaudy strip of expensive hotels, while Key Biscayne was, at least until the boom of recent years, a quiet, middle-class community. The Key Biscayne Hotel, which is comfortable but not at all lavish, is on the east, or ocean, side of the island. President Nixon's Florida home is less than a mile away, across the island on the west, or bay, side. Mitchell was staying in a house that, as I understood it, Bebe Rebozo had rented for him. It was about four houses up from the President's home, a comfortable house with a swimming pool and a lovely view of the bay, but by no means spectacular.

Fred LaRue warned me, on the short ride across the island, that Martha was on the rampage. He said that the Mitchells had not been out of the house since they'd arrived, and they'd had only one visitor,

Bebe Rebozo. I knew all about Martha's fear of assassination, but I couldn't imagine how all of them—John, Martha, their daughter Marty, Fred, Martha's assistant Kristen Forsberg, and their cook, Julia—could stay cooped up in that house day after day.

Fred LaRue was the only Mitchell associate who was ever able to get along with Martha for very long. He was a fellow Southerner, he was patient and understanding, and she would listen to him as she would to no one else. Fortunately for us at CRP, LaRue had entered the picture at about the time that both Porter and Sedam had given up on managing Martha. So LaRue took over the general supervision of The Account, with Martha's new assistant, Kristen Forsberg, handling the day-to-day details.

When we arrived at the Mitchells' house, with me carrying my two briefcases full of decision papers, I soon discovered that LaRue was right, Martha was indeed on the rampage. She flounced in and out all afternoon, making remarks like, "I don't know *why* they have to be here when we're on *vacation!*"

It was embarrassing to me, and as best I could I'd keep out of the way when she came around. Once, to get away from her, I went outside to talk to Kristen and Marty, who were fishing off the bulkhead. We chatted a few minutes, and when we went back in Martha called Kristen aside and stage-whispered: *"You'd better watch out for that Magruder."*

The implication was that I had designs on Kristen. She was a pleasant young woman in her twenties, but I certainly had no designs on her. It was just Martha's way of making us all uncomfortable.

Mitchell didn't want to work that afternoon. He was tired and nervous—he kept waiting for news broadcasts about the ITT case. He and LaRue and I sat around and talked, and eventually he went for a swim. Martha kept bursting in and out, tossing her sarcasms at us, and finally she announced that she didn't want to hear any more stupid talk about politics, so she and Kristen and Marty were going out for dinner. The three of us were relieved to see her go. Julia fixed us a steak dinner, and I made a point of leaving before Martha returned.

The situation was so bad that we agreed, before I left, that the next morning I'd come in the side door, one that entered directly into Mitchell's den, rather than enter the front door and risk encountering the lady of the house.

The next morning I had breakfast beside the pool at the Key Biscayne Hotel, then went over to meet with Mitchell and LaRue. I slipped in the side door, avoiding a confrontation with Martha, and the three of us soon got down to business.

The previous night I had left my two briefcases behind and LaRue had gone through them and arranged the thirty or so decision papers in the order we would discuss them. There were a number of major decisions, on the direct-mail program, on the advertising strategy, on a plan of Pat Buchanan's to set up "truth squads" to counter the Democratic candidate. Mitchell moved through them quickly. At lunchtime, Julia brought us sandwiches and we continued to work as we ate. The phone rang often, including several calls from Mardian about ITT, and LaRue would take the calls at the other end of the large den.

Finally we came to the Liddy espionage plan, which LaRue had put last in the pile of decision papers.

We discussed the proposal for ten minutes or so, and all of us expressed doubts about it. We feared that it might be a waste of money, and also that it might be dangerous. "How do we know that these guys know what they're doing?" Mitchell asked once.

But we were all persuaded of Liddy's competence, and beyond that we all knew of the atmosphere at the White House. Colson had been pushing for approval of the plan, and I assumed that Haldeman wanted it, because I had asked Strachan if Haldeman had any comments to make on the proposal, and Strachan replied that the plan was all right with Haldeman if it was all right with Mitchell.

Mitchell, as we talked, scribbled on the paper Liddy had prepared, which listed the amount of money he wanted, and the number of men and types of equipment he'd need.

Finally, Mitchell told me that he approved the plan, but that Liddy should receive only $250,000. We discussed the targets of the wire-tapping program, and it was agreed that Liddy should go ahead with the wiretapping of Larry O'Brien's office at the Watergate, then we'd see about the other possible targets.

I think Mitchell came close to rejecting the Liddy plan. I know he approved it only reluctantly. It was another of what I called his throw-away decisions, made under pressure to please the White House. But, nonetheless, the decision was made.

Not long thereafter, Harry Flemming arrived, stayed for a while, then he and I went back to the hotel and played tennis. We worked with Mitchell the next day, Friday, and that night Flemming and I went out to dinner with Ken Rietz, who was in Miami Beach working on the youth campaign, and Flemming's and Rietz's dates. The next morning, Saturday, I flew back to Washington to spend Easter with my family.

Why? Why did Mitchell approve such a plan? And why did others of us acquiesce in the decision?

I think the decision was the result of a combination of pressures that played upon us at the time.

For one thing, I think Liddy put his plan to us in a highly effective way. If he had come to us at the outset and said, "I have a plan to burglarize and wiretap Larry O'Brien's office," we might have rejected the idea out of hand. Instead, he came to us with his elaborate call girl/kidnapping/mugging/sabotage/wiretapping scheme, and we began to tone it down, always with a feeling that we should leave Liddy a little something—we felt we needed him, and we were reluctant to send him away with nothing. Whether by accident or design, Liddy had used an old and effective bureaucratic ploy: he had asked for the whole loaf when he was quite content to settle for half or even a quarter.

Secondly, Mitchell was operating under tremendous pressure. There were the ITT hearings, in which it was later alleged that he had perjured himself. No one was making more of the ITT affair than Larry O'Brien, and I think that the fact that O'Brien was a prime target of the Liddy plan was added incentive for Mitchell to approve it—he must have hoped that *something* could be found to silence his chief Democratic tormenter.

Moreover, Mitchell was affected by the terrible strain imposed on him by his wife. The woman's behavior was absolutely impossible, and it had to have a negative effect on his ability to concentrate on his work. I have mentioned one encounter with her at Key Biscayne, but there were many, many more. She would berate him loudly and endlessly—she didn't like his job, she didn't like his friends, she didn't like his salary, she didn't like Washington—there was no pleasing her. I thought Mitchell was amazingly patient with her. Once, at about the time he left the Committee to Re-elect in July, I asked Mitchell why he didn't divorce her. He shrugged and said something to the effect that it wouldn't be appropriate. Perhaps it would not have been, but there is no doubt in my mind that living with her distracted him and was a cause of some political misjudgments.

Finally, Liddy's plan was approved because of the climate of fear and suspicion that had grown up in the White House, an atmosphere that started with the President himself and reached us through Haldeman and Colson and others, one that came to affect all our thinking, so that decisions that now seem insane seemed at the time to be rational.

It was all but impossible not to get caught up in the "enemies" mentality. We believed in the President and what he was doing, and yet we were surrounded by critics and demonstrators. We had been shaken by antiwar demonstrations, the wave of bombings, the massive May Day attempt to shut down Washington, and by the theft and publication of the Pentagon Papers. Some of our opponents used illegal means, and we became inured to the belief that we, too, must use tough, even illegal means to achieve our ends. We wanted to win the election and we wanted to win it big. Just as a corporation wants to dominate its market, our reelection committee wanted to dominate that year's election, to do everything possible to win a stupendous victory. We were past the point of halfway measures or gentlemanly tactics.

We were wrong, of course, and our decision to approve the Liddy plan was inexcusable. It can only be said in explanation that it was made in a time of high national passion, by men who believed that their actions were necessary and their cause was just.

Gordon Liddy, whose James Bond fantasies might, with a little luck, never have left Dutchess County, New York, had made his way into the highest levels of the Nixon Administration. Perhaps it was just bad luck that he got there, or perhaps there was a certain historical inevitability to Liddy—perhaps if there had been no Liddy we would have created one. In any event, the impact of Liddy's fantasies upon some of us who should have known better, but who had come to share an exaggerated view of American political reality, was to be explosive and, for some, tragic.

CHAPTER X

Break-In

ONCE MITCHELL HAD APPROVED the Liddy plan, I tried to call Liddy from Key Biscayne to give him the news, but I couldn't reach him. I also called Gordon Strachan at the White House and told him of Mitchell's various decisions, including the approval of the Liddy plan. On Monday morning, back in my office in Washington, I told Reisner to call Liddy and tell him his plan was approved. Reisner did, and was surprised to hear Liddy respond:

"I can't do it. It's going to be hard. I've got to talk to Magruder."

Liddy rushed into my office later that day.

"I can't do it," he said. "There's not enough time. We've waited too late to put it together."

"It's your decision," I told him. "If you can do it, do it; if you can't, don't."

I didn't know if his complaint was legitimate or not. In a campaign, people always protest that they don't have enough time to do what you want done. If Liddy was right, and he didn't have enough time, he should have called off the plan. But that wasn't likely, once his $250,000 was approved.

On April 7, Hugh Sloan called and asked me if the $83,000 that Liddy was asking for was authorized. I said it was, but Sloan wasn't satisfied. He spoke to Stans, who called Mitchell, who asked me why Liddy needed so much money. I explained that this was Liddy's up-front

198

money, to hire the men and equipment needed to get his project started. Mitchell therefore told Stans the request was legitimate, and Sloan gave Liddy the money.

I didn't see much of Liddy in the next two months. He was supposed to come to my office at 8 A.M. each Monday to report to me, but usually one of us would cancel the meeting. When we did talk, it was on the basis of "How's it coming?" and "It's coming along fine." Liddy's project was such a minor part of our campaign plan, and Liddy himself was so distasteful to me, that I hardly ever thought of him that spring.

My thoughts in early April were much more on where we would hold the convention that summer. The previous summer we'd forced the Republican National Committee to accept the President's choice, San Diego, but throughout the winter we'd been more and more uncertain about that decision. We had information that antiwar groups would hold massive demonstrations during the convention, and San Diego was particularly vulnerable because of the thousands of indigenous antiwar activists in Southern California. And the hotel that would be our convention headquarters seemed vulnerable, because it was located on an island just offshore that was easily reached from the mainland. (This was the new Sheraton Hotel that ITT owned and had hoped that our convention would publicize.) We had a vision of an armada of thousands of wild-eyed hippies swimming across the inlet and overrunning our defenses. Our fear, of course, was that the antiwar demonstrators would turn our convention into a nightmare like the 1968 Democratic Convention in Chicago.

We were receiving estimates both from local police and from several federal agencies on the possible size of the demonstrations. One estimate was 100,000 demonstrators, which was bad enough, but we also had an estimate from Liddy of 250,000 demonstrators, which if true would have meant almost certain violence, on an even greater scale than Chicago.

We just couldn't take the chance, so Dick Herman, the National Committee's convention manager, recommended to Mitchell, and he recommended to the President, that we move the convention from San Diego to another city, preferably Miami Beach, which happened to be the city the National Committee's site-selection committee had urged on us the year before. There were two good reasons for choosing Miami Beach. One was that there were relatively fewer antiwar activists in the Florida area. The other was that the Democrats were holding their convention there in July, and many logistical problems would be solved if we used the same facilities. The television networks, for one thing, wouldn't have to make a costly and difficult move of their equipment.

The President approved the move, and we then faced two major problems. The first was a public relations problem. How did we leave San Diego without admitting the embarrassing fact that we'd been forced out by the threat of antiwar demonstrations? Obviously, we needed to put out a cover story that would explain the move in less embarrassing terms. Thus, I lunched at the San Souci one day with columnist Robert Novak and gave him an exclusive, inside story: we were about to move our convention because of San Diego's inadequate hotel and arena facilities. I let Novak read a memo that detailed San Diego's shortcomings. All this was true—San Diego's facilities presented serious problems—but it was not the whole truth, since our overriding concern was demonstrations. My talk with Novak resulted in a column that said exactly what we'd hoped it would say.

It was a good example of how we could often achieve our ends by effective leaks to the press. A good leak must go to a writer who had both credibility and mass circulation, and Novak had both. I might have leaked the story to a wire-service reporter, but a wire story ("Republicans Ponder Convention Switch") would probably have gotten less attention than an Evans–Novak column, with its aura of inside information. In this instance, the leak succeeded—it prepared the San Diego officials for what was coming, and it paved the way to our making the potentially embarrassing move with almost no public understanding of its real motive.

Our public relations effort could have been ruined if Governor Reagan of California or Mayor Peter Wilson of San Diego had stated publicly what they both knew to be the case, that we were moving the convention because we feared demonstrations. Mitchell sent Mardian to talk to Reagan, who agreed to say nothing about the real reason for the move. Someone also talked to Mayor Wilson, who voiced his displeasure that his city was losing the convention, but didn't discuss the real reason for the move.

Getting out of San Diego was easy compared to getting into Miami Beach. The problem there was political. We had to have the approval of the Miami Beach City Council, which had a Democratic majority. At the outset, the City Council seemed to be against us by 4 to 3 or even 5 to 2. We assumed there was some politics in this, with the Democrats out to give us a hard time, but there was also a genuine feeling among some residents of Miami Beach that one national convention in a summer was enough. Our prospects wouldn't have been helped if the word got out that we feared antiwar demonstrations; that was another reason to push our cover story.

Dick Herman spent several weeks in Miami Beach lining up local businessmen and political figures who could bring pressure to bear on the City Council to approve our convention. Bebe Rebozo helped with calls to his friends. Rarely had so much high-powered lobbying been focused on as minor a political entity as the Miami Beach City Council.

We simply didn't know what we'd do if Miami Beach rejected us. There was vague talk of a one-day convention in Washington. We considered several other cities, and even reached the point of considering the mountain resort town of Gatlinburg, Tennessee. We wanted the convention to launch our campaign, to set the tone, to be a prime-time PR extravaganza. If the Miami Beach City Council turned us down, the President's reelection campaign would start on a note of absurdity.

After a month of uncertainty, the Miami Beach City Council got around to voting, and we won by 4 to 3. I'd spent most of that afternoon with Mitchell and LaRue in Mitchell's law-firm office. LaRue's wife and my wife came by in the early evening to say hello to Mitchell and to have a drink before Gail and I and the LaRues went out to dinner. We were all tremendously relieved that the Miami Beach ordeal was finally behind us.

"Thank God that's over," I remarked. "Nothing worse than that can possibly happen to us in the rest of this campaign."

Mitchell sucked on his ever-present pipe and shook his head.

"You're wrong," he said. "This was a tough one, but before the campaign is over, something worse is sure to come along."

Our attention was riveted that spring by a national political drama that was unfolding more perfectly than we could have dreamed a year before. As the primary elections slipped by—New Hampshire on March 7, Florida on March 14, Wisconsin on April 4, Pennsylvania on April 25—the President's two Republican challengers dropped by the wayside, and the Democratic race became increasingly confused and bitter. Our hope had been that if the President stayed out of the political arena, the Democrats would turn on each other, and that was what was happening. Muskie stumbled, Humphrey never got off the ground, and to our amazement McGovern emerged as the frontrunner.

We had ambivalent feelings about the Democratic race. At first, we'd feared Muskie, but after his inept primary campaign we'd begun to hope he'd be the nominee. Humphrey was the Democratic contender that I personally respected the most, and yet politically we would have welcomed a Humphrey–Nixon rematch. McGovern was obviously running a strong campaign in the primaries, but he seemed to us to be the weakest of the Democratic contenders, because of his far-left record. He was our most-favored opponent, but for a long time we just couldn't believe we'd be that lucky. Our biggest fear was a deadlocked Democratic Convention and a draft of Senator Kennedy, because we felt that despite Chappaquidick he was the strongest Democratic candidate.

In April, in the weeks before the Pennsylvania primary, we received a fascinating report from Sedan Chair II, our man in the Humphrey campaign. After our first Sedan Chair quit, Bart Porter recruited a new "black advance man," a young private detective from Kentucky named Michael McMinaway, who was dubbed Sedan Chair II. In theory, Porter had turned the Sedan Chair operation over to Liddy, but Liddy was so often gone from Washington that Porter had to continue to supervise the project. I had, in effect, lost control of Liddy.

McMinaway was paid about $6,000 for about three months of activity, most notably in the Humphrey campaign in Pennsylvania. He was not disrupting the Humphrey campaign. That wasn't necessary. He was only reporting on it. He had walked into Humphrey's headquarters in Philadelphia, volunteered his services, and quickly risen to be the number-two person in the headquarters. He reported to us that the woman in charge of the headquarters, an old political pro, told him, "Mike, in every campaign one or two people like you turn up who really want to work and really understand politics."

Sedan Chair II sent us a report that described the Humphrey campaign as a disaster. There were few volunteers and no organization. There were conflicts with local Democratic leaders. The direct-mail program was a mess—they had the wrong lists and people forgot to put stamps on the envelopes, that sort of thing.

I showed Sedan Chair II's report to Mitchell and we had a good laugh at Humphrey's expense. That was how we regarded Sedan Chair II's activities, not as something that would bring us important information, but as comic relief in the serious business of reelecting a President.

California was the last and biggest primary, and we planned an all-out effort there, mainly as a final test of our campaign techniques. Lyn Nofziger had left the Republican National Committee to be the director of our reelection committee in California, and in mid-April he and Mitchell, Mardian, LaRue, and I met for a detailed discussion of our plans. One important decision we made that day was to use no media advertising in California. The decision was based on a recommendation from Phil Joanou, our very able deputy director of advertising, who had said in a memo:

> A four-week campaign consisting of radio, TV and newspaper, similar to the Wisconsin plan, would cost $750,000 plus production. I recommend that we do not spend this money during the primary. We are ahead and the California primary on the Democratic side could be very hot. We may be better off letting the Democrats cut each other up in this last primary, contrasted with Nixon in Russia. He will be getting plenty of prime time exposure.

It is, I might note, unusual to find an advertising man recommending *against* advertising. That was another reason it was good to have formed our own ad agency, rather than hiring one that was paid on commission.

We made maximum use in California of our Presidential spokesmen. By mid-March we estimated that twenty-eight surrogates would make sixty-six appearances in California between January 20 and the June 6 election. These included Vice President Agnew, Mrs. Nixon, Senator Dole, Secretaries Romney, Laird, Shultz, and Connally, and Finch and Klein from the White House. In effect, we saturated the state with newsmaking Nixon spokesmen.

Once we decided not to use newspapers or television advertising in California, our telephone and direct-mail programs became vitally important. Our telephone program was probably the most extensive any candidate had ever attempted in a primary and certainly the most extensive by an unopposed candidate. We set up nine telephone centers, each with ten telephones, with which we estimated that our volunteers could reach some 325,000 Republican households, or more than half a million Republican voters. The cost of these centers was estimated at $66,500, or about 16¢ per completed call.

Our callers would ask each voter if he or she intended to vote for the President on June 6, and the voters would thus be classified For, Against, or Undecided. The Fors would be contacted again in the get-out-the-vote drive, but the Againsts and the Undecideds would not be contacted again. This policy, of not trying to persuade the Undecideds, represented a major change from our procedure in the first primaries. This reflected the results of our follow-up surveys in New Hampshire, which indicated that follow-up calls to Undecideds did increase the number of them who voted, but not necessarily in the President's favor. Again, it seemed that an Undecided voter was probably an eventual non-Nixon voter, and we were moving closer to our no-persuasion policy for the general election.

Our direct-mail program in California was even more extensive. Mitchell approved a $342,000 program to reach two million Republican households, or about ninety percent of the state's Republicans. The plan included follow-up analysis to test the impact of personalized versus non-personalized mailings, one-page letters versus longer letters, one mailing versus two or more, and so on.

We were particularly interested in testing whether or not mailings and phone calls could win us votes among the traditionally Democratic black and Spanish-American communities. We assumed the black community would continue to vote heavily Democratic, but we hoped that by organizing, by getting the President's record before the blacks, and by using black celebrities from the worlds of sports and entertainment, we could increase the President's black vote in 1972 by fifty percent over what it had been in 1968.

We thought we might do even better among Spanish-American voters, and we directed a special program at California's more than three million Spanish-American voters. In their communities, we had bilingual volunteers making our phone calls, and we had an extensive mailing, with a letter from a campaign official named Manuel Quevedo, which said in part:

> President Nixon has focused his attention on bilingual education and has taken initiatives to address the most serious problem Spanish-speaking children face. He has put millions into migrant education programs throughout the country. He has increased aid to minority businesses and he has made sure that Spanish-speaking people get their fair share of the aid; in 1971 alone, 2,500 small business loans—a total of 58 million dollars—went to businesses owned by the Spanish-speaking people. To our people he has given not words but action. He is the first President to name dozens of Spanish-speaking Americans to high offices—more than four times as many as any previous President.

The eventual results of our efforts in the black and Spanish-American communities further convinced us that we were wasting our time going after undecided voters. We found that in low-income areas people were often highly suspicious of official-sounding callers, and as many as half the people refused to answer questions. The direct mail, at least in middle-class areas, showed some impact, but seemingly not enough to justify the cost.

But that was fine. Our purpose in the California primary was to learn, even if all the lessons weren't encouraging. And besides learning from our campaign, we also hoped to learn from the McGovern campaign, which peaked in California with a massive volunteer effort, one that Theodore White called "the most efficient technical apparatus ever fielded by any candidate in a primary." We believed that our campaign operation in California, if less colorful, was no less formidable, but there was no denying that the McGovern operation in the California primary had been magnificent.

We were intrigued by his success, and wanted to know more about his methods. Newspaper articles spoke in general terms, but didn't give us the technical details we wanted about his direct mail, his telephone calls, his door-to-door techniques, and so on. We wondered if he'd come up with any innovations that we should know about. We therefore sent a young man from our staff to poke around the McGovern campaign in California and see what he could learn. I forget how he operated; perhaps he posed as a reporter or a volunteer. In any event, he reported back to us that McGovern had no innovations, that he was following basic precinct-work procedures, and that his "secret" was simply the tremendous number of highly motivated volunteers he attracted—he had the people, and Gary Hart, his director of organization, saw that they were used effectively. I was particularly impressed by the report that whenever a volunteer entered a McGovern headquarters, he or she was put immediately to work. I had seen too many campaigns in which eager volunteers would walk in, only to be given a form to fill out, then sent away because nobody knew what to do with them.

It was about that time that Gary Hart was quoted in a newspaper as saying: "If the Nixon people underestimate us the way the Muskie people underestimated us, we'll kill 'em."

We had that quotation printed up and put on the walls of our CRP offices and all our local headquarters. We weren't going to underestimate McGovern. He had an impressive organization, but so did we, and we were not afraid to take him on in the fall.

J. Edgar Hoover died on the morning of May 2, and arrangements were made for his body to lie in state at the Capitol the next day. It happened that an antiwar demonstration was scheduled at the Capitol the same day. This combination of events caused Chuck Colson to spring into action.

Rietz and Porter both told me that Colson's office had called them, wanting them to provide young people to hold a counterdemonstration against the antiwar demonstration. Moreover Colson's plan called for the counterdemonstrators to tear down the Viet Cong flag that he believed the antiwar people would be waving. Colson apparently thought the publicity would hurt the antiwar movement, by making it seem that they'd come to demonstrate against J. Edgar Hoover (although in fact their demonstration had been scheduled prior to his death). Also, Daniel Ellsberg was to be among the antiwar leaders present, and Colson perhaps hoped he would be discredited.

Rietz had been reluctant to let any of his volunteers participate in Colson's plan, because of the possibility of violence. Finally, Colson called me.

"We've got to have some people there to demonstrate," he said, "and some people who can tear down that damned VC flag and protect our kids if it gets rough."

"Chuck, we can't send our kids out to get into fights," I told him.

We went through the usual hassle. He said the President wanted this done and if I wasn't willing I must be disloyal to the President. The problem was, once again, that often he was not bluffing, and the President *did* want what Colson said he wanted. I talked to Mitchell and we decided we'd have to go along with Colson's plan.

"We can send kids over there to demonstrate," I told Colson, "but we can't have them getting into fights."

"Okay, but if you don't want your kids going after that flag, get somebody else."

"I'll check with Liddy," I said.

I called Liddy and explained the problem—that we needed some strong-arm men to protect our kids and to go after the VC flag.

"No sweat," Liddy said. "I'll need some money to get the people up here and to use for bail if our guys are arrested."

Liddy went to Porter and drew some $5,000 for the operation. Part of the money, I learned later, went to fly up the Cubans whom Hunt had recruited for the Watergate break-in. At the time I knew nothing about the Cubans. I had the idea that Liddy used ex-FBI men for his missions.

Bob Reisner happened to be in my office during my talk with Colson and he expressed surprise that we'd agreed to send our people to the demonstration. Bob of course hadn't been around long and didn't know much about Colson and the White House pressures.

"It's a throw-away," I told him. "We have to do things like that so we can say no when it's important."

The operation went off more or less as planned. One of the Cubans later testified that he had been ordered to attack Ellsberg—"to call him a traitor and punch him in the nose, hit him and run." Ellsberg apparently avoided harm, but the Cubans went after the VC flag, got into fights with antiwar people, and were quickly arrested. They were just as quickly unarrested, however, when a mysterious "man in a gray suit" intervened with police. I assumed that was Hunt, perhaps using his old CIA credentials to persuade the police to free the Cubans.

I didn't see that the operation accomplished anything. It didn't receive much press, although possibly we got the antiwar demonstrators slightly more attention than they'd have gotten without the fights. Aside from the participants themselves, no one cared very much about a scuffle between antiwar activists and some Cubans. It only served to satisfy Colson and Liddy, and, if Colson was to be believed, the President.

At nine o'clock on the evening of May 8, the President went on television to tell the nation that he had ordered the bombing of Hanoi and Haiphong and the mining of North Vietnamese ports.

Suddenly, as with the Cambodian invasion two years before, the President seemed to have put his political life on the line. Liberal senators and commentators were quick to denounce the President for a reckless act of war, and to predict that it would fail militarily and would cause the Russians to cancel the forthcoming summit talks.

The morning after the President's announcement, Mitchell made one of his rare appearances at our regular weekly staff meetings. Mitchell was as poker-faced and unemotional as ever, but the very fact that he was there showed we were in a major battle.

"This is a test of our campaign organization," he said. "This committee has been in existence for a year, and now we find out if we can produce. I expect every one of you to give this all he's got."

And we did. This was, in a way, an even bigger push than Cambodia had been. Then, we had only a few contacts scattered around the nation, but now we had our full campaign organization in place, and we used it to the fullest to drum up support for the President. One obvious goal was letters and telegrams in support of the military action, and we drummed up so many of them that Ron Ziegler could soon announce that the White House mail was running six to one in the President's favor.

In Washington, a television station and a newspaper, the Washington *Star*, announced reader polls for or against the President's action. We had a dozen people working for several days filling out postcards for the television poll, which eventually announced 5,157 postcards in support of the President (probably half of them from us) and 1,158 in opposition. You voted in the Washington *Star* poll with a ballot that appeared in the newspaper one day. The *Star* must have broken all its records for newsstand sales that afternoon, because Rob Odle bought several thousand copies simply for the ballots.

As this battle for public opinion continued, Chuck Colson surfaced with a hard-line ad he wanted to run in the *New York Times,* the kind that accused our critics of treason. This was the same problem we'd faced with his negative ads in 1970, except that now we had professional ad men like Pete Dailey on hand and we were therefore able to keep Colson a good arm's length removed from our advertising program. In this instance, we were able to tone down the ad, although Colson had convinced Haldeman that some kind of ad should be run.

The ad that eventually appeared in the *New York Times* on May 17 was headlined "The People vs. the *New York Times*" and challenged a *Times* editorial assertion that the Vietnam action was "counter to the will and conscience of a large segment of the American people." The full-page ad declared that various polls showed from 59 percent to 76 percent of the people supported the President. I regarded it as an ad that didn't do us much harm but didn't do much good either. It presumably was good for Colson's ego, and perhaps for the President's, as a way of getting back at the *Times*, but to pay the *Times* $4,400 for an advertisement is an expensive way of getting back at them.

The important point is that the President won his gamble. The Russians did not call off the summit meeting, and the legitimate polls showed that a clear majority of the American people believed the mining of Haiphong would shorten the war. Nor was the operation the military disaster the liberals had predicted. The President had moved effectively to shorten the war in Vietnam, and just as effectively to present his case to the American people in the face of vocal criticism.

We could not know it at the time, but two events that May, the President's bold military action in Vietnam and the shooting of Governor Wallace a week later, had all but guaranteed the reelection of the

President. All we had to do was to sit back and wait for the Democrats to nominate George McGovern.

Unfortunately we were doing a good deal more.

Just after the Memorial Day weekend, Liddy came to my office and said a successful entry had been made at the Democratic headquarters in the Watergate, that wiretaps had been put in place and documents photographed. I told him that was fine, and to show me the results as soon as he had them. It was a brief exchange; I wasn't interested in Liddy's affairs until they produced some results.

A few days later, while Gordon Strachan was in my office discussing campaign business, Liddy came in, but not with news of the Watergate bugs.

"I was over at McGovern's headquarters last night," Liddy announced. "We had a little problem with a street light."

"So what did you do?" I asked.

Liddy gave us a little grin. "I shot it out."

"Shot it out?" I said. "You're supposed to keep away from these operations. You're damned sure not supposed to be shooting out street lights!"

Strachan was angry, too, but as much at me as at Liddy. "Jeb, you're supposed to keep these people under control," he said.

"Don't worry, don't worry," Liddy said. "I just had to go along and make sure everything was done right. I won't do it again."

In early June, Liddy brought me the first fruits of the Watergate entry —transcripts of wiretapped telephone conversations and photographs of some documents from Larry O'Brien's files. He explained that more material would be ready in a few days. I studied the material and soon realized it was worthless. The telephone calls told us a great deal more than we needed to know about the social lives of various members of the Democratic Committee staff, but nothing of political interest. I decided to wait for Liddy's second batch of material, hoping it would contain something substantial, before showing the material to anyone. But when Liddy brought me more photographs and transcripts a few days later, they were equally useless. The only thing that caught my eye was the transcript of a phone call between our own Harry Flemming and Spencer Oliver, a young assistant to Larry O'Brien.

My God! I thought. *Flemming's a double agent.*

But, as the transcript revealed, the talk was innocent—both were members of a bipartisan group called Young American Political Leaders, and they were discussing one of its activities.

I thought Strachan should see the material, if only to let the White House know we had made the promised entry. I didn't think, however, that I should send these documents over to Strachan by messenger, as I did most material, so I asked him to come examine them in my office. Strachan, who tended toward sarcasm, read the material and said something like, "This idiot is just wasting our time and money," and I had to agree.

The next morning I took the material to my regular 8:30 meeting with Mitchell.

"This isn't worth much," I said, as I handed the papers to him.

He studied the documents briefly. When he finished he was frowning.

"Get Liddy in here," he said.

I called Liddy, who appeared moments later.

"This stuff isn't worth the paper it's printed on," Mitchell told him.

"There's a problem," Liddy replied. "One of the bugs isn't working. And they put one of them on O'Brien's secretary's phone instead of O'Brien's phone. But I'll get everything straightened out right away."

Liddy dashed out, and Mitchell and I turned to other business. In retrospect, that would have been a fine time to abort the Liddy plan, but I don't think that occurred to anyone. His mission had acquired a certain bureaucratic momentum—the concept had been approved, the money expended, operations begun, and the first results obtained. True, there was a small problem, but Liddy, the professional, would take care of that.

The important news that week came from California. Senator McGovern, in winning the Democratic primary, had been mortally wounded by his old friend Hubert Humphrey. During a series of televised debates, Humphrey had raked McGovern over the coals about his welfare scheme, his proposed defense cuts, and other vague or dubious policies that McGovern endorsed. Before the debates, polls had indicated that McGovern might win California by as much as fifteen or twenty percent. In fact, he bettered Humphrey by only about six percent. He would still win the nomination, but we began to see what a vulnerable candidate he would be.

Our own primary campaign had gone extremely well in California, and we were looking ahead to the big victory we hoped to win there in November. To that end, we scheduled a series of meetings with California Republican leaders in Los Angeles on the weekend of June 17–18. Mitchell, Mardian, LaRue, and I were going out, and because there was a party planned with celebrities who supported the President, we invited our wives to join us. We flew out on Friday afternoon as guests on a plane owned by an oil company. Gail was bumped from the flight when Martha Mitchell decided at the last minute to bring a friend of hers. So Gail flew out on a commercial flight, and we all arrived at the Beverly Hills Hotel at about nine Friday night. We had an entire wing of one floor of the hotel for our group. We were all tired from the long flight, so after a nightcap we all went to bed, thinking we'd need plenty of rest for the busy two days ahead.

The next morning the Mardians, the LaRues, Gail and I, and Bart and Carol Porter were having breakfast in the Polo Lounge. Porter had flown out earlier to work on the celebrity party that was to be held that night. The Mitchells didn't join us for breakfast; as usual they ate in their hotel suite. The Polo Lounge was a favorite spot of mine in Los Angeles. It was one of the few places I'd found that served kippered herring for breakfast, and I was enjoying that treat when a waiter told me I had a phone call. He brought a phone to the table, and to my surprise it was Liddy.

"You've got to get to a secure phone," Liddy began.

"A secure phone?" I said. I thought he was joking. "I don't know where a secure phone is, Gordon."

"There's one at a military base at El Segundo, about ten miles from your hotel."

"I haven't got time to go to a military base," I said with some annoyance. This was no time for Liddy's cloak-and-dagger games. "What's so important?"

"Our security chief was arrested in the Democratic headquarters in the Watergate last night," Liddy said.

"*What?* Do you mean McCord?"

"That's right. Jim McCord."

I saw that I did need a secure phone, to say the least. I turned and asked LaRue if he knew where I might find one, because something confidential had come up. LaRue said that all I had to do was use a pay phone—they were secure.

"What's your number?" I asked Liddy. "I'll call you back."

I left the table in a state of shock. None of this made any sense. I knew Jim McCord slightly. He'd been our full-time security chief for about six months, and had worked for us part-time for a few months before that. He was a trim, balding man who didn't have much to say and seemed a thorough professional in his work. Both the Mitchells had become fond of him, and he often drove their daughter Marty to and from school. But I had no idea that he'd been in any way involved with Liddy's intelligence plans, and it didn't make any sense at all that he'd been arrested. Our people didn't get arrested. Our people were professionals.

As I left my friends and hurried out to find a phone, I wondered if they had seen the horror in my face. I couldn't believe what had happened, but I was beginning to sense that the fun and games were over, that a new reality was settling in.

CHAPTER XI

Cover-Up

I CALLED LIDDY back on the pay phone outside the Polo Lounge, and by the time I reached him I was angry.

"Liddy, what the hell was McCord doing inside the Watergate?" I demanded. "You were supposed to keep this operation removed from us. Have you lost your mind?"

"I had to have somebody on the inside to handle the electronics," Liddy said. "McCord was the only one I could get. You didn't give me enough time."

I couldn't believe it—Liddy was blaming his fiasco on me. But there was no point in arguing with Liddy, so I calmed down and asked him to give me all the facts he had. He explained that the four men arrested with McCord were Cuban "freedom fighters" whom Howard Hunt had recruited in Miami. He said all five men had given false names when arrested, but we had to assume that their true identities would be discovered.

"But don't worry," Liddy told me. "My men will never talk."

I didn't know what to tell Liddy. The situation was beyond my comprehension. I only knew that McCord's arrest was a disaster, because he was CRP's security chief; the Cubans might not even know whom they had been working for, but McCord would be very hard to explain away.

"I've got to talk to Mitchell," I told Liddy. "Stay by the phone. We'll get back to you."

I returned to the Polo Lounge and made a point of finishing my breakfast, so no one would think anything was wrong. Gail and the other wives were talking excitedly about their day of shopping and sightseeing, and about the gowns they would be wearing to the celebrity party we would attend that night. Breakfast seemed to drag on forever, but when we finally left the Polo Lounge I took Fred LaRue aside and said I had to talk to him in private.

We couldn't talk in our own rooms, because our wives might pop in, so we asked Steve King, Mitchell's bodyguard, if we could borrow his room, which was just across from Mitchell's. I could have gone directly to Mitchell, but I suppose I was putting off that inevitable step. LaRue was a close friend, someone I looked to for guidance, and I wanted his moral support. Quickly, I told LaRue the facts—McCord and the Cubans had been arrested in Larry O'Brien's office, and Hunt and Liddy might be next.

"Oh, God," I moaned. "Why didn't I fire that idiot Liddy when I had the chance? How could we have been so stupid?"

LaRue didn't say much. After all the tragic experiences of his life, he had learned to keep a tight check on his emotions. There was a certain fatalism to Fred.

"Maybe I'd better talk to Mitchell first," he suggested.

That was fine with me, so I waited in King's room while he went across to break the news to Mitchell. They called me to Mitchell's suite a few minutes later.

Mitchell must have been seething inside, but his outward behavior was calm and businesslike. I told him what I knew, and the three of us talked over the problem. At some point, we called in Bob Mardian. To my knowledge, Mardian was not then aware of the break-in plan, and we did not immediately explain it to him. Rather, we just said that McCord had been arrested and we were trying to decide how to cope with this potentially embarrassing situation. We all agreed that McCord was the heart of the problem.

"If we could just get him out of jail before they find out who he is," someone suggested. "Then maybe he could just disappear."

I don't recall who made what specific suggestions during this talk; but a consensus was reached. Perhaps we were grasping at straws, but we all believed that some way out could be found; after all, *we* were the government; until very recently John Mitchell had been Attorney General of the United States. It did not seem beyond our capacities to get one man out of the D.C. jail.

Someone recalled that McCord had once worked for the CIA. Perhaps that could be the handle—somehow we could say he was working on a special mission and whisk him out of there, just as, six weeks earlier, "the man in the gray suit" had convinced the police to free the Cubans who had beaten up antiwar demonstrators at the Capitol.

One of us suggested that Mitchell call Dick Kleindienst, his successor as Attorney General, and see if he could help us get McCord out of jail.

"No, that wouldn't be appropriate," Mitchell said. "It would be better if Bob called him."

That seemed logical, since Mardian and Kleindienst were close personal friends, but in retrospect it suggests to me that from the first Mitchell was trying to keep himself out of the cover-up activities.

Mardian placed a call to Kleindienst in Washington, only to learn that the Attorney General had gone for a round of golf at Burning Tree Country Club. Our anxiety by then was such that we came up with another plan: I would call Liddy, and we would have him go find Kleindienst on the golf course and explain that he must get McCord out of jail.

I had second thoughts about this plan, however. "I'm not the one to talk to Liddy," I said. "We don't get along."

It was agreed that Mardian would call Liddy, since the two were friendly. Then Mardian began to have second thoughts, not about calling Liddy, but about placing the call on the phone in Mitchell's suite. We were all becoming concerned about our own security. That McCord had been involved in the break-in, and that the men had bungled the job, seemed so incredible that we all shared a nagging suspicion that somehow the Democrats had set us up, that McCord might have been working for them, that at that very moment they might be tapping our phones.

Mardian therefore went to a pay phone to call Liddy about going to see Kleindienst. By then it was nearly ten o'clock, and we all went downstairs, where Governor Reagan was waiting with several limousines to take us to the day's political meetings.

Mitchell and Reagan climbed into the lead limousine. Mardian, LaRue, Steve King, and I got into the next one. Our destination was the Airport Marina Hotel, where we had two meetings scheduled, plus a 2 P.M. news conference for Mitchell. As we drove to the hotel, Steve King noticed that I was downcast. Steve was Mitchell's bodyguard, but he was no pug; he was a very bright, efficient, good-natured man in his early thirties whom we all enjoyed dealing with.

"Jeb, you look like you've got a problem," Steve said. "Is there anything I can do to help?"

I managed a grin. His question reminded me that I must maintain my usual outward self-confidence, no matter how disturbed I might be inwardly. "Thanks, Steve," I said. "But it's just a little PR problem back in Washington."

Our 10 A.M. meeting was a large one, with Mitchell and several California Republican leaders addressing about a hundred and fifty party figures from around the state, in a general discussion of the coming campaign. That was followed by a luncheon with about ten top California party leaders, primarily to discuss campaign finances. We were, of course, highly distracted that day. We went through the motions of talking politics and urging party unity, but we were also placing anxious calls to Washington and holding whispered conferences about each new scrap of information we received.

Cliff Miller, the Los Angeles public-relations man who frequently worked with us was on hand to help with the press arrangements, and he was drafted to help us prepare a statement for Mitchell to make if he was asked about the Watergate break-in at his news conference. Bart Porter has described how he stood guard at the door while Mitchell, Mardian, LaRue, and I huddled at a table in a huge hotel ballroom, and I think that must have been when we were working on Mitchell's statement.

As it turned out, no reporter asked Mitchell about the Watergate break-in, and he chose not to volunteer any comment. There was not a great deal he could have said, since McCord's identity had not yet been revealed, so there were no known ties between the break-in and CRP.

After the news conference, we returned to the Beverly Hills Hotel for further deliberations. By then Liddy had reported that he had approached Kleindienst on the seventeenth fairway at Burning Tree, but the new Attorney General had refused to talk to him about freeing McCord. By then, too, we had word that the police had found several thousand dollars on the burglars. That news left us dangling between fear and hope. Our fear was that the money was our money and could be traced to CRP. Our hope was that the money might prove to have come from Larry O'Brien and the Democrats, for we still somehow suspected McCord.

That the break-in had been bungled was undeniable. Liddy should have had a middle man between himself and the burglars, so they could have no idea they were working for us, and even if arrested couldn't implicate us. Even Ken Rietz had followed that principle when he had Fat Jack Buckley recruit the man who became Senator Muskie's driver. That McCord, *a CRP employee*, should be part of the break-in team defied our belief. Moreover, the burglary itself had been carried out in a slipshod manner that all but cried out for arrest. When McCord put the tape over the bolts on the doors of the Democratic offices, to keep them from locking, he didn't put it vertically, so that it would be invisible when the door was closed, but horizontally, so that it showed on both sides of the door and could hardly be missed by any security guard. We had to conclude that either McCord was an incredible bungler or he was a double agent, and the latter seemed at least possible.

Around 3:30 that afternoon I called my office and talked to Bob Reisner and Rob Odle about removing the Gemstone file and other political files from my office. Odle and Reisner, knowing nothing about the break-in plot, were convinced there was some sort of Democratic scheme afoot to embarrass the President, and they therefore took my files home that night as a security safeguard against whatever skullduggery might come next.

I also called Strachan. He had been calling me all day and I had put off returning his calls, partly because I didn't have anything new to tell him, and partly, I suppose, because I feared the wrath of Haldeman. But our talk was businesslike, a quick exchange of information.

Around four o'clock, my parents arrived for a visit with Gail and me. After my father's retirement in 1967, they had moved to an apartment in Santa Barbara, California, a community that attracts many retired people. They lived on their Social Security payments and about $100 a month my father received from the sale of his printing company. They enjoyed California's weather and informal life-style, and came back east only for visits with me and my family.

That afternoon, they visited us for about two hours in our suite. The calls from Washington had tapered off by then, but I remained nervous and distracted, and Gail did most of the talking for us.

"You're working too hard, Jeb," my mother said as they left. I kissed her good-bye and promised I would try to take better care of myself in the future.

The party that night was a memorable social event and, as far as our campaign plans were concerned, an important political event. It was held at the magnificent Bel Air home of Taft Schrieber, an official of MCA, the huge entertainment conglomerate, and its purpose was to assemble as many show-business celebrities as possible who supported, or might be persuaded to support, the President.

Bart Porter had helped plan the party and we had felt, through Haldeman, the President's intense interest in its success. Aside from a few stalwarts like John Wayne and Bob Hope, the President had never really had the show-business world behind him, but now, as an incumbent President, he was determined to add some glamour to his political entourage. I think this determination grew in part from his fascination with, and envy of, the Kennedys—we were trying to out-Kennedy the Democrats in 1972; that is, to give the Nixon campaign the show-biz sparkle that Kennedy campaigns traditionally possessed.

We knew, of course, that many show-business people were liberals who had spoken out against the war and would be supporting McGovern or whomever the Democrats nominated. But we also knew, or strongly suspected, that a good many movie stars and other celebrities weren't political or ideological, and that peer group pressure could be effectively applied to them, as Ken Rietz hoped to apply it to young voters. Thus, we hoped that a party like this one could help make it the "in" thing for Hollywood stars to support the President.

We tried to do our part by sending out some of our "stars." Henry Kissinger, the supposed "swinger" of our Administration, was supposed to attend, but he had to go abroad, and we sent Mrs. Nixon instead. Martha Mitchell was present too, on her best behavior and very much a star in her own right.

The party was held at poolside, and from Schrieber's hilltop home we had a magnificent view of the lights of Los Angeles. There was a dance band, Vikki Carr sang, the food and wine and service were outstanding —it was, even by White House or San Clemente standards, a lavish affair. There was, however, a certain stiffness about it. Gail's main memory of the party is of the two groups, the political elite and the show-business elite, gawking at each other in curiosity. Gail, who I thought looked magnificent, also felt that she and the other Washington wives were positively dowdy alongside the Hollywood women in their stunning gowns and jewelry.

The guests that night included Charlton Heston, who was a center of attention because he was a Democrat, and being avidly wooed by us Republicans; Governor Reagan, tall and self-confident, the one person present who moved easily between the political and entertainment worlds;

John Wayne and his wife, Pilar; Arlene Dahl; Zsa Zsa Gabor; Jack Benny; Terry Moore, looking very sexy and not at all like the girl-next-door I remembered from fifties movies; and quite a few actors and actresses whose names and faces were only dimly familiar to me. We had learned, as we planned the party, that many of Hollywood's lesser luminaries were anxious to attend, less for political reasons than in hope of gaining a little free publicity.

At dinner, Gail sat between John Gavin, the actor, who struck her as an egomaniac, and Herb Kalmbach, whom she had not met before but liked immediately. My dinner partner was a stunning creature whose name I have forgotten, but who was identified to me as one of Rory Calhoun's ex-wives. We danced once, and I tried to make conversation, but her knowledge of politics was as limited as my knowledge of Hollywood, and communications were difficult.

I was, of course, preoccupied. I excused myself several times to call Washington. I talked to Odle when he obtained a copy of the first edition of Sunday's Washington *Post*, because we were intensely interested in how they would play the break-in story. We were pleased that the *Post* carried only a brief story, by-lined by two reporters we'd never heard of, Carl Bernstein and Bob Woodward. As I made my phone calls, Mitchell and Governor Reagan spoke to the guests, urging their wholehearted support for President Nixon in the fall. Then there was dancing until the party ended, in the small hours of the morning. Gail and I, and Bart and Carol Porter, stayed until all the guests had left, so we could have a nightcap with our host, Taft Schrieber, and could thank him again for his hospitality.

We returned to the hotel, where there was a final discussion in progress in Mitchell's suite. Mitchell felt that Mardian should fly back to Washington the next day to take charge of the situation—to direct the cover-up. I assumed he favored Mardian because he was a lawyer and because he could get along with Liddy. I had neither of those qualifications, but I wasn't entirely pleased to trust my future to Mardian. On that uncertain note, the first day of the Watergate cover-up ended.

My life had changed that day. For the first time I realized, and I think we all realized, that we were involved in criminal activity, that if the truth became known we could all go to jail. During the spring, when Liddy was presenting his break-in plan, I should have been aware that it was illegal, but somehow it seemed acceptable, perhaps because we were discussing it in the office of the Attorney General of the United

States. But at some point that Saturday morning I realized that this was not just hard-nosed politics, this was a crime that could destroy us all. The cover-up, thus, was immediate and automatic; no one ever considered that there would *not* be a cover-up. It seemed inconceivable that with our political power we could not erase this mistake we had made.

At that point, LaRue was only marginally involved in the break-in conspiracy, in that he was aware of discussions of it, and Mardian was not to my knowledge involved at all. Either of them might have saved themselves great difficulty by walking away from the whole affair. That they did not was due to personal loyalty to Mitchell and political loyalty to the President. In all our discussions, there was a great deal said about "protecting the President." We were trying to do that, certainly, but it is also true that Mitchell and I hoped to save our own skins in the process. We were in so deep there seemed to be no turning back, no alternative but to plunge ahead. I suppose I considered, if not that first day then in the days ahead, that if I wanted to go to the Justice Department and tell the prosecutors all I knew, I could probably walk away from the mess a free man. But that was never a serious consideration. My fellow conspirators were also my friends, and you didn't save yourself at the expense of your friends.

A call from Haldeman woke me the next morning, Sunday morning.

"Do you think this phone is safe?" he began.

"I don't know. I guess so."

"Okay, what happened?"

Haldeman was as brisk and businesslike as ever. I told him what I knew about McCord's arrest, the Cubans, the money, and so on. We discussed the press statement we had drafted, but never released. McCord's identity had by then become known, and we agreed that a statement must be issued minimizing McCord's ties with CRP. Later that day we issued a statement by Mitchell which stressed the fact that McCord was not technically an "employee" of CRP, since we contracted with his McCord Associates to handle security for CRP. The statement described McCord as "the proprietor of a private security agency who was employed by our committee months ago to assist with the installation of our security system" and who had "a number of other business clients." Mitchell's statement added: "This man and the other people involved were not operating either on our behalf or with our consent."

I told Haldeman of Mitchell's plan to have Mardian return to Washington to take charge of the situation.

"No, the President doesn't trust Mardian," Haldeman said. "You come back and take charge."

"Do you want to tell Mitchell that?"

"No, you tell him. If he has a problem, he can call me."

It was a short talk. I gave him the facts and got my instructions. I spoke with the assumption that he knew about the break-in plan, and nothing he said indicated he did not.

I went to see Mitchell and he accepted Haldeman's proposal that I return to Washington, instead of Mardian, to take charge of the cover-up. I had no objection to the assignment. There was an element of self-protection involved. I was already in such deep trouble that it didn't seem it could be much worse.

I called the airlines and discovered I couldn't get a direct flight back to Washington that day. A strike was set for the next day and all the flights were booked. The best they had was a flight to Chicago, followed by a long wait for a plane to Washington. It was an absurd and maddening situation—the Nixon Administration was threatened, and I couldn't get back to Washington.

"For God's sake, I'll call Sedam and he can charter you a flight from Chicago to Washington," LaRue said, and that is what we did.

The four of us—Mitchell, LaRue, Mardian, and I—walked out into the hotel's bright, flowering gardens for a final talk. We were there less to admire the flowers than to avoid the bugs that in our anxiety we imagined might be hidden in Mitchell's suite. Mitchell stressed that I must find out more about the status of Hunt and Liddy, that I must reassure the CRP staff that all was well, and that I should talk to John Dean about legal aspects of the situation.

Thus instructed, Gail and I packed and a limousine took us to the airport for our flight to Chicago, where a chartered plane was waiting to take us to Washington. Gail was confused by this sudden change in our plans, and by my obvious preoccupation with this burglary in Washington, but our plans had often changed, and I had often been preoccupied, in the past three years, so she took it all in stride. It was past ten when we finally arrived home, too late to do anything more than go to bed.

When I arrived at my office the next morning I stepped immediately into the double life I would live for the next ten months. On the one hand, I spent much of the morning moving about our offices and reassuring CRP's staff that nothing was wrong, that we had no idea what McCord had been up to, that the best thing was for everyone to get back to work. I was cheering up the troops, but I could have used some cheering up myself. I was learning how hard it is to live a lie. I had always been, relative to the norms in the corporate and political worlds in which I moved, an open and direct person. I trusted people and they usually trusted me. To have to lie day after day, to live with a cover-up story that grew more and more complex and difficult to control, became a terrible mental strain.

When I wasn't reassuring the staff that morning, I was meeting with people who had information I needed to sort out the tangled Watergate mess.

The first person I talked to was Hugh Sloan, our treasurer. We knew by then that several thousand dollars in $100 bills had been found on the burglars. What we did not know, and I hoped Sloan could explain, was whether the money had come from CRP and, if so, if there was any way it could be traced to us.

Sloan was nervous when he came to my office, obviously very shaken, and his reply to my question left me shaken too. He said the money found on the burglars was money he had given to Liddy, and that it could probably be traced to us. (Sloan didn't explain how he knew that; I assumed he had spoken with Liddy and gotten the bad news from him.)

The reason the $100 bills could be traced to us resulted from a complex sequence of events. The new campaign-financing law had gone into effect on April 7. Before that date, large political contributions could be made in cash and anonymously; after April 7 all contributions had to be reported. Many donors, particularly those who contribute to both parties, treasure their anonymity, and in the final days before the new law went into effect our Finance Committee was flooded with cash contributions—some $6 million in the last two days.

Two of these last-minute contributions came in the amounts of $89,-000 and $25,000. The $89,000 was originally a cash contribution by some Texas oil men. It was "laundered" through a Mexican bank and brought to Sloan by an oil company executive in the form of four cashier's checks. The $25,000 was originally a cash contribution by Dwayne Andreas, a Minnesota businessman who in 1968 was a major contributor to Hubert Humphrey's campaign. Andreas gave the cash to Kenneth Dahlberg, the Midwestern chairman for the Finance Committee to Re-elect the President, who converted it into a cashier's check which he gave to Maurice Stans, who passed it along to Hugh Sloan.

Sloan and Liddy proceeded to "launder" these two contributions again. Sloan gave Liddy the five cashier's checks, which totaled $114,000, and Liddy gave them to Bernard Barker, the Miami businessman who was to become one of the Watergate burglars. Barker deposited the cashier's checks in his Miami bank in mid-April, and over the next few weeks he withdrew the money in $100 bills. In mid-May, he gave the money back to Liddy, who passed it on to Sloan, minus $2,500 in "expenses."

What no one considered in this process was that Barker's bank, like all banks, was required by law to keep records of the bills it issued in denominations of $100 and above. The bank therefore had a record not only of the Dahlberg and Mexican cashier's checks going into Barker's account, but of the serial numbers of the more than a thousand $100 bills it had paid out to Barker.

Sloan put the $111,500 in identifiable $100 bills into his safe, along with a good deal of other money. By coincidence, when Liddy went to Sloan for more money for his intelligence-gathering operation, Sloan happened to give him several packages of the identifiable $100 bills from Barker's bank. Thus, by chance, the circle was completed—the money that Barker had laundered and returned to the Finance Committee was returned to Barker and the other burglars for the Watergate break-in. If Sloan had picked up another package of $100 bills, or if Sloan or Liddy or Barker had broken the $100s into smaller bills, the Watergate story might have turned out quite differently.

But that was not what happened, and once I had spoken to Sloan I knew our problem had grown more serious. McCord might keep silent, but the fact that the burglars carried money that came from the Finance Committee to Re-elect the President would be hard to explain away.

My talk with Sloan was brief. We had never gotten along well, and I sensed that he blamed whatever had gone wrong on me and the others on the political side of the campaign.

Next I called in Liddy, and it was a new Gordon Liddy who entered my office a moment later. The starch was gone from his spine and the gleam gone from his eye. James Bond had been exposed as a bumbling clown. I almost felt sorry for him. Our talk was brief and almost friendly. There was no point in my berating him.

"It looks like we've got a problem, Gordon," I told him.

"Yeah," he admitted, eyes downcast. "I goofed."

"Gordon, let's face it, you and I can't work together. Why don't you talk to Dean? He's going to help us on this problem."

"Okay."

"You don't have any records that would cause us a problem, do you?"

"I've shredded them all."

"Okay, Gordon. I'll talk to Dean and ask him to call you."

"Okay," Liddy echoed, and left my office.

I called Dean, who'd just returned from a trip to the Far East, briefed him on the situation, and asked him to talk to Liddy. Then I called Strachan and passed on the bad news I'd gotten from Sloan.

"I assume you're not going to have any documents in your files that would cause us a problem," I said to Strachan.

"We won't," Strachan said. "I assume you won't either."

After I finished with Strachan, I asked Hugh Sloan to return to my office. I was worried about him and concerned to see him so shaken. As I understood the new campaign-finance law, he might be personally responsible, as our treasurer, for any infractions of the law. I wondered if he understood that, and I asked him if he had reported the disbursements that he'd made to Liddy.

Sloan said he had not, and that the reports had already been filed with the Government Accounting Office.

"Hugh, you may have a problem," I said. "You may have to find some other way to explain that money."

"Do you mean commit perjury?"

"You might have to."

Sloan shook his head and departed, a very despondent young man, and one who was to be the source of many problems for us and many leaks to the newspapers.

I received a call that afternoon from Lee Jablonski, Mitchell's secretary, who told me that Martha had found out about the arrests—which they'd managed to keep from her for two days—and that she was extremely upset, particularly about our firing McCord, whom she'd known and liked. Lee said that Mitchell and LaRue and Mardian were on a plane returning to Washington, and that if Martha called me I should talk to her and try to calm her. She did call me, not long after that.

"Why are you firing Jim McCord?" she demanded. "Why are you throwing him to the wolves? You know he couldn't have done anything wrong."

"Martha, we'll do what we can for him," I assured her. "We don't know *what's* going on. But we can't keep him on the payroll after he's been arrested in the Democratic headquarters."

But I didn't succeed in calming Martha, and a few days later Steve King and a doctor had to overpower her and give her a shot to calm her down, at least as Martha told the story.

Also that day, I received a call from Roy Gooderall, one of Vice President Agnew's political aides, who asked me to explain to him what the Watergate break-in was all about, so he could brief Agnew.

"I'm sorry, Roy," I said, "but I can only talk to the Veep directly about this. Have him call me."

I got word that Mitchell wanted me to meet with him and Mardian and LaRue when he returned to his Watergate apartment about 6 P.M. Rob Odle had returned the Gemstone file to me; I put it in my briefcase and at the appointed hour I had Carl Foster, my driver, take me to the Watergate.

Mitchell's apartment was like a morgue. John Dean had arrived a few minutes before I did, and he, Mitchell, Mardian, and LaRue were sitting there drinking and talking in bitter, despondent voices. Dean reported on his talk that afternoon with Liddy.

"He said it was all Jeb's fault for cutting his budget," Dean said drily. "But he said he was a good soldier and he'd never talk. He said if we wanted to shoot him on the street he was ready."

There was general discussion of the situation, but nothing of substance was said. We had lost control of events—we were passive bystanders now, waiting to see what others would do, the Cubans, McCord, Liddy, the police, the newspapers, the Justice Department. More drinks were passed around, and I could see a long evening of booze and self-pity shaping up. The prospect was not an inviting one, and I was pleased to receive an unexpected call from John Damgard, the Vice President's appointments secretary, who asked if I wanted to round out a tennis foursome with Agnew that evening. That sounded more inviting than the foursome of Mitchell, Dean, Mardian, and LaRue, so I accepted.

Before I left, however, I addressed a final question to Mitchell.

"I have the Gemstone file," I said. "What do you want me to do with it?"

"Maybe you ought to have a little fire at your house tonight," Mitchell replied.

I nodded and left. I had Carl drive me to my office, where I picked up my tennis clothes, then out to the Linden Hill indoor courts in Bethesda, Maryland. I sent Carl home, and went inside, carrying my tennis togs and the suitcase with the Gemstone file. It was around nine o'clock, and I'd missed dinner, but dinner was the least of my worries.

For three years, I'd seen Agnew from time to time and one of us would say, "We've got to play some tennis," but we never had. At the time, I was so glad for the diversion that I assumed his invitation on this particular night was only a coincidence; it was only later that I realized that Agnew had wanted a chance to ask me about the Watergate break-in. I must have seemed his best source of information, since we'd always gotten along well, while most of the White House people had scorned him.

We played three sets, with Damgard and me beating Agnew and his partner, a man from the State Department. I left my clothes and the briefcase on the floor beside the court while we played. When we finished, around eleven at night, Agnew called me aside.

"Jeb, what the hell is going on?"

My instinct was to be candid. "It was our operation," I said. "It got screwed up. We're trying to take care of it."

Agnew frowned and looked away. "I don't think we ought to discuss it again, in that case."

Damgard gave me a ride home. It was close to midnight when I arrived. Gail and the children were asleep. I went to the kitchen and drank a glass of milk, then I walked into the living room to burn the Gemstone papers in our fireplace.

The file was about four or five inches thick, about half photographs and half transcripts of telephone conversations. I couldn't just toss the whole thing in; I had to get the fire going and feed the papers in, a few at a time. I sat cross-legged on the floor in front of the fireplace, glancing at the Gemstone papers before I tossed them into the fire, chuckling at Harry Flemming's unexpected conversation with the Democratic official, and at the graphic details of the social lives of some of the Democratic Committee staff people. The photographs, I discovered, blazed brightly, the way Christmas trees and certain kinds of paper do; for a moment the fire seemed to leap out at me. A sudden thought crossed my mind: what if a passing policeman saw the blaze through the window and came to investigate? Commit a crime and the world is made of passing policemen.

No policeman came, only Gail, awakened by me or perhaps by the crackling of the fire.

"What in the world are you doing?" she asked. "You're going to burn the house down."

"It's all right," I said. "It's just some papers I have to get rid of."

Gail, of course, knew nothing of the break-in plot. There had been one awkward exchange between us that spring, at the time when Liddy's plan was under consideration and when we were worried about demonstrations if we held our convention in San Diego.

"If the convention is in San Diego," I remarked to her one night, "we may have to grab some of the radical leaders and take them to Mexico."

"How would they get back?" Gail asked incredulously.

"They might not get back," I said.

My remark was meant as a joke, but Gail was horrified.

"What are you talking about?" she cried. "You can't do things like that. That's insane."

I realized I had spoken out of turn, and I said no more to her about our cops-and-robbers schemes.

Now, as she watched me sitting by the fireplace in my tennis togs, trying to keep my bonfire under control, she asked with some annoyance:

"Jeb, what would we tell the firemen if you burned the house down in June?"

"I don't know," I admitted, and Gail sat down beside me as I finished my chore. As I watched the last of the Gemstone file going up in smoke, I thought of how much those papers had cost, and how worthless they had been, and I wondered how much more they might cost, and how much else might go up in smoke, before this insane affair was ended.

When all the documents were burned away, I poked at the ashes, lest some phantom passing policeman might yet discover the charred evidence, and when Gemstone was all ashes I said good night to Gail and took a bath and, finally, got to bed.

CHAPTER XII

The Cover Story

ONCE WE AT CRP DENIED any involvement in the Watergate break-in, it became necessary for us to develop a complicated cover story that would place the full blame on Gordon Liddy and would show that he had misappropriated for his own illicit ends money we had given him for legitimate purposes.

The basic cover story was developed in a series of meetings held in Mitchell's office in the four weeks following the break-in. Normally, Mitchell, LaRue, and I would attend those sessions on the cover story, and sometimes Dean and Mardian joined us. There were many other meetings that I did not attend that dealt with other aspects of the problem—the PR end of it, for example, or the raising of money for the defendants and their lawyers.

My involvement focused on our explanation of why we had authorized Liddy $250,000 for a program of security and intelligence-gathering— our explanation of why this was for legal, rather than illegal, ends. In effect, we had to invent a legitimate program that Liddy might have been carrying out. We all discussed the cover story at length, but I was its principal author, since I was the one who was going to tell it to the FBI, the grand jury, the prosecutors from the U. S. Attorney's Office, and eventually to the judge and jury in the Watergate trial.

The basic goal of the cover story was to make Liddy solely responsible for the break-in. We assumed that Hunt and Liddy would soon be implicated, because of the money and the address books found on the original five burglars. We assumed that Liddy, Hunt, and McCord (and the four Cubans, if they knew) would keep silent about the break-in having been approved by Mitchell. Our all-consuming fear was that if the blame moved past Liddy it would swiftly reach the President himself and endanger his reelection.

I was the next line of defense after Liddy. I told Mitchell that if necessary I would take the blame by telling the prosecutors I had authorized the break-in without his knowledge. Mitchell did not reject my offer immediately. I later discovered that he discussed it with Dean and Ehrlichman at the White House, and that Ehrlichman initially thought it was a rather good idea. However, once they discussed the matter fully, they realized that blaming me wouldn't work. Too many people knew that I had no authority to approve $250,000 for anything. Thus, if the blame moved past Liddy, it swiftly bypassed me and reached Mitchell. And if it reached him, the President's close friend and campaign manager, it would in effect touch the President himself. Thus, as we struggled to hide the truth about the Watergate burglary, we could tell ourselves that we were "protecting the President," and to a degree that was true.

Mitchell resigned as campaign director on the first of July, and after that almost all the cover-up meetings I attended were held in his office in his law firm, which was just across the hall from CRP at 1701 Pennsylvania Avenue. I was still working an eleven- or twelve-hour day as deputy director of the campaign, but a summons from Mitchell took precedence over all but the most urgent campaign business.

The meetings in Mitchell's office were calm, low-keyed, and businesslike. Sometimes we discussed the campaign as well as the cover-up. Sometimes there were long pauses in our deliberations, as we confronted questions that seemed to have no answers, but there was no sense of embarrassment or shame as we planned the cover-up. If anything, there was a certain self-righteousness to our deliberations. We had persuaded ourselves that what we had done, although technically illegal, was not wrong or even unusual, and that our enemies in the press and in the political world were trying to make a mountain out of a molehill, trying to use this minor incident as a means to destroy Richard Nixon. After the Democrats nominated Senator McGovern, we felt that we were protecting the honorable peace that the President was bringing to Vietnam and avoiding the national disaster that would follow if McGovern became President. We were not covering up a burglary, we were safeguarding world peace. It was a rationalization we all found easy to accept.

We did not discuss the Watergate affair in terms of perjury or burglary or conspiracy. We would refer, rather, to "handling the case" and "making sure things don't get out of hand." Essentially, we used management terms to discuss a legal problem. Yet we were not dealing with a tidy managerial problem. There were many loose ends and much confusion to the Watergate cover-up. We often didn't know what was coming next, and for a while the federal prosecutors seemed to be as confused as we were. It was a time, for me and I think for all of us, of intense pressure and pervasive fatalism. Fred LaRue and I used to joke that as the cover-up continued, our drinking was increasing and our sex drives were diminishing.

Fred was the only person I could discuss the Watergate affair with in any detail. Mardian and I were not close and I avoided him because I thought he was erratic and might make some blunder that would blow the cover-up. Dean and I would sometimes discuss the case on the basis of, "Well, this is insane, but here we are," but Dean was not a personal friend of mine in the sense that LaRue was. LaRue and I would often end the day with a drink in his office and a discussion of the complexities of the case. Fred saw little hope for us; he would say, in more or less these words:

"No Administration can withstand the kind of investigation we're going to be put through—there'll be Congress, the grand jury, the civil suits, the newspapers, investigations going on for years. There are just too many bodies buried, too many problems, too many loose ends. We may make it, but I doubt it."

He was right, of course, and I think that at bottom we all sensed the futility of the cover-up, but we saw no alternative to it except the unthinkable one of admitting our guilt, both to ourselves and to the world.

On Tuesday, June 20, Larry O'Brien announced that he was bringing a civil lawsuit against the various officers of the Committee to Re-elect the President. This would allow the Democrats to probe our files via the legal "discovery" process, and it caused us to take two actions. First, Mitchell agreed that we must retain lawyers to defend us in the civil suit and other Watergate-related matters. We soon retained two outstanding Republican lawyers in Washington, Kenneth Parkinson, an expert on civil law, and Paul O'Brien, who was known as an astute "political" lawyer. They were our "outside" lawyers, and Bob Mardian served as our "in-house" counsel on Watergate, with assistance from Dean, LaRue, and Mitchell. CRP's general counsel, Glenn Sedam, was furious at having been "passed over" in favor of Mardian; only later did he realize what a favor we had done him.

Our other response to Larry O'Brien's lawsuit was to make sure that we destroyed all possibly incriminating documents. Bart Porter balanced out his cash accounts and destroyed all records of his cash payments to Liddy. Bob Reisner went through my files and removed all sensitive political material. I called Gordon Strachan and we assured one another that our respective files had been sanitized.

I also mentioned to Mitchell that morning the exchange I'd had with Agnew the night before.

"You shouldn't have done that," Mitchell said. "Don't do it again."

"I didn't know what else to do," I said. "He's the Vice President and he asked me so I told him."

"Well, just don't discuss the facts with anyone," Mitchell told me.

Our basic problem in that first week concerned the money we had authorized for Liddy. We knew that the five burglars had $5,300 of our money on them when they were arrested and that the money could probably be traced to us. We knew that the investigation would soon move from the five burglars to Liddy, and we would soon be called on to explain why we had given Liddy the $5,300 and how much more we had given him. We knew that we had authorized $250,000 to Liddy, much of it for an illegal wiretapping and burglary operation. What we *didn't* know, and this was a major problem for several weeks, was how much of the $250,000 had actually been disbursed to Liddy by Hugh Sloan, the treasurer of our Finance Committee.

Our first need, therefore, was to find out from our campaign treasurer how much of the authorized $250,000 he had given Liddy. A rather incredible problem arose when Sloan refused to answer the question. I spoke to Sloan twice that week and he simply wouldn't give me a figure. He would say that he didn't have it, or hadn't figured it out yet, or that he had to talk to his boss, Maurice Stans, or something. The situation with Sloan was complex and delicate. We didn't know how much he knew. I suspected that he knew something about the break-in plan— and thus knew what the money was going for—because he was friendly with Liddy, who had probably boasted to him about his project. It eventually turned out that he'd given Liddy an amazingly large portion of the $250,000, and I suspected that was the reason he had been so reluctant to reveal the figure to us.

On Friday of that week, Chapin called me to say that he'd seen Sloan at a party the night before and that Sloan had been telling people he thought Mitchell and I were involved in the Watergate break-in. Sloan later charged that I had tried to persuade him to perjure himself to help us hide the payments to Liddy.

I never felt that Sloan's actions were motivated by any high-mindedness, but by personal animosity and by a desire to protect himself from any involvement in wrongdoing. Sloan felt he had been shunted aside by the White House, resented the fact that Mitchell wouldn't deal with him directly, and seemed to resent me and the authority I had in the campaign. He seemed to be bitter that he didn't have a bigger role, but the fact was that he hadn't sufficient experience. Rob Odle, who was friendly with Sloan, would often come to me and say Sloan was upset about this or that affront. I would tell Rob that I just didn't have time to worry about Sloan's sensitivities. But, once the cover-up began, I would have to spend a good deal of time worrying about them.

If Sloan had been someone we trusted, we might have sought his assistance in the cover-up. If Sloan had said he had given Liddy $20,000, for example, that would have been a great deal easier to explain to investigators than $200,000. But we didn't trust Sloan and we certainly weren't going to ask him to perjure himself. In my discussions with him that week, I told him we needed a figure, that it would be helpful if it was a low figure rather than a high one, but that I could live with any figure if he'd just give me one. But he wouldn't give it, so a basic element of our cover story was left dangling for three weeks. This led us to solve the problem by constructing a cover story that assumed a large figure, rather than a low one, so that we didn't need Sloan's cooperation.

I discussed the Sloan problem with Mitchell on Saturday, the 24th, and he summoned Sloan to his office. Once again, Sloan claimed he didn't know how much money he'd given Liddy. Sloan was extremely nervous and distraught. He looked as if one puff of air might make him crumble like a dry leaf. He told Mitchell that the FBI wanted to interview him and asked Mitchell what he should do. That was when Mitchell made his comment, "When the going gets tough, the tough get going." That didn't seem to be what Sloan had wanted to hear, and he wandered off looking more dejected than ever.

Sloan apparently went downstairs to the Finance Committee offices and talked to Stans, because Stans called and told Mitchell he wanted to come up and see him. I offered to leave, but Mitchell said I should stay. Stans came in and asked Mitchell to tell him what this Watergate business was all about. Mitchell replied that Liddy had been the cause of the problem and we'd probably have to fire Liddy.

"We have this problem with Sloan," Mitchell continued. "We need to know how much money he gave Liddy, and he won't give us a figure. I wish you'd ask him to be more cooperative."

Stans said he'd speak to Sloan, but in fact Sloan left that very day for a vacation in Bermuda without ever giving us a figure. The first full week of the cover-up ended on that confusing and frustrating note.

By the next week, FBI agents were questioning members of our staff. On Wednesday, June 28, they tried to interview Liddy. He refused to answer their questions, and Mitchell fired him. Liddy had, of course, assured us of his silence—he had goofed, but he would be a good soldier to the end, as indeed he was.

It was obvious that the FBI agents would soon get to me, and so, in meetings that week, Mitchell, Mardian, LaRue, Dean, and I nailed down several key elements of our cover story:

—We would not try to conceal the fact that we had authorized $250,000 to Liddy for intelligence-gathering operations. Too many people knew that—people at the Finance Committee, Reisner and Porter, various secretaries—for us to think it could be concealed. Rather, we would admit the $250,000 had been authorized, but claim it was for legitimate activities, some of which we would have to invent, and claim the break-in was some wild scheme Liddy had carried out on his own.

—Pending a figure from Sloan, we would assume we had to account for at least $100,000 that had been given to Liddy. I knew that Bart Porter had advanced him some $35,000 for various investigations and trips to San Diego, Miami Beach, and elsewhere. My best guess was that Sloan had given him between $40,000 and $70,000 for the first two months of Liddy's operations. I had forgotten the figure of $83,000, which was the original up-front money I had authorized Sloan to give Liddy. The prosecutors would later press me very hard on my forgetting that figure, but the truth was that it was a very minor element of the campaign and the figure simply slipped my mind.

—To make our cover story as plausible as possible, we would volunteer that Liddy's work had included such things as investigating Jack Anderson and the Muskie contributor who was supposedly a polluter. We would also stress Liddy's legitimate work, such as gathering information on the demonstrations that radical groups planned for our convention, but we would exaggerate the amounts involved, as a means of covering the amounts actually spent on the Watergate break-in.

—We all agreed that we badly needed someone to corroborate my account of Liddy's activities. We agreed the corroboration should not come from Mitchell, for we hoped to keep him out of the investigation entirely. We succeeded to some extent, in that Mitchell was not called to testify in the Watergate trial early the next year. Mardian or LaRue might have corroborated my story, since they were already involved in the cover-up, but that did not make much sense because their roles in the campaign would not logically have involved them in the matter of Liddy's finances.

We discussed various people on the staff who might be called upon to back me up, and we kept returning to the head of our surrogate program, Bart Porter.

It made sense. Porter had handled money for us and, as we were ready to admit, had given Liddy money for several intelligence-gathering activities. Porter was in charge of the surrogate speakers program, and I was coming to think that we could devise a story that much of the money to Liddy had gone to protect the surrogates. Moreover, Porter was attractive and articulate, and I thought he would make a persuasive witness.

There remained the question of whether Porter would commit perjury for us. To be candid, I thought there were several people on the staff who would, because they would not consider it committing perjury, but protecting the President from enemies who were out to destroy him. But I was most confident of Porter, for he was famous for his loyalty to the President—it was Porter who once spoke of how he had worn his first Nixon button at age eight, when his parents were working in an early Nixon campaign.

Besides loyalty, Porter was extremely ambitious, both socially and politically. Unlike most of the young men at the White House and CRP, he cared a lot about Georgetown dinner parties and the Washington social scene. And we were all well aware that Porter had a consuming desire to get ahead in the Nixon Administration. He'd been in the White House and gotten a taste of the limousines and all the other amenities and he wanted eagerly to have them for his own. He and I often discussed his ambitions, which if not well focused, were nonetheless large.

Porter's problem was that he had performed well as one of my project managers in the White House, and he handled the surrogate program well, but people like Higby and Chapin were forever complaining to me about Porter—they just didn't like him personally. I liked Porter. I saw a good deal of him socially, and I was often cast in the role of his defender. Porter knew this, and knew that his future in the Administration might depend on the kind of support I gave him.

So, one day that week, either Thursday or Friday, I called him into my office, shut the door, and asked him to sit down.

"Bart," I began, "I've just come from a meeting with Mr. Mitchell and Mr. LaRue, and your name was mentioned as someone we could count on in dealing with this Watergate case."

Porter nodded eagerly. This was, of course, at a time when most of the people on our staff were eager to help out in the Watergate defense— Rob Odle, for example, was furious with me because I wouldn't involve him in the matter.

"Bart," I continued, "you know that we just fired Liddy."

"Sure," Porter said.

"It's apparent that this break-in was something Liddy cooked up on his own. Doesn't that sound like the sort of stupid thing that Liddy would do?"

Porter laughed. "It sure does," he agreed.

"I want to assure you, Bart, that I didn't know anything at all about this break-in, that Mr. Mitchell didn't, that none of us did."

"I know that, Jeb."

"The thing is, Bart, we still have a problem about the money. Gordon was authorized money for some dirty tricks. You knew about Sedan Chair, but there were some other things you didn't know about. Nothing illegal, but things that could be very embarrassing to the President, and to Mr. Mitchell and Mr. Haldeman and others. Do you follow me?"

"Sure. Sure, Jeb."

"So, I was talking to Mr. Mitchell about this problem, and your name came up as someone who's loyal to the President and whom we could count on to help out."

"You know I'll do anything I can, Jeb."

"Bart, you know that the Democrats have filed a suit against us and they're seeking immediate discovery, and we've got the grand jury and the FBI investigations, and if all these people start getting into our records we're going to have some real problems."

"Just tell me what I can do, Jeb. Be specific."

"Well, as the person in charge of our surrogate program, you've been concerned about radicals disrupting our rallies. Right?"

"Right!"

"Suppose, then, that we'd authorized money to Liddy, not for the dirty tricks, but to infiltrate the radical groups, as a way of protecting the President and the surrogates. Suppose we had started that program last December. Could such a program have cost $100,000?"

"Jeb, that's easy. You could have hired ten college students and paid them a thousand dollars a month, $500 for salary, $500 for expenses, for ten months. That's $100,000 right there, and that's not very much money in a $45-million campaign."

"That's true, Bart. That's certainly true."

I paused a moment. It had gone about as I had expected.

"Bart, would you be willing, if I told the FBI that Liddy was authorized to spend $100,000 that way, to corroborate my story? To say that I came to you last December, and said we needed a surrogate protection program, and that you estimated it would cost $100,000?"

"Yes, I probably would do that."

"Bart, you've got to understand that you'll have to tell this story to the grand jury, and you could have a problem if anything went wrong. On the other hand, we expect everything to go well, and if it does I have assurances from Mr. Mitchell that people like you who were loyal to the President will be very well remembered in the next Administration."

Perhaps it hadn't occurred to Porter that anything could go wrong, for he hesitated a moment.

"I need some time to think about it, Jeb."

"Fine, Bart. You take all the time you want."

I tried to get away from Washington as often as possible for long weekends with my family, and on Friday, June 30, we flew down to the Sea Pines Plantation on Hilton Head Island, South Carolina, for the Fourth of July weekend.

We had barely unpacked when LaRue called and said I must return to Washington the next morning to meet with Mitchell. He didn't say why, but we all knew what a serious problem Mitchell was having with his wife, who that week had been calling reporters and saying she was a "political prisoner."

I flew back to Washington Saturday morning and met with Mitchell and LaRue in Mitchell's CRP office at about 10 A.M. Mitchell got right to the point—he was resigning as campaign director.

Even though I'd suspected this was coming, I was stunned. Tears came to my eyes. I'd worked closely with Mitchell for more than a year, I'd come to have great affection for him, and the prospect of his leaving was a terrible jolt.

We talked for quite a while. Mitchell said that Clark MacGregor, the former Minnesota congressman who'd been serving as the White House director of Congressional Relations, was coming over to replace him as campaign director. He said that the White House wanted me to continue in my same capacity with the new title of deputy director (I had been called chief of staff), and that Fred Malek would also be made a deputy director and would direct our trouble-ridden field operations. Mitchell stressed that he was not leaving because of the Watergate case, but because of the problems with his wife, and also because he believed his daughter Marty needed more of his time and attention.

When I left Mitchell's office, I went to my own office and called Larry Higby. I was terribly upset by Mitchell's departure, and it occurred to me that he might not have been telling me the whole story, that perhaps the White House wanted my resignation along with his, but had been afraid to ask for it because of my knowledge of Watergate.

"Larry," I told Higby, "you tell Bob that if he wants me to resign all he has to do is say so. I won't cause any problems. Just say so if that's what you want."

"Nobody wants you to resign," Higby assured me.

We left it at that, then a minute later, Higby called back and said Haldeman wanted to talk to me.

"No, I'm too upset to talk to him now," I said.

"Well, Bob wants you to know that he and the President want you to stay."

"Okay," I said. "If that's what they want, I'll stay."

After that talk, and despite that talk, I sat alone in my office for nearly an hour in a state of total depression. I was upset because of Mitchell's leaving, and because of Watergate hanging over me, and by my uncertain status at CRP with MacGregor and Malek coming in. The reelection campaign that had started out so well fourteen months before was starting to look like a disaster, and my own future looked pretty bleak as well.

There was speculation that the President fired Mitchell because of Watergate, and that Mitchell used his wife's behavior as a convenient cover story. I doubted that. At the time Mitchell resigned, the Watergate affair seemed to be under control, but Mitchell's problems with his wife, and with his daughter as well, were very real. It might be that Nixon did nothing to discourage Mitchell's departure, but if nothing else, Nixon needed Mitchell's cooperation in the cover-up.

I know nothing to indicate that Nixon was aware in advance of the plan to break into the Democratic headquarters. It is possible that Mitchell or Haldeman told him in advance, but I think it's likelier that they would not have mentioned it unless the operation had produced some results of interest to him. Based on my knowledge of how the White House operated, I would suspect that once the burglars were arrested, Nixon immediately demanded and got the full story, and that thereafter he kept in close personal touch with the cover-up operation, through Mitchell and Haldeman. It's possible that they kept the truth from him, either to shield him from involvement or out of fear of his wrath, but I think it much more likely that he would demand the truth and they would provide it.

I think the White House always assumed that Mitchell would hold, that he would protect the President no matter what happened. I suspect they were less certain of me, and thought it best to keep me at CRP where they could exercise some control over me. I was told later that John Dean urged that I be let go when Mitchell resigned. If that had happened, it would have created a presumption of my guilt that would probably have led to my being indicted and tried along with Hunt, McCord, Liddy, and the others. If that had happened, I think I would have held to the cover story, but the White House had no way of knowing that, so they chose to keep me.

Also, if the White House had given any indication of throwing either me or Mitchell overboard, it might have discouraged Hunt and Liddy, and everything depended on their keeping silent. I was often told, by Dean and others, "It's not just Watergate, Jeb, there's more that we can't let come out." At the time I didn't know what he meant. In retrospect, I think Dean had in mind the plumbers program, involving Hunt and Liddy, which included the break-in at the office of Daniel Ellsberg's psychiatrist. Thus, I think that making sure that Mitchell and Magruder held on Watergate was tied in with making sure Hunt and Liddy held on the plumbers program—the whole thing had become a fantastic house of cards, one the slightest gust of wind from any direction might send tumbling down.

When I made my first appearance before the grand jury investigating the Watergate break-in, on the morning of Wednesday, July 5, we had agreed to the broad outlines of the cover-up story, but many of the details were still fuzzy. I was prepared to bluff the story if necessary, but the grand jury was just getting started, other CRP people who'd testified had not been pressed very hard, and we hoped I wouldn't be either.

Rob Odle had been one of the first to testify. As our director of administration, Rob was asked to explain who did what at CRP. Rob was completely innocent of any involvement in, or knowledge of, the Watergate break-in, but despite his innocence he proved to be a bad witness. He was nervous, and he had a habit of answering a question with a question of his own. We were told that as a result of his demeanor, plus the fact that he was McCord's immediate superior, the prosecutors for a time suspected that Odle might be the mastermind of the Watergate plot.

My testimony was brief and uneventful. I sat in a witness chair in a large room in the Federal Courthouse, with the prosecutors behind a table on my left and the twenty-odd members of the grand jury on a raised platform on my right, some of them seeming bored by the proceedings. I explained what I did at CRP, how we were organized, and how we related to the Finance Committee. The investigation was still in a very basic stage, and it appeared that I was not under any kind of suspicion. One of the prosecutors asked if I'd been interviewed yet by the FBI. I said I had not. The prosecutors preferred for an FBI interview to precede grand jury testimony, so I was told I would be excused for the time being.

At the end of work that day, at Mardian's insistence, I had a drink with Hugh Sloan, who had returned from Bermuda and still hadn't given us a figure on his disbursements to Liddy. I saw Sloan reluctantly, for by then I knew he was blaming me and Mitchell for Watergate, but Sloan remained a central figure in the situation and Mardian, for some reason, thought I should talk to him.

We drove over to the Black Horse Tavern, a quiet restaurant a few blocks from my office, and once again he claimed he didn't have a figure yet. He said he'd try to get one the next day. At that time, I still thought he might have given Liddy as little as $45,000 and I asked if that might be the figure he might tell the investigators. Sloan apparently knew the figure was larger than that, because he told me:

"If I'm asked point-blank, did Mr. Liddy ever receive $45,000, of course I'll say yes. But I won't stop there. If I'm asked if he got more than that, I'll say yes. If they ask what the total figure is, I'll answer to the best of my knowledge."

"I have no problem with that," I told him. "All I'm asking for is a figure. I'd like a low figure, but I can live with any figure, if you'll just give us one."

"I'll try to get you one tomorrow," Sloan promised.

In fact, he never did give me a figure. A few days later he told Mardian he'd given $199,000 to Liddy, an incredible amount, given the fact that Liddy was only two and a half months into his operation when it was terminated. I had to assume that Sloan had been stalling us because he knew he couldn't justify a $199,000 outlay to Liddy. But Sloan's $199,000 figure didn't matter much, because we'd gotten around the problem by developing a story that could account for Liddy's full $250,000 if necessary.

By then, the FBI had asked to interview both me and Bart Porter. I went to Porter to get his decision on corroborating my story, and, as I had expected, he said he would do it.

Three FBI agents came to see me one day late that week. Like the grand jury, they were just getting into the case and didn't have a good grasp on it. They were extremely interested in the cash disbursements Sloan had made to Liddy, which they seemed to think violated the campaign-finance law. I explained that we at CRP had authorized payments to Liddy, but that they would have to talk to Sloan at the Finance Committee about the payments and the records of them.

"But they were giving him *cash*," one of the agents said.

"There's nothing wrong with that."

"But why did you deal in cash?"

"Liddy asked for cash. He said the people he dealt with wanted cash."

"But weren't you suspicious?"

"I assumed Liddy knew what he was doing."

It was part of our strategy to concede the undeniable fact that our bookkeeping had been sloppy. It was also part of our strategy to point the finger at Liddy, by volunteering that he'd been involved in intelligence-gathering operations. We knew that would come out eventually, and it would enhance our credibility if we helped the investigators along.

The FBI interview did not touch any vital areas. At that point, we had the advantage of a certain built-in confusion. Our operation and its finances were so complex that it took the investigators several weeks to decipher them. It was hard for them to know whom to talk to and what questions to ask. Neither the FBI nor the prosecutors ever interviewed Bob Reisner in 1972; if they had, it might have blown the entire cover-up sky high. The investigators knew that the transcripts from the wiretapping of the Democratic headquarters had gone into a file called the Gemstone file. I assume they learned this from Alfred Baldwin, who had monitored the phone calls for Liddy and who had cooperated with the prosecutors. Bob Reisner had seen the Gemstone file on my desk, although he did not know what was in it. He also knew that I'd taken the Gemstone file to one of my meetings with Mitchell. Reisner didn't know the importance of the information he had, but if he'd been asked the right questions, his answers would have taken the wiretapping scheme directly to me and Mitchell.

We probably profited, too, by a reluctance on the part of the FBI, and the prosecutors too, to charge in like gangbusters to the Committee to Re-elect the President and start grilling men who had high-level influence in the Nixon Administration. But the prosecutors, if cautious, were thorough, and eventually got the job done.

The next week, around July 12 or 13, I had an unexpected conversation with Ken Parkinson, one of the lawyers we'd retained to handle the Watergate suits. Parkinson was in his mid-forties, very precise and self-confident, a partner in a leading Washington law firm and an expert on civil law. Another lawyer once told me, in praising Parkinson as a courtroom tactician, that he was "a master of delay."

Bob Mardian brought Parkinson to my office, and once they were settled, Mardian said to me:

"Jeb, I want you to tell Ken the truth about Watergate."

I looked at Mardian in surprise. Aside from my slip-up with the Vice President, I hadn't told *anyone* outside our circle the truth about Watergate. The cover-up story had become our official "truth."

"Do you mean *the* truth?" I asked Mardian.

"Yes."

"Bob, Mitchell told me not to do that."

"No, he said this was all right."

I shrugged and proceeded to spend two hours telling Parkinson the truth about Watergate. The lawyer listened intently and took notes. My recitation was punctuated only by Mardian's anguished comments: "Oh, God, no!" . . . "You didn't meet in *Mitchell's* office?" . . . "How could you be so *stupid*?" For Mardian, although aware of the basic facts, had apparently never heard all the grisly details. Or, if he had, he was putting on a good show for Parkinson's benefit.

When I finished, the two men thanked me and left, Mardian looking aghast, Parkinson looking concerned.

Mitchell called me to his office a little later that day. Mardian was with him.

"Jeb," Mitchell said gravely, "I gather that you told Ken Parkinson the true story."

I was astounded.

"Mardian *told* me that you wanted me to tell him the true story," I said.

"No, we shouldn't discuss it with the lawyers," Mitchell said. "We have to protect the lawyers."

Our exchange ended on that inconclusive note. To this day I don't know why Mardian had me tell the story to Parkinson, but it was typical of Mardian's erratic behavior. As I understood it, the lawyers had been kept in the dark until then—Mardian and LaRue hadn't even let them interview Mitchell. But, once I told Parkinson the truth, he went straight from my office to Mitchell's office, and confronted Mitchell with what I had said. Mitchell promptly denied it.

Those events later caused Parkinson legal problems. Lawyers can knowingly defend guilty men, but one thing lawyers can't do is knowingly be a party to perjury. Parkinson's problems arose from his continuing to represent us even after I had told him I was perjuring myself. His defense was that Mitchell had denied my story, and that he'd believed Mitchell's account rather than mine.

We finally wrapped up the cover story that weekend. Parkinson told me he needed a written account of our version of Liddy's activities for the prosecutors. Bart Porter and I wrote our account on a Friday and took it to Parkinson's law office on the morning of Saturday, the 15th. He said it needed more detail, and we decided to discuss it further over lunch. We walked over to Gusti's Restaurant on M Street and had a beer and Italian food on their sidewalk cafe while we discussed the statement and the situation in general. I must have been depressed that day, because Porter and I discussed what would happen if we were indicted. In those days, I could not imagine going to prison; when I worried it was simply about the disgrace of being indicted.

That afternoon Porter and I rewrote the cover story into its final form. As it turned out, Parkinson never turned our report over to the prosecutors, but at that point, in mid-July, the cover story was complete. For better or worse, we were stuck with it.

Our story began with the admission that Mitchell, as director of CRP, had authorized the Finance Committee to give Liddy $250,000 for a program of security and intelligence-gathering. Of this, we said, $100,000 was for a surrogate protection program wherein ten young people would be paid $1,000 a month for ten months to infiltrate radical groups that might endanger our thirty-odd surrogate speakers as they traveled around the country. This was necessary, we said, because several of our headquarters had already been firebombed, our speakers had been heckled and threatened, and if we were going to send them around the country we had a responsibility to protect them.

The remaining $150,000, we said, was primarily to provide security for our convention, and also for such things as Liddy's investigation of Jack Anderson, and of Senator Muskie's water-polluting contributor. Convention security would include such things as hiring and equipping agents to infiltrate radical groups that might disrupt the convention, as well as Liddy's own expenses. We stressed that convention security had become doubly expensive when we had shifted the convention from San Diego to Miami Beach.

All the activities we outlined were legitimate and logical. The problem with our story was that we couldn't document a dime's worth of it, much less a quarter of a million dollars. The fact was that on the Saturday the break-in was discovered, Liddy, hoping he could disassociate himself entirely from his intelligence-gathering role, had shredded all his receipts and documents, not only the ones relating to his illegal activities, but the ones that documented his legitimate intelligence-gathering work and that would have been useful to us in supporting the cover-up.

Our position was that we had authorized the $250,000 to be spent during the campaign and that if Sloan said he had advanced $199,000 of that we were surprised but that was within Sloan's authority. We admitted that we had practiced shoddy bookkeeping. When pressed for proof of how Liddy had spent the money, all we could say was, "Talk to Liddy." And Liddy, of course, wasn't talking.

Several weeks went by and we became increasingly worried because I had not been called back before the grand jury. It appeared that the grand jury was taking its time, building its case carefully. At some point in early August the prosecutors told our lawyers that I was a target of the grand jury investigation, a warning they are required to give if that is the case. As far as I knew, all they had against me was Sloan's charge that I had asked him to perjure himself, which I knew to be false, or at best a misunderstanding. As the days went by, we began to fear that the grand jury might simply indict me without calling me to testify again. That was upsetting, for I at least wanted a chance to sell the story I'd taken such pains to concoct.

During this period, when it seemed possible that I might be indicted, both Dean and Mitchell assured me that if I was tried, or imprisoned, I would receive financial support and there was a good chance that the President would exercise executive clemency to keep me out of prison. I recall Dean coming to my office one afternoon, after he had attended a meeting with Mitchell, and reassuring me on this issue.

I was standing at my window, looking out at Pennsylvania Avenue, and Dean said:

"Jeb, the President is very pleased with the way you've handled things. You can be sure that if you're indicted you'll be taken care of."

He went on to say that executive clemency would be exercised in my behalf. I took Dean's assurances with a grain of salt. Certainly I *wanted* to believe him. And, as I was aware, a great deal of financial support was going to the seven Watergate defendants and/or their lawyers. Still, I knew how the White House worked, and I knew that what Dean might say—or even what Mitchell might say—and what the President would do were very different things.

I was beginning to sense that I was in a very lonely and vulnerable position. The others had conspired with me, but I was the one who had agreed to go perjure himself before the grand jury. If I was caught, either for conspiracy with Liddy or for perjury, I intended to keep quiet to protect Mitchell and the President. I had volunteered for my role in the cover-up, out of ambition and loyalty and self-protection, yet to some extent the others used my ambition and loyalty to set me up, just as I used Porter's ambition and loyalty to set him up. But in both cases, Porter's and my own, we were willing to be used.

There were, of course, successive lines of defense in the cover-up—the Liddy line, the Magruder line, the Mitchell line, the Haldeman line. I might argue that Mitchell and Haldeman used my loyalty to set me up, but it might also be argued that at the same time the President was using their loyalty to set *them* up as his last line of defense.

As we waited for the grand jury to act, another unexpected problem arose. Hugh Sloan had resigned on July 14, and his and Stans's activities at the Finance Committee were under investigation by the FBI and the grand jury. Some of the secretaries at the Finance Committee began to leak information to the FBI and the press that they hoped would be harmful to me and Mitchell. They apparently were motivated by a belief that we were the cause of Stans's and Sloan's difficulties; in fact, the Finance Committee was a logical place for the investigators to begin their work, given the large amounts of cash that had gone to Liddy.

The most harmful series of leaks was items from a copy of Sloan's list of cash disbursements. Sloan had destroyed the original but one of the secretaries had a copy. Eleven disbursements, totaling just over a million dollars, were on the list, and several of them opened up new areas of investigation for the prosecutors. In addition to the $199,000 to Liddy, Sloan's list of cash disbursements included:

—A $250,000 payment to Herb Kalmbach, part of which went to pay trickster Donald Segretti.

—A $350,000 payment to Strachan, supposedly for polls, but part of which later went to the Watergate defendants and their lawyers.

—A $20,000 payment to me, which I passed on to conservative writer Victor Lasky. Dick Howard, Chuck Colson's aide, had called me one day and told me to give the money to Lasky, who had written an extremely favorable book about the President. In fact, it was so favorable that Lasky's publisher refused to issue it, so we were giving him the $20,000 his publisher wouldn't give him.

—A $10,000 payment to Lyn Nofziger for the ill-fated scheme to reregister Wallace voters in California.

—A $25,000 payment to Bob Hitt, Secretary Rogers Morton's political aide, which was passed on to William Mills, who had been Morton's administrative assistant in Congress and then had succeeded Morton as the Republican congressman from the Eastern Shore of Maryland. This money went to help finance Mills's 1972 campaign. In the spring of 1973, when the unreported donation became known and Congressman Mills thus seemed to be implicated in the Watergate scandals, he committed suicide.

We asked Stans to take action to stop his secretaries from leaking harmful information, but he claimed there was nothing he could do. And in truth, he was right. The women already had the documents or the knowledge, and if you disciplined them or fired them, it only worsened matters. The irony of the situation was that the leaks did no particular harm to me or Mitchell, their intended victims, but did create a number of problems for Stans himself, as well as for Haldeman, Kalmbach,

Strachan, and others against whom the secretaries presumably held no grudge.

We felt some concern as our own secretaries at CRP were being interviewed by the FBI, because we simply didn't know how much they knew or remembered. For example, Liddy's secretary, Sally Harmony, had typed up the transcripts of the wiretapped Democratic telephone conversations for the Gemstone file, and if she had testified that she made a copy for me the whole cover-up story would have been in danger of collapse.

The Finance Committee secretaries had tried unsuccessfully to enlist Sally Harmony in their anti-Mitchell, anti-Magruder campaign. In August, after Sally went with us to the Republican Convention in Miami Beach, the Finance Committee secretaries told the FBI and the grand jury that she hadn't done any work down there, that the trip had simply been a pay-off for her cooperation with us. That was the kind of problem we faced, and it was a maddening one. One of my cohorts used to mutter darkly that he would get those blankety-blank little blankety-blanks at the Finance Committee if it was the last thing he ever did.

Our dealings with our secretaries were delicate. You couldn't just ask one of them to perjure herself, because if she reported that to the FBI you had just created a new problem for yourself. What we could do, before a secretary went to testify, was to suggest to her very gently that she be careful, that she not let herself get tripped up, that we certainly hoped she wouldn't say anything that caused us problems. As it turned out, none of our CRP secretaries said anything that hurt us.

The leaks were going to Carl Bernstein and Bob Woodward, the two young Washington *Post* reporters who had covered the initial break-in story and had been on the Watergate story ever since. We respected Woodward and Bernstein's tenacity. We told other reporters the cover story, but we had a policy of never talking to Woodward and Bernstein, because they knew too much—there was too great a risk of their asking a question that would trip up one of us. I altered that policy only once. Woodward called and said—obviously on the basis of a leak from the Finance Committee—that he had information that I'd handled $50,000 in cash. The correct figure was $20,000, the money I'd given to Victor Lasky for the book he'd written but not had published. I talked this over with Van Shumway, CRP's press officer, and we agreed that I should try at least to get the figure corrected. There was no use in having the higher figure appear, and also if we could convince Woodward he was wrong, that might make him more cautious in the future.

I therefore called Woodward and told him the $50,000 figure was wrong, nevertheless he went ahead and printed it.

One afternoon while I was awaiting my second grand jury appearance, Larry Higby called and began to apologize about my not being invited to the cruise that night.

"What cruise?" I asked. "What are you talking about?"

It developed that the President was taking some people who were involved in the campaign for a cruise on the *Sequoia,* the Presidential yacht, that night. The guest list included Colson, Ziegler, Chapin, and Malek, and would have included me, except for my little problem with the grand jury. The White House, Higby explained, thought it best to keep me away from the President at this particular point in time.

The more I thought about it, the madder I got.

Those bastards, I thought, *they want me to perjure myself for them but they won't invite me on their lousy cruise.*

Still, I understood the problem, and I remained a good soldier.

Three young Assistant U.S. Attorneys, Earl Silbert, Donald Campbell, and Seymour Glanzer, were serving as the prosecutors in the grand jury investigation of the Watergate break-in. It was their procedure, when a CRP employee was to testify before the grand jury, to have him or her come in first for a private interview with the prosecutors. This interview would then be followed by the witness's formal testimony before the full grand jury. We assumed they followed this procedure because they could more intensively and effectively interrogate a witness in private than they could in the formal proceeding with the twenty-odd grand jury members present and interrupting with questions of their own.

Witnesses were not allowed to have a lawyer present when they went before the grand jury. However, we had been sending our lawyers along when our people went for the preliminary sessions with the prosecutors. We had initiated this practice and, while we suspected the prosecutors didn't like it, they had tolerated it.

My second grand jury appearance was scheduled for August 16, and a private session with the prosecutors was set for the day before that, the

15th. However, the prosecutors informed us that I would not be allowed to bring a lawyer with me. I could decline to see them in private, but if I came I must come alone.

I took this as a very bad sign, and the decision became a major one for me. Should I go in cold to be cross-examined by three skillful prosecutors? Or should I decline the honor? I discussed the matter with Mitchell, Dean, and LaRue, and in the end I decided to take my chances with the prosecutors. I had my story and I had to go with it; to do otherwise would amount to an admission of guilt.

On the day before my meeting with the prosecutors, Mitchell went over my testimony with me for a half hour in his office. The next morning, I went to John Dean's office in the Executive Office Building for a dress rehearsal for my session with the prosecutors that afternoon. I paced nervously around the large office while Dean sat at his desk firing questions at me, the toughest ones he could come up with, particularly on the money and Liddy's role at CRP. We discussed in great detail how I should speak of Liddy. On the one hand, we wanted to suggest that Liddy was the sort of erratic individual who was capable of having planned and carried out the Watergate burglary on his own. We also felt I should indicate the ill will that had existed between me and Liddy, and underscore the idea that I would not become involved in a criminal conspiracy with someone I so disliked. On the other hand, Dean and I agreed that I should not be too harsh on Liddy in any personal way, lest he learn of it and become angry and decide to speak out instead of remaining silent.

Dean knew Earl Silbert, the chief prosecutor, and he stressed to me that he was a smart, shrewd prosecutor, that he would probably like nothing better than to nail me to the wall, and that I should keep my guard up regardless of how well the meeting might seem to be going. Dean was at his best that morning. He was not a warm person, not someone I ever fully trusted, but he too was, as he said of Silbert, a smart, shrewd lawyer, and the advice he gave me was excellent. As it turned out, he had a very good fix on what the prosecutors would ask me, and his two-hour interrogation of me was time well spent.

Paul O'Brien accompanied me to the Federal Courthouse for my 2 P.M. meeting with the prosecutors, even though he could not be present during the examination. We arrived on time, but the prosecutors greeted us with an unsettling ploy. They kept me waiting. Silbert's secretary indicated he'd be with me any minute, but the minutes turned into hours. O'Brien and I waited on a wooden bench in the hallway outside Silbert's office. We talked for a while, until we ran out of things to say. O'Brien was a short, chunky Irishman, normally the most genial of men, but after a couple of hours of this treatment he was fuming. He kept going in to check with Silbert's secretary, and she kept assuring him it wouldn't be much longer. Three o'clock passed. We went for coffee. We read newspapers. Four o'clock passed. By then I was pacing the hallway in frustration. If the wait was deliberate, and designed to unnerve me, it almost succeeded. When the secretary finally called me in at five o'clock I was a nervous wreck. And yet, as I entered Silbert's office, I pulled myself together, and I felt fine.

Earl Silbert, a slender, intense man of about my own age, was known as one of the Justice Department's bright young men, and he had been friendly in the past with John Dean and other of the Administration's rising young lawyers. But in this situation we had to assume Silbert and the other prosecutors would do us no favors, for their reputations were on the line, just as ours were.

Silbert and Donald Campbell, also in his mid-thirties, rose and greeted me with a formal handshake. Then Silbert sat down behind his cluttered desk. I took the chair across from him, and Campbell took a seat off to one side. Throughout the interview, Silbert would take the lead and Campbell was more the detail man, checking facts and figures in his notebook when necessary. Seymour Glanzer, the third of the prosecutors, was not present, which was just as well, because he was an expert in white-collar crime and was considered an exceptionally tough and re-sourceful interrogator.

I faced Silbert for a moment. No one was smiling. Silbert began the interview with a blunt reminder of my status:

"Mr. Magruder, you realize you are a target of the grand jury's investigation."

"Yes, I understand that."

"We want to advise you that you have the right to remain silent."

"I understand that, Mr. Silbert, but I want to cooperate with you in any way I can. I'm just as anxious to see this matter cleared up as you are."

"All right, then, let's talk about Gordon Liddy and his role in your campaign."

For an hour the two men asked tough, probing questions that were intended to shake my story. It seemed to me that the unspoken tone of their questioning was, "All right, you son of a bitch, you're guilty and we know it."

They pressed me hard on why we had authorized the $250,000 to Liddy for intelligence-gathering and security. They implied that $250,000 was an outrageously high figure. My reply, in essence, was this:

"Mr. Silbert, you have to realize that in a campaign the size of ours, involving some forty million dollars, $250,000 isn't a great deal of money. Liddy's operation was a minor part of the campaign, one that we left largely up to Liddy because he was considered an expert in the field. His operation became doubly expensive when we had to move our convention from San Diego to Miami Beach. And the truth is that we moved the convention from San Diego because of the threat of radical demonstrations there, and we had told Liddy to spend whatever was necessary to find out what the radicals planned to do. If you consider the damage the radicals did to the Democrats in Chicago in 1968, you'll realize that it was easily worth $250,000 to us to prevent that sort of problem at our convention in 1972."

Naturally, they pressed me on our lack of controls over Liddy's spending, our giving him cash, and our lack of documentation of how he'd spent the money.

To a large extent, I blamed that on the Finance Committee—they handled the money, not I. I added that Mitchell's preoccupation with the ITT case in the spring had caused a certain loosening of controls at CRP. I noted that I had a particular problem in that I didn't get along well with either Liddy or Sloan, so perhaps that had caused me not to watch them as closely as I should have. I mentioned the fact that Liddy and I strongly disliked one another. That could easily be documented, and was a strong point—it didn't make sense that I'd be involved in a criminal conspiracy with a man who had once talked about killing me.

They questioned why we had used Liddy for intelligence-gathering rather than using the FBI or other federal agencies. I replied, quite truthfully, that we didn't have faith in the federal agencies.

They pressed me hard on my alleged attempt to get Sloan to perjure himself. I told them that all I had done was suggest to Sloan that he might have a serious problem if he'd filed false reports about unreported campaign donations. I added that Sloan had never liked me and that perhaps he had misunderstood or misinterpreted my statement.

We went into great detail on all aspects of Liddy's activities, real and imaginary—the Jack Anderson investigation, the surrogate protection plan, and so on. The point is that I knew my story, that there was a lot of truth to it, and that I had an answer to all their questions. The prosecutors may not have believed me, but they couldn't shake me.

After about an hour of questioning, the tone of the meeting began to change. I saw that I had taken the initiative. I was leading the prosecutors, not vice versa. At some point it quit being "Mr. Silbert" and "Mr. Magruder" and became "Earl" and "Jeb." We even reached the point of swapping Liddy stories—it was the prosecutors who told me about Liddy burning his hand on the candle, rather than a blow torch, while trying to impress some people.

When I left Silbert's office at 8 P.M., I felt very good, very confident. I thought I'd pulled it off, that I wouldn't be indicted. Paul O'Brien had waited for me outside Silbert's office and we rode back to CRP and had a few stiff drinks as we discussed my apparently successful performance.

My appearance before the grand jury the next day was anticlimactic. The tone of the prosecutors' questions indicated to me that I was no longer a subject of their investigation.

The next day, August 17, John Dean called me and said that his Justice Department sources had confirmed what I already suspected— that I was not going to be indicted. The indictments would stop with the four Cubans, McCord, Hunt, and Liddy. The cover-up, apparently, had held.

I was tremendously relieved by Dean's news. I had been at my "best" in those three hours with the prosecutors—well-informed, self-confident, persuasive—and apparently I had sold them our story. To do so seemed all-important at the time, for selling our story seemed crucial to the re-election of the President. In retrospect, perhaps his reelection would have occurred even if I had been indicted, but we did not assume that then. The two months after the break-in had been a bad time for me, but when I got the news from John Dean it seemed as if it had all been worth it.

That night, Fred LaRue and I celebrated with dinner at Billy Martin's Carriage House Restaurant in Georgetown. Our mood was a strange one. We laughed and joked and unwound, celebrating this apparent victory after two months of intense pressure. But there were times during our celebration when we lapsed into silence, when we found our depression returning, when we grimly asked each other if we could possibly get

away with this incredible cover-up, when I realized that I had only suc-
ceeded in compounding my already serious legal and ethical dilemma.
Before the evening was over, I did something I've done rarely in my life.
I got roaring drunk.

CHAPTER XIII

The Campaign

MEANWHILE, Richard Nixon was running for reelection, and I was one of the people directing his campaign.

The new campaign director, Clark MacGregor, was a man about whom I had mixed feelings. Essentially, I considered MacGregor a typical politician—hearty, imposing, excellent at speechmaking and handshaking, generally pleasant to deal with, but not a man of great substance, not a good manager, not someone who wanted to concern himself with the details of our sophisticated campaign operation. MacGregor struck me as an excellent front man—fine at public relations, fierce in defending CRP from encroachments by Stans, Ehrlichman, and other empire builders, and generally a good campaign director as long as he concentrated on speechmaking and didn't try to direct the campaign.

MacGregor had been a congressman in Minnesota until he ran for the Senate against Hubert Humphrey in 1970. Following his defeat he was brought into the White House to replace the departing Bryce Harlow. In effect, MacGregor was put in over Bill Timmons in the Congressional Relations operation, but most of us went to Timmons if we wanted something done. MacGregor had made a serious mistake during his first weeks in the White House. He kept criticizing the work of his predecessor, until word of his criticism got back to Harlow, who confronted him about it. Harlow later told me he said to MacGregor:

"Clark, I've known you a long time and I bear you no ill will. You've

253

got the job now and you don't have to knock me to succeed in it. I have my friends in this town and you have yours, and I think we'd both be better off if you'd be more careful in what you say."

It seemed to many of us that MacGregor had only hurt himself by criticizing the popular and respected Harlow, and the episode suggested to me that MacGregor was not as astute as one should be to succeed in Washington's corridors of power.

One result of MacGregor's replacing Mitchell at CRP was to increase Haldeman's role in the campaign substantially. For one thing, Haldeman began treating me as his employee again. If Higby called me and said Haldeman wanted something done, and I protested that MacGregor wanted something else done, Higby would say, "You do it Bob's way," and the only remaining question was how to get around MacGregor.

One such conflict arose when Haldeman wanted us to pay for a half-hour television appearance by John Connally, the chairman of Democrats for Nixon. MacGregor, acting on information from Maurice Stans, protested that we didn't have enough money to show the Connally film. In this instance, it might have been that MacGregor was reluctant to see Connally get such extensive exposure, since Connally was already overshadowing MacGregor in the campaign. But Haldeman wanted the film shown, so finally we simply had to tell MacGregor to talk to Bob about it, and the money was found. MacGregor had a shrewd instinct for knowing where he stood in the campaign pecking order. He knew that he could not win a fight with Haldeman (no one could) but that, on campaign matters, he probably had more clout with the President than Ehrlichman or Stans, and when conflicts with them arose he stood firm.

MacGregor was in a difficult position. He had been thrown into the campaign very late, there was much about it he did not understand, and he must have felt unsure of himself. He tended, therefore, to overreact during his first month or so. He was fine for the first few days; everything was, "Great to be aboard; boy, what a great campaign this is going to be." But soon he decided that things weren't being run to his satisfaction. MacGregor considered himself a practical, action-oriented politician, and he got the idea that CRP was too planning-oriented. He would pound his fist on his desk and tell us, "By God, we need some *action;* we've got to get things *moving!*"

There were some areas where action was needed, but by and large the campaign was proceeding on the schedule we'd mapped out a year before. Most campaigns operate in a state of crisis, and I think it took a while for MacGregor to adjust to a campaign that was moving along in an orderly, almost tranquil manner. Part of the initial problem was that MacGregor had never run a large organization before, and his political experience, in Congressional campaigns in Minnesota, had not prepared him for the sophisticated techniques we were using in advertising, direct mail, polling, and so on. He was fine when he did his homework, but he tended to jump from one thing to another, to overreact to complaints from state chairmen, and not to focus on details. He was better in making speeches about action than in actually producing action.

One area of the campaign that he understood and made a major contribution to was our surrogate speakers program. As a veteran speechmaker himself, MacGregor could make many useful suggestions to Bart Porter on ways the program could be improved. He and his wife, Barbara, came up with the idea for our surrogates' wives program. We invited the most articulate of the surrogates' wives—Joyce Rumsfeld, Mary Richardson, and Barbara MacGregor herself were among the most effective of them—to speak around the country on behalf of the President. We generally sent them to smaller or medium-sized cities where a visit from a Cabinet member's wife would make news, and we handled the advance work, provided them with material for their speeches, and so on. Barbara MacGregor supervised the program, which won us a good deal of publicity and eventually won the ultimate tribute—compliments from the President.

On most mornings when MacGregor was in town, Fred Malek, Fred LaRue, and I would meet in his office to discuss the day's activities. LaRue's status had not changed when MacGregor replaced Mitchell. He got along with MacGregor, and he continued as a floating campaign adviser, as well as spending a lot of time working on the Watergate defense. LaRue used to joke, as we entered MacGregor's office, "Well, which speech do we get today?" He was referring to MacGregor's tendency to lean back in his chair, look out the window, and deliver a monologue. Sometimes he would parrot the President's words ("You know, fellows, I was thinking last night, this really *is* the first President who's had a generation of peace . . .") and sometimes we would realize that he was rehearsing a speech he would be giving later in the day. I didn't mind MacGregor's speeches—I had a lot else to think about in those days—but they would drive Fred Malek up the wall, because Malek really *was* action-oriented and couldn't stand to waste a half hour every morning listening to a monologue.

Malek and I had some conflicts in July and August. As I'd expected, he came charging into the campaign with all the finesse that he'd exhibited the time he drove his Mercedes through the tourists to see the bears at the garbage pile. Malek made it clear to me that, although we both held the title of deputy director, he considered himself the senior deputy director. In fact, he generously informed me that there'd been talk in the White House of firing me but he'd intervened to save my job. I found that hard to believe. If I'd been fired, it wouldn't have been because of my work at CRP, but because of Watergate, and Malek wouldn't have been involved in those deliberations.

Malek and I had different roles, of course. He directed the field operation and I supervised the advertising, direct mail, and polling programs. I think that at the outset he hoped to take over my part of the campaign, but eventually he realized he had his hands full simply doing his own job. To his credit, Malek did do much to bring order to the field operation that had been so disorganized under Harry Flemming's direction. I felt a certain sympathy for Malek as he tried to gain control over the field program. I had realized when CRP was first being set up that its "inside" activities, such as the advertising, the polling, and the direct mail, would be controllable, but that its "outside" function of dealing with fifty state campaign organizations would be extremely difficult to direct, because you had to rely on state chairmen who simply might not follow instructions. It had therefore been my instinct, from my first meetings with Mitchell in the spring of 1971, to take charge of the inside programs and to let other people struggle with the fifty state organizations. Flemming could not handle that job, and Malek probably did as much as was possible under the circumstances.

Malek and I had one sharp conflict when he tried to expand his program at the expense of mine. Malek told the state chairmen to increase the door-to-door canvassing program, which he directed, and to cut back on the telephone canvass, which I directed. I won that battle by going out into the field and documenting that my telephone program was working and his door-to-door program wasn't working as well. I talked to state chairmen, visited dozens of our storefront headquarters, talked to volunteers, and was able to show that the available volunteers could be better used on the telephone. There is, for one thing, a far greater element of control in a telephone program. The volunteers are in your headquarters under your direct supervision. When you send a fellow out to knock on doors, he may have a few doors slammed in his face and decide to go drink beer for the rest of the afternoon and fake his reports. Moreover, since we were stressing identification rather than persuasion, the telephone canvass was more suited to our campaign; McGovern's campaign necessarily stressed door-to-door persuasion. Once I got back to Washington with my facts and figures, Malek accepted my conclusions and for the remainder of the campaign we got along well enough, with him running his area and me running mine.

To an extent, working for MacGregor had brought Malek and me together, despite our differences. By mid-July we agreed that the campaign might become a disaster unless we could gain some control over our new boss. MacGregor tended to shoot from the hip, to disrupt carefully laid plans, to confuse the staff, to overreact to complaints from political figures, and generally to bring disorder to an extremely well organized campaign. Malek and I therefore cooperated on what we considered a major coup. We arranged for Bob Reisner, my able administrative assistant (whom Malek had originally recommended to me) to become MacGregor's special assistant. By so doing, we were able to keep ourselves informed on MacGregor's activities, and often the presence of Reisner would prevent MacGregor from making mistakes. Typically, for example, a state chairman would call to demand more money for programs in his state and MacGregor, ever the affable pol, would want to oblige him. The problem was that as the campaign progressed we had more than forty of the states locked up, and to spend more on advertising or direct mail in those states was simply a waste of money. Reisner, at MacGregor's elbow and understanding the campaign strategy, was often able to say, "Excuse me, Mr. MacGregor, but I believe there's already been a decision made to . . ." and thus prevent many problems. Reisner's performance satisfied everyone. MacGregor himself often declared, "By God, bringing Bob Reisner in here is the smartest thing I've done in this campaign!"

MacGregor and I usually got along quite well. We had a joke about our being relatives, since the names MacGregor and Magruder trace back to the same Scottish clan. We did have one unpleasant scene, however. We had arranged a dinner at Camp David at which MacGregor, Malek, and I—the Three M's, they called us—briefed the Cabinet on the campaign. During dinner, in front of two or three Cabinet members, MacGregor chewed me out for a mistake I'd allegedly made. I couldn't believe it. It was a crude thing to do, the sort of thing Mitchell would never have done, and to make it worse I was innocent of the wrongdoing he accused me of. He claimed I hadn't gotten a new direct-mail report to him, when in fact it was on his desk and he hadn't bothered to read it. I didn't think I should argue with him in front of the Cabinet, so I swallowed hard and promised to take care of the matter. Inwardly, I was furious. Haldeman could chew you out with class, but MacGregor's performance was simply unpleasant.

The Republican National Convention in Miami Beach in late August was outwardly a near-perfect display of party unity and inwardly a typical political convention with all the typical political conflicts.

Two of the conflicts that we managed to keep from public view concerned MacGregor—first, his fending off an attempt by Ehrlichman to seize control over the campaign, then his efforts to find out the truth about Watergate.

We already knew that one of MacGregor's strong points was a readiness to protect his prerogatives. When he had first become campaign director, Maurice Stans had tried to push him around a few times, declaring that we didn't have the money for this or that program, but we had learned that if we briefed MacGregor he was very good at telling Stans, "By God, we've *got* to have that money, and there's no two ways about it!"

The Ehrlichman challenge was more serious, however. As the party leaders assembled at Miami Beach, a number of them were grumbling about our field operation. Malek was making improvements, but there were still problems left over from the months when Flemming was in charge. Some state chairmen had been saying to Ehrlichman, in effect: "We need some help from the White House, John; those boys at CRP aren't handling things right."

The complaints prompted Ehrlichman to come up with what we at CRP called the Three Stooges Plan, whereby three of his deputies, Bud Krogh, Ed Morgan, and John Whitaker, would travel around the country and "monitor" the campaign and report back to Ehrlichman in the White House. Malek, LaRue, and I discussed this proposal with two of the potential stooges, Morgan and Whitaker, not long after we arrived in Miami Beach. We objected to it vigorously. The obvious problem was that state chairmen are never satisfied, and once their requests were turned down at CRP they would turn to the White House and try to play us off against Ehrlichman, and in the process throw the campaign into chaos.

But Ehrlichman was not easily dissuaded, and a few mornings later he insisted on a face-to-face meeting with MacGregor about his plan. The meeting was held over breakfast one morning in MacGregor's suite at the Doral Hotel, with MacGregor, Ehrlichman, LaRue, Malek, and myself present.

Breakfast was not cordial that morning. Ehrlichman had a technique he used to get his way—attack, attack, attack. In effect, he said to us: "You guys are doing a lousy job. I know, because the state chairmen tell me so. I'm here to help you. My men can go out in the field and get things straightened out. You need help, so why are we arguing?" Ehrlichman's style of attack was much like Colson's, except that he didn't challenge your patriotism in the process.

Ehrlichman came alone, confronting the four of us, and he added one clever wrinkle to his argument. He tried to split me off from the others by saying, "Now, it's obvious that Jeb's got his operation in good shape; it's just this field operation that's a problem." But I didn't bite. I supported Malek all the way, because it was obvious to me that Malek on his own would do a better job than Malek with the Three Stooges looking over his shoulder. The success of my telephone canvass depended in large part on the efficiency of Malek's volunteer program, so I had every reason to oppose anything that would impede Malek.

The final word went to MacGregor, however, and he stood firm.

"We won't even consider it," he told Ehrlichman. "We've got things under control and your people would just cause confusion."

"The President wants it," Ehrlichman insisted.

"Then let him tell me that," MacGregor said firmly. That ended breakfast and, we hoped, the Three Stooges Plan.

But when the convention was over, and the President went to San Clemente for a rest, Ehrlichman summoned MacGregor and Malek there, supposedly to discuss his plan with the President. However, upon his arrival, MacGregor went to Haldeman and declared that he would not accept the Ehrlichman plan, and the meeting with the President was canceled. Apparently either Haldeman or Nixon just didn't want to get into a fight with their campaign director.

There was, I suspected, another level to the MacGregor–Ehrlichman jousting over the campaign, in that both of them were widely viewed within the Administration as wanting to replace Richard Kleindienst as Attorney General in the second Nixon Administration. Kleindienst's appointment had been engineered by Mitchell, but he had become a liability because of his role in the ITT controversy and he wasn't expected to be kept as Attorney General very long after the election. No one doubted that Ehrlichman wanted the job. As for MacGregor, he so frequently declared to us, "Gentlemen, I can't worry about the Attorney Generalship; I've got to run this campaign," that no reasonable man could doubt that he lusted mightily for the appointment.

The other thing MacGregor lusted for was the truth about Watergate. I had existed with that problem ever since he joined the campaign and I first told him the cover story. The problem was that from time to time someone would suggest to MacGregor that there was more to the Watergate story than we had told him, and he would come to me and solemnly declare:

"Jeb, I have information that there's more to this affair than you've told me, and I think it's time for you and me to have a straightforward discussion. I'm having a terrible time with the press. They're making a fool of me, and if I'm made a fool of, the whole campaign is made a fool of."

"Certainly, Clark," I would say, and I would proceed to tell him the cover story once more.

The problem, as MacGregor suggested, was the press. In his ignorance, MacGregor kept letting things slip unnecessarily. For example, he blurted out the fact that the cashier's check from Dahlberg had been part of the money that went to Liddy.

On several other occasions, when asked about some new report or allegation, he would say, "No, I've checked that with Mr. Mitchell [or Mr. Colson or Mr. Haldeman] and he's assured me it's not true." We didn't want to get into that kind of specific denial by specific individuals. We tried to persuade MacGregor to say "No comment" or "I don't know" to questions about Watergate, to refer them to the Justice Department or the FBI, but it wasn't in MacGregor's nature to say "I don't know" to reporters.

Watergate surfaced in two unexpected ways while we were in Miami Beach. First, quite unexpectedly, Mardian came up to me one day at our command post on the top floor of the Doral Hotel, and said:

"Jeb, I just wanted you to know, we're going to put a memo into the files outlining a theory of your involvement in the Watergate affair. This is simply to protect Mitchell, if anything goes wrong."

"You're *what?*"

"Don't get excited. It'll just say that although we have no evidence, we suspect that you may have authorized the break-in, and later perjured yourself about it. We'll say we accept your story, but we do have some doubts."

"You're crazy as hell," I said. "I won't agree to that."

"Well, you *said* you'd take the blame."

"I will, if it comes to that, but that doesn't mean you guys should put memos in the files that set me up."

"We're just trying to protect Mitchell."

"I'll talk to Mitchell," I said. I talked to LaRue, then called Mitchell, who was in New York, and who said the idea had seemed like a good one, but that if I objected they would drop it.

Watergate surfaced a second time in Miami Beach when MacGregor called me to his suite well past midnight one night and once more demanded the truth about Watergate. I was annoyed at the late-hour call, as well as being exhausted, but I could see that I would have to go through the whole ritual again. MacGregor was pacing the floor in his pajamas and bathrobe; apparently he'd been upset because of some new allegation that reporters had asked him about that day. His wife was also present, and also in a robe, although she soon went to bed. Bob Reisner was there, and as soon as I saw what I was in for I called La-Rue, awakening him, and asked that he join us. I wanted him there both for moral support and, given the problems that were arising, for verification of exactly what I'd said. LaRue arrived, we all had a drink, and I went through the cover story once more, in great detail, to an increasingly sleepy audience.

MacGregor had an annoying habit of asking you a question, then, when you had begun your answer, of interrupting you. "Now wait a minute, Jeb," he would say. "Just wait a minute. What about this . . . ?" LaRue tried to help me out, and I tried to keep my annoyance under control, because MacGregor had a hot temper and there was no sense in arousing it. Also, I felt sympathy for MacGregor's difficult position. He must have sensed that something was rotten at the Committee to Re-elect, and that his own position was a potentially dangerous one, yet no one could confirm his fears. "Jeb," he would say, "you must understand that it's essential to the reelection of the President that I know the truth."

The problem was that *we* thought it was essential to the reelection of the President that he *not* know the truth. Mitchell and Dean and I had discussed the matter and agreed that the last thing we should do was to level with MacGregor. It seemed too likely that he'd let the whole thing slip at his next news conference. As a result, despite all his pleas, MacGregor probably knew less about Watergate than any senior official of the campaign.

Despite our internal problems, the 1972 Republican Convention was virtually flawless as a PR effort—it was, indeed, the culmination of four years of the President's intense concern with public relations. It succeeded because we realized we must minimize the "convention" aspects of our convention, and treat it instead as a television show. The people watching in their homes do not want to see roll calls and parliamentary debate. They want to see drama, spectacle, celebrities, and speeches that don't drone on forever.

We realized that our convention lacked drama—everyone knew that Richard Nixon and Spiro Agnew would be renominated—so we tried to make up for that lack with timing, variety, and spectacle. Under Dwight Chapin's direction, a minute-by-minute scenario was prepared, and it was followed. Speeches were written in advance, approved, and timed so they would not run over. The less interesting, parliamentary aspects of the convention were held during the day, so the prime-time hours could be used for dramatic events—the films of the President's trip to Russia and China, demonstrations by several thousand enthusiastic young people, and finally the President's acceptance speech. An estimated sixty million Americans watched some part of our convention, and while they may have occasionally been bored (we joked about staging a few fist fights on the convention floor to keep people awake) they could not help but contrast the efficiency and unity of our convention with the confusion and conflict of the Democratic Convention a month earlier.

In July, several of us had taken a room in a Washington hotel so we could watch the Democratic Convention in privacy each evening. I thought Larry O'Brien did a smooth, professional job of running it, but that he or someone blundered spectacularly when they let the nomination speeches for Vice President run on and on until McGovern had to deliver his acceptance speech at three in the morning. That may have been democracy in action, but it was a poor way to present the party's new candidate for President to the American people. It was the kind of blunder that could not have happened at our convention.

The convention, coming as it did just after my apparently successful grand jury appearance, was a pleasant break for me. Gail and the children came down and I was able to get my thoughts off Watergate, at least part of the time. The children stayed at the Key Biscayne Hotel and

Gail spent some nights with them and some nights with me at the Doral. I arranged for a car and driver for Gail, and she would bring the children over two at a time for the convention events. They were upset by the hippies who were gathered outside the Convention Hall and chanting obscenities at the people who went inside. Once, when police used tear gas to break up the demonstrators, Gail and two of the children arrived in the hall choking, crying, and terrified. But, once inside, they enjoyed themselves. They had a front-row box near the podium, near Jo Haldeman and Jean Ehrlichman and other wives Gail had gotten to know. Gail was fascinated by the comings and goings of the various political and show-business celebrities, and by the rush of the reporters to interview each new one. She noted the contrast between Charlton Heston, one of our prize Democrats for Nixon, who regally declined interviews, and the Rockefellers—Nelson and Happy—who obviously loved the media attention. All the children joined us on the night of the President's acceptance speech, and when the convention was finally over we stayed on in Key Biscayne for a few days, relaxing and soaking up the sun.

But Watergate did not stay buried for long. A few days after my return to Washington, the grand jury subpoenaed my office diary, and a few days after that I was told I was wanted for further testimony. The demand for the diary threw us into panic, because its entries for January 27 and February 4 said something like: "AG's office—w/Dean & Liddy."

The diary thus carried Liddy directly into the Attorney General's office—not once but twice—and raised the question of whether the four of us might have been discussing political espionage.

Soon after the subpoena came, I took the diary and went to Mitchell's law office, where I found him meeting with Dean, Mardian, LaRue, and several other men on another aspect of the case. Dean, Mitchell, and I went to a nearby office in the law firm for a private look at my diary. The two entries were in pencil, which led Dean to suggest that we erase them. His plan had the virtue of simplicity, but, as I pointed out, the FBI certainly had experts who could tell if a diary entry had been erased. I therefore came up with another proposal. We could say that the January 27 meeting had been canceled at the last minute, and rescheduled for February 4, and that when we met we had introduced Liddy to Mitchell and had discussed only the legal questions of the new campaign law.

The others agreed that this was the best solution to the diary problem. We didn't think that anyone's secretary would remember whether a meeting six months earlier had been held or canceled. The only people who knew were the four of us who had attended. That fact led me to tell Dean and Mitchell:

"If I testify to this, that there was no January 27 meeting, and it comes up later, you've both got to support me."

Both men nodded their full agreement, but getting that support a few months later would not be so easy.

Thus, when I made my third grand jury appearance, on September 6, I told the new story about the canceled meeting. I was also asked about Donald Segretti's harassment of Democratic candidates, and I could truthfully say I knew nothing about it. The prosecutors seemed friendly, I was not pressed hard on anything. A few days later, the grand jury handed down its indictments, and they were limited to the basic seven defendants—the four Cubans, McCord, Hunt, and Liddy. The cover story seemed to be holding, and I could focus again on the Presidential campaign.

For me, one of the most satisfying aspects of the 1972 campaign was my relationship with John Connally, the former governor of Texas, who had served in the Nixon Cabinet as Secretary of the Treasury and who during the campaign became the chairman of Democrats for Nixon.

It had been apparent for some time that Connally was going to support the President in 1972, and that he would probably switch to the Republican Party to make his own bid for the Presidential nomination in 1976. There was a good deal of discussion in the spring of 1972 about whether Connally would do us more good by heading a Democrats for Nixon group, or by making a dramatic switch to the Republican Party. Eventually, the McGovern nomination, and the resultant alienation of many moderate Democrats, convinced us that Connally would be most effective as a moderate democrat going after other moderate Democrats, rather than as a Democrat-turned-Republican.

In mid-July I got a call from Chuck Colson asking me to help Connally set up his Democrats for Nixon office, which at the outset was in the Madison Hotel, where Connally was staying. My first thought, when Colson called, was: *Oh, God, here we go again; another fight with Colson.* But it didn't work out that way. Colson didn't have the free-wheeling role in 1972 that he'd had in 1970. With the extremely tough and independent Connally running Democrats for Nixon, Colson wasn't about to take *that* over, and the same was true of the advertising campaign, with the able Pete Dailey in charge. Colson largely confined himself to the "attack group" activities in the White House, which planned the line that various administration spokesmen would take in criticizing McGovern. I had three people from our office, a writer, a press man, and a man whose job was to monitor Senator McGovern's every word, go over each day for meetings of Colson's "attack group." Our main concern was to see that the attacks on McGovern were coordinated with our advertising, so that if we were stressing one week the ad that criticized McGovern's welfare scheme, the Administration spokesmen would also stress that line. Colson was very cooperative about this.

In fairness to Colson, it should be said that he had been the first person to see, and then to sell to the President, the vast potential the President had for cutting into the traditionally Democratic vote in 1972. Colson's efforts in 1970 and 1971 had paved the way for the President's success with unions, Catholics, ethnics, and other special-interest groups in 1972.

From our point of view at CRP, Connally's Democrats for Nixon organization could be an extremely important element of the campaign, if it could be kept under control. If our target was disaffected Democrats, then Democrats for Nixon was the ideal vehicle for many of our advertisements and mailings. The problem was that citizens' groups of this sort are often disasters, because their leaders have the idea they can operate independently of the campaign high command.

That was not the case with Connally. He was independent, but he was also shrewd enough to see at once that we at CRP had the tools he needed to accomplish what he wanted. He met with us, he listened to our explanations of our advertising and direct-mail programs, he asked questions, and within a week or two he had a complete mastery of what we were doing. I became his liaison with CRP and I was continually impressed by his intelligence, his energy, and his concern with every detail of our program.

He *did* have a temper, as everyone learned who had occasion to displease him. I did only once. Democrats for Nixon had a number of Democratic figures who were speaking around the country on the President's behalf, and Connally had laid down the law that no one was to be used as a speaker without Connally's personal approval. One day, however, he arrived in Los Angeles and discovered that Dr. James Theberge, a foreign policy expert, was also in Los Angeles speaking on behalf of Democrats for Nixon. Minutes later, I got a call from Connally in New York, where I was meeting with our advertising people.

"Jeb, you and I have gotten along pretty well, haven't we?"

"Yes, sir."

"That's right, we've gotten along fine, and that's why I can't believe you've gone behind my back like this."

"Gone behind your back? Governor, what do you mean?"

"What do I mean? I mean what in the hell is this guy Theberge doing in Los Angeles without my permission?"

"Governor, I can explain . . ."

"This isn't you, Jeb. I know that either Colson or Haldeman is behind this. Don't you try to cover for them."

It went on like that for a while, until I could persuade him that I had approved the professor's speech in Los Angeles, and it was not part of a Colson plot somehow designed to embarrass him. My mistake—for which Connally berated me at length and in great volume—was in not getting his approval for the Theberge speech. Actually, I'd sent some material on the man to one of his assistants, but that wasn't good enough. So Connally chewed me out for five minutes or so, with class, the way Haldeman did, and we never had any problem after that.

Perhaps the most important function of Democrats for Nixon was to sponsor advertising that would be critical of McGovern and that might lure traditional Democrats to vote for Nixon. Not long after Connally joined us, I wrote a memo that set out my and Pete Dailey's views on the kind of advertising strategy Democrats for Nixon should follow. It said in part:

> The advertising objective should be to persuade traditional hard-line Democrats to vote for Richard Nixon in November. Care should be taken that this objective is not diluted by other less vital goals. For example, no attempt should be made to gain converts to the Republican Party—this is too big a jump to ask most people to take and it would take years to accomplish.

> No attempt should be made to persuade Democrats to vote the Republican line. It's too tough a sale. It will happen in many cases, anyhow.

> No attempt should be made to broaden the Committee to include traditional ticket-splitters and/or independents. The Committee to Re-elect will be concentrating most of its energies on this group. The Democrats for Nixon should concentrate on Democrats.

The basic thrust of the advertising message should be:

> Senator McGovern does not reflect the philosophy of most Democrats or of most Americans. He is leading the party in the wrong direction and would the country as well.
>
> It is necessary that you (the Democrat) put country ahead of party in 1972.
>
> Richard Nixon more adequately represents the philosophy of the American people. He has been a good President and deserves support.

Advertising copy must be restrained both in condemnation of McGovern and praise of the President. There is no need to resort to excess emotionalism, distortion, or innuendo to point out the dangers of a McGovern administration. His positions on defense, welfare, taxes, and peace terms are in conflict with the thinking of most Democrats and should simply be exposed as such.

On the other hand, overly lavish praise of the President will probably turn the target audience off faster than you can say Democrats for Nixon. Remember, these are *Democrats*. Many of them can be persuaded to vote for the President because they honestly believe he is the better candidate. But we can't expect them to be happy about the situation that has forced this choice.

The Democrats for Nixon sponsored three major anti-McGovern television spots, and later polls documented that they were highly effective advertisements. One showed a McGovern poster on a weather vane, flip-flopping in the wind, as a voice suggested that McGovern shifted his positions from day to day. Another showed a hand knocking model ships and planes off a table, to dramatize what we regarded as McGovern's ill-considered proposals for cutting the defense budget. The third showed a construction worker eating a sandwich and thinking about McGovern's $1,000-a-year welfare scheme. Finally the worker asks, "Say, who's going to pay for this?" and with a gulp he answers his own question: "Me!" It was tough, effective political advertising, and no one appreciated it more than Connally, who had nothing but scorn for McGovern and his wing of the Democratic Party.

I found Connally tough, well-informed, cordial when not aroused, extremely intelligent, and fascinated by every detail of political campaigning. All in all, I would have to say he is the most impressive political figure I've ever known, and if things had worked out differently I would have been delighted to have worked on a Connally for President campaign in 1976.

By September, the campaign was moving along smoothly. MacGregor by then saw that we were in good shape, and he was spending a lot of his time on the road. Malek by then was leaving me alone and concentrating on his own responsibilities, and he was also spending an increasing amount of his time on White House personnel matters. The President had decided to get rid of a great many political appointees after the election, and Malek was involved in determining who stayed and who did not.

For me, despite all my problems and distractions, the campaign was an immensely satisfying time. We had spent more than a year preparing for it. We had been criticized, first by Haldeman and Colson and others at the White House, then by MacGregor, for overemphasis on planning. But now, finally, we saw our plans paying off, we had our people and our programs in place, virtually every element of the campaign was moving ahead on schedule, and it was a beautiful process to behold.

The 1972 Nixon campaign has not, in my opinion, received the attention it deserves, both because of Watergate and because the Democratic candidate, Senator McGovern, ran such a poor campaign that analysis has tended to focus on his mistakes rather than on our successes. I think that's unfortunate, and I'd like to suggest here at least a few of the elements of our operation.

We had, from the outset, run a dual campaign, combining a national campaign for all fifty states with a target-state strategy of special emphasis on ten crucial states: Pennsylvania, Michigan, Maryland, California, New York, Ohio, Illinois, Texas, New Jersey, and Connecticut.

In effect, all states were equal but some were more equal than others. All fifty states benefited from our television advertising, but there was extra coverage on stations in the target states. All states got a minimal number of surrogate speakers, but the target states were saturated with these Administration spokesmen. The nontarget states were given a phone-at-home telephone canvass plan, but in the target states we funded expensive telephone centers from which some six and a half million households were called.

By October, as our prospects began to look very good, we began shifting to a fifty-state strategy, one that assumed the possibility of something close to a fifty-state sweep by the President. On the basis of our own polls and public polls, we began to see that certain once-uncertain states were locked up, and that some states we'd once thought beyond our reach were becoming serious prospects for the President. From day to day, we would shift our priorities, never slackening off on the ten target states, but increasing our emphasis on states like Rhode Island, McGovern's home state of South Dakota, and even Massachusetts, which by the final week we were making a serious effort to carry, and which was, of course, the only state we didn't carry.

By the final weeks, it was too late to begin a telephone canvass or a direct-mail program in a new state like Massachusetts or South Dakota. What we could do, and did, was to saturate such states with last-minute advertising and surrogate speakers who could get us free television publicity. Even at the end, when we were hoping for a fifty-state sweep that would carry in a Republican Congress, we were haunted by the memory of Truman's upset of an overconfident Dewey in 1948 or, for that matter, of Humphrey's strong finish in 1968. We didn't think we could take anything for granted. Even when the polls showed Nixon far ahead of McGovern, there was a high percentage of undecided voters, and we had to assume that most of them were traditional Democrats who would return to their party in the voting booth. MacGregor, Malek, LaRue, and I had some discussions in October of whether we should simply cut off campaign spending to save money, but we agreed that we couldn't risk either the loss of momentum or the adverse public response to such a confident action. Not the least of our concerns was that some break in the Watergate case—one of the defendants talking, perhaps, or the grand jury reopening its investigation—might blow the campaign sky-high.

McGovern's young antiwar volunteers were well publicized throughout 1972, and I think the point should be made that in the actual fall campaign we had a bigger and better volunteer program than McGovern's. His volunteers had worked effectively in the primaries, but after the Eagleton affair and a few other fiascoes McGovern found it hard to get new volunteers or even to keep the ones he had. The movement among young people was toward Nixon, and thanks to Ken Rietz's efforts many months earlier we had a youth organization that could make use of them.

Nor was there any way for McGovern to match our telephone or direct-mail programs. He had enough money by the final months of the campaign, but those programs, to be done correctly, must be set up in the spring, and at that point McGovern had neither the money nor the plans to establish them. McGovern had his storefronts and his telephone calls going out, but not as part of a national plan and not on anything like the scale of our operation.

By October 1, we had some two thousand storefront headquarters in operation across the nation. In California alone, we had 170 storefronts, forty-five telephone centers, and 30,000 volunteers. Each center was expected to make a minimum of 1,500 calls per day, and all the callers asked the same questions, so the results could be reported to Washington and evaluated on a national basis.

Our direct-mail program continued to supplement the phone calls and door-to-door visits. On the final weekend of the campaign, on the basis of literally millions of calls and visits, we sent "mailograms" signed by the President to some six million Nixon supporters asking them to vote. A telegram from the President seemed a little corny to some, and it took several memos to the White House to sell the idea, but those mailograms were viewed by most recipients as a personal contact by the President (many were later framed) and they helped our voter turnout on Election Day. In addition to those mailograms by the President to committed Republicans, Connally's organization was sending millions of letters to potential Democrats for Nixon in the final weeks of the campaign and they too had their impact. I may be prejudiced, but I believe the 1972 Nixon campaign was the best-planned, best-organized, best-run Presidential campaign in American history, and there was no way that Senator McGovern, with the time and money at his command, could come close to equaling it.

Election night was anticlimactic. We took over much of Washington's huge Shoreham Hotel for a victory celebration for about five thousand invited guests. This was no casual affair. It had a carefully selected guest list, a strict pecking order, and a definite political intent. The early-evening victory celebration being televised in Washington was designed to influence the vote on the West Coast (thanks to the time change) and then to provide a suitable forum to the President's first postelection appearance. The guests were divided into three categories: Maurice Stans's Fat Cats, who got the best food and drink in their own private enclave; other VIPs, who got good food and drink; and, finally, everybody else, who had access to the hotel ballroom and cash bar.

I took Gail and the children to the celebration, and we got VIP treatment, of course, but the evening was strangely unexciting for me. We had won our great victory, a bigger one than we'd expected, and I was proud of it, yet part of me felt that it was a hollow triumph. When, finally, the President made his appearance at the Shoreham and the crowd cheered wildly, I felt cut off from the celebration around me. Elections are a kind of fantasy world; that is part of their appeal. You bring together the best people and the best facilities, you have action and power and suspense, and if you are very lucky you may win the kind of historic victory we won in 1972. But I knew as well as anyone in that crowded, echoing ballroom how high the cost of our victory had been, and I sensed that for me the fantasy was almost over.

CHAPTER XIV

The Cover-Up Fails

IN EARLY OCTOBER I had a visit from the President's friend
J. Willard Marriott, whom I had gotten to know in 1970 when he was
chairman of the Honor America Day committee and I was the White
House liaison with that committee. Marriott had also been chairman of
the 1969 Inaugural Committee, and he came to see me to discuss the
need to begin planning for the 1973 Inaugural. He had come to me, he
said, because he'd been unable to arouse any interest at the White House.
He pointed out that we were talking about a multimillion-dollar event,
with perhaps three hundred staff people, three thousand volunteer workers, and thirty thousand guests at the various balls, concerts, and receptions, as well as the Inaugural Ceremony itself and the parade that
traditionally follows it. If we waited until after the November 7 election
to begin planning for the January 20 Inaugural, we wouldn't have time to
do the job right.

I agreed, and I contacted Haldeman. His initial reaction was to put
off Inaugural plans until after the election, lest we divert our energies
from the campaign. I persisted, however, and eventually Haldeman
agreed that some basic decisions on staff and logistics should be made in
October. Haldeman asked if, once the election was past, I would like to
direct the Inaugural Committee staff. Haldeman and I both knew that
the Watergate situation complicated the question of my job in the second
Nixon Administration, and it seemed to me that working on the Inaugural

272

Committee would be an interesting way to spend a few months while I waited for Watergate to cool down. I had anticipated this offer and had already discussed it with Mitchell, who agreed it would be a good idea, so when Haldeman offered me the job I accepted it.

Haldeman and I also discussed the question of whether Marriott should again be asked to be chairman of the Inaugural Committee. Haldeman at first thought not. Haldeman's view was that while the President liked Marriott personally, he didn't want to have to deal with him on the Inaugural because Marriott, an extremely successful, self-made businessman, tended to approach the President as an equal, sometimes to disagree with him, and that wasn't how the President liked to do business. The fact was that the President and Haldeman wanted to control all important decisions on the Inaugural and they didn't want to debate them with an independent figure like Marriott. We knew, both from the 1969 Inaugural and from Honor America Day, that we could expect to have certain philosophical differences with Marriott. For one thing, as a businessman, he tended to be concerned about profit and loss, whereas from the White House point of view the Inaugural was a celebration of Richard Nixon and making a profit wasn't a consideration. Also, we could anticipate that Marriott would see the Inaugural more as a Washington civic event, whereas to the President it was a national political event— invitations to it were a form of patronage, and beyond that it was a television spectacular.

I had great respect for Marriott, and felt I could work with him effectively and could get around the problems Haldeman raised. I talked to Mitchell, who shared my regard for Marriott, and felt I could solve the problems Haldeman raised. Mitchell called Haldeman about the Marriott appointment. I added a memo of my own, and eventually Haldeman and/or the President agreed that Marriott should have the post.

I asked Bart Porter, Ken Rietz, and some other people I had confidence in, to join the Inaugural staff and we began some initial planning in October. On the day after the election I met with our key staff people at our Inaugural offices at Fort McNair in southwest Washington. Once our planning was in motion Gail and I departed for a ten-day vacation, along with Bart and Carol Porter, Joan and Bob Marik, and Glenn and Charlotte Sedam. On our way to the Bahamas, Gail and I stopped in Daytona Beach for a visit with Bill France, the one-time garage owner who'd founded the Daytona Beach 500 stock car race. France was a George Wallace supporter and fund raiser, a big, genial, bearlike man in his fifties. One highlight of our visit came when France took us out in his Oldsmobile for a ride around his Daytona 500 track. The track is banked on the curves, and as we roared into a curve at 110 miles an hour, France laughed and took his hands off the steering wheel to show us how perfectly designed the track was. That was Gail's most enduring memory of the visit—screaming in the back seat as she zoomed around a curve at 110 miles an hour with a driver who'd let go of the steering wheel.

We flew from Florida to the Bahamas. Gail says that on this holiday Bart Porter and I didn't really unwind, that at most we seemed to unwind about halfway from the pressures of the campaign, but I felt myself to be as relaxed and happy as I'd been in a long time.

Back in Washington, we faced two basic problems: which 15,000 or so of our supporters did we honor with Inaugural invitations, and what did we do with them once they arrived in Washington?

First, we sent out some 200,000 "honorary" Inaugural invitations. These were large, handsomely engraved, suitable for framing, but if you read the small print you realized that they didn't admit you into anything. We planned on sending out enough "real" invitations to yield about 30,000 Inaugural guests. Each state reelection committee chairman was told he could submit a list of so many invitees—perhaps a hundred or two, depending on the size of the state—and people like Stans, Agnew, Connally, and Colson had separate lists of their own. Each person who submitted a list was asked to rank the people in order of priority, then we at the Inaugural Committee made the decisions on what people got into the exclusive Inaugural affairs and what people got invitations only to the large events.

The standard invitation was to one of the five Inaugural Balls—we intended to squeeze all thirty thousand guests into those. Most people also got an invitation to one of two large receptions, each of which was planned for about 10,000 guests. Beyond that, there was room for only higher-priority individuals to attend some of the smaller dinner and concerts. I don't recall a great deal of difficulty in the negotiations over invitations. The most delicate situation came when we were dealing with the Rockefeller forces and the Reagan forces over seats for the two governors and their parties at the Friday night symphonic concert at the Kennedy Center. We wound up with what might be called separate but equal facilities, with each governor having a box that flanked the President's box at the concert.

None of these events was free. We charged admission, ranging from

$10 for the big receptions to $500 for tickets to the most exclusive of the Friday night dinners and concerts. We took in some $4 million and, to Mr. Marriott's delight, showed a small profit.

We made several innovations in the 1973 Inaugural. For one thing, we managed to end the parade before dark by reducing the distance between the floats and bands and by assigning monitors to see that they stayed the desired distance apart. Another innovation was to use government buildings, such as the Kennedy Center and the Smithsonian buildings, for the Inaugural balls, instead of hotels. We expanded the number of Inaugural events and thus were able to invite more people than had attended any previous Inaugural. Following our usual procedure, we geared the events for television, so that the nation could enjoy them, and so that they would be helpful to us politically.

The highlights of the Inaugural Week were these:

—The Vice President's Reception, held on Thursday, January 18, from 5 to 9 P.M. at the Smithsonian Museum of History and Technology, with some 10,000 people attending, and Vice President and Mrs. Agnew as host and hostess.

—On Thursday night, we held two "Salute to the States" variety shows in the Opera House and the Concert Hall of the Kennedy Center, with a total of about 4,000 people attending.

—Friday afternoon, at the Corcoran Gallery of Art, we had a "Salute to America's Heritage" reception, which was done in the style of a neighborhood block party and featured the music, food, and art of the nation's various ethnic and minority groups. It was a festive event, marred only by a hard rain that soaked the several thousand people who were waiting in line to get in.

—On Friday evening we held two formal dinners and three Inaugural Concerts at the Kennedy Center, one in each of the Kennedy Center's three main halls. There was a youth concert, with popular entertainers; an American music concert; and a symphonic concert, featuring Van Cliburn and the Philadelphia Symphony Orchestra, under the direction of Eugene Ormandy. There had been some controversy about the symphonic concert, with officials of the Washington Symphony thinking it should perform, but the Philadelphia Symphony was chosen, at the President's own insistence, because of his great personal admiration for it and Eugene Ormandy.

—On Saturday night, after the Inaugural Ceremony at the Capitol and the afternoon parade, Inaugural Balls were held at the Kennedy Center, the Smithsonian Museum of History and Technology, the Smithsonian Museum of Natural History, the Pension Building, and a youth ball at the Sheraton Park Hotel. Gail and I attended the ball at the Museum of Natural History. One of the ironies of the evening was that many people wanted to attend the Kennedy Center Ball, thinking it would be the most glamorous one, but we'd packed some ten thousand people in there, it didn't have parking or other facilities, and the whole thing was a mob scene. The President made an appearance at each of the five balls and he was almost crushed by the churning sea of humanity that overflowed the Kennedy Center.

—Finally, on Sunday morning, the official Inaugural activities ended with a White House worship service for about two hundred political VIPs. As Gail and I went through the receiving line, the President stopped us and talked to us for four or five minutes. He told us that this was without question the finest of the six Inaugurals he'd attended. (He went in 1949 as a congressman; in 1953, 1957, and 1961 as Vice President; and in 1969 and 1973 as President.) He praised the parade for moving quickly enough so that people could enjoy it before they froze. And he also praised the symphonic concert and particularly Eugene Ormandy, whom he said he considered the finest conductor of our time. He was generous with his praise of my work, and, as usual, he was quite specific about what he had liked.

I was pleased, naturally, by the President's compliments. It was good to know that I was no longer in the limbo of the previous August, when I'd been kept away from the President's cruise because of my Watergate problem. The Inaugural had been an exciting and satisfying three months for me. I'd had an excellent staff and I thought we'd done a first-rate job. I'd enjoyed all the amenities that went with the job, like driving around in my Mustang with special Inaugural license plate #4 on it (just behind the President, the Vice President, and Marriott), and getting VIP treatment as I took Gail to the Inaugural events. Just before the Inaugural I'd been the subject of a long, favorable feature article in the Washington *Post*. The Watergate affair seemed, in those early weeks of the new year, to be fading from the public consciousness and it was possible to think it might somehow be forgotten in the aftermath of the President's stunning electoral victory. I had been receiving a number of feelers about jobs in the private sector, and there was even some talk of my running for office in California. My real desire, however, was to have an important position in the new Administration, and as the

Inaugural interlude neared an end, I began to give that question serious thought.

Several weeks before the Inaugural, I had gone to New York to talk to Mitchell about the positions several people would receive in the new Administration. We had lunch at his club and then went to his law office to finish our talk. I wanted to be sure that several men who had worked for me at CRP and on the Inaugural Committee were taken care of. I was concerned about people like Odle, Sedam, Marik, and particularly Bart Porter, the one person I had specifically promised a good job. The White House personnel office had seemed to be dragging its feet about these people, and I thought it best to talk to Mitchell, so that if necessary he could say a word to Haldeman or even to the President.

Mitchell and I also discussed my own plans. I mentioned that I had an opportunity to be the $75,000-a-year president of a medium-sized corporation, but that I was much more interested in staying in the Administration and perhaps running my own agency. Mitchell puffed on his pipe and commented that perhaps I should consider the corporate opportunity. That bothered me a bit, particularly since John Dean had recently made a similar comment, and I was also bothered by my exchange with Mitchell about Bart Porter.

"We really have to take care of Bart because of what he did for us on the Watergate case," I told Mitchell. "I told him that if he'd support my story, we'd see that he got a good job, and we owe it to him to deliver."

Mitchell's response was disturbingly vague, as if he didn't know what I was talking about. But in general he had been very positive and helpful that afternoon so I put his vagueness about Porter from my mind.

A few days later, however, I had a talk with John Dean. We discussed Watergate from time to time, with Dean filling me in on the upcoming trial of the seven defendants and on the efforts being made to guarantee that they would plead guilty and remain silent. During this January talk, however, John indicated surprise that anything as bizarre as the Watergate break-in could have happened.

"Look, John," I said, "I know you remember those meetings we attended in Mitchell's office."

But Dean didn't seem to remember those meetings. He, too, was becoming vague about Watergate.

I began to get worried. If Dean and Mitchell were having memory lapses about the meetings at which we'd discussed the Liddy plan, I thought it might be scapegoat time and I might have been chosen for that honor. In retrospect, I suspect that Dean and Mitchell had indications that the grand jury was going to reopen the investigation, and that they were indeed trying to position things so I could take the blame. I also suspect that the meeting with Dean, when he couldn't recollect our discussions of the Liddy plan, was being taped, so that he might later use it as evidence of my guilt and his innocence. I know that several of my later talks with Dean and Haldeman in their offices were taped without my knowledge.

I had volunteered, in the first days of the cover-up, to take the blame, if necessary, to protect Mitchell and the President, but now I was no longer willing. Too much had happened—the vagueness, my suspicions about my conversations being taped, the White House personnel office not taking care of my people, Colson's telling a reporter that there was no place for me in the second Administration. I was beginning to feel that I had been loyal to the team but the team wasn't being very loyal to me. Moreover, even if I had been willing to be a scapegoat, it was no longer feasible. The case had grown too big. Besides the original conspiracy, there was now perjury, obstruction of justice, the various efforts to buy the silence of the seven defendants; I couldn't have accepted the guilt for all that if I'd wanted to.

After Dean had his lapse of memory, I decided I should have a talk with Haldeman. I was already planning to talk to him about my job situation and I decided that at the same time I should make sure he had the facts about the Watergate affair. I realized that he and I had had only one direct conversation about the case, during the call he made to me in Los Angeles on the weekend of the break-in. For all I knew, Dean and Mitchell might have told Haldeman that I authorized the break-in. I was confused. I didn't know what the grand jury might do or what my friends might do. I talked to LaRue, and he agreed that I should talk to Haldeman. I think he too was curious about what Haldeman might say, because LaRue was a Mitchell man and had never been close to Haldeman. If I was being tossed overboard, LaRue had to ponder whether he might expect the same fate.

So I sat down with Haldeman and went over the facts with him—the three meetings with Mitchell, then the cover-up, the perjury, all the people who had been involved in the affair. In essence, I said: "Look, Bob, I've been a good soldier, but I want to be sure you know it wasn't just me in this thing, it was a lot of people."

Haldeman, too, was vague. He said this was the first he'd known about some of these matters. He said he hadn't known about the break-in in advance. That was possible, if Strachan hadn't passed on to him the material I'd sent over on the Liddy plan, but I thought it was most unlikely.

Haldeman made one unexpected and interesting comment. He said that, in retrospect, it would have been better if they'd let Mitchell take the blame for the break-in back in June when it occurred. That way, he noted, no cover-up would have been necessary. He tossed that comment in, and I didn't pursue it, but I think that in retrospect, from his and the President's point of view, there's no question that he was right.

If you assume, as I do, that Nixon didn't know about the break-in plan in advance, and that approving it was a blunder Mitchell made, then the White House would have been far better off to put all the responsibility on Mitchell. Presumably I would have been included too, although perhaps a way could have been found to extricate Dean, since he worked in the White House. Mitchell and I would have gone to trial for conspiracy, and there's at least some chance that we could have been acquitted, if we had protested our innocence and blamed Liddy, and Liddy had remained silent. The President's reelection probably wouldn't have been affected.

The main flaw with this scenario may be the one I suggested earlier—if the White House deserted Mitchell, that might have discouraged Hunt and Liddy, and once either of them decided to talk all of the plumbers' exploits would have come to light.

In any event, after I talked to Haldeman about Watergate, we discussed job prospects for both me and Porter. Haldeman promised to see that Porter was taken care of; in fact, he called Higby on his intercom and asked Higby to remind him to speak to Malek about Porter. As for my job, I'd be willing to return to the White House on a temporary basis, but Haldeman didn't seem interested in that. He brought up the possibility that I might direct the planning for the Bicentennial Commission. I was interested, and agreed to talk to several people about the commission's work. I left my meeting with Haldeman feeling encouraged. I had told him the Watergate story and I had received his assurances about my and Porter's jobs. There seemed nothing more for me to worry about, at least for the time being.

On Tuesday, January 23, just three days after the Inaugural, I testified in the Watergate trial in Judge John Sirica's courtroom. My testimony could hardly have been less eventful. I went in, took the oath, was questioned for about forty-five minutes, and left. Neither the prosecutors (and I was their witness) nor the defense lawyers challenged my story. It may be, of course, that the prosecutors were laying the groundwork for a later perjury case against me; certainly Earl Silbert got me firmly on record in this exchange:

Q. Mr. Magruder, did you ever give Mr. Liddy any assignment concerning the Democratic National Committee?

A. No.

Q. Did you ever receive any report of any kind from Mr. Liddy concerning the Democratic National Committee offices and headquarters at 2600 Virginia Avenue, Northwest, here in the District?

A. No.

Q. Did you ever give Mr. Liddy any assignment concerning Senator McGovern's Campaign Headquarters at 410 First Street, Southeast, here in the District?

A. No.

Q. Did you ever receive any intelligence information from him concerning those headquarters?

A. No specific intelligence, no.

Bart Porter followed me to the witness stand, and told the story about the surrogate protection plan that we'd developed the previous July:

Well, it was along about that time [December of 1971] that I began to become concerned about the possible disruption of some of our appearances by some of the extremist groups across the country both from the right and left, but principally from the left, disruptions at appearances or rallies which could cause embarrassment and could cause the press to perhaps report more on the disruption rather than on the substance of the particular speaker . . . There was a general discussion [at a meeting with Liddy and Magruder] on what something like that might cost and I figured right off the top of my head, figured it might cost as much as a hundred thousand dollars from that period of time until the actual election. I based that on perhaps the use of about ten college-age people who might be able to assimilate themselves into such organizations as the Yippies and the SDS and other such radical troops and perhaps paying them $500 a month for ten months and another $500 expenses which would be about $10,000 a month and for ten months would be around a hundred thousand dollars, so that figure was discussed, yes.

The most memorable moment in my appearance at the trial came when I left the witness stand and Gordon Liddy, sitting at the defense table, smiled at me and winked.

Soon after I testified at the trial, I flew out to California to test the political waters there. The incumbent Secretary of State, Edmund Brown, Jr., was expected to run for governor in 1974, and I had considered the possibility of running for that office if he did vacate it. My preference was to have a good job in the Administration, and I considered running for office in California something of a fallback position if things went wrong in Washington. I had discussed the idea with Mitchell, Haldeman, Lyn Nofziger, Herb Kalmbach, and others, and most of them thought it was a good idea. Haldeman had commented that I was both personally attractive and knew how to run a campaign—an unusual combination in political candidates. I was not a native of the state, and I'd been away since 1969, but I knew a lot of Republican leaders there, and if enough of them thought I looked like a winner I might be able to preempt the field on the Republican side.

I assumed before I went that I would find support among the Reagan wing of the California Republican Party and little support among the Finch wing, and that was how it turned out. I had worked with Reagan's people when I was in the White House, as well as at CRP and on the Inaugural, and we were on good terms. They thought of me as "a Mitchell man" and Mitchell and Reagan were friendly. I had a half-hour talk with Reagan and he was quite encouraging, although I didn't ask for any commitment and he didn't offer any. It was too early for that. I also had a talk with Finch, but it was a typical disjointed Finch conversation, with him jumping from one topic to another, and nothing of substance ever being said. Insofar as Finch and Reagan represented liberal and conservative ideological poles in the party, I considered myself somewhere in between them, but I was more personally comfortable with Reagan and his people. I had worked with Finch in the past and he knew I had reservations about him, so I didn't expect much from him or his people, nor did I think that would hurt me.

I came away from my California trip feeling that unless Reagan backed some other candidate in the primary, I could probably win the Republican nomination. I already had promises of $100,000 in campaign funds, a good start in a state where running for office is extremely expensive. I felt that I could do well on television and that my family would be an asset. I knew a lot of young business and professional men who would like to become involved in my campaign, and I felt that I knew how to put together a first-rate political campaign. The biggest question in my mind was whether I wanted to run for office, or whether I could get a job in the new Administration that would be more attractive to me.

Gail didn't accompany me to California, and after my trip I took her and the children skiing in Colorado. Gail's attitude about my future was that whatever I decided to do—run for office, stay in government, or return to the business world—was fine with her, but she wanted me to make my decision so she'd know whether we'd be moving and whether the children would be changing schools. I agreed with her, and when we returned to Washington I was determined to get the matter settled. I was still on the Inaugural Committee payroll, completing some work there, but it was time for a decision.

The problem was that I had reached the point where most of the jobs I was qualified for required Senate confirmation, but Haldeman and I agreed that I should not be exposed to the confirmation process. It wasn't a question of my getting a majority vote in the Senate; I probably could have done that. The problem was my going up for hearings under oath in which the Democratic senators could question me about Watergate and perhaps summon others like Mitchell to testify. We had the unhappy precedent of the Kleindienst confirmation hearings, when the ITT case had been reopened, and we didn't want to run the risk of that happening on Watergate.

Normally, I would have expected an appointment either as the Undersecretary of one of the Departments or, preferably, as the head of an agency like ACTION or the Environmental Protection Agency, but those were out because they required Senate confirmation. The simplest answer to the situation would have been for me to take a corporate job, where I would have made twice the money I could expect in government, but I enjoyed government and after my four years as a staff man I wanted an opportunity to run a program of my own.

Haldeman summoned me to his office on a Friday in early March to discuss my situation. He'd kept his promise to find Bart Porter a good government position—although Porter had chosen to go with a private corporation—and I was curious to see what he'd come up with for me. John Dean was with Haldeman when I arrived. I found out later that Haldeman had ordered the White House personnel office to come up with a list of ten possible jobs for me. Eight of them would have required an Executive Order changing them to non-Senate confirmation posts, and two others did not require confirmation. It was one of these two that Dean and Haldeman outlined for me first—Director of Policy Planning at the Department of Commerce. It was more a policy than a management job, directing a staff of economists and statisticians who advised the Secretary of Commerce on policy matters. The job paid $38,000, and while it obviously wasn't what I wanted it sounded interesting and I thought it might do on a temporary basis. Haldeman stressed that this would be temporary, until Watergate had died down and they could risk sending me up for Senate confirmation. I agreed to talk to the new Secretary of Commerce, Fred Dent, a textile executive from South Carolina, and after having a friendly conversation with him that Saturday I took the job.

Somewhat to my surprise, I greatly enjoyed my rather brief stay at the Department of Commerce. Secretary Dent was agreeable to work with, I had an excellent staff, and my background in business and economics was broad enough so that I could deal comfortably with the various policy issues that arose. My real value in the job, however, was that I knew both the people and the processes of the Nixon Administration. At the White House, at CRP, and at the Inaugural Committee, I had functioned as a high-level bureaucrat, someone who knew how to get things done. I had experts on my staff whose knowledge of economics far exceeded my own. What I could add was the ability to call John Ehrlichman or George Shultz or Bill Simon or Peter Flanigan and get answers to our questions. In our staff discussions, I could say with some confidence, "No, the President won't like that approach," or "Ken Cole in Ehrlichman's office is the guy to talk to about that."

We worked on such issues as oil imports and East-West trade. Our people saw the possibility of an energy crisis, but we were repeatedly told by the White House and the Treasury Department not to worry about it. We became involved in a decades-old dispute between our Department and the State Department as to which should have authority over commercial attachés in U.S. embassies. When we were asked to undertake a new study of the issue we discovered there had been innumerable other studies of it over the years, and what it boiled down to was that State had control of the commercial attachés and it wasn't about to give them up. I did what I could to get my people plugged into the right circuits in the Administration, and I enjoyed myself in the process. Unfortunately, my stay at the Commerce Department was to be even briefer than I'd expected.

On the afternoon of Friday, March 23, I received a call at my Commerce Department office from Van Shumway, CRP's press officer.

"Have you heard about McCord's letter?" he asked.

"Oh, my God," I said. "What letter?"

"He wrote a letter to Sirica. It's in this afternoon's Washington *Star*."

"What did he say?"

"A lot," Shumway said, and read me the letter. In brief, McCord charged that he and the other Watergate defendants were under "political pressure" to plead guilty and remain silent, that perjury was committed at the trial, and that higher-ups were involved in the break-in plan.

McCord's charges were, of course, correct, and I had to assume he would name me as one of the higher-ups in the plot. I had no reason to think that McCord would protect me. Two months earlier, when the *Post* had run the article on me, McCord had bitterly told John Dean, "I'm going to prison and Magruder's getting his picture in the papers." McCord was fighting for his freedom, and by implicating me he might save himself. Judge Sirica, by threatening the Watergate defendants with long sentences, had cracked one of them, and that was the beginning of the end for the cover-up. Except for Judge Sirica, I think the cover-up might have held. We had come a long way from the time, the previous year, when Sirica took the Watergate case and John Dean commented, "Well, I don't know much about him, but he's a Republican so he'll probably be okay."

I mumbled something to Shumway, hung up, and called John Dean at the White House. His secretary told me he was there and said she'd get him for me, but then she came back on the line and said he couldn't speak to me right that moment. I told her it was very important, and she left the line, then returned and said she was sorry, but Mr. Dean would have to call me later.

I was starting to panic. I wanted to know what was happening, what the McCord letter meant, what we should do, but Dean wouldn't talk to me. I called Paul O'Brien, CRP's lawyer.

"Paul," I said, "I called Dean about the McCord letter but he wouldn't take my call."

"I know," O'Brien said. "I don't think he wants to talk to you."

I knew that. We discussed the letter for a minute, but O'Brien didn't seem to have anything helpful to say, so I called Fred LaRue, who was one of the few people I felt I could trust.

"What's going on?" I asked LaRue. "Dean won't talk to me."

"I know," he said. "I'll try to get that straightened out."

"We can't handle this thing if we don't *talk* to each other!"

"I know, I know," LaRue told me. "Why don't you come over here and we'll go over it?"

I went to LaRue's Watergate apartment that afternoon, and again the next morning, and at both meetings we tried to evaluate the situation as best we could. The more I thought about it, the more I was convinced that McCord's testimony, by itself, would not be fatal to us. All McCord could know was whatever Liddy had told him—presumably that Dean, Mitchell, and I had been in on the break-in planning—and that was secondhand evidence, or hearsay. So long as Liddy remained silent, McCord's secondhand information could not convict us.

The problem was that McCord's letter would almost surely cause the grand jury to reopen its investigation, and I didn't think the cover story could survive additional scrutiny. The prosecutors would almost surely call Bob Reisner the second time around, and his testimony would probably link me and Mitchell to Liddy's Gemstone file. Moreover, as LaRue pointed out, there were other aspects of the case, involving money and promises of executive clemency to the defendants, that McCord might have firsthand information about. Also, the Senate hearings were about to begin, and they posed another serious threat to our fragile cover story.

I should have realized by that Saturday that the cover-up had been shattered, that there was no way to put Humpty-Dumpty together again. The instinct for self-protection still guided me, the illusion that we might somehow escape the inevitable, but I think I was increasingly realizing that I couldn't go through it all again. The previous summer we had all been a team, united by the goal of the President's reelection. Now that motivation was gone, the team was scattered—Mitchell in New York, Mardian back in Arizona, me out of the White House orbit—and we seemed to be reaching the point of every man for himself.

The next day, Sunday, a reporter from the Los Angeles *Times* called me at home for my comment on a story that McCord had named me and Dean as having had prior knowledge of the Watergate break-in. I declined comment, but after I hung up the phone I was a basket case, a complete wreck. That was it. The truth seemed destined to come out, and all I could see ahead was the wreckage of my life.

A friend in Los Angeles called and read me the *Times* story the next morning. It was the lead story on the front page, with pictures of me and Dean, and it began:

"Convicted Watergate conspirator James W. McCord has told Senate investigators that White House counsel John W. Dean III and former Presidential aide Jeb Stuart Magruder had prior knowledge of the bugging of the Democratic National Committee headquarters last year, the *Times* learned Sunday."

When I reached my office that morning I called Dean and this time he spoke to me. He let me do most of the talking, as I outlined my theory that all McCord could know about the break-in plan was hearsay. Dean and I commiserated about the Los Angeles *Times* story, and the pressures of having the press on your trail, and we agreed that we'd keep in close touch. I later learned from the prosecutors that he'd taped this conversation.

I called Ken Parkinson and said I wanted to talk to him about my legal situation and asked if he could continue to represent me. He indicated that he would, and asked me to come talk with him and O'Brien. But when I reached his office, Parkinson said that perhaps it would cause a conflict for him to handle my case. As CRP's lawyer, his chief client at that point seemed to be Maurice Stans, and I was later told that Parkinson talked to Stans, who didn't want Parkinson representing me. Paul O'Brien was also in Parkinson's office that afternoon, and we discussed lawyers I might retain. They mentioned James Bierbower, whom they said was a Republican and had an excellent reputation. One of them called Bierbower's office, but he was in Bermuda attending a bar convention, and no decision was made about my legal representation.

Gail's and my bedroom overlooks our front yard, and the next morning, as I was waking up, I heard strange noises outside. Then, when Gail arose and pulled open the shades, she suddenly screamed and threw herself to the floor. There, on our lawn, were twenty or so reporters and photographers with their cameras focused on the house. My car was in the driveway, so I had no choice, when it was time to leave for work, but to make my way through them and mutter my "no comment" to their questions. But the representatives of the media are not easily discouraged, and they became a fixture on my lawn for the next two months, sometimes just two or three, sometimes twenty or thirty. Eventually I could anticipate, depending on the day's Watergate developments, how many reporters would be out front the next morning. Sometimes, when it was obvious that a big morning was ahead, Gail and I would take the children and spend the night with our closest friends, the Gillespies. It became quite a cat-and-mouse game. After a while I began parking on the next street over and going out the back door and over the back fence to make my morning getaway. The reporters caught on to that and began stationing people in strategic points around the neighborhood where my comings and goings could be observed. Some of the reporters were particularly diligent about poking around our back yard and peering in the windows to see if I might be hiding inside. One of my few triumphs in the next few months was that the press never caught me after that first morning.

When I finally reached my office that Tuesday morning I had a call from Mitchell, who asked if I would fly up to talk to him in New York that afternoon. I assumed Parkinson or O'Brien had told him that I was becoming anxious about my legal situation. On the flight up to New York I wrote on a yellow legal pad all the questions that I hoped Mitchell would answer for me: Would my legal expenses be taken care of? If I went to prison would there be money for my family? Would I get help in finding a job after prison? Was there a chance of executive clemency by the President?

When I met with Mitchell in his office, I went through each point, and he assured me that everything I asked for could be provided. He was extremely confident and solicitous about my concerns. "Don't worry, Jeb," he said. "We'll take care of you."

I was glad to have his assurances, but I realized that he was in New York now, and I told him I would feel better if I could have assurances from Haldeman as well. Mitchell said that was no problem, that he was going to be in Washington the next day and he would arrange a meeting with Haldeman for the two of us.

He did so, and the next day, Wednesday, the 28th of March, when I arrived at Haldeman's office, Mitchell was already there. I told Haldeman again how serious I felt my legal problems were, and explained my hope that if I was indicted and brought to trial, I would receive financial support and, if necessary, executive clemency. Haldeman, too, was extremely reassuring to me. He stressed that he and the President considered me one of the Administration's best people, and they wanted to help me in every way they could. However, he was careful to say that they could only help me as friends, not in any governmental way.

I brought up a crucial issue—the need for Dean and Mitchell to back up the story we'd agreed to, and that I'd told the grand jury, that our January 27 meeting with Liddy had been canceled. I trusted Mitchell, but I didn't trust Dean, and he had made comments to me that suggested he was having second thoughts about the story we'd agreed to when my diary was subpoenaed.

Haldeman said he couldn't settle that matter, but he suggested that Mitchell and I meet with Dean that afternoon, when he returned from a trip to Camp David. Dean had been at Camp David several days, supposedly writing a report for the President on Watergate; I assumed he'd been mostly avoiding the press, which was pushing him not only about McCord's statement but about Pat Gray's remark before his Senate confirmation hearing to be FBI director that Dean probably lied to FBI agents about Howard Hunt's job at the White House.

Mitchell and I met with Dean that afternoon in Higby's office, and Dean refused to say he'd support me on the canceled meeting if he was called to testify before the grand jury. He was evasive. Perhaps the question was premature, he said. Perhaps he wouldn't be called, or could decline to testify on grounds of executive privilege.

"But, John," I insisted, "what if you *do* have to testify?"

But Dean wouldn't say. Mitchell tried to be a conciliator, saying he was sure Dean would cooperate when the time came. I wasn't so sure. I was furious with Dean and, rather than have it show, I left the meeting, saying I'd let Dean and Mitchell discuss the matter further. Months later, I began to see that Dean by then already realized that to support my perjury would only lead him deeper into the quagmire, and that he was thinking seriously about going to the prosecutors, which he did a few days later, in hopes of winning immunity. Dean, as a lawyer, had a far better grasp of the realities of the situation than I did. The chronology of the affair proves that he was about ten days smarter than I was. I was still dealing openly with the others, thinking they were my friends, thinking that somehow we could still hold things together, and meanwhile Dean was negotiating with the prosecutors and he and Haldeman were taping their talks with me. It was common knowledge in the White House that Colson taped many of his phone calls, but it never occurred to me that my friends would tape mine.

On Thursday I called Bierbower, the lawyer that Parkinson and O'Brien had recommended, and made arrangements to fly to Bermuda and see him on Saturday. Mitchell had urged me to talk to a lawyer, but he had added that of course I should not tell the lawyer the truth.

On the next morning, a rainy Friday, I read in the paper that Bob Reisner was about to be called to testify before the grand jury. That seemed to be the end of me. Reisner knew I had seen the Gemstone file and had taken it to a meeting with Mitchell. Moreover, I had heard somewhere (I don't remember how) that Reisner remembered searching for an easel for Liddy just before we left for the January 27 meeting with Mitchell. His memory of the search for the easel would chip away at my sworn testimony that the meeting had been canceled. I was tremendously frustrated. I had forgotten all about the damned easel, so why did Reisner have to remember it?

I called Reisner at home, said I wanted to talk to him, and suggested that I pick him up and give him a ride to work—he had by then gone to the White House to work in the personnel office. Reisner was friendly and courteous, but he said he didn't think it would be a good idea for us to talk.

When I got to my office, I was becoming more and more agitated about Reisner's testimony and I called him at his office and insisted that I had to talk to him. He was reluctant, but finally said he'd talk to me if there was a third person present. I said that was fine and arranged for us to meet at Paul O'Brien's office. But when I reached the lawyer's office, Reisner had called and said he'd decided not to come. I had asked O'Brien to feel out Reisner about the easel, and he had discovered that Reisner did remember about it. I called Reisner from O'Brien's office and I was extremely upset.

"Bob, what are you doing?" I demanded. "There wasn't any easel. Forget about the easel. I can't understand this. Aren't you going to cooperate? Everyone else is cooperating. It isn't just me. If this gets out of hand they're going to impeach the President."

Reisner said that he didn't want to hurt me or anyone else, but that he would have to tell the investigators the truth about what he knew.

When I cooled off, I realized that Reisner was right, that he had to tell the truth and that it was silly of me to expect him to do anything else. I'd gotten enough people in trouble without trying to add Reisner to the list. I didn't want Bob to think I'd tried to make trouble for him, so I called him back at the White House. I couldn't reach him, so I phoned his wife and asked her to have him call me at home that evening. Reisner later described our evening conversation to the Senate Watergate Committee this way:

> Now, in that evening phone call, the entire nature of the phone call was different. I think he said that he was upset, that he was sorry if he was overly anxious. He said he just wanted me to realize that there were some extremely serious matters concerned here and that I should treat them in that way.
>
> I said I intended to treat them in that way.

I should have gone to the prosecutors immediately, but I hadn't even talked to a lawyer yet. I think the main reason I held back was my fear that if I told the truth I would harm Mitchell. I was more or less resigned to my own fate, I wasn't worried about Dean, and I hadn't yet realized that my testimony would harm Haldeman, but I didn't want to do anything that would harm Mitchell. I still looked upon him as a kind of father figure, the man in government I had felt closest to, the one I still called "Boss" when we talked.

The next day, Saturday, Gail and I flew to Bermuda, so I could talk to James Bierbower and so both of us could have a vacation from the reporters who were camped on our lawn.

Bierbower joined us for dinner that evening, and I told him the cover story, explaining about my possible problems with McCord, Dean, and Reisner. Bierbower said it sounded like a difficult case, but said he'd represent me. With that settled, Gail and I proceeded to enjoy ourselves for a couple of days. The next day we won our flight in the mixed doubles tennis tournament at the Coral Beach Club, although we lost the championship match.

We returned to Washington on Tuesday, April 3. One day later that week Mitchell came to Washington and I talked with him in his law office. Once again, he told me that I must hold, that if I did we could see this through. I wanted to believe him but I couldn't. The fact was that you could no longer have a rational discussion with Mitchell about the Watergate situation. All Mitchell had left was blind faith. When you'd bring up specific points—Dean's waffling or Reisner's testimony— he wouldn't say, we'll do this or that, he'd only say, "We'll handle it somehow." But that wasn't good enough. LaRue and I agreed that Mitchell simply wasn't facing reality anymore. He was only believing what he wanted to believe.

I felt tremendous sympathy for him. He had approved the Liddy plan only reluctantly, in a time of personal distraction over his wife and the ITT affair, and only, I think, because of the mood that prevailed in the Administration. Mitchell had been an extremely successful Wall Street lawyer, then the Attorney General of the United States, and now he stood face to face with disgrace and possibly prison because of one ill-considered decision. It was a hard reality for him to face, but LaRue and I were facing it, and we agreed that the whole thing had fallen apart and we'd probably have to tell the truth soon. LaRue had stressed that it was time for us both to think about protecting ourselves and our families instead of continuing to worry about protecting Mitchell and the President.

Also that week Clark Mollenhoff, the big, gruff investigative reporter whom I'd known when he served at the White House in 1969–70, came to my office for a talk about the Watergate affair. I stuck to my cover story, which led him to comment that perhaps I ought to reread one of his books, *Washington Cover-Up*. Just in case I didn't get the point, he added in parting:

"Jeb, I don't know what your part was in this mess, but the best thing you can do is to come clean."

That Saturday, April 7, I met with my lawyer, Jim Bierbower, for our first full discussion of the case. Bierbower introduced me to a young lawyer named Jim Sharp, who had just joined his firm and who would also be working on my case. Sharp was about thirty, a wiry, sun-tanned Oklahoman with thick black hair. He'd just come to Bierbower's firm from the U.S. Attorney's Office. As an Assistant U. S. Attorney, Sharp had obtained the bribery conviction of former Maryland Senator Daniel Brewster, and also a conviction in the celebrated case of a Washington civil servant named Robert Ammidown who had hired another man to murder his wife.

As I went over my story—the cover story—with Bierbower and Sharp, the latter began asking me a prosecutor's tough, skeptical questions. It was obvious to me that Sharp didn't believe me. Bierbower was an excellent lawyer, who gave me valuable advice, but I think that at the outset he wanted to believe my story, whereas Sharp, perhaps because he had just come from the U. S. Attorney's office, saw through it from the first.

Bierbower reported to me that earlier that day, before seeing me, he'd talked to John Dean's lawyer, who'd said in effect: "Well, of course John doesn't have any legal problem, but Jeb has a very serious problem, and we don't know if we can help him." That made me furious. I had a problem, but so did Dean, one at least as serious as mine.

Early the next week, Larry Higby called and said that they had information that I'd leaked something to a reporter that linked Ehrlichman to Watergate. I hadn't, and the charge enraged me. "You people are out of your minds," I told Higby. "You're sitting in the middle of a criminal conspiracy and you're worrying about a PR problem." I couldn't believe it; I was facing prison and Higby was calling me about Ehrlichman's image.

That same morning, I called Bart Porter in New York. I sensed that it was only a matter of time until I would have to go to the prosecutors, and I felt that Porter should do the same thing, the sooner the better. I felt a responsibility about Porter because I had gotten him into this mess.

"Bart," I told him, "things aren't looking very good for me."

"What do you mean?"

"Well, let's just say that things are getting a little hot down here."

"Jeb, I don't know what you mean. You always told me you weren't involved in doing anything wrong."

"That's true," I admitted.

"I don't want you to go into anything," he said.

Perhaps Porter thought that if he didn't know anything about Watergate, it would go away. He was in New York in a new job and the events of the previous summer must have seemed a long way off. I didn't want to push him, so I told him I would keep him informed on what was happening, and we left it at that.

Jim Sharp came to my office later that day and we talked about the cover story again. He listened with obvious skepticism, and when he left he commented: "Jeb, pretty soon you're going to have to tell me the truth."

His words struck home. The whole thing had become ridiculous. I was up to my ears in a criminal conspiracy, I had a lawyer who was trying to help me, and I was lying to him. The grand jury was reopening its investigation, the Senate investigation was about to start, McCord had named me, Reisner would implicate me, Dean might challenge my sworn testimony—all in all, my story hadn't a chance of surviving. Nor did I have the heart to keep on lying, even if there was a chance. I was sick of lying, to my wife, to my friends, to the press, even to myself. The strain was just too much. I was nervous and distracted and irritable.

Often, with my family or with my colleagues at work, I just wasn't there. I was beginning to drink too much to calm my nerves, and taking a tranquilizer every night to get some rest. I couldn't take any more, in mind, in body, or in spirit. I still didn't want to hurt Mitchell, but that wasn't the issue anymore. The next morning, April 10, I went to Jim Sharp's office and told him the truth about Watergate. When I finished he shook his head and said the only thing he could say:

"Jeb, you've got no choice. It's just a matter of time before they know the whole story and right now they need us. We should go to the prosecutors and make the best deal we can."

He explained my legal situation to me. I could go to trial, plead not guilty, and not take the stand, but that would be an extremely weak position, given the evidence against me. Sharp pointed out that this was no ordinary criminal case. This case was part of history, it might go on and on, and for me, considering my guilt, to try to fight it in the courts would be a tremendous drain on my mental, physical, and financial resources. I could ponder those alternatives, he said, but the best advice he could give me was to admit my guilt and let him seek the best arrangement he could with the prosecutors. After an intensive discussion of all the alternatives open to me, I agreed that he was right. And once I had made that decision, I felt a tremendous sense of relief, I felt almost happy, to be finished with the cover-up and all its lies. I felt as if I'd been seized by madness for a long time and suddenly I had become sane again.

The next day, Wednesday, I called Porter and again urged him to go to the prosecutors and tell them all he knew.

"Jeb," he protested, "you're asking me to put one of your feet in a six-foot hole."

"I know that," I told him. "But I got you into this and the least I can do is help you get out of it."

That day, or perhaps the next, I had another call from Higby, who reached me at LaRue's apartment. I had been trying to reach Haldeman but he wouldn't talk to me. I had asked Higby, "Is there any direction Bob can give me?" Now, Higby told me, in more or less these words: "Bob wants you to know that the President wants you to tell the truth."

Higby also asked me who would be implicated by my testimony. I told him Mitchell, and to a lesser degree Mardian and LaRue at CRP, and Dean, Strachan, and possibly Colson at the White House.

"Then you won't implicate Bob?" Higby asked.

I said I didn't think I would. It hadn't occurred to me that Haldeman would be legally implicated by my having told him in January about the cover-up and my perjury.

I felt much better after my talk with Higby. He said the President wanted me to tell the truth, and I was telling the truth. Everyone was pleased. I didn't learn until later that our talk had been taped; then I realized that the assertion about the President's wanting me to tell the truth and the leading questions about Haldeman were intended to be part of Haldeman's defense.

On Thursday, Sharp and Bierbower opened negotiations with the prosecutors. The idea was that, in exchange for my testimony and co-operation, the prosecutors would agree to a reduced charge against me. I told my lawyers in advance that I didn't expect to escape punishment, that obviously I wanted them to strike the best bargain they could, but that they had my authority to agree to a one-count felony indictment, which, in this case, meant a maximum sentence of five years. As a practical matter, given the usual parole policies, a five-year sentence meant about twenty months in prison. And, of course, I could hope that the judge would sentence me to something less than the five-year maximum.

Earl Silbert took a hard line with my lawyers that first day. He implied that he might not need my testimony and he might choose to nail me with the toughest sentence he could. (At that time we didn't know that Dean had already approached Silbert with an offer to tell the whole story in exchange for total immunity.) Negotiations resumed the next day in Bierbower's office (so the press wouldn't get wind of what was happening) and went on for three hours while I waited anxiously in a nearby office. I had made my decision and now I wanted the matter settled; it was agony to sit there for three hours while in another room men were debating for how long I would go to prison. I kept thinking about what my imprisonment would mean to Gail and the children, whose interests I'd ignored for so long while I was worrying about Mitchell and Nixon. For the first time in my life I considered suicide. I could see how, if a situation became bad enough, if someone faced twenty years of prison instead of two, suicide would seem one solution to the problem. But suicide didn't really make sense. I still had my family to think of, even if I went to prison for a while. It wasn't my style to give up—throughout my life, if I did my best, things had always seemed to work out.

Sharp came in and said Silbert wanted to hear part of my story, to have a better idea of what evidence I had. We agreed that Sharp and Bierbower would guide what I said, so as to give Silbert a taste of my testimony but not all of it. I went into Bierbower's office and confronted Silbert, the prosecutor I'd lied to for so long. I had to assume that nothing would please Silbert more than to nail me, since I as much as anyone had frustrated the first Watergate investigation.

I began by apologizing to Silbert. "Earl, I'm sorry about what happened," I told him. "I know I made it difficult for you. I did it because I thought it was necessary. But that's not the case anymore and I want to cooperate with you."

Silbert accepted my apology graciously and I began telling him the highlights of my story. My impression was that Silbert was surprised by the complexity of the break-in plan and the cover-up, and the number of high-level people involved in them.

The afternoon ended without Silbert and my lawyers reaching any agreement about my plea. I went home and that evening Gail and I went to a dinner party that an admiral was giving for Gail's aunt and uncle, who were visiting in Washington. Throughout the evening, Jim Sharp was on the phone negotiating with Silbert. The prosecutor was holding out for a two-count indictment, which meant I would face a maximum of ten years in prison. Sharp was seeking a misdemeanor count, which would mean a maximum of a year in jail. I left the dinner party several times to call Sharp and get his report on the progress of the negotiations. Finally, Sharp called me and said Silbert had agreed to a one-count felony indictment. I said that was fine and returned to the dinner party.

As we drove home that night I finally told Gail the truth about my role in Watergate. I think she had guessed at the truth for months, but chose not to accept it. Now she had to know. At first she didn't understand how serious the situation was, and she thought I should not go to the prosecutors if it meant harming friends like Mitchell and LaRue. But finally I made it clear that we were talking about serious crimes, and that people were going to prison, perhaps including myself. Once she understood, she agreed that I had no choice but to tell the truth and accept the consequences. This was not an easy time for Gail. No one she had known had ever been involved in a crime or gone to prison. She had had doubts about politics and now her worst fears about political life had been confirmed. But we agreed that we must do everything we could to make the best of this, and minimize the harm to our children.

Throughout the difficult months that followed, Gail was unfailingly understanding and considerate.

The next day, Saturday, I spent most of the morning telling my story to the prosecutors in Bierbower's office. While I was there, I received a call from Higby asking if I would come and see Ehrlichman in the White House that afternoon. The prosecutors had no objection, so I said I would. In fact, I had already told the prosecutors that I wanted that weekend to inform Haldeman, LaRue, Mitchell, O'Brien, and Parkinson of what I had done. I regarded that as a courtesy to friends, to let them hear the story from me rather than from reporters or the prosecutors. The prosecutors had agreed; they perhaps hoped that my becoming a prosecution witness would encourage some of the others to do the same.

My two lawyers accompanied me to Ehrlichman's office. I think they were getting concerned about my making statements that might later be used against me. Ehrlichman began the meeting by explaining that the President had assigned him to find out the truth about Watergate. He knew I was cooperating with the prosecutors, and I spent about twenty minutes relating to him the highlights of what I was telling them—about my three meetings with Mitchell and the subsequent cover-up, including my perjury. Ehrlichman expressed surprise at all this, but said he wished me well and he was glad I had two such fine lawyers. He added that of course none of this had anything to do with *him,* but I think that Bierbower shook his confidence a little when he remarked, "You know, Mr. Ehrlichman, the prosecutors are very interested in you and Mr. Haldeman."

Ehrlichman's office was on the second floor of the West Wing of the White House, and as the lawyers and I left we passed Haldeman's first floor office. I asked the two lawyers if they would wait for me a minute while I went in and said hello to Haldeman. Actually, it was more like saying good-bye, because it wasn't likely that I'd be seeing him again.

I went into Haldeman's office and found him at his desk and Higby sitting nearby. I told Haldeman that I had enjoyed working for him, that I was sorry about the way things had worked out but I was in serious trouble, that I had committed perjury, and I had to cooperate with the prosecutors for the sake of my family.

Haldeman, when I said I had committed perjury, showed surprise, just as Ehrlichman had.

I had told him about my perjury three months earlier, but I wasn't there to argue with him, so I shrugged and said something like, Okay, Bob, whatever you say.

That exchange, I later learned, had been taped and presumably would be used as part of Haldeman's defense. My talk with Ehrlichman earlier that afternoon had also been taped, I was later told by the prosecutors. I don't think that anything about the whole affair made me angrier than learning that Dean, Haldeman, and Ehrlichman had been taping my conversations. I had been acting in good faith, with people I thought were my friends, and they were asking me leading questions and making self-serving observations in an effort to set me up and save themselves. Of course, while I had not taped any conversations, I had not hesitated to use Bart Porter's loyalty to involve him in the cover-up, and he was my friend too.

As far as I know, Haldeman's only advance knowledge of the break-in plan came through my reports to Strachan, assuming Strachan passed them on to Haldeman. I find it easy to understand how Haldeman could have considered the Watergate break-in Mitchell's problem, and how he could have become involved in the cover-up to protect the President. My impression was that Haldeman, a nonlawyer like myself, didn't realize until late in the game that he was involved not in hard-nosed politics but in a criminal conspiracy.

When I left the White House about 5 P.M. I crossed Lafayette Park and encountered Bart Porter outside St. John's Episcopal Church. Following my advice, Bart had come down to Washington and had talked to Parkinson and O'Brien, but still had not made up his mind what to do. I said that I had just come from the White House, that the cover-up was all over, that I had told the truth to the prosecutors, and that he should do the same as soon as possible. He finally did, a few days later.

That night I called Paul O'Brien and Ken Parkinson to tell them I was cooperating with the prosecutors. O'Brien called me back the next morning, Sunday the 14th of April, and asked if I could come to his home in Bethesda, Maryland, a short drive from my own home, to talk about the situation. When I arrived, O'Brien gave me some coffee and we went out on his sun porch to talk. O'Brien was normally a genial, happy-go-lucky Irishman, but this morning he was extremely nervous and upset. He said he wanted to discuss what I had told the prosecutors about his role in the case. He stressed how serious it was for any lawyer to become involved in improper activity, because if a lawyer was disbarred, he had no other way to make a living. My lawyers had told me to be careful about what I said to anyone about the case, but O'Brien was a friend and I told him I'd help him any way I could.

"Jeb, I've got an idea," O'Brien said. "Suppose I write down some questions about what you've told the prosecutors, and then we can talk about your answers, just to make sure we've got everything straight."

"Okay, Paul, that sounds all right."

He seized a yellow legal pad and wrote down his first question, which had to do with what I had told him about the cover-up activities. The truth was that I had not discussed the cover-up with O'Brien, until my meeting with him and Parkinson in late March. He wrote down my answer, and then asked his next question, relating to some other aspect of the cover-up, and again I said he had not been involved and he wrote down his question and my answer.

Eventually he had filled the sheet of paper with questions and answers which made clear that I had no knowledge of his having been involved in the cover-up. When we had finished with his questions, he said, "Well, Jeb, would you just sign this for me?"

I wanted to help him, but I was concerned about what my lawyers had told me.

"I don't know, Paul. My lawyers told me to be careful about what I said to people, so I don't guess they'd want me to sign anything."

"I understand perfectly," O'Brien said. "That's good advice and you're smart to follow it. But, look, there's just one thing that bothers me. If I have to show these questions and answers to the prosecutors, and you haven't signed them, you won't have any way of proving if it's the same piece of paper or if I've changed anything. Why don't you just make an X at the bottom of the page, so you can be sure I haven't changed anything?"

"Well, I guess there's nothing wrong with that," I said. O'Brien gave me a friendly smile and handed me a pen, and I made my X at the bottom of the sheet of legal paper.

Later that day, I talked on the phone to Jim Sharp.

"I had a strange meeting with Paul O'Brien this morning," I told him. "He wanted me to sign a statement about what I'd told him about the cover-up."

"My God, you didn't do that, did you?" Sharp asked.

"No, no, I wouldn't sign it," I said.

"Good," Sharp said. "You're using your head for a change."

"All I did was make an X at the bottom of the page," I explained.

"*An X!*" Sharp shouted. "You idiot, don't you know an X is as good as your signature if you use it to identify yourself on a document?"

"No," I admitted. "I didn't know that."

I spent the rest of that Sunday in a state of gloom. For all I knew, I might have fouled up the arrangement we'd worked so hard to make with the prosecutors; Silbert might say, "Magruder, the deal's off—you're too stupid for us to use as a witness." But as it turned out, nothing more was ever said about the paper with my X on it.

I called Mitchell at his law office on Monday to tell him that I was cooperating with the prosecutors. I hadn't called him over the weekend because I was afraid Martha might answer. Actually, I suspected that LaRue had already told him what I was doing, but I felt he deserved a personal call from me. Our brief talk was difficult, but not unpleasant. For me, it meant telling a man for whom I had great affection that I was giving evidence that might send him to prison.

"I'm sorry," I told him, "but I've got to think of my family and I don't have any other choice."

"I understand," he said. "You understand, of course, that I'll have to go the other way."

In other words, he would deny my charges and we might end up in court calling each other liars.

"I understand that," I told him. "Good luck, Boss."

"Good luck, Jeb."

That was that. He went his way and I went mine.

CHAPTER XV

Waiting

DURING THE MONTHS after I began cooperating with the Watergate prosecutors in April of 1973, some people would ask: If Magruder admits guilt, why is he walking the streets a free man while the Watergate burglars are in prison?

The answer was simple. I was free as a convenience to the prosecutors. They wanted to question me at length about Watergate-related activities, and it was more convenient for them if I was at home than if I was away in prison. Prison could wait until they were finished with me.

For my part, I found myself torn between a normal instinct to remain free and a growing desire to get my imprisonment over with. But I had little choice except to do what the prosecutors wanted, since I hoped that when I eventually went before Judge Sirica for sentencing they would state that I had cooperated fully, and that might be a mitigating factor in the sentence he gave me.

I faced, however, the question of how I would support myself while I awaited sentencing. I resigned from the Commerce Department on April 26. There was no question of my not working. Our savings would not have lasted long, and I had to think of putting money away to support the family while I was in prison.

Gail and I had decided that we would stay in Washington. Most other Watergate figures, such as Haldeman and Ehrlichman, left Washington soon after they resigned their government jobs. We decided we would

300

stay. The children were in school and didn't seem to have any serious problems, despite the publicity. We knew we would be losing some of our political friends, but we had many nonpolitical friends we could count on.

As for work, I'd received many job offers in the months before Watergate broke, and it seemed at least possible that I could find a full-time position with some company. But since I knew I would have to be available to the prosecutors, and I didn't know how long my legal limbo would continue, it seemed unlikely that a full-time job would work out, even if I could get one.

I decided, therefore, to set myself up as a consultant in the marketing field. Even before I left Commerce, I began calling business executives who'd previously expressed interest in hiring me if I left the government. These were people who knew I had considerable knowledge of general marketing techniques, including direct mail, advertising, demographics, and related areas.

In essence, I told each of them: "I've pleaded guilty and I'm probably going to jail. No one knows that yet, but you should know before you make a decision. If you use me as a consultant, I think I can help your company, and my price will be right. I don't think that hiring me would cause you any serious public-relations problems if you handle it correctly."

I got varied responses. A couple of men never took my call. A few others talked to me once but chose not to pursue the matter. In some instances, a company president encouraged me, but later said that others in the company feared "a problem with the stockholders" if they employed me; I took this to reflect a fear of adverse publicity.

One of the people I called was Charles Fraser, the founder and president of the Sea Pines Company at Hilton Head Island, South Carolina. I had gotten to know Fraser in the early 1970's when I'd taken my family to his Sea Pines Plantation for vacations. Fraser was a Southerner in his early forties, a Yale Law School graduate, and, in my view, a brilliant businessman, who has built what is perhaps the finest resort community in the United States. He is the only major recreational developer who is widely respected by environmentalists because of the ecological concern he has shown in developing the Sea Pines Plantation, as well as his new Amelia Island Plantation in Florida and Palmas del Mar resort in Puerto Rico.

I called Fraser in late April, explained my situation, and flew down to Charlotte, North Carolina, to talk to him. He said he thought there would be no problem in using me as a consultant, but that he felt he should discuss the matter with a few other people. He talked to his old friend Harry Dent, who had left the White House and returned to South Carolina to practice law. Harry told him, in effect, "You can help Jeb and Jeb can help you, so why not?" Fraser also spoke with Mike Maloney, who did some consulting for him in Washington, a Democrat with ties to Senator Humphrey, who also said he saw no problem in using me.

I therefore began as a part-time consultant to the Sea Pines Company, working with its marketing people on demographic studies, site selection, an improved direct-mail program, and studies of new retail opportunities. It has been, for me, an entirely pleasant arrangement. There have been one or two references in the newspapers to my work with the company, but thus far its stockholders have not risen up in revolt because of me.

A friend of mine in New York, a wealthy entrepreneur who had promised me financial support if I ran for office in California, became my second client. Because his companies are regulated by the government, he thought it best not to publicize the fact that I was working for him.

I obtained a third client more or less by accident. I was having lunch one day in May with Nick Ruwe, the Assistant Chief of Protocol, and David Cudlip, the president of Mohave Management Corporation, a Los Angeles firm that is involved with travel clubs and charter flights. Cudlip mentioned that he was having some marketing problems and suggested that perhaps I could help with them. I jumped at the chance, and his company became the third client of Metropolitan Research Services, as I called my consulting firm.

All things considered, that seemed like a decent start. I was able, in my time as a consultant, to keep my earnings close to the $38,000 I would have earned if I'd stayed in government. Business was not exactly booming, however, and it eventually became clear that I would not be in a viable position until I got prison behind me.

Besides getting my business started that spring, I also had to think about the press, about the ill-health of some members of my family, and about my appearance before the Senate Watergate Committee.

We still had reporters and photographers in front of our house many mornings, and on our doorstep many evenings. I might have become resigned to these uninvited guests, except that it was a problem with the children, who didn't understand why people waited in front of our house to take pictures of their father. One morning when Whitney left for school, he was confronted by a group of reporters and photographers, and rather than walk through the middle of them he cut across the edge of the yard. But he was met at the sidewalk by a young woman who is a reporter for one of the television networks. She stuck a microphone in his face and asked that he tell her my whereabouts.

Gail was watching in horror from the doorway. She was afraid to run to Whitney's aid, lest that scene be filmed for the evening news. So she shouted to the woman: "You get away from my child! If you want something you come to me, but leave my children alone."

The young woman withdrew, apparently surprised by Gail's ferocity, as indeed was Gail, who rarely raises her voice. It was not to be Gail's last unpleasant encounter with the press. There was a *New York Times* reporter who came to our house several times around midnight, while I was away on trips, and would bang on the door and demand to see me and demand proof when Gail said I wasn't there. There were also unpleasant incidents with Maxine Cheshire, the Washington *Post*'s gossip columnist, who had an endless curiosity about Watergate-related trivia, and once called one of our neighbor's homes and tried to pump an eleven-year-old child for information about the Magruders.

During this period, almost all our neighbors were tremendously understanding and helpful. We lost, as we'd expected, some of our political friends, but our nonpolitical friends were wonderful. And, for that matter, I remained on good terms with some of my political associates, including Fred LaRue, Rob Odle, Glenn Sedam, and others. One of the worst consequences of the Watergate affair, to those involved, is the many broken friendships left in its wake. In some cases, as between me and Haldeman or Mitchell, friends find themselves in direct contradiction on their testimony. In other instances, I discovered that because of Watergate, I'm *persona non grata* with people I once considered my friends.

I once commented that one result of my notoriety was getting the best tables in Washington restaurants. That was good for a laugh, but it gave a misleading picture of my situation. I had achieved a certain celebrity but it was not one I enjoyed. It wasn't that people were unpleasant. I had only one bad experience with a stranger, one evening when I was in a restaurant in the South and a drunk Republican woman berated me for "ruining the President." I have learned to treasure my anonymity, and I hope I can recapture it before too many years have passed. Connie Chung of CBS called me one day in the fall to inform me that I had been dropped from the Green Book, Washington's "social directory," and to ask if I had any comment. I told her that if all I had to worry about was being dropped from the Green Book, I would be the happiest man in America.

Early in May my mother entered the hospital. She was in her early seventies but she had always been a robust woman, and we had assumed she would outlive my father, who had a number of health problems. But she was also a heavy smoker, and had signs of emphysema. I talked to her that week and she expressed far more concern about my problems than about her health. However, she had cancer tests while she was in the hospital. I talked to her doctor on the morning of Friday, May 11, and he said that her condition was serious, but not critical, and there was no need for me to come to California immediately. She died that night.

Her death was a great blow to me and Gail, and it was followed in early June, just before my Senate testimony, by Gail's father suffering three heart attacks. The third was a massive one that would probably have killed him, except that he was already in the hospital and the doctors were able to keep him alive by artificial means. Gail and I had to assume that his heart attacks, and perhaps my mother's sudden death, were to some degree related to their anguish over my difficulties. Certainly that thought did not make my situation any easier to bear.

The Senate Watergate hearings opened on May 17 and I testified on June 14. I was, I believe, the fifteenth witness, coming just after Hugh Sloan, Bart Porter, and Maurice Stans, and just before John Dean and John Mitchell.

I was terrified at the prospect of appearing on national television to confess all the stupid and criminal acts I had committed while in government. It was like going to church to make your confession—but in front of a hundred million people. Still, I felt that I should make the best of the situation. I began with the assumption that while the hearings had a valid legislative purpose, and were a good way to inform the nation about Watergate, they were also a show, and the show belonged to the senators, not to the witnesses. For the witnesses, it was a no-win situation; the best you could do was to tell the truth, conduct yourself with dignity, and not try to argue or to give a lot of excuses.

At least that was how I saw it. Various other witnesses approached the hearings in different ways. Bart Porter, who had admitted committing perjury, tried to claim that he hadn't known he was breaking the

law because he'd been blinded by his loyalty to the President. I sympa-
thized with Bart, but it's very hard to talk your way around repeated
acts of perjury, and I thought he made a mistake in trying to do so.
John Dean, when he testified, chose to begin with a prepared statement
that took two days to read. I had a lot of memos I could have read too,
but I didn't see any point in that approach. I decided, instead, to make
a brief opening statement, then to let the senators guide the discussion,
instead of trying to guide it myself. Dean and I at least had the advantage
of being cooperative witnesses; Ehrlichman, when he testified, chose to
be combative with the senators, and it was a fight he could only lose.

Gail accompanied me to my testimony and sat just behind me. She
was terrified by the TV cameras and the news photographers, but I had
told her that I very much wanted her moral support. (We got additional
moral support from our friend Joan Gillespie, who sat with her and
joined us for lunch during the noon recess.) My opening statement to
the Committee is perhaps worth reproducing here:

> I helped organize the Committee to Re-elect the President be-
> ginning in May 1971 and I remained there throughout the entire
> campaign. Unfortunately, we made some mistakes in the campaign
> which have led to a major national concern. For those errors in
> judgment that I made I take full responsibility. I am, after all, a
> mature man and I am willing to face the consequences of my own
> acts. These mistakes were made by only a few participants in the
> campaign. Thousands of persons assisted in the campaign to reelect
> the President and they did nothing illegal or unethical. As far as I
> know at no point during this entire period from the planning of the
> Watergate to the time of trying to keep it from the public view did
> the President have any knowledge of our errors in this matter. He
> had confidence in his aides and I must confess that some of us
> failed him. I regret that I must today name others who participated
> with me in the Watergate affair. This is not through any desire to
> implicate others but simply to give you the facts to the best of
> my recollection. Thank you.

My testimony was completed in one day, as I had hoped it could be.
I had no complaint about my treatment by the senators. I was the first
witness to get into the details of the break-in planning and the cover-up,
and I think most of them were fascinated by my story. That was the
one thing I had going for me: I was there to tell the truth. I had nothing

to hide and little to lose. One thing I had learned in my dealings with the prosecutors was that once you agreed to tell the truth you had to tell it all. There was no holding back. I think that when I first went to the prosecutors I had the idea that I could confess everything I had done, but perhaps could go easy on some of the other people. But that is not how the game is played. You tell it all.

Senator Howard Baker had tried, in his questioning of the various witnesses, to probe their motivations. I anticipated his question, and in my answer I tried to point out the frustrations we in the White House had felt in trying to cope by legal means with antiwar people who resorted to illegal acts—the draft-card burning, the leak of the Pentagon Papers, the May Day attempt to shut down Washington, the bombing of the Capitol and so on.

I specifically mentioned the case of William Sloane Coffin, who had been indicted for counseling young men to resist the draft—in effect, to break the draft law. I went on to say:

> Now, here are ethical, legitimate people whom I respected, I respected Mr. Coffin tremendously. He was a very close friend of mine. I saw people I was very close to breaking the law without any regard for any other person's pattern of behavior or belief. I believed as firmly as they did that the President was correct in this issue. So, consequently—and let me just say, when these subjects came up and although I was aware they were illegal, and I am sure the others did—we had become somewhat inured to using some activities that would help us in accomplishing what we thought was a cause, a legitimate cause.
>
> Now, that is absolutely incorrect; two wrongs do not make a right. For the past year, I have obviously had to consider that and I understand completely that that was an absolute incorrect decision. But that is basically, I think, the reason why that decision was made, because of that atmosphere that had occurred and to all of us who had worked in the White House, there was that feeling of resentment and of frustration at being unable to deal with issues on a legal basis.

Perhaps I did not make my point clearly, for some commentators later criticized me for trying to justify the Watergate crimes by equating them with Bill Coffin's antiwar activities. I understand the difference between a crime committed in secret by government officials and an act of civil disobedience by someone who is prepared to accept the consequence of his act. I was not trying to say that the antiwar activities justified our offenses, but that they created an atmosphere in which we could wrongly convince ourselves that they were justified. Obviously, our actions were not justified.

Several of the senators made generous comments to me when they had finished questioning me. There was one exchange with Senator Montoya that I would like to reproduce here:

SENATOR MONTOYA: Well, Mr. Magruder, I believe that you have told a very complete story. I believe you have been most frank. I believe you have comported yourself in an admirable fashion before this committee. I want to say to you that the tragedy of Watergate is that it has affected many fine young men who dedicated themselves to a President and it has affected their families more. Now, I ask you this final question: Does it not amaze you that after all this allegiance and blind devotion to duty, now you have been relegated to solace and to stew in your own juice?

MR. MAGRUDER: Well, Senator, let me just say I have had to take the attitude and I have taken the attitude that this is certainly a very unfortunate period of my life. I am not going to let it destroy me. I have a wonderful wife and four children.

SENATOR MONTOYA: I understand that you do, Mr. Magruder.

MR. MAGRUDER: And I am not going to lay down and die because of it. I think I will rehabilitate myself, I guess is the best word. I think I am in that process and I hope to be able to live a useful life. I would not recommend this as a method of reemergence, but in this case, I think I can and I will.

SENATOR MONTOYA: I want to wish you well in your future endeavors.

MR. MAGRUDER: Thank you, Senator.

SENATOR MONTOYA: Thank you.

The pressure on me let up a little after my Senate testimony. Public attention turned to John Dean, the next witness, who charged, as I had not, that the President was involved in the cover-up. Gail and I wanted to get away from Washington for the summer, and we were fortunate to be able to rent a large Victorian house in the old resort community of Blue Ridge Summit, Pennsylvania, which sits atop a mountain near the Maryland-Pennsylvania line. I would drive to Washington to see the prosecutors, and to my work, but I was usually able to spend two or three days a week with my family, which was perhaps the most I'd ever spent with them on a regular basis. The phone didn't ring so much in Blue Ridge Summit, and people mostly accepted us for what we were. I began to relax a little; after a year of needing tranquilizers to get to sleep each night, I quit using them entirely. Gail said I had begun looking better the day I went to the prosecutors; certainly I felt better.

We couldn't escape Watergate entirely, of course. When we rented the house, its owner asked the officers of the little country club there if we might join it, as most people who took houses did. The club said no, and the refusal was clearly because of my association with the Watergate scandal. Some of our new neighbors, who were members of the club, were upset by this, and invited us to be their guests for dinner at the club one night. We met many of the members, and after that a special membership meeting was called and we were invited to join. It was a pattern we often saw: people thought I had horns until they met me, but after that there would be no problem.

I might add that the ubiquitous Maxine Cheshire found out about this minor controversy, and was poised to do a story if we were blackballed. When we were admitted to the club, that, of course, was not a story.

I sometimes watched the Watergate hearings that summer. I can't say that I enjoyed them, but they held a certain irresistible fascination. I didn't particularly mind when Mitchell contradicted my testimony about his approving the Liddy plan. I knew what he was going to do anyway. But I must say I was annoyed when Gordon Strachan, who had been a friend of mine, launched a personal attack on me. He pictured me as a scheming bureaucrat who would deliver full reports to the White House on matters that were going well and would report little or nothing if a project was in trouble. Strachan's point apparently was that the Liddy plan was a fiasco and I therefore would not have given the White House a detailed report on it. The flaw in Strachan's story was that you just didn't get away with making that sort of slipshod report to Haldeman.

Strachan also suggested that I was trying to "deliver" him to the prosecutors in order to gain better treatment for myself. The fact was that in my long, sometimes exhausting sessions with the prosecutors, they made it clear they wanted only the truth—they were eager for every detail I could possibly remember, but nothing that was invented. The worst thing I could have done for my own interests was to lie to the prosecutors.

In the weeks following my Senate testimony, I received hundreds of letters from friends, acquaintances, and strangers. All but a handful of them were friendly and many of them were religious in nature—people would say they were praying for me and my family and that with God's help we could still make a good life for ourselves. During this same period the *New York Times* published an article about me by Bill Coffin on the op-ed page. In this piece Bill philosophized on my moral dilemma. Although I can hardly term it a flattering appraisal, it wasn't unsympathetic. I called him to thank him for his concern, and he invited Gail and me to New Haven for a visit. We flew up and spent a night with Bill and his family. Bill and I had a long talk about my situation, and essentially what he said to me was this:

"You've got to look on this as an opportunity to make adjustments in your moral and ethical structure. You can benefit from this or you can be destroyed by it. It's up to you."

One of the things I learned, as the months went by, was that the way people responded to me had nothing to do with their politics, or with their religion or financial status or any other single factor. Some people are simply generous and compassionate, and others are not. Bill Coffin was helpful, despite our political differences, as was Edward Bennett Williams, the criminal lawyer and Democratic figure, who gave me advice and encouragement on several occasions. Such businessmen as J. Willard Marriott, whose political philosophy is similar to my own, were particularly helpful.

One day I was talking to columnist Art Buchwald and he urged me to think about lecturing, both as a way to ease my financial problems and to make some constructive use of my experience. Buchwald gave me the name of his lecture agent and insisted that I call him. His urgings, following those of Bill Coffin, and coming at a time when my finances were increasingly uncertain, persuaded me I should explore lecture possibilities.

I found that I was in demand as a lecturer, and that the money was very good. After the agent's fee and my expenses, I might clear as much as $1,500 per lecture. That was welcome news. The money from my lectures could provide for my family when I was in prison. I therefore let my new agent arrange me a lecture tour of college campuses, beginning when school opened in September. I couldn't talk about the evidence in the Watergate case, but I thought I could deliver a meaningful lecture on the causes of Watergate and the moral lessons to be learned from it.

But once my lecture tour was announced, a controversy broke out. The *New York Times* carried on its op-ed page on August 28 an article by Victor Gold, Vice President Agnew's onetime press secretary, which was headed "Jeb Magruder, Superstar," and in which Gold variously compared me to John Dillinger, the bank robber, and Arthur Bremer, the disturbed young man who shot George Wallace; the point of Gold's article was that a confessed perjurer should not be allowed to profit from his wrongdoing. The Vice President's legal problems were beginning to surface then, and I assumed that Gold hoped to detract a little from Agnew's troubles by attacking me. It was, in any event, a clever and effective attack. I saw Gold in restaurants a few times after that but he would never look me in the eye.

At about that time, also, the Doonesbury cartoon strip began a series of cartoons that concerned "the Jeb Magruder Show" coming to campus. They were pretty amusing, actually. In one of them, the hippie priest was finally able to get a date with the women's libber because he had two tickets to the sold-out "Jeb Magruder Show."

Then something less amusing happened. On August 16 I had pleaded guilty before Judge Sirica to a one-count conspiracy charge. The judge deferred sentencing at the request of the prosecutors, but my activities thereafter were under his jurisdiction. Jim McCord was also under the jurisdiction of the court, and Judge Sirica had required him to cancel a lecture tour. McCord's lawyers protested that their client should not be denied the right to lecture if Magruder was allowed to do so. Judge Sirica responded on September 5 by ordering me not to give any lectures.

I had no choice but to cancel my tour. My lawyers felt that, as a legal matter, I could probably have won an appeal from the order, for I still had the basic right of free speech. But as a practical matter I couldn't risk offending the judge who eventually was going to decide for how long I would go to prison.

Only two voices were raised in my behalf in this episode. Nicholas Von Hoffman, the Washington *Post*'s liberal columnist, declared that Judge Sirica was no more right in silencing me and McCord than we in the Nixon Administration had been right in trying to silence our critics. And the American Civil Liberties Union also protested the judge's action, although my lawyers made clear that we planned no appeal. I couldn't help but think that, had the person involved been anyone but a Watergate defendant, such voices as the editorial pages of the *New York Times* and the Washington *Post* would have cried out against this denial of free speech.

Although I understood Judge Sirica's reasoning, his prohibition of my lectures was both a financial and a psychological blow. For a couple of weeks, I had let myself think I had solved my financial problems; suddenly the lecture money was gone and I was worried about my consulting business. It appeared that I might lose one or two of my three clients, and when I made calls trying to find new ones, I had no luck. Some potential clients were men who in the spring had said "maybe later." Some were men who had written me after my Senate testimony and said they'd like to help. But none would use me as a consultant. The Watergate case had grown increasingly worse, and no one wanted anything to do with it. I was desperate. I told one corporate executive that he didn't have to use me in a top-level job; that I was willing to be a clerk. But he didn't want me even in that capacity.

The summer months at Blue Ridge Summit had been idyllic, but once we had returned to our Washington home in September both Gail and I entered a period of depression. We realized that the children were going to have certain problems in school. We realized that our social lives had changed in a number of subtle and not so subtle ways that were impossible to ignore. I had my financial worries, and I began to realize that my legal limbo might continue a long time. I went through the charade of making plans and decisions, but the fact was that I had lost control of my life. I had a feeling of helplessness. I saw that I wasn't being judged by what I could do, but on the basis of one mistake I'd made, and there didn't seem to be anything I could do to change that.

Sometimes it seemed to me that many people did not simply want to see me punished, they wanted me destroyed. The "Superstar" column and the other public outcries that led to Judge Sirica's forbidding my lectures struck me that way. As Von Hoffman said in his column on the incident, to deny me the lecture income was not really punishing me so much as it would punish my family. The media kept pounding away at me and the other Watergate figures. It became routine to hear, for example, David Brinkley describe me as a "Watergate crook." *Esquire* magazine gave me the title "Brown-nose of the Year." A fellow writing an article on consulting firms for the Washington *Post* began by saying that it was people like Jeb Magruder who gave consulting a bad name. Maxine Cheshire kept dishing out trivia about us. There was nothing I could do about these attacks; Judge Sirica, in banning my lectures, had also forbidden me to grant interviews to the media.

I understood what was happening. Our Administration had been at war with a large and powerful segment of the media. For a time we had the advantage. Then, post-Watergate, they got the advantage, and once they had us down it wasn't their instinct to let us up. I suppose that was understandable, but my feeling was that I was out of it, I wasn't a threat to anyone anymore, I was just trying to survive.

I hope that in time, when tempers have cooled, some writers will begin to view the Watergate figures and their families not as pawns in a larger political struggle, but as people with feelings and virtues and lives to lead. I suspect that will happen. In February of this year the *New York Times* carried an interview with Gail, one that enabled her to express her feelings about what we have been through, and perhaps there will be similar articles about others in the case. That same month, *Rolling Stone*, the rock-music magazine, carried a long, sad piece about the difficulties that Howard Hunt's children had experienced while he was in prison. Articles like that seem to me to be the interesting ones today: the fact that Hunt and I are "Watergate crooks" is hardly news anymore.

My apparently endless sessions with the prosecutors were another source of depression. Jill Volner, my main contact, was reasonable to deal with, but some of the others made no secret of their contempt for the Watergate figures. I sometimes saw in certain members of the Special Prosecutor's staff the same kind of arrogance and self-righteousness that I and others in the Nixon circle had been guilty of not long before. When I proposed in October to take Gail with me for a business-and-pleasure trip to Europe, Special Prosecutor Archibald Cox's lawyers argued before Judge Sirica that I should not be allowed to go because I might be planning to flee the country. It was ridiculous to think that Gail and I would flee without our children, and Judge Sirica agreed that I could go, but required that I post $5,000 bond. I was glad that Sirica, at least, understood I was not planning to flee the country. Then I found that no professional bondsman wanted to do business with me. It was only hours before our departure that Jim Sharp was able to arrange bond and thus make the trip possible. I began to understand what poor people mean when they complain about the judicial system. You lose your humanity; you become a number being shuffled through an impersonal, indifferent system. Certainly one of Gail's emotional low points came the first time she went down to the courthouse to meet with my probation officer, who was preparing his presentencing report. He was considerate to her, but it was not the sort of experience her life had prepared her for.

And so it went in the last months of 1973. I remember Gail saying at Christmas, not bitterly but sadly, that so many of our friends had written on their Christmas cards that they hoped that 1974 would be a better year for us, not realizing that it would be a much worse year because it was the year I would go to prison.

We saw the New Year in at our old Victorian house in Blue Ridge Summit, banging pots and pans with our children and the Gillespie family because our regular noisemakers didn't seem loud enough.

As the new year began, we entered a period of resignation. It seemed that the prosecutors would soon be finished with me and that my sentencing was drawing close. When Bud Krogh, who faced a maximum of ten years in prison, received a six-month sentence, I couldn't help hoping that I might receive similar treatment. It seemed to me that the worst was behind me, that prison could not be any worse than waiting for it and fearing it had been.

Moreover, both Gail and I felt that there had been a positive side to the experience we had been through. While everything else fell apart, our family life had become stronger and closer than it had ever been before. Gail once said I should be thankful for Watergate, because she couldn't have lived with me any longer as I had become—obsessed with my work, too tired and distracted to share in the give and take of real family life. In my work, I had acquired the habit of telling people what to do, and that habit had spilled over into my home life; now I tried to give fewer orders and to pay more attention to what Gail and the children had to say. It took me a while to adjust to my new life—I no longer had to put on a business suit every morning and hurry off to work—but I came to enjoy it. I like to cook and putter in the kitchen, and most of all I relished the time I was able to spend with the children.

Our greatest concern was to try to minimize the damage that my problems would cause the children. Each of them is different, an individual who responds to the problem in a different way. Whitney, the oldest, is a tall, conscientious boy who is both a good student and a good athlete. He was in the seventh grade at St. Alban's, a private school in Washington, when the Watergate scandal broke in the spring of 1973. One of his classmates, a larger boy, called him "Watergate Whit" and got knocked down for his trouble. But, far more important to us that spring, at the height of my difficulties, Whitney was nominated to be one of his class's twelve prefects, the highest honor open to students. And the following fall he was elected president of his eighth grade class at St. Alban's.

We explained to the children that their father had made a serious mistake and might go to jail, but we didn't dwell on the matter. We wanted our family life to continue as normally as possible. It was hard to know just how much they understood. Eleven-year-old Justin is a tall, blond, creative boy, who has always had a talent for drawing and for making things. Early in 1974 Gail took him to be tested for possible admission to the Sidwell Friends School. When the tests were over, and Gail asked him what they had been like, he explained that there was an essay test in which he had the choice of writing on "The most interesting person I know is . . ." or "As the car pulled out of the driveway . . ." Justin said he'd started to write that the most interesting person he knew was his father, but he'd changed his mind and written instead on the other subject.

Gail asked what he had written, and he told her that the essay began like this: "As the car pulled out of the driveway, I waved good-bye to my brother, who was being taken away in a police car. He was being taken to Joliet prison. He had been convicted of a mass murder. He was being taken to Joliet to die in the gas chamber." Gail was shaken, because it seemed to her that Justin was really writing about his father, that all the press attention had made him think my crime was worse than it was and that I would die in prison.

The incident depressed us, because if Justin didn't understand the nature of the problem, if his fears were that great, we weren't at all sure what was going on in the minds of the two younger children. Nine-year-old Tracy has always been a cheerful, outgoing child, one with unusual musical talents, but in recent months Tracy has been withdrawn and quiet, as if she is trying to understand what is going on around her. Gail is concerned that Tracy, as the only girl, may be the child most vulnerable to damage by this experience.

We worry, too, about Stuart, a big, cheerful seven-year-old, who's at the stage where he's very close to his father; we don't know how he may be affected by my absence for a long period. It's very hard to know how much a seven-year-old understands. Stuart came home one recent Saturday and told us:

"I don't like that family behind us."

"Why not?" Gail asked.

"The girls came up to me a while ago and started saying, 'Your daddy's going to prison, your daddy's going to prison.' "

He tried to imitate the cruel singsong the girls had used.

"That's not true," I said.

"It might be true," Gail told him. "Your father may have to go to prison."

"I know that," Stuart said.

We try to deal with the problems as they arise, and to give the children the love that can carry them through this.

When Watergate broke, three of the children were in private schools. Given my financial problems, one obvious economy would have been to put one or more of the others in public schools. But we felt that should be a last resort. We feared that having to switch schools, coming on top of all the Watergate publicity, might be more than they could take.

I think the children can come through this. They're strong and healthy, and they have a mother who will do all that she can for them while I'm away. In later years, I'll try to deal honestly with their questions, so that they can understand what I did and why.

One of the letters I received after my Senate testimony was from Dr. Louis Evans, the new minister of the National Presbyterian Church, and his wife, Colleen. Mrs. Evans, who actually wrote the letter, said that she had watched my testimony while moving into her new house. She mentioned that she and her husband lived not far from us and they'd like to get to know us and to help us in any way they could. In time Gail and I got to know the Evanses well, and Dr. Evans and I had many long talks about my life, about the imperfect nature of man, about his capacity for both good and evil. The Evanses and other friends in church were a great support to us during a difficult time.

Many people were skeptical when articles appeared saying that Chuck Colson had become deeply religious as a result of his Watergate-related difficulties. I never doubted Colson's sincerity. It would be difficult to pass through something like Watergate without experiencing basic changes in your values.

In my own case, I found that I had lost the ambition that once drove me to push myself so hard in the corporate and political worlds. I no longer care about being the president of a corporation or making $100,-

000 a year. For fifteen years I fought to reach the pinnacle of our society, I got very close to the top, and I found that it wasn't all it was supposed to be. To get there and to stay there you have to pay too high a price in your private life. Obviously, in my case, ambitions led to disaster. But I think that even if there hadn't been a Watergate, and I'd gone on to corporate success, it still wouldn't have been worth it—but I would have been unable to see any alternative to what I was doing.

I don't know what the years ahead will hold for me. Perhaps I will return to the corporate world, but with the knowledge that I will no longer be fighting to be president of the company. Perhaps I may start some small business of my own; Gail and I have discussed the possibility of buying a small inn somewhere. I've also thought that I would like to teach. I can't know now what opportunities may present themselves when I get out of prison. I do know that my work, whatever it is, is only going to support my life, and is not going to dominate my life as it did for so long.

Why did it happen?

I've tried, throughout this book, to suggest some of the personal and political factors that led to Watergate. In summary, I think there were three major causes.

First, the fact that over the past third of a century too much power has accumulated in the White House. There are too many people working there who are not confirmed by the Senate and are not responsible to anyone but the President. In recent months I have seen this view expressed in several articles. I can only add that I have observed the Imperial Presidency up close, as a member of the royal court, and while life there is pleasant, it is also unreal. People with vast power at their disposal get cut off from reality, and their power is inevitably misused. One Administration will have its Watergate, another its Vietnam. Clearly, there is a need for the Congress, the courts, the media, and the general public, each in its own way, to work to lessen both the power and the aura of divine right that now surround our President. I agree with Professor Philip Kurland, who wrote in the *Wall Street Journal,* "It was exactly when the White House became what it is now, a fourth branch of government, that we started down the road to Watergate."

I think the second cause of Watergate was the peculiar nature of Richard Nixon, a man of enormous talents and enormous weaknesses. Without question, Nixon had the potential to be the greatest conservative political leader of his time; he knew his goals and he had the skills required to achieve them. Yet he had a fatal flaw, too, an inability to tolerate criticism, an instinct to overreact in political combat.

I don't know which came first, the liberals' loathing of Nixon or Nixon's loathing of the liberals, but the passions fed on one another, grew more and more bitter, until once he achieved the Presidency, Nixon could not resist the urge to use his awesome powers to "get" his enemies. A President sets the tone for his Administration. If President Nixon had said, "I want each of you to do his job, to obey the laws, and not to worry about our critics," there would have been no Watergate. Instead, the President's insecurities, aggravated by the constant opposition of the media, liberal politicians, and the antiwar activists, led to an atmosphere in the White House that could create the plumbers, the enemies lists, and Watergate.

Finally, Watergate happened because some of us who served the President served him poorly. It is not enough to blame the atmosphere he created. No one forced me or the others to break the law. Instead, as I have tried to show, we ignored our better judgment out of a combination of ambition, loyalty, and partisan passion. We could have objected to what was happening or resigned in protest. Instead, we convinced ourselves that wrong was right, and plunged ahead.

There is no way to justify burglary, wiretapping, perjury, and all the other elements of the cover-up. In my own case, I think I was guilty of a tremendous insensitivity to the basic tenets of democracy. I and others rationalized illegal actions on the grounds of "politics as usual" or "intelligence gathering" or "national security." We were completely wrong, and only when we have admitted that and paid the public price of our mistakes can we expect the public at large to have much faith in our government or our political system.

Too often, we view our Constitutional rights as abstractions. I must admit that I did not fully consider just how wrong our act of wiretapping was until I learned that Haldeman, Dean, and Ehrlichman—my *friends* —had secretly taped their talks with me. I went into a rage. Those were *private talks*. They had no *right* to do that. Finally I realized, not just intellectually, but in my gut, that we had no right to wiretap Larry O'Brien's phone, either. Nor, I eventually came to see, can society tolerate the act of perjury, which strikes at the heart of our system of justice.

I have sometimes been asked if I think I have a flaw of character that led me to make the mistakes I made. Obviously, someone who knowingly breaks the law has some flaw of character or of judgment or of sensitivity to right and wrong. Yet I think, too, that if we consider how many people broke the law in the Watergate affair, men who were usually model citizens in their private lives, we must ask if our failures do not somehow reflect larger failures in the values of our society.

I think that, as Bill Coffin suggested, I am a fairly representative member of my generation. And, looking back over my life, I think that I and many members of my generation placed far too much emphasis on our personal ambitions, on achieving success, as measured in materialistic terms, and far too little emphasis on moral and humanistic values. I think that most of us who were involved in Watergate were unprepared for the pressures and temptations that await you at the highest levels of the political world. We had private morality but not a sense of public morality. Instead of applying our private morality to public affairs, we accepted the President's standards of political behavior, and the results were tragic for him and for us.

One of the great misfortunes of Watergate is that it has wiped out a generation of men who had the ability and the commitment to be future leaders of the Republican Party, men like Bud Krogh, who has already entered prison, and Dean, Porter, and myself, who are awaiting sentencing, and Chapin, who is awaiting trial on a perjury charge. Other men who had no involvement in the scandal have been injured as well; one example is Rob Odle, who lost a job because a particular Cabinet member didn't want a person on his staff whose name had in any way been mentioned in connection with Watergate.

I have described many things I did that I'm now deeply ashamed of. I've tried to relate them candidly, and I've not attempted, as I detailed each wrongdoing, to express to the reader my retrospective shame and sorrow. But the reader is assured that there has been a great deal of shame and sorrow. I've damaged my own life, I've hurt those I love most, and I've helped deal a terrible blow to the political cause I believe in. I hope that young people who are in politics, or who may enter politics, may view this book as a cautionary tale. I won't tell them, as Gordon Strachan did, to stay away from politics. I would tell them, rather, to play the game hard but clean, and to bring to public life the same high standards they would apply in private life. I didn't do that, and I feel that I owe an apology to the American people for having abused the position of public trust that I was given.

I have no regrets about anything that has happened since I began cooperating with the prosecutors. I think the agreement I reached with the prosecutors was a reasonable one. John Dean fought for months to trade his testimony for immunity from prosecution, but in the end he accepted a one-count indictment, just as I did. Other of my colleagues, as I write this, have been indicted and are awaiting trial. Perhaps, by one legal means or another, they may escape punishment. Even if they do, even if I might have done the same, I still think I made the right decision in pleading guilty and accepting the consequences. Better to admit the truth and pay the penalty.

Others can make their own decisions; I've made mine. As I write this, it appears that Judge Sirica will soon pass sentence on me. I wouldn't be honest if I said I expect to benefit from prison. If I never went to prison, I would have been changed by this experience. I've been living in a kind of prison for almost two years, ever since the day the burglars were arrested in the Watergate. Yet if society's laws are to be respected, people who break them must be punished, and prison is one tangible form of punishment. I hope that my prison term will, in society's eyes, wipe my record clean and give me a chance to start anew. As I told the senators, I don't intend to be destroyed by this experience. I will still have a long life ahead of me, and I think it can be a good life, for me and my family.

INDEX

Abernathy, Robert, 10
Accardo, Anthony J. ("Tough Tony"), 44
Advertising: by Democrats for Nixon, 266–267; in 1970 Congressional campaign, 93, 125–127; in Presidential campaigns, general, 50; in Presidential campaign of 1968, 4–5, 91, 156, 157; in Presidential campaign of 1972, 148, 152, 155, 156–158, 203, 208, 256, 264–265, 266–267, 268, 269
Agnew, Spiro T., 59, 97–98, 107, 225–226, 274, 310; on "Face the Nation," 113; lack of access to Nixon, 59, 128; 1972 renomination of, 262; 1973 Inaugural Reception of, 275; role in 1970 Congressional campaign, 128, 129; role in 1972 Presidential campaign, 149, 203; speeches of, 64, 123, 125, 128; spokesman for "Silent Majority," 128; and Watergate news, 225, 226, 231
Air Force One (plane), 129–130
Allen, James, 39
Allott, Gordon, 59
Alsop, Joseph, 117
Ambassadors, foreign, first audience with President, 57
American Civil Liberties Union, 310
American Independent Party, 188
American Nazi Party, 189
Ammidown, Robert, 291
Anderson, Jack, 171, 175; Dita Beard memos, 181; Liddy's investigation of, 190, 233, 243, 251
Anderson, Martin, 99–100
Andreas, Dwayne, 222
Antiwar movement, 53–54, 58, 66, 72, 197, 199–200, 306, 317; Alsop column on, 117; and Cambodian invasion, 113–114, 115; Chapin memo on PR response to, 81–83; civil disobedience by, 306–307; Communist funding alleged, 166; demonstration coinciding with Hoover funeral, 206–207;

Antiwar movement (*continued*)
Haldeman attitude toward, 101, 166; McGovern volunteers, 269; Moratorium rallies (Oct. 1969), 54, 73, 75, 79, 81; Nixon's PR memo on counteroffensive, 74–75; Washington Monument rally (Nov. 1969), 54, 73, 81, 83, 114; White House PR campaigns against, 79–83, 113–118
Apollo XI astronauts, 6, 86
Ashbrook, John M., 157, 186

Baker, Howard H., 110, 306
Baldwin, Alfred, 241
Barker, Bernard, 223
Barr, Charles, 41
Bayh, Birch, 111
Beard, Dita, 181
Benny, Jack, 219
Bernstein, Carl, 219, 246
Bierbower, James, 286, 289, 290, 291, 294–295, 296
"Black advances," 167, 202. *See also* "Dirty tricks"
Blacks: alienated by Nixon Administration, 98; vote courted in California, 204
Blair, C. Stanley, 80
Blessing, Ed, 49
Blount, Winton, 102
Booz, Allen and Hamilton, 35, 39
T. R. Braun & Co., 62
Bremer, Arthur, 310
Brewster, Daniel, 291
Brinkley, David, 105–106, 108, 311
Broadway-Hale department stores, Calif., 45, 46, 47, 48, 51, 52
Brock, William, 150, 158–159
Brookings Institute, 87
Brown, Edmund, Jr., 281
Brown, Sam, 86
Buchanan, Patrick, 53, 54, 70, 71, 73, 74, 195; NBC News coverage analysis by, 105, 106; role in 1972 campaign, 148

321

Nixon, Edward L., 182–183

Nixon, Pat (Mrs. Richard M.), 203, 218

Nixon, Richard M., 32, 135, 229, 316–317; Agnew frozen out by, 59, 128; antimedia stance of, 5, 55, 77, 84, 86; and antiwar movement, 53–54, 58, 74–75, 79–83, 114, 117, 166, 206; and antiwar rally at Washington Monument (Nov. 1969), 83; appointment changes, second Administration, 268; basic flaws of, 317; blamed for Watergate climate, 196–197, 316–317, 318; and cabinet members, 59, 101–102; and Cambodian invasion, 109, 112–114, 115; and Carswell nomination, 109, 110, 111–112; Colson's influence with, 64, 65, 66, 77, 111, 117, 122, 135, 138, 206; crisis proclivity of, 72; desire to be *Time* Man of the Year, 86; desk of, 177; dislikes disagreement and independence in his associates, 273; domestic advisers of, 67, 68; domestic programs of, 67, 97, 103–104, 140–141; dual personality of, 168; "enemies" mentality of, 60–61, 86, 197, 317; executive clemency promises made in his name, 244, 285, 287; and Finch, 147; government reorganization plan of, 140–141; Haldeman as mouthpiece for, 59–61; ill-at-ease in face-to-face meetings and on TV, 4, 57; image building, 100, 139; improved in group and mass meetings, 57; inaccessibility of, 59, 102; inner circle of, 65; insularity of, 137; and intelligence-gathering, 166; and Kennedy write-in scheme for New Hampshire, 187; Kent State tragedy views, 113; "kitchen debate" with Khrushchev, 76; and Klein, 59, 63, 64, 112, 135–136, 138; leadership potential, 316–317; liberals seen as his enemies, 5, 53, 86, 317; Lincoln Memorial meeting with antiwar demonstrators, 114; and MacGregor, 259; Magruder's attitude toward, 6, 9, 34; a manager rather than politician, 137; Mitchell and, 121, 122, 237–238; 1960 Presidential campaign, 34, 168; 1968 Presidential campaign, 4–5, 51, 70, 71, 137, 156, 168; 1970 Congressional campaign role of, 95–96, 122, 128–133; and 1972 Convention site, 150–152, 199–200; in 1972 primaries, 171–172, 186–187; in

Nixon, Richard M. (*continued*) 1972 public opinion polls, 269; at 1972 Republican Convention, 262; 1973 Inaugural of, 273, 275–276; "Now More Than Ever" slogan in 1972, 154; "Open Door" slogan of, 139–140; opposes "open door" policy toward campus critics, 115; paranoid about criticism, 77, 168, 317; Phoenix speech of (1970), 130–132; physical awkwardness of, 4, 57; in plane delay incident, 71; preoccupation with Kennedys, 73, 218; PR concepts and instincts of, 5, 57, 73–77, 93–94, 159; PR problem of, 4–5; question of advance knowledge of Watergate break-in, 238, 279, 305; question of knowledge of Watergate cover-up, 238, 307; rarity of personal appearances, 93–94; in regional press briefings, 96–97; reception of foreign ambassadors by, 57; and revenue sharing, 140, 141; San Clemente estate of, 3, 4, 6, 8–9; secrecy obsession, in polling, 155–156; State of the Union Message of 1970, 140; taping of his conversations, 8; trails Muskie in 1971 polls, 133, 146; "Tricky Dick" label forgotten in 1972, 154; trip to China, 146, 262; trip to Russia (1972), 146, 203, 207, 208, 262; trivial complaints about media, 84–85, 86; Vietnam policy of, and PR campaign, 74–75, 79–83, 113–118; Vietnam troop withdrawals announced by, 53; Vietnam (North) bombing and mining ordered by, 207–208; voter opinions of, 153, 154; and Watergate truth, 293–294, 296; and youth vote in 1972, 158, 159–160, 269

Nofziger, Lyn, 59, 74, 79, 87, 110, 116, 126, 281; member of P.O. group, 78; 1972 campaign jobs of, 189, 202–203, 245; proposal for Institute for an Informed America, 87–88

North Vietnam, 74, 113; U.S. bombing of, 207–208; U.S. mining of ports, 207–208

Northbrook *Star*, 43

Novak, Robert, 132, 166–167, 200

O'Brien, Larry, 149, 155, 191, 196, 216, 262; civil suit against CRP, 230–231; wiretap target, 180, 181, 195, 196, 209, 210, 317